CURRICULUM
A Comprehensive Introduction

FOURTH EDITION

John D. McNeil
University of California, Los Angeles

SCOTT, FORESMAN/LITTLE, BROWN HIGHER EDUCATION
A Division of Scott, Foresman and Company
Glenview, Illinois   London, England

ISBN 0-673-52021-8

Library of Congress Cataloging-in-Publication Data

McNeil, John D.
    Curriculum : a comprehensive introduction / John D. McNeil.—4th
  ed.
      p.   cm.
    Includes bibliographical references.
    ISBN 0-673-52021-8
    1. Education—Curricula. 2. Curriculum planning I. Title.
  LB1570.M3178 1990
  375′.001—dc20

1 2 3 4 5 6 KPF 94 93 92 91 90 89

PREFACE

This book is designed as a tool for the study of curriculum. Although it is intended primarily for use in college and university courses in curriculum, it may also prove of interest to practicing teachers, administrators, parents, and concerned citizens who wish to engage in serious reflections about curriculum. You are not expected to bring to the reading of this book a knowledge of the technical skills of curriculum making. The necessary curriculum concepts and methods are explained and developed as required.

The book has several distinctive features. First, it is comprehensive. Several perspectives of curriculum are treated in some detail. There is no intention of narrowing the field of curriculum into a study of history, sociology, or any other specialization. Instead, the outlooks from many disciplines are sought for their contributions to our understanding of curriculum. This approach is in contrast to one in which individual scholars find the curriculum problem too complex and, therefore, try to redefine the problem narrowly in terms of their own disciplines.

This is a textbook. It is not a monograph dealing in depth with a small corner of the curriculum field. As a result of reading this book, responding to the discussion questions at the end of each chapter, engaging in the suggested supplementary reading, and questioning and adapting the ideas and prescriptions presented in the chapters, students of curriculum will be drawn into new paths for determining why certain procedures are superior to others. Although I have striven for a realistic concept of what constitutes curriculum and have suggested ways to better implement the things that are now necessary, I have intentionally left much to the reader and instructor. Everything that ought to be known about curriculum has not been put into the book. My aim was brevity and simplicity of treatment.

Second, the presentation is not rhetorical. Curriculum, like many other fields, has had in recent years its share of books advocating particular concepts and solutions. My purpose is not to argue the case for one favored view but rather to demonstrate that many factors need to be considered in any reflective analysis of curriculum questions. I seek to evoke a quality of response and make a deliberate attempt to show the strengths and weaknesses of competing points of view. Indeed, although each of the views presented here has merit, it would be a loss for any one of them to dominate. A straightforward analysis of the different positions is given in every chapter. Usually, my opinions are reserved for a concluding comment.

A third feature of the book is its topical division and order. Each topic has been given a certain degree of independence as a separate unit of study appropriate for one or more class sessions. The order of the topics may be changed. For example, it is possible to start with the last part of the book, if it is preferable to define the curriculum field before embarking on its study.

Part I examines four prevailing concepts of curriculum. The assumptions underlying these different orientations with respect to curriculum purpose, method, organization, and evaluation provide a framework for relating many subsequent topics. Part II features the technical skills of curriculum development—the core of curriculum knowledge. The chapters in this part help answer questions such as "*what* should be taught" and "*how* should it be taught." By examining various curriculum models, techniques, and practices, we can gain important insights into the task of making curriculum decisions. This part also focuses on important problems concerning how best to organize the curriculum.

Part III treats curriculum as seen by governmental policy makers, institutional leaders, and classroom teachers. It is timely in that it centers on the restructuring of schools, innovation and change, evaluation, and policies as they bear upon curriculum.

Part IV examines curriculum in a wider context and from a broader point of view. In this part, one chapter deals with curriculum issues such as international comparisons of curriculum and achievement, the teaching of thinking, and curriculum in a multicultural context. Another chapter reveals trends in the teaching of the subject fields, including new developments in the science, math, social studies, and arts curriculum.

Finally, Part V is devoted to curriculum as a field of study. The first chapter in this part brings a historical perspective to the field, showing our inherited ways of thinking about curriculum problems. A second chapter describes the work of the growing edge of scholars in the field of curriculum. The content of this chapter indicates the kind of studies that will explain the nature of "the curriculum" and delimits the domains and processes of curriculum inquiry.

This revised edition contains the major principles and concepts that were featured in the previous editions. The content, however, is different in that it includes fresh descriptions of recent developments in curriculum practice, particularly those experiencing rapid change—evaluation, current issues, directions in the subject fields, politics, and research. The text has been strengthened by adding material that clarifies basic ideas. For example, I have made a differentiation between curriculum as social reconstruction and curriculum as social adaptation.

I want to express grateful appreciation to the following reviewers for helpful suggestions in revising the text: Reuben Hilde, Loma Linda University; Albert Lindia, Central Connecticut State College; John McClure, The University of Iowa; James Walter, University of Nebraska–Lincoln; Daisy F. Reed, Virginia Commonwealth University; E. John Kleinert, University of Miami; and Robert Williams, Indiana State University. The guidance of Christopher Jennison at Scott, Foresman and the initial support from Mylan Jaixen have been significant in developing the present text.

CONTENTS

I□CONCEPTIONS OF CURRICULUM.................... 1

1□Humanistic Curriculum   3
Characteristics of the Humanistic Curriculum   5
  Purpose   5
  Role of the Teacher   8
Basis for Selecting Learning Opportunities   8
  Organization   10
  Evaluation   11
Directions in Humanistic Curriculum   12
  A Confluent Curriculum   13
  Consciousness and Transcendency   16
  Responses to Depersonalization   18
Criticisms of the Humanistic Curriculum   24
Concluding Comments   26

2□The Social Reconstructionist Curriculum   29
Characteristics of the Social Reconstructionist Curriculum   31
  Purpose   31
  Role of the Teacher   31

Basis for Selecting Learning Opportunities 32
Organization 33
Evaluation 34
Social Reconstruction in Practice 34
Changing the Community 34
Paulo Freire's Practice of Social Reconstructionism 36
Neo-Marxists 39
Futurologists 43
Social Adaptation 45
Criticisms of Social Reconstructionism 46
Concluding Comments 47

3 □ Technology and the Curriculum 51
Technology and the Ideal of Efficiency 52
Examples of Technological Curriculum 53
Systems Technology 53
Instructional Alignment 54
Personalized Systematic Instruction in Higher Education 54
Mastery Learning 55
General Characteristics of Classroom Technological Systems 56
Objectives 56
Methods 57
Organization 57
Evaluation 58
Technology in the Development of Curriculum Materials 59
Technical Innovations 61
Computers 61
Interactive Video 63
Issues in a Technological Approach to Curriculum
Development 63
Special Problems 64
Concluding Comments 67

4 □ The Academic Subject Curriculum 69
Approaches to the Academic Curriculum 70
The Forms of Knowledge Approach 71
Structure in the Disciplines Approach 73
Reaction Against a Structure of Knowledge 75
Revival of the Disciplines Approach 77
Liberal Arts and the Academic Core 78
Cultural Literacy 82

Characteristics of Curriculum as Academic Subject Matter 84
  Purpose 84
  Methods 85
  Organization 85
  Evaluation 88
  Making Subject Matter More Appealing to Growing Minds 89
Concluding Comments 92

II ☐ CURRICULUM DEVELOPMENT.....................97

5 ☐ **Deciding What Should Be Taught 99**
  Arenas for Deciding What to Teach 100
    Levels of Decision Making 100
    Different Curriculum at Different Levels 103
  Contents for Development of Curriculum 104
    Range of Activity 104
    Institutional Purposes 105
    Functions of the Curriculum 106
  Determining What to Teach 108
  Rational and Technical Models in Curriculum Decision
      Making 110
    Needs Assessment Model 110
    The Futuristic Model 115
    The Rational Model 117
    The Vocational or Training Model 121
    Disjointed Incrementalism 125
    Emergent Approaches in Curriculum Decision Making 126
  A Comment on Models for Curriculum Building 128
  Concluding Comments 130

6 ☐ **Developing and Selecting Learning Opportunities 133**
  Principles for Developing Learning Opportunities 135
  Learning Opportunities for Higher Order Thinking 140
    Problem Solving 140
    Creativity 142
  Procedures for Developing Learning Activities 144
    Major Orientations 144
  Criteria for Selecting Learning Activities 153
    Philosophical Criteria 153

Psychological Criteria   154
Technological Criteria   154
Political Criteria   156
Practicality as a Criterion   157
Criticisms of Criteria for Selecting Learning Opportunities   158
Concluding Comments   159

7□Designing and Organizing Classroom Learning
Opportunities   163
Organizing Structures   164
Structure at the Institutional Level   164
Structure at the Classroom Level   165
Centers and Course Development   170
Organizing Elements   171
Common Organizing Elements   172
Principles for Sequencing Content and Activities   174
Traditional Principles of Sequence   174
Newer Principles of Sequence   176
Categorizing Sequencing Principles   181
Principles for Integrating Content   183
Integration   183
Issues in Curriculum Organization   186
Concluding Comments   188

III□MANAGING CURRICULUM 191

8□Administering Curriculum   193
The Context of Restructuring   193
Roles in Restructuring Curriculum   195
The Principal as Director of Learning   195
The Principal in Shared Leadership   195
Department Heads in Curriculum Management   197
Administrative Arrangements   198
Stratifying Students   200
Staffing Patterns and Scheduling   201
Supplementary Personnel   203
Nongrading   203
Facilities   204

The Middle School 204
Alternative, Magnet, and Specialized Schools 205
Directions in the Reform of School Organizations 208
Options in the Schools 208
Administration for Instructional Effectiveness 209
Coordinating the Curriculum 209
Shared Values 211
Effective Principals 211
Effective Classroom Practices 212
Effective Research and Curriculum Policy 212
Concluding Comments 215

9□Implementing Curriculum Change 217
Conceptualizations of the Change Process 218
Kinds of Changes and Difficulties in Implementing Them 218
Sociological Findings About Change 219
Conditions Conducive to Change 221
Strategies for Change 222
Top-Down Strategies 222
Research and Development 223
Multiple Element Strategies 223
Bottom-Up Strategies 225
Middle-Up Strategy 227
Suggestions for Successful Implementation Through Staff
Development 227
Networking for School Renewal 229
Introducing New Materials into the Classroom 230
Concluding Comments 232

10□Evaluating the Curriculum 235
Models for Evaluation 237
Consensus Models 237
Pluralistic Models 242
Controversial Technical Issues in Curriculum Evaluation 245
The Form of Objectives 245
Measurement of Intended Outcomes Versus Goal-Free
Evaluation 247
Norm-Referenced Tests and Criterion-Referenced Tests 248
Tests and Invasion of Privacy 250

Techniques for Collecting Data 251
  Measuring Affect 252
  Sampling 253
  Technical Hazards 254
Concluding Comments 256

11□The Politics of Curriculum Making 259
Curriculum Policy 260
  The Politics Involved 260
  Decisions About What Will Be Taught 261
Concepts for Interpreting the Process of Political Decision
    Making 262
  The Professionalization of Reform 262
  Forces of Stability 263
  Constraints on Policy 264
Participants in Determining Curriculum Policy 266
  School-Based Participants 266
  Community Participants 271
  State Agencies 273
  Testing Agencies 275
  Publishers 275
  The Courts 276
  The Federal Government 277
  Foundations 280
  Pressure Groups 281
Conflicts in Curriculum Control 282
Concluding Comments 284

IV□ISSUES AND TRENDS 287

12□Current Issues Demanding Responses 289
Curriculum for Thinking 290
  The Focus of a Thinking Curriculum 292
Curriculum Competition: An International Comparison 295
  Invidious Comparisons 295
  Validity of Invidious Comparisons 299
Vocational Education 301
  Contrasting Purposes for Vocational Education 301
  Access to Vocational Education 303

Content of Vocational Education   305
Restructuring Vocational Education   306
Trends in Vocational Education   307
The Hidden Curriculum   308
The Informal System Within the School   308
The Sociology of Knowledge   309
Hidden Curriculum and Moral Growth   311
Moral Education   312
Kohlberg's Theory of Moral Development   314
Value Clarification   315
Cultural Pluralism   318
Approaches to Multicultural Education   319
Bilingual Education   321
Concluding Comments   322

13 □ Directions in the Subject Fields   327
Mathematics   327
Mathematics in Our Schools   327
Trends in Mathematics   329
Science   332
Evolution of Science Teaching   332
New Approaches in Science Education   335
Recommendations for the Future Science Curriculum   336
Physical and Health Education   338
Its Place in the Curriculum   338
Guidelines for Future Physical Education Programs   339
English   341
English as a Subject   341
Trends in the Teaching of English   343
Reading   346
The Curriculum for Reading   346
Trends and Directions   346
History and Social Studies   347
History as a Subject   347
An Evaluation of History Curriculum   348
History and Geography in the 1990s   349
Social Studies   350
The Future of Social Studies   351
Foreign Language   353
The Rise and Fall of Foreign Language   353
Efforts to Revive Language Instruction   354

The Arts   356
  Fine Arts in the Curriculum   356
Concluding Comments   360

V□RESEARCH THEORY AND CURRICULUM 365

14□A Historical Perspective of Curriculum Making   367
  Context for Formulation of the Curriculum Field   368
  Herbartism and the McMurrys   371
    Basic Tenets of Herbartism   371
    The McMurrys' Thinking   372
  John Dewey Opposes Herbartism   376
    Dewey's School   376
    Dewey's Curriculum   377
  Scientific Curriculum Making   378
    Societal Influences   378
    Key Ideas   379
    Bobbitt's Contribution   379
    Charters' Contribution   383
  Improvement of Instruction   384
    Local Development of Curriculum   384
    The Course of Study Movement   385
    Caswell's Influence   386
  Rational Curriculum Making   388
    Tyler's Curriculum Inquiry   388
    Criticisms of Tyler's Rationale   389
  Concluding Comments   390

15□The Promise of Theory and Research in Curriculum   395
  State of the Field   396
    The Need for Curriculum Theory   396
    The Need for Curriculum Conceptions   399
    The Need for Studies of Correlation and Integration   403
    The Need for Studies of Sequence   405
    The Need for Analyzing Educational Objectives   405
    The Need for Process–Product Research   407
  Future Directions in Curriculum Theory   409
    The Soft Curricularists   409
    The Hard Curricularists   410

Directions in Curriculum Research 412
   Comprehensive Curriculum Inquiry 413
   Synoptic Activity as Curriculum Inquiry 413
   Conceptualization as Curriculum Inquiry 414
   Qualitative Inquiry in School Settings 416
   Action Research as Curriculum Inquiry 417
Concluding Comments 420

Index 423

Conceptions of Curriculum

Prevailing conceptions of curriculum can be classified into four major categories: humanistic, social reconstructionist, technological, and academic. Proponents of each have different ideas about what should be taught, to whom, when, and how.

Those with a humanistic orientation hold that the curriculum should provide personally satisfying experiences for each person. The new humanists are self-actualizers, who view curriculum as a liberating process that can meet the need for growth and personal integrity. They should not, however, be confused with those persons in the liberal arts tradition who regard the humanities as separate disciplines, such as art, music, and literature, and who attempt to deal with the human being solely through cultural creations.

Social reconstructionists stress societal needs over individual interests. They place primary responsibility on the curriculum to effect social reform and generate a better future for society. They emphasize the development of social values and their use in the critical thought process.

The technologists view curriculum making as a technological process for achieving whatever ends policymakers demand. They consider themselves accountable by producing evidence which indicates that their curriculum attains intended objectives. Efficiency and accountability are overriding values to the technologist. Theirs is not a neutral orientation, for the technologists espouse commitment to a method that in turn has consequences for curriculum goals and content.

Persons with an academic orientation see curriculum as the vehicle by which learners are introduced to subject matter disciplines and to organized fields of study. They view the organized content of subjects as a curriculum to be pursued rather than as a source of information for dealing with local and personal problems. Persons who fall into this category as-

sume that an academic curriculum is the best way to develop the mind—
that mastery of the kind of knowledge commonly found in such a curriculum contributes to rational thinking.

In the chapters that follow, each of the four categories are described,
analyzed, and evaluated. Students of curriculum who understand these
four positions will be better able to formulate their own ideas regarding
purpose, content, method, organization, and evaluation of curriculum. The
extent to which one or more of the conceptions applies at a given time and
place is a unifying thread in the organization of this text.

1

Humanistic Curriculum

The term *humanistic curriculum* may evoke a number of negative connotations—easy therapeutic gimmicks, antiscientific affinitives, preoccupation with the esoteric rather than with everyday life, and the countercultural movement of the 1960s with its antinomian and drug-oriented features, to name a few. With the 1980s came a mighty wind of change away from a child-centered curriculum based on interests, natural mode of growth, and impulses for pupil action. In its place were strong pressures for a subject-oriented curriculum consisting in the high school of five basics—four years of English, three years of mathematics, three years of science, three years of social studies, and one-half year of computer science. Arguments for this shift away from the child-centered curriculum rested on the belief that our nation was at risk because foreign competitors overtook American preeminence in commerce, industry, science, and technological innovations. Charges were made that educational institutions lost sight of the basic purposes of schooling; that the curriculum was homogenized, diluted, and diffused; and that a curriculum smorgasbord allowed for extensive student choice, which resulted in declining achievement scores in mathematics, science, and ''higher order'' intellectual skills.

In view of the negative connotations and the imperatives for academic mastery, more rigorous standards and firm codes of discipline, can we simply write off a humanistic orientation to curriculum? Such a dismissal would be unfortunate, for there are strong arguments in favor of the humanistic approach.

The American people have a commitment to self-actualization. Repeatedly, parents express their interest in self-understanding, and in fostering the emotional and physical well-being of their children as well as the intellectual skills necessary for independent judgment. The humanistic curriculum supports the American ideal of individualism, helping students discover who they are, not just shaping them into a form that has been designated in advance.

Americans place a premium on innovation and creativity. Thus it is a mistake for educators in the United States to respond to competition from Japan by imitating the Japanese curriculum with its emphasis upon shaping a whole population to a high level of rigorous discipline and its focus upon the same basic academic subjects for all. Although in Japan the average amount of learning is higher, the range of knowledge is narrower, and Japanese educators themselves are uneasy about Japan's emphasis on rote learning at the expense of critical thinking.

Instead of adapting curriculum so that pupils score higher on multiple-choice examinations, Americans should be concerned with maintaining their advantage in creativity, problem-solving skills, and innovation. The humanistic curriculum features activities that are exploratory, puzzling, playful, and spontaneous—all of which are vital for innovation and self-renewal. The best interests of Americans lie in providing students with a curriculum that is fixed on the future—on what is possible and potential, not on what is merely utilitarian or what will make the learner a helpless captive to what is already known.

The humanistic curriculum goes a long way toward solving a fundamental problem facing educators today: that much of what is taught is not learned and much of what is presented and tested for is not assimilated. Critics who think that greater learning is achieved by pouring more facts into children's minds are mistaken. Earlier reformers who tried to raise standards in the curriculum with rigorous academic programs met with failure. What went wrong? The new programs were often too far removed from the backgrounds of both students and teachers and did not take into consideration how learners might construct meaning. This should not be interpreted to mean that subject matter must be easy. Rather, it must be brought to life, taught in a way that demonstrates its relevance to the learner. The humanistic curriculum offers an alternative to dull courses and depersonalization.

Widespread dissatisfaction with much of the present curriculum is evidenced by high dropout rates, vandalism, and discipline problems among the bored, the unhappy, and the angry. The problem is not just one of motivating students to acquire academic content. A larger concern is determining the appropriate educational response to students who live desperate lives—students who lack a purpose for living, good personal relations, and self-regard. The humanistic curriculum addresses this concern.

There are signs that the '90s will see a revival of humanistic curriculum. Current reforms in medical education, for example, introduce a blend of humanism and science. Medical educators recognize that one-eighth to one-fourth of their students suffer from serious depression, and they see a need for doctors who are more skilled in human relations. Hence, many of the nation's 127 medical schools are designing humanistic curricula. Instead of using a lecture hall with the sole mission of transmitting anatomy, biochemistry, and physiology, there are human values courses, which focus upon emotional skills and understanding.[1] Students in the Albert Einstein College of Medicine helped to design their values curriculum so that they could learn how to respond to their psychological needs at various stages of life and to understand their own feelings.[2] In this curriculum, students may face each other in a circle and talk about a topic once almost taboo—their fears about talking with dying patients, their fears of dying themselves. In learning to face an inability to cure every problem, doctors are more likely to avoid overaggressive treatment and prolongation of a patient's pain.

This chapter describes how humanists respond to the central questions of what and how to teach. Examples illustrate ways in which the humanistic curriculum promotes personal development, learning, and self-actualization. In the next few pages, we will examine humanistic methods of learning—the idea of subject matter as a source of personal development—and how the humanistic curriculum allows learners to consult themselves and to enjoy their capacity to discriminate and sense the world.

CHARACTERISTICS OF THE HUMANISTIC CURRICULUM

Purpose

Humanists believe that the function of the curriculum is to provide each learner with intrinsically rewarding experiences that contribute to

---

[1]*Clinical Education and the Doctor of Tomorrow*, New York Academy of Medicine, 2 East 103rd Street, New York, NY 10029.

[2]Joseph Berger, "New Medical Schools Challenge: Human Values," *New York Times Education* (November 16, 1988): B9.

personal liberation and development. To humanists, the goals of education are dynamic personal processes related to the ideals of personal growth, integrity, and autonomy. Healthier attitudes toward self, peers, and learning are among their expectations. The ideal of self-actualization is at the heart of the humanistic curriculum. A person who exhibits this quality is not only coolly cognitive, but is also developed in aesthetic and moral ways, i.e., one who does good works and has good character. The humanist views actualization growth as a basic need. Each learner has a self that is not necessarily conscious. This self must be uncovered, built up, taught.

Third force psychology is closely associated with the humanistic curriculum. This psychology is largely a reaction to what some psychologists found to be inadequacies in behaviorism and Freudian psychologies. The third force psychologist believes that behaviorism is mechanistic and that behaviorists view the learner as a detached intellect, ignoring affective responses and higher order aspects of the personality such as altruism. Likewise, to the third force psychologist, Freudian psychologies appear overly cynical about the motives of persons and emphasize humankind's pathological and unconscious emotion forces.

The late Abraham Maslow was a key figure in the development of third force psychology. Maslow viewed self-actualization as having several dimensions. He saw it as a life achievement, a momentary state, and the normal process of growth when a person's deficiency motives are satisfied and his or her defenses are not mobilized by threat. Maslow assumed that the human being has a biological essence. Hence the search for self means attending to impulses from within which indicate that a person is a part of nature as well as a unique being.[3]

If third force psychology is its foundation, it follows that the humanistic curriculum must encourage self-actualization, whereby learners are permitted to express, act out, experiment, make mistakes, be seen, get feedback, and discover who they are. Maslow thought that we learn more about ourselves by examining responses to *peak experiences*—in other words, those experiences which give rise to love, hate, anxiety, depression, and joy. For Maslow, the peak experiences of awe, mystery, and wonder are both the end and the beginning of learning. Thus, a humanistic curriculum should value and attempt to provide for such experiences as moments in which cognitive and personal growth take place simultaneously.

---

[3]Abraham H. Maslow, "Some Educational Implications of the Humanistic Psychology," *Harvard Educational Review,* 38 (Fall 1968): 685–696.

Consider this anecdote from a biology class: "The teacher was trying to teach us about sugars, and we yawned as he added glucose to some Fehling's solution. But when he heated the mixture and the blue solution turned into a red solid, I sat up straight and recognized the moment as a turning point in my life. Within a day I had bought a Gilbert chemistry set and began threatening my attic and the peace of mind of my parents."[4]

Influenced by Maslow's concepts of peak experience and the need to discover one's potentialities and limitations through intense activity, Csikszentmihalyi began his studies of optimal and enjoyable experiences in which there is a deep concentration on the activity at hand—the person forgetting his or her problems and losing temporarily the awareness of self.[5] Such experiences are termed "flow" and at their most challenging level allow the person to transcend self. "I am so involved in what I am doing I don't see myself as separate from what I am doing." Those who find their activities to be intrinsically enjoyable (in flow) develop their intellectual ability to the fullest. Flow experiences occur when environmental challenges match one's competencies and skills. In contrast, negative experiential states occur in overchallenged situations (anxiety) or when one is overskilled for the task (boredom). As one's capabilities grow, he or she must take in increasingly greater challenges to stay in flow.

How can the curriculum contribute to flow experiences? Although persons differ in their ability to experience flow—it is easier for some people to enjoy everyday life and to transform routine and threatening situations into opportunities for action—the ability to experience flow may be learned. Meditation and spiritual discipline help a person to control consciousness. Yoga helps to train a person to concentrate attention, control memory, and to focus on specific goals. Offering a range of learning opportunities increases the possibility of matching appropriate challenge and competency. A curriculum goal might be to educate students so that they will be able to experience flow and avoid boredom and anxiety, regardless of social conditions. To this end, students would learn to recognize challenges, to turn adversity into manageable tasks, and to trust their skills.

---

[4]R. M. Ramette, "Exocharmic Reactions," *Journal of Chemical Education* 57, no. 1 (January 1980):68–69.

[5]Mihaly Csikszentmihalyi and Isabella Selega Csikszentmihalyi, *Optimal Experience: Psychological Studies of Flow in Consciousness* (Cambridge: Cambridge University Press, 1988).

Role of the Teacher

A humanistic curriculum demands the context of an emotional relationship between students and teacher. The teacher must provide warmth and nurture emotions while continuing to function as a resource center. He or she should present materials imaginatively and create challenging situations to facilitate learning. Humanistic teachers motivate their students through mutual trust. They encourage a positive student teacher relationship by teaching out of their own interests and commitments while holding to the belief that each child can learn. Those who assume a leadership role in affective approaches to learning must get in touch with themselves; they must know how the teaching role affects both the teacher and the pupil.

Three essentials for the humanistic teacher as seen by students are the following:

1. Listen comprehensively to the student's view of reality. ("She cares about my feelings and understands what I wish to say when I have difficulty in expressing it.")
2. Respect the student. ("He used my idea in studying the problem.")
3. Be natural and authentic, not putting on appearances. ("She lets us know what she feels and thinks and is not afraid to reveal her own doubts and insecurities.")

Manipulative methods are out; the humanistic teacher does not coerce students. Although numerous techniques are associated with humanistic teaching, not all who use these techniques can be called humanistic teachers. Only those who are committed to the ideas underlying the techniques are considered truly humanistic. Conversely, teachers who are kind and humane to students are not necessarily implementing a humanistic curriculum. Kindness may, in fact, be associated with any curriculum conception.

BASIS FOR SELECTING LEARNING OPPORTUNITIES

In the recent past, many resources offered exercises, techniques, and activities for advancing the humanistic goal of psychological growth. One way to select from among these resources was to identify a concern, theme, or topic, such as self-judgment, and then to select procedures or exercises that appeared to be related. Another way was to leave the content open-ended and to let themes and issues arise spontaneously from the teaching procedures and instructional materials. For the teacher who follows the latter mode, procedures and materials should match the learner's willingness to risk self-disclosure and give up privacy. Such willingness can, in turn, be increased when the procedures create trust in the group situation, thus helping students view comfortably their own discomfort.

The encounter group is an approach used in business and education to further human relations and personal functioning. In an encounter group there is very often little imposed structure. Group members decide upon the purposes. The teacher facilitates expression and clarifies the dynamics that are at work. After an initial warm-up period, members express themselves to each other. Facades give way, defenses are lowered, and hidden feelings and concerns are revealed. Group members give positive and negative reactions to these revelations. Usually the experience is valuable, resulting in better communication and self-understanding as well as increased understanding of others.

Self-awareness is believed to be best attained by observing one's own feelings. Examination of one's own thought—sentences, dialogue, and fantasies—is a means of achieving self-awareness. So, too, is the study of personal actions, movements, and physical expressions.

The humanistic curriculum increases self-awareness; it allows learners to seek typical personal patterns in their own responses to a series of activities. Acceptance rather than denial of one's own patterns is necessary in order to change an aspect of self. Under the humanistic approach, the learner is taught to distinguish ends from means. For example, an activity might provoke a silent member who wants to be viewed as intelligent to reveal that he or she thinks silence creates such an impression. If he or she discovers, however, that silence is seen by others as reflecting intimidation rather than intelligence, the silent one may be willing to attempt a different approach to achieve the desired goal. The teacher should at this point provide activities that permit learners to experience alternative ways of behaving and to evaluate these behaviors in terms of their consequences, such as the reactions of friends. These consequences will enable learners to decide whether to keep all, some, or none of the new responses.

Humanistic curriculum is today characterized less by contrived and game-like activities aimed only at aspects of personal growth and more by examination of the inner life of students in the learning process, as in the context of acquiring knowledge of subject matter, vocational training, or basic skills. Whether providing instruction in typing, computer programming, or chemistry, the humanistic teacher creates opportunities for the learners to deal with their affective concerns, i.e., beliefs, values, goals, fears, and relationships. For example, a sixth-grade teacher might give her pupils an opportunity at the end of each week to evaluate themselves and their work in terms of accuracy, what has been accomplished, and the usefulness of what they have learned. Students in this situation acquire new personal goals and form new attitudes about learning such as the following: (a) the number of errors is not a sufficient criterion for determining failure or success; (b) errors can be useful in learning; and (c) consistently perfect scores may signal the need for more challenging tasks.

Organization

One great strength of the humanistic curriculum appears to lie in its stress on integration. *Integration* refers to the learner's increased unity of behavior. In helping learners integrate emotions, thoughts, and actions, humanists achieve an effective organization. Humanistic schemes do much to resolve the weakness of the traditional curriculum in which the logical organization of subject matter, as defined by an expert, fails to connect with the learner's psychological organization. The humanist's concerns for wholeness and Gestalt lead to a curriculum that encourages comprehensiveness of experience, thus counteracting the prevailing practice of fragmented curricula.

It is true, however, that at times a humanistic curriculum lacks sequence. Students may have little opportunity to broaden and deepen a single aspect of their development. There is danger in a smorgasbord curriculum of minicourses such as The Jazz Age, Sexism in America, Writing Poetry, and Zen and the Western World, in which the total program seems to be just an unsystematic collection of bits and pieces.

Sequence requires centering on a single element such as concern, value, concept, attitude, or problem, and then arranging activities so that the student becomes increasingly able to deal with or exhibit that element. In the case of the smorgasbord, if self-understanding had been the focus or element, activities within each minicourse could have been cast to have a cumulative effect upon self-knowledge. Schemes for ordering activities so that the pupil derives the maximum benefit from each include providing opportunities for (a) dealing with preconceptual feelings before being asked to verbalize feelings and (b) taking action in a situation before trying to explain or understand the situation.

A particularly interesting scheme for sequencing dimensions of affective experiences has been proposed by Shiplett.[6] His strategy is to order experiences as follows: (1) Arrange activities to reveal concerns and blockages. Use experiences that help students deal with fears and unmet needs such as security and self-worth. (2) Introduce materials with orientation loadings, i.e., arrange for activities that focus on topics, subject matter, and learning tasks likely to help make pupils want to learn. Activities that stimulate curiosity are cases in point. (3) Present engagement loadings (activities that are rewarding in and of themselves). The student should be given pleasurable experiences, such as movement and novelty. (4) Introduce accomplishment loadings (the effects of completing a learning task). Mastery and satisfaction are examples of accomplishment loadings.

Evaluation

Unlike the conventional curriculum, which is objectively defined and in which there are criteria for achievement, the humanistic curriculum stresses growth, regardless of how it is measured or defined. The humanist as evaluator emphasizes process rather than product. Humanistic evaluators do, however, ask whether activities are helping students become more open, independent human beings. Humanists view activities as worthwhile in and of themselves and as a possible contribution to future values. The good classroom provides experiences to help pupils become more aware of themselves and others and develop their own unique potential. Humanistic teachers pride themselves on knowing how students are responding to activities, either by observing their actions or by seeking feedback after the activities are completed.

When asked to judge the effectiveness of their curricula, humanists usually rely on subjective assessments by teachers and pupils. They also may present outcome measures, such as students' paintings or poems, or talk of marked improvement in pupil behavior and attitudes. The late Carl Rogers summarized many of the research results showing positive association between affective classrooms and growth, interest, cognition, productivity, self-confidence, and trust. Rogers documented evidence that students learn more, attend school more often, and are more creative and capable of problem solving when the humanistic curriculum is

---

[6]John M. Shiplett, ''Beyond Vibration Teaching: Research and Curriculum Development in Confluent Education,'' in *The Live Classroom*, ed. George I. Brown (New York: Viking, 1975), pp. 121–131.

employed.[7] His evidence comes from studies in the military and other settings, in eight countries, at all levels of education and with students of different race, sex, and socio-economic status. By way of example, in a study on the effects of giving young children choices, pupils in an "educationally handicapped" third grade classroom were given the chance to design their own reading program. At first the pupils found it difficult to believe that they really could design their own program. Initially their responses were negative: "We don't want to do workbooks every day." But they also came up with constructive suggestions: "Could we have a quiet time when everybody just reads?" "Can we just read to you to hear, teacher?" "Can we read something else more than the reading book?" Students were given the opportunity to tell the class anything important about themselves, and time was set aside so that students could come individually to the teacher to talk about anything they wanted her to know, such as something bothering them about school or themselves or something exciting they wanted to share. At the end of a year, not one of these children, all of whom had been one or more years below grade level, made less than eleven months' progress in reading; some made three years' growth. Furthermore, the fact that increased self-awareness was achieved is evidenced by their comments: "It's all right to be me." "Everyone has feelings and it's OK to express them." "Doing things that are important *to me* is worthwhile."

DIRECTIONS IN HUMANISTIC CURRICULUM

The 1970s saw two prevalent forms of humanistic curriculum—confluence and consciousness. In the 1980s humanists planned curriculum with a focus on human development, while at the same time being responsive to public pressure for achievement. Currently, the humanistic curriculum is bridled by both.

Academicians who realize that the emotional qualities of the humanistic curricula, such as flow, are necessary for improving complex achievement, as well as social reconstructionists who want to take advantage of the humanists' success in increasing student personal power and sensitivity to feelings (consciousness of self), are building upon it to develop *critical awareness* of patterns in the society so that it can be changed (consciousness of society).

---

[7]Carl Rogers, "Researching Person-Centered Issues in Education," in *Freedom to Learn for the '80s* (Columbus, OH: Merrill, 1983), pp. 197–221.

A Confluent Curriculum

Rationale for Confluence. The essence of confluent education is the integration of an affective domain (emotions, attitudes, values) with the cognitive domain (intellectual knowledge and abilities). It is an *add-on* curriculum, whereby emotional dimensions are added to conventional subject matter so that there is personal meaning to what is learned. Confluentists do not downplay objective knowledge, such as scientific information, in favor of subjective or intuitive (i.e., direct and immediate) knowledge. The confluent teacher of English, for example, links affective exercises to paragraphing, organization, and argumentative and other discursive forms of writing. By beginning with the student's personal, imaginative, and emotional responses and working out from these, the confluentist helps learners both to acquire language skills and to discover themselves.

Confluentists do not believe that the curriculum should teach students what to feel or what attitudes to have. Their goal is to provide students with more alternatives to choose from in terms of their own lives, to take responsibility for appreciating the choices available, and to realize that they, the learners, can indeed make choices.

Shapiro and others have analyzed examples and nonexamples of confluence, concluding that a confluent curriculum includes the following elements[8]:

1. Participation. There is consent, power sharing, negotiation, and joint responsibility by coparticipants. It is essentially nonauthoritarian and not unilateral.
2. Integration. There is interaction, interpenetration, and integration of thinking, feelings, and action.
3. Relevance. The subject matter is closely related to the basic needs and lives of the participants and is significant to them, both emotionally and intellectually.
4. Self. The self is a legitimate object of learning.
5. Goal. The social goal or purpose is to develop the whole person within a human society.

Gestalt psychology is one of the bases for confluent education. The theory behind it is existentially based; that is, it focuses on what is happening here and now rather than on interpreting one's history. With

---

[8]Stewart B. Shapiro, "The Instructional Values of Humanistic Educators: An Expanded Empirical Analysis," *Journal of Humanistic Education and Development* 24, no. 3 (June 1987): 155–170.

respect to the curriculum decision of what to teach, the Gestalt theory forces one to question goals, and to ask about our heritage such questions as: "Is it of value to us now? Does it make us more alive or does it deaden us and tend to keep us hung up on outmoded ways of thinking and perceiving? Does it tie us to old models and goals for ourselves and for our children that are . . . counterproductive to a (healthy) society?"

Activities Within the Confluent Curriculum. Confluent curricula have been prepared by teachers at various levels and in most fields. These curricula include goals, topics, materials, and texts. Confluent lessons, units, and course plans have been field-tested and are available for inspection.[9, 10]

Many of these materials use *affective* techniques. George I. Brown has given us forty examples of such affective techniques, including the following:

1. Dyads. As an exercise in communication, two persons—new friends—sit back to back and try to communicate without turning their heads. Next, they face each other and, without talking, try to communicate using only their eyes. They are to be aware of how they feel as they do this (for example, silly, embarrassed, fascinated). Later, they close their eyes and communicate by only touching hands; and, finally, they communicate any way they wish. The pedagogy of the exercise is to move participants from little risk to more. That is, one reveals more of oneself and becomes more vulnerable as the exercise proceeds.

2. Fantasy body trip. Members of a group are asked to close their eyes, be comfortable, move into themselves. Each person is asked to concentrate on different body parts, beginning with toes, moving up to the head, experiencing any sensations felt emanating from the separate parts of the body. After this fantasy trip, the group shares their experiences. Applications of this technique can be used in discussing such concepts as: "What is a person?" and "Who am I?" Students begin with rediscovering their bodies. Other exercises concentrate on other parts of the person or on the experience of being a whole.

3. Rituals. A large group is divided into five subgroups and asked to create a new ritual. A ritual is a custom or practice—such as shaking

---

[9]Ger. Metz, "Gestalt and Transformation," in *The Live Classroom*, ed. George Brown (New York: Viking, 1975), p. 21.

[10]George I. Brown, "Examples of Lessons, Units, and Course Outlines in Confluent Education," *The Live Classroom*, ed. George Brown (New York: Viking, 1975), pp. 231–295.

hands. The idea is to invent a ritual either to replace one we already have or for a situation in which no ritual at present exists.

4. Gestalt "I have available" technique. This technique is to help persons get in touch with their own strengths or resources. Each participant completes a sentence beginning with "I have available . . .", and gains understanding by being aware of whatever emerges. For example, one may recognize personal characteristics, other persons, and things that can help one cope with the world.[11]

Unlike most curriculum writers, the authors of confluent materials do not expect others to carry out the suggested plans exactly or even roughly as described. Whoever uses the confluent materials should make them a part of their own philosophy; they should not regard them merely as techniques. Ideally, teachers create new approaches for their own classrooms. To design such approaches, however, the rationale underlying the techniques should be understood and accepted.

The "curriculum of concern" is a type of confluent education in which students' basic concerns determine what concepts will be studied. A *concern* differs from an *interest*. Concerns are the basic physiological and sociological drives of students. Interests are the activities that attract students. A student might be *interested* in cars because he or she is *concerned* with feelings of powerlessness. Thus, the proper approach to the student is not necessarily *Hot Rod* magazine but some way to help the students explore an understanding of power.

As an illustration of a curriculum of concern, self-identity is the concept and students explore the disparity between what they think about in school, what they are concerned about in their own lives, and the way they act. The curriculum outline consists of a series of questions designed to lead the student to a personal sense of identity and finally to an examination of the actions that would express that sense of self. Some of the questions are What is human about human? Who am I? How can we find actions to express our thoughts and feelings?

Such a curriculum can include a variety of activities, such as a trip to the zoo to contrast humans with animals, improvisational drama to imitate the movement of animals, discussion of animal metaphors in the characterization of humans, and debates about animal and human groups. Note that these activities can be undertaken without changing the orientation of the school in any major way. They can supplement the commitment to teaching reading, writing, and arithmetic.

---

[11]George I. Brown, *Human Teaching for Human Learning* (New York: Viking, 1971).

Students draw generalizations as a result of these experiences. For example, students conclude that self-consciousness allows persons to use their own diversity for their own benefit. Thus, "If a consciousness of self is one of the major differences between animals and humans, then one of the most effective ways to make persons more human, or more humane, would be to help them explore the significance of their own diversity."[12]

Consciousness and Transcendency

Mysticism. Although humanistic psychologists typically emphasize the affective and cognitive domains, some humanists are interested in treating higher domains of consciousness as well. Accordingly, the curriculum involves not only a cognitive mode of consciousness but an intuitive receptive mode—guided fantasy and various forms of meditation. For example, *transcendental meditation* (TM) is concerned with altering states of consciousness, voluntary control of inner states, and growth beyond the ego. It has been tried as an adjunct to the high school curriculum partly because it is seen as a way to diminish drug abuse among students. Essentially, TM is a simple technique for turning attention "inwards toward the subtler levels of thought until mind transcends the experience of the subtlest state of thought and arrives at the source of thought. This expands the conscious mind and at the same time brings it in contact with the creative intelligence that gives rise to every thought."[13] TM has been used to reach some very commonplace curriculum goals, such as reduction of social tension, increased learning ability, and improved athletic performance. It has also inspired more novel goals, such as growth in consciousness and in other ways of knowing.

The Maharishi International University (MIU) at Fairfield, Iowa, offers degrees in a number of fields, such as physics, mathematics, biology, business, and education. However, as a university founded on a philosophy that uses transcendental meditation, it also offers opportunities for students to experience higher states of consciousness. Everyone—faculty, students, staff—at MIU practices a twice-daily hour-long routine of meditation. In addition, in all courses an effort is made to foster a principle of interdependence by which personal individuality is related to con-

[12]Terry Borton, *Reach, Touching, and Teach: Student Concerns and Problem Education* (New York: McGraw-Hill, 1970).

[13]Maharishi Mahesh Yogi, *Maharishi Mahesh Yogi on the Bhagavad-Gita, A New Translation and Commentary* (Baltimore: Penguin, 1969), p. 470.

sciousness of whatever subject matter has been taught. As concepts are introduced in one course, students and teachers seek to recall corresponding concepts in other disciplines and how the concepts might be experienced in meditation. The probable consequence of this practice is a sense of personal relevance to knowledge and an integration of the different academic disciplines.[14]

One caution concerning transcendental meditation, practiced in such courses as the Science of Creative Intelligence, is that its inclusion in the curriculum may violate legal precedents opposed to sectarian indoctrination. The "science" of TM is held by some to be essentially a religious philosophy because its presuppositions about the source of life and energy reflect monistic Hinduism with pantheistic consciousness.

The religious concept of transcendence (i.e., the experience of going beyond any state or realization of being) has implications for curriculum. It suggests that students should learn how a particular mode of investigation in a subject field relates to other specializations. A transcending consciousness also helps us recognize the incompleteness of any subject. To learn that no discipline provides the full and final disclosure of the nature of things may help learners discern new possibilities, new directions, and new questions. A curriculum of transcendence should foster a spirit of criticism toward existing practices and encourage undeveloped potential and hope in improving one's existence.

Other Transpersonal Techniques. Biofeedback for controlling brain waves, deep hypnosis, yoga, and the use of dreams are additional transpersonal techniques that have implications for curricula. In English, for example, dreams may be used as a basis for creative writing because they contain the emotional impact of messages from the unconscious. Physical education, too, may use aspects of the transpersonal in learning to control one's body for optimum health and physical fitness through biofeedback and yoga.

The use of such techniques as relaxation and imaginary journeys are sometimes used in academic courses. A high school shop teacher relaxed his class and had them imagine they were electrons being pulled and pushed by the fields around induction coils. The students read the chapter in the book dealing with induction coils. The students said they had no trouble visualizing the forces described in the book, and the quality of their lab work seemed to bear this out.

---

[14]Robert Berrettini, "Pure Consciousness and Transdisciplinarity" (Paper delivered at American Educational Research Association [AERA] Annual Convention, Montreal, April 1983).

A review of hundreds of studies regarding self-improvement techniques led the National Research Council (NRC) to conclude that many nonconventional techniques, such as sleep learning and mental imagery, can help people improve their abilities and that other techniques, such as extrasensory perception and psychokinesis (mind over matter), exist only in the minds of believers.[15] Mental imagery and mental rehearsal help a person to perform better on skills that require a thoughtful, systematic approach. Some techniques like biofeedback and cohesion (the process by which members of a group become committed to each other and their common goals) have useful application but do not improve a person's abilities. Biofeedback can reduce muscle tensions, but the relaxed state it produces doesn't necessarily make for better performance. Although cohesive groups exhibit loyalty, altruism, and a willingness to take risks, no clear evidence exists that cohesion is linked to sharper skills.

Responses to Depersonalization

Self-Directed Learning. Self-directed learning is one response to the threat of depersonalization brought about by narrow focus on basic skills in reading, writing, and arithmetic. Humanists believe that the basics should include a sense of ability, clarity of values, positive self-concept, capacity for innovation, and openness—characteristics of the self-directed learner.

Key ideas to consider in planning a curriculum for self-directed learning are the following:

Achievement motivation. Those persons who are motivated by hope of success have an incentive to learn when the task is not too easy and when there is an expectation of success. Persons motivated by fear of failure, on the other hand, tend to select tasks that are either so easy they cannot fail or so difficult that no embarrassment results when they do.

Attributive theory. Achievement-oriented individuals are more likely to see themselves as a cause of their success.

Children's interests. When children find schoolwork distasteful and yet are driven to engage in more of the distasteful work, they acquire learned helplessness, having no interests related to learning. Freedom to undertake a self-directed study of something that concerns the

---

[15]Daniel Druckman, *Study 7—Self Improvement Techniques* (Washington, DC: National Research Council, 1988).

learner seems to be an important condition for developing channeled effort.

Locus of control. Locus of control is the extent to which persons feel they have control over their own destiny. Internal control is highly correlated with achievement.

A curriculum model for self-development has been proposed by Evan Keislar.[16] The goal of this curriculum is to optimize future growth and development of the individual learner. Learners are helped to mediate key decisions by reflecting on their level of cognitive development and testing proposed courses of action. Resources are provided for helping learners deal with uncertainty, take risks, try out ideas, and profit from mistakes. The teacher's role is to make sure that the student faces situations that arouse questions and lead to exploration. Challenges are matched to the child's pattern of development. Although the teacher is available to help the pupils find needed resources, the teacher does not do so when information is readily available. Because growth proceeds through encounters with conflict and tension, this curriculum promotes an optimum level of uncertainty.

As with other humanistic curricula, the self-directed curriculum aims at development in several areas:

Cognitive. Children respond to the requirements of problematic situations, not simply to external directions. By anticipating consequences, they learn to make wise choices about goals. Allowances are made for those children whose thinking is tied to immediate perceptions and for those who are ready for inferential thought.

Affective. Children learn to deal at an emotional level with such uncertainties as social conflicts, evaluation, and challenge. They learn to view failure as a learning experience.

Social. Assertiveness training, role training, experimenting with competitive and cooperative groups are among the activities provided.

Moral. Moral development is fostered through consideration of moral conflicts that arise from the social activities of the class and the wider community.

Ego development. The development of self-respect and self-confidence occurs through a social climate in which a person's world does not depend on ability or level of maturity. Each individual has an opportunity to attain success for there is no scarcity of rewards.

---

[16]Evan R. Keislar, ''A Developmental Model for a Curriculum in the Primary Grades'' (Unpublished paper, UCLA Graduate School of Education, Los Angeles, 1983).

In many ways, self-directed curriculum is consistent with what John Dewey suggested more than sixty years ago, i.e., a curriculum that poses problems rooted within the present experience and capacity of learners, problems that arouse an active quest for information and invite the production of new ideas.[17]

Finding the Personal in the Academic. In concentrating on academic knowledge, the learner may be depersonalized. To counteract this danger, there are two courses of action: (a) recognizing the limitations of academic knowledge while acknowledging other forms of knowledge and (b) finding personal meaning in subject matter.

The optimally developed person has not merely accumulated encyclopedic knowledge, but can live well, acting wisely in a wide range of circumstances and situations. The kind of knowledge that permits optimal development is not likely to be found in the conventional academic curriculum. More likely, it is found in personal knowledge—know-how achieved through active expression of one's existence and by interactive engagements with others and the natural environment. Walking and talking are illustrations of great achievements acquired by active expression. Good manners and the skills of mechanics, artisans, physicians, and engineers are examples of knowledge acquired by emulating master practitioners. In short, there are many ways to gain knowledge other than through the academic fields.

Although academic knowledge is not sufficient for personal development, under some circumstances, it can enhance personal knowledge, and enable a person to live better. What are these circumstances? Kenneth Resch identifies one and Philip Phenix gives suggestions for personalizing four more fields.[18,19]

1. *Literature.* Resch believes that it is imperative for teachers to find their own personal connections in subject matter, to share these connections with students, and to hope that students will share their understanding. In reading Wordsworth's *The Prelude* (in which Wordsworth picks up a piece of stone rubble left from the destroyed Bastille and begins to muse of his youthful and lost past), Resch shares with his

---

[17]John Dewey, *Experience and Education* (New York: Macmillan, 1939).

[18]Kenneth E. Resch, "Wordsworth, Whitman and Us: Finding Personal Relationships," *English Journal* (April 1988), 19–22.

[19]Philip H. Phenix, "Promoting Personal Development Through Learning," *Teachers College Record* 84, no. 2 (Winter 1982): 301–317.

students some of his own seemingly trivial possessions and the memories they evoke. In turn, students share their memories sometimes by bringing things to class or by simply talking about possessions and the memories associated with them. In such an approach, poetry is related through personal experience to students who begin to sense their own relationships and the romantic notion of responding to the past to find relevance in the classroom.

2. *The Arts.* There is personalization when the arts—music, art, dance— are taught with the idea of knowing how to produce patterns of the field and competencies in expressive movement or at least taught so that the learner is able to emphatically participate in the activity.

3. *Mathematics.* Unless the student is helped to become a participant in the process of mathematics, symbol-making, and manipulation according to the accepted canons of the mathematics community, the study of math is likely to be depersonalized.

4. *Science and Social Science.* Personalization is enhanced through application and transcendency. Students see how knowledge of the material may be applied to the satisfaction of human need through technology and through use of knowledge of science in understanding self or seeing how the natural world supports personal life. Personalization exists when students are helped to see mysteries yet unprobed by scientific undertakings as well as by shifting perspectives and alternatives.

5. *History.* Personal development occurs in the study of history when the past is dramatically re-created, making the past available for participation by persons now living, and when the students feel personally involved in the historical happening. History as only chronicle is depersonalizing.

An outstanding example of teaching history as personal development is found in Arye Carmon's curriculum, *Teaching The Holocaust.*[20] This curriculum helps the students formulate a set of moral rules for self through a confrontation with the Holocaust. The curriculum, which has been introduced in three countries—the United States, Germany, and Israel—places the adolescent at the focal point of the education process. The Holocaust serves as subject matter for responding to the needs of today's adolescents.

---

[20]Arye Carmon, "Problems in Coping with the Holocaust: Experiences with Students in a Multinational Program," *AAPSS, Annals* 450 (July 1980).

The theory of Erik Erikson underlies the construction of this curriculum.[21] Erikson felt that persons are confirmed by their identities and societies regenerated by their lifestyle. To enter history, students must be able to relate their childhood to the childhood experiences of former generations. They must be able to identify with the ideals conveyed in the history of their culture. According to Erikson, in youth, childhood dependence gives way; no longer is it the old teaching the young the meaning of life. It is the young who by their actions tell the old whether life as represented to them has some vital promise.

The major objective of this Holocaust curriculum is to heighten the student's awareness of the critical function of adult responsibility. This objective is achieved by fostering awareness of the human tendency toward stereotyping, prejudice, ethnocentrism, obeying authority, and thus escaping responsibilities.

The subject matter is organized into units—the socialization of a German adolescent in Nazi Germany, the socialization of a secret service man, the moral dilemmas of individuals and groups during the Holocaust, and the meaning of life in the post-Holocaust era. In each unit, students are given documents from the historical period. These documents provide historical background and serve as stimuli for discussion of the moral dilemma. The method of instruction is a combination of individual inquiry and group integration. Each person deals with a specific document; students form small groups to exchange feelings and opinions regarding the topics and their individual studies; then the entire class completes the discussion of the topic at hand. The content is not alien to the students and they cannot remain apathetic to it. Students face questions that are relevant to their own lives—Why sanctification of life rather than martyrdom? What are the dilemmas that confronted the individual and which confronted Jews as members of a community? Which of these dilemmas touch you personally? Why? What is the common denominator of the dilemmas? Discussion manifests a dialogue between the student and his or her conscience, and between students and peers.

During the first phase of the curriculum, resistance toward the subject matter increases. Students tend to resist giving up their stereotypical attitudes and other protective mechanisms. Gradually this resistance fades, only to be replaced by a feeling of helplessness. At this point the study has opened students to the possibility of critical thinking and

---

[21]Erik Erikson, *Identity, Youth and Crisis* (New York: W. W. Norton, 1968).

moral judgment. Students then begin to formulate the universal rule of confronting moral dilemmas: "How would I have behaved if I had been in this situation? How should I have behaved?"

Connecting Individual Learning and Social Learning. Although the humanistic curriculum enables students to become knowledgeable about self and feelings, it has been faulted for not offering the societal perspectives necessary for social change. Instead of giving sole attention to the psychological factors that shape people, humanists are asked to reveal social, political, and historical connections to inequality and evil in the world.[22]

An example of how curriculum can be developed to synthesize personal and social change is found in the work of Lee Bell and Nancy Schniedewind.[23] In their curriculum, the teacher focuses upon personal competition and uncritical acceptance of competition in the larger society. Questions as to why students need to feel superior to others and their uncritical belief in the superiority of American institutions and values are treated. The teacher begins by creating a trusting classroom and tries to develop the student's sense of personal power. Affirmative activities are implemented by which students validate their own and others' strengths. Students explore put-downs and how put-downs weaken personal power. Group support is developed through cooperative activities involving shared leadership and conflict resolution. Students examine the costs of competition on self-esteem and interpersonal relationships as well as on political and economic relationships in society.

This curriculum is ordered so that the concepts of personal power, group support, critical consciousness, and action are applied first to the personal level and then to the community, nation, and world. At the personal level, students explore their feelings about ability grouping and standardized grading procedures. They consider alternative procedures that will validate everyone's strengths. At the community level, students explore the effects of cooperation and competition in the workplace. At the national level, they study examples of political cooperation, like the successful farmworkers' boycotts. At the global level, students engage in high level activities, such as comparing personal egotism to social egotism.

---

[22]Ronald May et al., *Politics and Innocence: A Humanistic Debate* (Dallas: Saybrook, 1986).

[23]Lee Bell and Nancy Schniedewind, "Reflective Minds/Intentional Hearts: Joining Humanistic Education and Critical Theory for Liberating Education," *Journal of Education* 169, no. 2 (1987): 55–79.

CRITICISMS OF THE HUMANISTIC CURRICULUM

Four charges are commonly made against the humanists. (1) Critics charge that humanists prize their methods, techniques, and experiences instead of appraising them in terms of consequences for learners. The humanists, they say, have been lax in seeing the long-term effects of their programs. If they were to appraise their systems more thoroughly, the humanists might see that their use of emotionally charged practices such as sensitivity training and encounter groups can be psychologically or emotionally harmful to some students. The self-awareness they encourage is not always a change for the better. (2) Critics maintain that the humanist is not concerned enough about the experience of the individual. Indeed some programs appear to demand uniformity of students and appear to regard open questioning as a dangerous deviance, getting in the way of development.[24] Although humanists say that their curriculum is individualistic, every student in a given classroom is actually exposed to the same stimuli. For example, everyone may be expected to take part in group fantasy, hostility games, and awareness exercises. (3) On the other hand, as we have shown, critics also charge that humanists give undue emphasis to the individual. These critics would like humanists to be more responsible to the needs of society as a whole. (4) Critics charge that the theory on which humanistic curriculum rests is deficient. Instead of advancing unity and relatedness among the psychological principles from different schools of psychology, they say the theory increases the disconnectedness of scientific knowledge. Third force psychology does not bring together the collected knowledge of behaviorism and psychiatry.

Rebuttals to these attacks take varied forms. Humanists admit that their educational approach can be misused. However, as George I. Brown points out, teachers who would abuse their teaching role would do so whether or not they had affective techniques available. Furthermore, because humanism helps teachers learn more about themselves, those teachers are likely to demonstrate fewer instances of negative and destructive behavior. Not all students should have to participate in the humanistic curriculum because it may not be appropriate for everyone at the curriculum's present stage of development. This curriculum promises a fuller realization of the democratic potential of our society. The goals of the humanistic curriculum call for students who can perceive

---

[24]Richard Adams and Janice Haaken, "Anticultural Culture: Lifespring's Ideology and Its Roots in Humanistic Psychology," *Journal of Humanistic Psychology* 27, no. 4 (Fall 1987): 501–517.

clearly, act rationally, make choices, and take responsibility both for their private lives and for their social milieu.

The in-house differences of opinion regarding underlying theories of humanistic education attest to its intellectual vitality. Efforts to revise Maslow's concepts are one indicator. Chiefly, these efforts center on difficulties with the concept of self-actualization on which the whole personal growth movement is based.[25] Humanists must realize that vice and evil are as much in the range of human potentiality as virtue. Some humanists challenge the notion that our biology can carry our ethics and recognize that self-actualization may not always lead to the common good.

F. Hanoch McCarty believes it is necessary to combat the perceptions of humanistic education as chaotic, lacking in purpose and a set of common goals. He would change the phrases of the '70s—"If it feels good, do it" and "Do your own thing"—by adding "as long as it does not rob others of their dignity and potential."[26] In other words, McCarty believes that humanists must be involved with the welfare of others and that one should not seek personal pleasure while others slave.

Shortly before his death, Maslow addressed the question of whether we can teach for personal growth and at the same time educate for competence in academic and professional fields.[27] He thought it was possible, though difficult, to integrate the two goals. (The teacher's role of judge and evaluator in competency education is often seen as incompatible with the humanistic role.) In his last article, Maslow expressed uneasiness over some practices in curricula of the ESALEN type, particularly trends toward anti-intellectualism and trends against science, discipline, and hard work. He worried about those who considered competence and training irrelevant. For Maslow, the learning of content need not be the denial of growth. He thought subject matter could be taught humanistically with a view to enlightenment of the person. Study in a subject field could be a help toward seeing the world as it really is, a training in sensory awareness, and a defense against despair. To believe that real knowledge is possible and that weak, foolish human beings can band together and move verified knowledge forward toward some small mea-

---

[25]Michael Daniels, "The Myth of Self-Actualization," *Journal of Humanistic Psychology* 28, no. 1 (Winter 1988): 7–88.

[26]F. Hanoch McCarty, "At the Edges of Perception: Humanistic Education in the '80s and Beyond" (Paper delivered at AERA Annual Meeting, Montreal, Canada, April 1983).

[27]Abraham H. Maslow, "Humanistic Education," *Journal of Humanistic Psychology* 19, 3 (Summer 1979): 13–27.

sure of certainty encourages us to count upon ourselves and our own powers.

There is a concern that many Americans view the humanistic approach negatively. Although most people would support increased human potential and self-worth as ends, they may be suspicious of what appear to be bizarre procedures, such as exploring the senses through touch/feel exercises and emphasizing the sensual, if not the sexual. If thought, feeling, and action cannot be separated, then neither should feelings be separated from injustices faced by one's fellows. Rather than *feel* the "joy" of a "blind walk," students might *feel* the "revulsion" and "outrage" of abused children.

Critics of the humanistic curriculum reveal their own bias as social reconstructionists by demanding that the humanists do more than strengthen present courses. New teaching techniques that involve learners and their feelings in each lesson are not enough. They want to broaden the boundaries of the humanistic curriculum from self-study to political socialization; they would like humanistic curriculum to include such problem areas as medicine, parental care, sexism, and journalism. These critics want humanistic curriculum to deal with the exposure of injustice so that the learner's growth would be less restricted. The blending of humanism and social reconstructionism tries to answer this complaint.

CONCLUDING COMMENTS

Listening, self-evaluation, creativity, openness to new experiences, and goal setting are important curriculum goal areas. Learners have a real concern about the meaning of life, and curriculum developers should be responsive to that concern. Putting feelings and facts together makes good sense. We should also help our learners acquire different ways of knowing. Still, few persons would want the humanistic curriculum to be the only one available or to be mandated for all. We have much to learn before we can develop a curricula that will help pupils become self-directed.

Our best thinking today suggests that self-direction may follow from a climate of trust, student participation in decisions about what and how to learn, and efforts to foster confidence and self-esteem. The obstacles to be overcome are a desire by some institutions and persons to maintain power over others, a distrust of human nature, and a lack of pupil experience in taking responsibility for their own learning.

A fruitful approach to improving humanistic curriculum has begun. It includes focusing on the physical and emotional needs of learners and attempting to design learning experiences that will help fulfill these needs. The idea that curriculum objectives and activities should match emotional issues that are salient at particular stages of life is powerful. Curriculum developers should ask how particular subject matter might be structured in order to help pupils with developmental crises. Adolescents, for example, who are experiencing an identity crisis and trying to reconcile conflicts with parents might study history to illuminate the origins of parents' attitudes and beliefs, considering the present validity of these origins. They might use the sciences in meeting their needs for coherence in which objects of study are not represented as isolated substances. Or, they might use the arts to express their feelings and their natural desire to be themselves.

QUESTIONS

1. Consider a subject matter of interest to you. How could this subject matter be taught to avoid depersonalizing learners?
2. What is your response to those who believe that schools should not undertake the complicated responsibilities that an affective curriculum implies and that such programs may infringe on the civil liberties of children?
3. What are the expected outcomes from a primary classroom in which there is a "sad corner"; an "I feel" wheel with an arrow that points to "fine," "tired," "sick," "scared," and a plant that is ignored while another is loved so that pupils can see that "if we love it more, it will grow more, like people"?
4. Designers of affective programs have been accused of equating good mental health with conformity. They are said to promote compliance with school routines and instruction and to discourage the kind of initiative, individuality, and creativity that demands changes, "rocks the boat," and gives learners control over the institution in which they must exist. To what extent are these accusations true?
5. Reflect on some of the ideas, concerns, and activities associated with the humanistic curriculum. Which of these are likely to prove fruitful and have a continuing effect on what is taught? You may wish to consider (a) psychological assumptions about the importance of freedom, learning by doing, and risk taking; (b) views of knowledge such as

those stressing subjective or intuitive knowledge and the idea that the subject that matters is one in which the learner finds self-fulfillment; and (c) instructional techniques (value clarification, cooperative games, use of dreams, etc.)

6. What is your stance on the nature of the individual? Do you believe evil is inherent in human nature or are persons essentially constructive? What are the curricular implications of your answer?

SELECTED REFERENCES

Berman, L. M. and Roderick, J. A., eds. *Feeling, Valuing and the Art of Growing: Insights into the Affective,* ASCD Yearbook. Washington, DC: ASCD, 1977.

Csikszentmilhalyi, Mihaly and Csikszentmilhalyi, Isabella Selega. *Optimal Experience: Psychological Studies of Flow in Consciousness.* Cambridge: Cambridge University Press, 1988.

Della-Dora, Delmo and Blanchard, Lois Jerry, eds. *Moving Toward Self-Directed Learning: Highlights of Relevant Research and Promising Practices.* Alexandria. VA: ASCD, 1979.

Johnson, D. *Reaching Out: Interpersonal Skills and Self-Actualization.* Englewood Cliffs, NJ: Prentice-Hall, 1986.

Journal of Humanistic Education and Development (current issues). Falls Church, VA: American Personnel and Guidance Association.

Journal of Humanistic Psychology. Association for Humanistic Psychology (current issues).

Levine, Sarah L. *Promoting Adult Growth in Schools.* Newton, MA: Allyn and Bacon, 1988.

Rogers, Carl K. *Freedom to Learn for the '80s.* Columbus: Merrill, 1983.

Schneidewind, N. and Davidson, E. *Cooperative Learning, Cooperative Lives: A Source Book of Learning Activities for Building A Peaceful World.* Dubuque, IA: William C. Brown, 1987.

Weinstein, G. and Alschuler, A. ''Educating and Counseling for Self Knowledge Development,'' *Journal of Counseling and Development* 64 (1985): 19–25.

2

The Social Reconstructionist Curriculum

Social reconstructionists are interested in the relationship between curriculum and the social, political, and economic development of society. Optimistic social reconstructionists are convinced that education can effect social change, citing, for example, literacy campaigns that have contributed to successful political revolutions. Pessimists, on the other hand, doubt the ability of the curriculum to change existing social structures but want the curriculum to be a vehicle for fostering social discontent. They want learners to understand how the curriculum is used to consolidate power and to define society.

Aspects of reconstructionism appeared in American curriculum thought in the 1920s and 1930s. Harold Rugg was concerned about the values for which the school should work. He tried to awaken his peers to the "lag" between the curriculum, a "lazy giant," and the culture, with its fast-paced change and its resultant staggering social dislocations. Rugg's textbooks, teaching, and professional leadership had one overriding quality—the spirit of social criticism. He wanted learners to use newly emerging concepts from the social sciences and aesthetics to identify and solve current social problems. Rugg and his colleague, George Counts, author of *Dare the School Build a New Social Order?*, were among the pioneer thinkers who called on the school to begin creating a "new" and "more equitable" society.[1]

---

[1]George Counts, *Dare the School Build a New Social Order?* (Yonkers, NY: World Book, 1932).

In the early 1950s, the late Theodore Brameld outlined the distinctive features of social reconstructionism.[2] First, he believed in a commitment to building a new culture. Brameld was infused with the conviction that we are in the midst of a revolutionary period from which the common people will emerge as controllers of the industrial system, of public services, and of cultural and natural resources. Second, Brameld felt that the working people should control all principal institutions and resources if the world is to become genuinely democratic. Teachers should ally themselves with the organized working people. A way should be found to enlist the majority of people of all races and religions into a great democratic body with power to enforce its policies. The structure, goals, and policies of the new order must be approved at the bar of public opinion and enacted with popular support.

Third, Brameld believed that the school should help the individual, not only to develop socially, but to learn how to participate in social planning as well. The social reconstructionist wants no overstating of the case for individual freedom. Instead, the learners must see how society makes a people what they are and must find ways to satisfy personal needs through social consensus. Fourth, said Brameld, learners must be convinced of the validity and urgency of change. But they must also have a regard for democratic procedures. Ideally, reconstructionists are opposed to the use of intimidation, fear, and distortion to force compromise in the attempt to achieve a "community of persuasion." However, the reconstructionists take sides and encourage all to acquire a common viewpoint about crucial problems, to make up their minds about the most promising situations, and then to act in concert to achieve those solutions. The social reconstructionists believe they are representing values that the majority—consciously or not—already cherish. Most people are not now able to act responsibly, they say, because they have been persuaded and stunted by a dominating minority—those who largely control the instruments of power. Hence most persons do not exercise their citizenship on behalf of their own interests—their cherished values—but on behalf of scarcity, frustration, and war.

This chapter presents the premises of social reconstruction and the different directions taken by different social reconstructionists: revolution, critical inquiry, futurism. A distinction is also made between a curriculum of reconstruction, which attempts to change the social order, and a curriculum of social adaptation, which helps students fit into a world they never made.

---

[2]Theodore Brameld, *Toward a Reconstructed Philosophy of Education* (New York: Dryden, 1956).

CHARACTERISTICS OF THE SOCIAL RECONSTRUCTIONIST CURRICULUM

Purpose

The primary purpose of the social reconstructionist curriculum is to confront the learner with the many severe problems that humankind faces. Social reconstructionists believe that these problems are not the exclusive concern of "social studies" but of every discipline, including economics, aesthetics, chemistry, and mathematics. We are now in a critical period, they claim. The crisis is universal, and the widespread nature of the crisis must be emphasized in the curriculum.

The social reconstructionist curriculum, however, has no universal objectives and content. For example, the first year of such a curriculum might be devoted to formulating goals for political and economic reconstruction. Activities related to this objective might include the following: (1) a critical survey of the community (for example, one might collect information on local patterns of savings and expenditures), (2) a study relating the local economy to national and worldwide situations, (3) a study treating the influence of historic causes and trends on the local economic situation, (4) an examination of political practices in relation to economic factors, (5) a consideration of proposals for change in political practices, (6) a determination of which proposal satisfies the needs of the most people.

Objectives in later years of the curriculum might include the identification of problems, methods, needs, and goals in science and art; the evaluation of the relationship between education and human relations; and the identification of aggressive strategies for effecting change.

Role of the Teacher

Teachers must relate national, world, and local purposes to the students' goals. Students thus use their interests to help find solutions to the social problems emphasized in their classes. If a community wants to encourage participation of different ethnic groups in public meetings, for example, a foreign language class could help facilitate this participation by interpreting. Such a program provides an opportunity for students to use their special skills and interests to promote community goals in discussion groups, general assemblies, and other local organizations.

The teacher stresses cooperation with the community and its resources. Students may, for example, spend time away from the school participating in community health projects (for science classes) or in community acting, writing, or dance programs (for arts and literature classes). Even the arts must be integrated with other concerns in the program. The interconnection between art and science and art and economics, for example, might be strengthened as the art student looks at art in home and city planning, contrasts unhealthy communities with ''ideal garden cities,'' and attempts to see how the desire for business profits affects the quality of life.

In the primary school, the emphasis is on group experiences. Projects demand interdependence and social consensus. Children of different ages join in community surveys and other cooperative activities. The curriculum of an upper elementary school keeps the utopian faith by providing generous exercises in social imagination. It might allow children to create rough models of future and more just institutions, such as imaginary hospitals, television, or schools, and thus stimulate the children's awareness of grave contemporary problems and how special structures might be modified to address these problems.

Also, as a resource person and catalyst, the teacher seeks opportunities for youth to work as equals with adults in social projects and political activities. The school and neighborhood project of Boston, for instance, channels funds to students who, with adults, make grants to deserving neighborhood undertakings, such as attempting to clean up Boston Harbor and serving meals to homeless women.[3] However, more than encouraging social service, the teacher should challenge the beliefs of students and develop their critical consciousness.

Social reconstructionists hold that all teachers are political persons who must choose either to serve whoever is in power (conservatives) or present options to those in power (social reconstructionists). This is not to say that the teacher neglects course content simply to politicize students but that students learn to recognize that content is never neutral and to continually ask ''In favor of whom and for what do we use our knowledge?''[4]

BASIS FOR SELECTING LEARNING OPPORTUNITIES

For the social reconstructionist a learning opportunity must fulfill three criteria: it must be *real*, it must require *action*, and it must teach

---

[3]*The Forgotten Half: Pathways to Success for America's Youth and Young Families* (Washington, DC: William T. Grant Foundation on Work, Family and Citizenship, 1988).

[4]Paulo Freire, ''Letter to North American Teachers,'' in *Freire for the Classroom*, Ira Shore, ed. (Portsmouth, NH: Boyston/Cook, 1987), pp. 211–216.

values. First, learners must focus on an aspect of the community which they believe they can change and to which they will devote their efforts. Passive study, simulations, and role playing do not meet this criterion. Furthermore, the learners must have the opportunity to recognize the real importance of what they are to do. Second, learners must act on an issue or problem, not merely study it. Responsible action on a matter of public concern may include working with community groups, informing people about social problems, and taking a stand on controversial issues. Third, learners must form a coherent system of values. A learning activity must offer an opportunity to use a sense of what is right and wrong, desirable and undesirable and to supply the person with a sense of purpose and a basis for both individual and collective effort.

Henry Giroux implies that learning opportunities should provide an idealistic vision of a moral community, i.e., paint a picture of what life should be and insist that practical programs be measured by the degree to which they create this kind of society. As a utopian, he wants learning opportunities that exemplify the importance of critical democracy, solidarity, caring, and hope.[5]

Organization

A social reconstructionist organizes learning activities around such questions as these: Can the ordinary human being fulfill his or her own capabilities in the face of depersonalized forces? Can neighborhoods learn to work together to solve their own problems? Can the economic and political establishments be rebuilt so that people everywhere have access to environmental and cultural resources? Such questions are intended to invite explorations into learning, not only by means of books and laboratories, but by firsthand involvement in the experiences of people in communities.

A secondary school may organize with a common focus for integration of learning experiences such as Theodore Brameld suggested. He likened his system to a wheel: The "hub" consists of a general assembly (the entire school) engaged in studying one of the central critical questions. The "spokes" are courses composed of discussion groups, content and skill studies, vocational training, and recreation. These courses support the topics treated in the hub. Less concrete but still clearly delineated in the curriculum plans is the "rim," or unifying theme for the

---

[5]Henry A. Giroux, "Schooling and the Politics of Ethics: Beyond Liberal and Conservative Discourses," *Journal of Education* 169, no. 2 (1987): 9–34.

enterprise. The theme might be a principle, predicament, or aspiration for all mankind. The rim synthesizes the questions treated in the general assemblies, binding the whole.

Instructional sequence typically follows these stages: (1) identifying issues that appear most problematic, (2) examining the realities of the students' lives, including constraints and root causes of their problems, (3) linking issues to institutions and structures in the larger society, (4) relating social analysis to the visions and ideals students have for their world, community, and themselves, and (5) taking some responsibility (action) for putting the realities more in accordance with the ideal.

Evaluation

Evaluation covers a broad spectrum of students' abilities—articulation of issues, generation of possible solutions, redefinition of their world views, willingness to take action toward an ideal. Students are expected also to evaluate their own learning and to reflect as a group about the actions they have taken.

Social reconstructionists are also interested in the effect of the curriculum upon the community. Factors to be weighed include the growth of community consensus, increased political power of the working class, and an improved quality of life.

SOCIAL RECONSTRUCTION IN PRACTICE

Changing the Community

Few schools have tried to develop a curriculum completely within the framework of social reconstructionism. Within the United States, such efforts chiefly have been in poor communities. Similarly, worldwide, the Peace Corps and the Third World countries have attended to the concept and have tried to apply it, primarily in rural areas. The recent trend of involving the community in establishing goals for their neighborhood schools and in participating in the conduct of learning opportunities in pursuit of these goals is consistent with social reconstruction.

Project Ixtliyollotl in the community of San Andres, Mexico, is an alternative to conventional schooling.[6] The project began with members

---

[6]Ixtliyollotl Education Center, Cholula, Puebla, Mexico, 1989.

of the community recognizing that their high loss of human resources, illiteracy, family disorganization, and poverty was not being addressed by educational agencies. Shortly thereafter, more than 600 persons—children, youth, and adults—pooled their limited resources and formed their own school with related community activities. Subject matter is taught in the context of improving the social and economic conditions of San Andres. Science is taught in relation to local health improvement and history to understand the origins of their situation and to create a future. As an example of the close tie between school and daily life, one learning opportunity involves youth analyzing the political orientations of newspapers (social studies) and then issuing their own newspaper (writing) to serve the particular interests of San Andres. Under the leadership of the school, community members meet to acquire the mental outlooks, knowledge, and skills for establishing new industry central to the development and self-sufficiency of the community. Building upon traditional understanding of cattle, textiles, and agriculture, adults find ways to adapt this knowledge to a changing world. The project focuses upon strengthening the economic, political, and social capacities of women because they are seen as the key to the quality of life. Success has been hard won. The financial sacrifices of those on the brink of survival comprise one hurdle; another is harassment (vandalism, threats upon life, legal challenges) instigated by political powers who fear an empowered community and educational bureaucrats who are uneasy by Ixtliyollotl's achievement with tasks that they should address but don't.

Some features of social reconstructionism can be found as early as the 1940s. For example, the school program in Holtville, Alabama, a consolidated rural high school located in a poor area, had as its ideal better living conditions in the community.[7] In Holtville, the students were challenged to study their local economy. They found many problems: heavy meat spoilage in the stores, purchase of canned fruits and vegetables from outside the community as opposed to purchase of the same fruits and vegetables grown in the community, and an overemphasis on the production of a single crop.

With the cooperation of local farmers, the students secured a loan from a governmental agency to construct a slaughterhouse and refrigeration plant. Guided by a teacher, the students began processing meat and renting lockers to the farmers. Soon, they had paid off the loan. Then

---

[7]*The Story of Holtville: A Southern Association Study School* (Nashville: Cullum and Ghertner, 1944).

they did more. They started a hatchery and arranged to sell chicks to the farmers and buy back eggs below the market price, making money on the enterprise. Subsequently, they undertook to manage a cannery at the school, installed a water supply; helped install modern facilities in homes, restored homes; purchased modern machinery, which they rented or used in working for the farmers; planted over 65,000 trees to prevent erosion; planted, sprayed, and pruned 50,000 peach trees for farmers; and set up woodwork and machine shops, a beauty shop, a local newspaper, a movie theatre, a game library, a bowling alley, and a cooperative store in which many of their own products were sold, including toothpaste made in their chemistry department.

In a similar fashion, Myles Horton founded Highlander Folk School in Tennessee, a leading educational center for activists in labor, civil rights, and other social struggles.[8] Horton's curriculum guidelines call for starting with the people's problems. (They may not be able to state what they want in educational terms, but they know what they want in practical terms.) The program must be based on the people's perception of the problem, not the educator's. The curriculum maker must induce the people to use what they already know and to share it. The curriculum maker helps people diagnose their problem and helps learners supplement their knowledge. Limited use is made of the professional when the need for technical advice is obvious. At Highlander, participants are encouraged to take action, such as picketing the welfare office, and then analyze the action to understand its importance and to internalize it.

Student activities conducted according to reconstructionist principles are also found in volunteer programs in which students attempt to solve local poverty problems, to organize community resources to aid consumers, to help foreign-born nursing home residents, to correct discriminatory employment practices, to determine community needs, to establish facilities for mental patients, and to reform state utility laws.

Paulo Freire's Practice of Social Reconstructionism

Today, the leading social reconstructionist in both theory and practice is Paulo Freire.[9] Although Freire has concentrated on the challenges

---

[8]John N. Glenn, *Highlander: No Ordinary School 1952–1962* (Lexington: University of Kentucky, 1988).

[9]Paulo Freire, *Pedagogy of the Oppressed* (New York: Herder and Herder, 1970).

facing Latin America and one African country in this time of change, he believes that other areas of the Third World differ only in small details and that they must follow his "cultural action for conscientization" if they are to be liberated from political and economic oppression.

Conscientization. Conscientization is the process by which persons, not as recipients but as active learners, achieve a deep awareness both of the sociocultural reality that shapes their lives and of their ability to transform that reality.[10] It means enlightening people about the obstacles that prevent them from having a clear perception of reality. One of these obstacles is a standardized way of thinking—acting, for example, according to the prescriptions received daily from the communications media rather than recognizing one's own problems. Other obstacles are dehumanizing structures that control learning from the outside, educational systems whose schools are an instrument for maintaining the status quo, and political leaders who mediate between the masses and the elite while keeping the masses in a dependent state. Conscientization means helping persons apprehend the origins of facts and problems in their situations rather than attributing them to a superior power or to their own "natural" incapacity. Unless people see these facts objectively, they will accept the situation apathetically, believing themselves incapable of affecting their destiny.

Freire has put his philosophy into action. For example, his plan and materials for teaching reading to adult illiterates aims at transformation not reproduction. Table 2–1 shows the contrast between Freire's approach and the conventional approach to teaching reading in adult literacy campaigns.

Freire contends that oppression comes from within the person as well as from without. Hence, the felt needs of each person must be challenged if they are to be freed from blind adherence to their own world views as well as to the uncritically examined views of others. If farmers come to Freire demanding a course in the use of pesticides in order to increase yields of their crops, for example, Freire assists them by examining the causes of their felt need for such instruction, thereby rediagnosing their need for the course. Probing into causes might lead the participants to conclude that a course in use of pesticides, as initially perceived, is not needed as much as a course on marketing practice.

---

[10]Paulo Freire, "Cultural Action and Conscientization," *Harvard Education Review* 40, no. 3 (May 1970): 452–477.

TABLE 2–1 Contrasting Approaches to the Teaching of Reading

Conventional Approach	*Freire Approach*
The teacher chooses words and selections to read and proposes them to the learner.	Poor people create texts that express their own thought-language and their perceptions of the world.
Primers feature word selections that have little to do with the students' sociocultural reality. Literature is defined from a Eurocentric perspective, which does not reflect the lives and experiences of minority children.	Words are chosen for their (1) pragmatic value in communication with one's group. "Dangerous" words (i.e., *love* and *lust, lease* and *license, prison* and *power*), for example, the significant concepts that exist among the most broken of the poor; (2) connotations of indignation; (3) generative features, such as syllabic elements by which learners can compare and read new words of importance to themselves.
The teacher implies that there is a relationship between knowing how to read and getting a good job.	The teacher stresses that merely teaching persons to read and write does not work miracles. If there are not enough jobs, teaching reading will not create them.
Learning to read is viewed as memorizing and repeating given syllables, words, and phrases or as reproducing generalizations (main ideas) in passages rather than constructing personally relevant meanings from text.	Learning to read is viewed as important to reflecting critically on the cultural milieu and to awakening students to the dehumanizing aspects of their lives.

The aim of education in Freire's approach is not to accommodate or adjust learners to the social system, but to free them from slavish adherence to it.[11]

Eradicating Illiteracy. Despite attempts to cope with illiteracy, adult illiterates in the United States exceed 25 million. A recent report on the efforts to eradicate illiteracy in the United States attests to the inadequacy of curricula that are not immediately relevant to people's lives. The book recommends that illiterates help design a literacy program based on their own needs.[12] Creating a network of community-based literacy programs in poor neighborhoods could potentially win the confidence of people

[11]Paulo Freire and Donaldo Macedo, *Literacy: Reading the Word and the World* (South Hadley, MA: Bergin and Garvey, 1987).

[12]David Marman, *Illiteracy: A National Dilemma* (New York: Cambridge Book Co., 1987).

who would otherwise be suspicious of solutions that they perceive as imposed on them from the outside.

National literacy campaigns in Cuba, Nicaragua, and China using many of Freire's techniques, such as volunteer teachers and the participation of the peasants and the poor in their own education, have resulted in great gains in literacy and laid the foundation for social development.[13] Although the leaders of these campaigns are optimistic that curriculum can develop a critical consciousness in students and prepare people to reinvent society, others are more pessimistic.

Wendy Griswold maintains, for instance, that curriculum has not altered very much the structural problems of inequality, poverty, or the domination of the many by the few.[14] She finds little evidence that educational reform has had a positive influence on economic development; most curriculum reforms support the status quo. Even leaders of revolutionary régimes use the curriculum to consolidate their power. In fact, the political revolutions in Cuba and Nicaragua preceded literacy; literacy did not contribute to revolt. Curriculum can, however, contribute to the building of a social order by promoting political awareness and strengthening challenges to the existing society.

Neo-Marxists

A new left evolved in the '70s that sought social reforms using the schools to awaken allies in labor, civil rights, and other groups with the need for control and power. These revolutionaries accused older social reconstructionists of being naive in the belief that they could transform society by using a "new wave of students who have been nurtured (in the schools)." According to the neo-Marxist, the older reconstructionists failed to recognize that oppression and exploitation are a fundamental characteristic of class structure in the United States and cannot be altered by tinkering with the school. These neo-Marxists advocated that curriculum specialists recognize that the success of the schools is tied to conditions in the larger society. Just as the conflicts over the curriculum arise outside the school, so the solutions to these problems require efforts by the larger society. Parents, concerned citizens, organized labor, students, and other groups must be involved in studying, for example, the prevail-

---

[13]Special issue: "Education: A Transformation, Identity, Change and Development," *Harvard Educational Review* 51 (February 1981).

[14]Wendy Griswold, "Education and Transformation," *Harvard Educational Review* 52, no. 1 (February 1982): 45–53.

ing patterns of financing, ways to create more jobs, and the possibility of redistributing income.

1975 Manifesto. Indeed, in 1975, an ASCD Yearbook committee presented a call to action, encouraging educators to protect their own living standards by uniting with other educators, students, workers, and minority organizations. The manifesto in the yearbook urged educators to demand democracy for students and a curriculum designed to serve the interests of the dominated: the broad working class. Public school educators were given guidelines for action:

1. Develop a core of progressive teachers in each school for the purpose of examining instances of class discrimination—materials, tests, methods, policies—that show differential bias.
2. Encourage students to study the presence or absence of democracy in the school and to report whose interests are being served by existing policies and procedures.
3. Present the findings of dominant class interests at meetings with progressive parents, members of other schools, the teachers' union, and other professional organizations.
4. Expose the class content of your school program publicly—for example, at PTA and union meetings.
5. Enlist the help of community and working-class organizations in developing a curriculum based on the interests of the working class. The curriculum at a minimum would include (a) the teaching of modern history focused on the struggles of Western-dominated Third World countries, the working classes, oppressed minorities, and women against exploitation; (b) full equality for the language and culture of oppressed national minorities; (c) instruction in fundamentals of socio-economic analysis of social relations; and (d) development of cultural activities aimed at the acceptance of working-class culture.
6. Establish an areawide committee for a curriculum based on the interests of the dominated groups, enlisting students in the struggle for liberation.
7. Introduce a plan for disseminating revolutionary demands and form a united front among all dominated groups against the increasingly centralized and rigid control by the power structure.[15]

"Reproductive" Critical Theory and Knowledge. Recently, Michael Apple and Henry Giroux have argued that the knowledge "reproduced" in

---

[15]James A. MacDonald and Esther Zaret, eds., *Schools in Search of Meaning,* ASCD Yearbook (Washington, DC: National Education Association, 1975): pp. 158–161.

schools produces a stratified social order and perpetuates the values of dominant social class interests. Only rarely has the curriculum not reflected what is happening outside of school.[16] Both authors believe that we should broaden the curriculum to include community action. Through community action, they hold, students develop social and political responsibility and skills while learning to question the ethic of their institutions and to criticize them when they fail to meet ideals. Giroux wants teachers to change the nature of schooling so that it is more emancipatory and less a feeble echo of the demand for social order.[17] He holds that teachers have the potential to overcome the social form that oppresses them. Giroux feels that schools are sites where personal opinions and beliefs are formed and reformed. Conflict must be made part of the curriculum both because it is a legitimate means of getting recourse in unequal societies and a positive source of vitality and renewal.[18] Teachers may oppose the official curriculum based upon their own experiences, critical reading, and discussion with others. Although it is naive to think that the school can create the conditions for changing the large society, teachers and students must try to transform their own practices and consciousness as part of a larger strategy to change society.

By way of example, in Marilyn Frankenstein's curriculum "Statistics for the Social Science," students learn to understand the importance of quantitative reasoning in the development of critical consciousness and the ways in which math anxiety sustains hegemonic (power) ideologies.[19] Students explore the fact that statistics are not neutral and the reasons why official statistics are more useful to conservative than to radical thinkers. Students analyze statistical knowledge to reveal underlying interests and methods of collection as well as to consider what new knowledge might be produced which is consistent with humanization and with the improvement of their own lives. By way of illustration, students learn how the government makes the proportion of the federal budget for military spending appear smaller by such practices as including funds "in trust" as social services while placing war-related expenditures, such as the production of nuclear war heads, the space program, and veterans' programs as part of various nonmilitary categories like the Department of Energy budget. Frankenstein's students address such

---

[16]Michael Apple, *Education and Power* (Boston: Routledge & Kegan Paul, 1982).

[17]Henry Giroux, *Ideology and the Process of Schooling* (Philadelphia: Temple University Press, 1981).

[18]Henry Giroux, "Critical Pedagogy: Cultural Politics and the Discourse of Experience," *Journal of Education* 67, no. 2 (1987): 23–41.

[19]Marilyn Frankenstein, "Critical Mathematics Education," in *Freire for the Classroom*, Ira Shore, ed. (Portsmouth, NH: Heinemann, 1987), pp.180–204.

myths as the belief that social welfare programs are responsible for a declining standard of living by asking students to research, using arithmetical operations, the amounts given to the poor versus the amounts given to the rich to uncover the fact that ''welfare'' to the rich dwarfs subsidies to the poor.

In seeking to understand the causes of math anxiety, students learn how structures in our society result in different groups being more affected than others by this anxiety, and how people participate in their own mathematical disempowerment. Students see how differentiated treatment based on race and class is related to math avoidance and question why research on math anxiety focuses only on the relationship between sex and mathematics learning.

Evidence in support of the ''reproductive'' theory of curriculum, i.e., that the knowledge taught in school perpetuates existing political and economic structures, has been provided by Jean Anyon.[20] In her case study, Anyon collected data on school knowledge in five elementary schools in contrasting social class settings. Her data suggest that while topics and materials are similar among working-class, middle-class, affluent, and elite schools, dramatic differences exist in pupils' experience of the curricula in these schools.

In the working-class schools, students were not taught their own history—the history of the working class, and the curriculum emphasized rote behaviors rather than creative thinking. The dominant theme was student resistance. The teacher had to discipline the class physically at times in order to impose a curriculum, which consisted only of the basics and worksheets. In contrast, the middle-class school students viewed knowledge as facts and generalizations which could be exchanged for college entrance or a better job. Possibility was the dominant theme.

In the affluent school, students perceived knowledge as a personal activity related to things or ideas. They were taught ways of using ideas for their own interests. The dominant theme in the affluent school was individualization. Because students thought for themselves and engaged in creative projects and personal discovery, their schooling stressed individual values over collective ones.

In the executive elite school, excellence was the theme. Students viewed knowledge as the result of rational rules, not personal discovery. Children were provided with socially prestigious subject matter and were given analytical insights about the social system.

---

[20]Jean Anyon, ''Social Class and School Knowledge,'' *Curricular Inquiry* 11, no. 1 (1981): 3–41.

Though Anyon concluded that the curriculum reproduced the maintenance of class roles in society, she felt it also offered possibilities for transformation. The resistance of working-class pupils might lead to a restructuring of capitalistic ideology. The middle-class students, on the other hand, might become disillusioned with false promises about big rewards for working hard and might become critics of the system. Students in the affluent school might recognize irrationalities in society as they engage in their individual efforts at making sense of the world. Pupils in the elite school might discover the difference between using knowledge for pleasure and using it to maintain power in the face of competition from others. Furthermore, elitist learners might perceive a need for destroying the system because they might see how under capitalism one must exploit others.

Anyon's optimistic view that transformation through resistance is possible in the face of reproduction signals a new direction in critical theory. Whereas previous critiques of curriculum have been too deterministic, offering weak roles to human actors, today some critical thinkers are recognizing that schools do more than reproduce dominant social relations or serve capitalistic demands. The language of critique is being modified to include the language of possibility.

Futurologists

Curriculum futurologists advocate making deliberate choices about the world of the future (utopia). They would study trends, estimate the social consequences foreshadowed by the trends, and then attempt to promote probable futures seen as ''good'' and prevent those seen as ''bad.''

There are many futurologists in society at large. The World Future Society alone, a nonprofit, nonpolitical organization, has 16,000 members from economists and philosophers to Venus watchers. Generally, futurologists do not attempt to predict what is going to happen in 10 or 15 years but attempt to decide on what they want to happen so that they can then make more intelligent choices.

The Use of Future Planning. Harold G. Shane, professor at Indiana University, is representative of those social reconstructionists who would use future planning as a basis for curriculum making.[21] He urges planning the future, not planning for the future. As with other social recon-

---

[21]Harold G. Shane, *Educating for a New Millennium* (Bloomington, IN: Phi Delta Kappan, 1981).

structionists, he stresses the power of persons to shape their own destiny and to believe that they are not bound to an inescapable future to which they must conform.

Shane would obligate curriculum developers to study trends first. Trends may be technological developments that have been identified with the help of specialists in academic disciplines. Such trends include reduction of hereditary defects, increase in life expectancy, chemical methods for improving memory, and home education via video and computers. Trends also may be inventoried problems such as those found in the literature of disaster (for example, famine, dwindling resources, pollution). Shane would have educators who have studied trends engage with a wide number of participants in analyzing their consequences. Such consequences might be mandatory foster homes for children whose natural homes are harmful to their physical or mental health, psychological prerequisites for candidates seeking public office, use of biochemical therapy for improving mood, memory, and concentration, reversal of counterecological trends, and controlled growth. Professional specialists (those with expert knowledge) would decide whether the promised consequences would humanize or dehumanize. Final judgment about desirability, however, must rest with the people concerned. (Procedures used by futurists in setting purposes are described on pages 115–117).

Most social reconstructionists are very clear about the role of the professional expert in the determination of social policy. Although they use experts in analyzing complicated social problems, they do not entirely relegate the solution of these problems to the experts. "In the realm of social policy, the decisions of the whole people, when they have full access to the facts, are in the long run typically wiser than those made by any single class or group. The cult of the expert is but the prelude to some form of authoritarian society."[22] Reconstructionists favor pressing society for decisions and for the development of a clearer social consensus as to what the "good life" is. In achieving this consensus, the ideas of children, parents, administrators, and teachers should be considered. Those ideas that the group sees as having merit must become the basis for "mutual coercion," control for a socially worthy purpose.

Typical Recommendations. Futurist curriculum focuses on the exploitation of resources, pollution of the air and water, warfare, the effect of

---

[22]B. Othanel Smith et al., *Fundamentals of Curriculum Development* (Yonkers, NY: World Books, 1950), p. 638.

the population increase and the unequal use of natural resources, propaganda, especially in press and screen, and self-control in the interests of one's fellow man.

For example, in his view of the future, Neil Postman responds to TV as a dangerous curriculum—an information system specially constructed to influence, teach, train, and cultivate the mind and character of the young—competing with the school's curriculum. It is a dangerous curriculum because it is (a) present-centered (does not encourage deferred gratification), (b) attention-centered (entertainment takes precedence over content), (c) image-centered (weakens ability to use abstract, propositional reasoning), (d) emotion-centered (nonintellectual), and (e) largely incoherent (it creates discontinuity). Postman would create a future in which the curriculum of the school would counter TV, offer a sense of purpose, meaning, and the interrelation of disciplines. The historical development of humanity, for instance, could be used to integrate the teaching of philosophy, science, language, religion, and cultural expression.[23]

Social Adaptation

Both social adaption and social reconstruction derive aims and content from an analysis of the society that the school is to serve. Curriculum development in response to social needs, such as AIDS and sex education, parenting programs, antidrug campaigns, are often more adaptive than reconstructive. Such curriculum represents a mechanism for adjusting students to what some groups believe to be an appropriate response to critical needs within society. Social adaption differs from social reconstruction in that usually no attempt is made to develop a critical consciousness of social problems and to do something about them. The approach of social adaptionists is to give students information and prescriptions for dealing with situations as defined rather than to seek a fundamental change in the basic structure of society underlying the problems. Whereas social adaptionists look at society to find out what students need to achieve and to protect themselves in the real world to fit into society as it is, social reconstructionists look at society with the intent of building a curriculum by which students can improve the real world.

---

[23]Neil Postman, "Engaging Students in the Great Conversation," *Phi Delta Kappan* 64, no. 5 (March 1983): 310–317.

CRITICISMS OF SOCIAL RECONSTRUCTIONISM

Reconstructionism is appealing because of its faith in the ability of humankind to form a more perfect world. Furthermore, it claims to use the best of science in determining status and possibilities. Among the reconstructionists' difficulties, however, is the fact that scientific findings permit varied interpretations. Established empirical conclusions are scant. Even the futurologists have been divided into the "bleak sheiks" (pessimists) and the "think-tank utopians" (optimists). Also, there are no direct implications for curriculum. What one sociologist or economist considers true may be refuted by another. Few agree about which conduct is best for a planned society.

Reconstructionists with a Marxist orientation fault older reconstructionists for failing to recognize that oppression and exploitation are fundamental characteristics of class structure in the United States and cannot be altered by teachers within the schools. Although older reconstructionists did not speak of the school as remaking the society in any total sense, they did believe that the school might influence behavior in regard to social problems. They realized that attitudes and beliefs would not be sustained unless supported by changes in the structure of society. However, older reconstructionists thought that the primary task of the school was a moral and intellectual reconstruction. Unlike the neo-Marxists, they did not believe that the school should be an instrument for subversion and political revolution. Instead, they wanted to use the school to extend the ideals to which the people were already committed.

Neo-Marxists also have been faulted. Their theory of cultural reproduction has been challenged because no evidence shows that schools have been deliberately oppressive in the interests of the larger society. Indeed, the neo-Marxists have introduced the concept of "resistance," indicating that the curriculum may not function solely to prepare students for stratified points in the capitalistic social order. Daniel Liston has faulted Marxists for not providing sufficient evidence in support of their claims and for associating a particular consequence without showing that it is the practice itself which produces the result.[24] With respect to tracking, for example, little evidence exists that this grouping arrangement was selected for capitalistic purposes or that it persists because of its positive effects for capitalism.

Although the work of Freire in developing curriculum through dialogue with learners is generally highly regarded, he, too, has his critics.

---

[24]Daniel Liston, "Faith and Evidence: Examining Marxists' Explanations of Schools," *American Journal of Education* 96, no. 3 (May 1988): 323–351.

Jim Walker, for instance, doubts that Freire's educational ideas and methods are truly liberating because they do not give enough attention to effecting a revolution. Freire has little to say, Walker charges, about the nature of political leadership and how to achieve unity among a divided people.[25]

C. A. Bowers, on the other hand, believes that Freire's approach reflects Western culture and therefore might undermine the traditional world view of people in non-Western cultures. Brown questions whether Western assumptions such as knowledge is power, change is progressive, and people are the masters of their own fates are appropriate in non-Western traditional societies.[26]

CONCLUDING COMMENTS

Social reconstructionists are concerned with the relation of the curriculum to society as it *should* be as opposed to society as it *is*. Many tenets of this group are consistent with our highest ideals, such as the right of those with a minority viewpoint to persuade those of a majority viewpoint, and with faith in the intelligence of the common people and in their ability to shape their own destiny in desired directions. Neo-Marxists within the social reconstructionist ranks would pit class against class, disregarding the differences within classes, groups, and genders. The futurists in the movement are far less ideologically oriented and would be happy if the curriculum would help learners "want well," i.e., conceive of a desirable future after taking into account crucial social trends.

The reconstructionist commitment to particular social ideas determined by "social consensus" may have difficulty being accepted in an individualistic United States. Americans have so many competing interests and different views regarding moral, religious, aesthetic, and social issues that it is difficult for them to agree on an ideal. Some also voice concern about the reconstructionists' efforts to create a collective society in which solutions are reached through social consensus.

We can expect accelerated curriculum development along reconstructionist lines whenever a resolution of conflict in values is needed. Such a need often exists in multicultural neighborhoods. Cultural groups

---

[25]Jim Walker, "The End of Dialogue," *Literacy and Revolution*, Robert Mackie, ed. (New York: Continuum, 1981), pp. 120–151.

[26]C. A. Bowers, "Cultural Invasion in Paulo Freire's Pedagogy," *Teachers College* 81, no. 4 (Summer 1983): 935–955.

frequently have different interpretations of history, different conceptions of nature, different levels of aspiration, and different views of social conduct. The prediction also applies whenever there is a breakdown in the barriers that isolate the school from the community. Accelerated curriculum development should thus occur when parents and community members become involved in teaching and social service roles, when students and adults participate in effecting changes outside the school building, when community members assess local social and economic needs or deficiencies and decide how the institutions in the community can contribute to the improvement of the selected priority needs.

It is difficult to implement social reconstruction in state schools in which conservation of the political status quo and social adaptation is the rule. Furthermore, social reconstruction isn't viable as long as teachers view teaching as subject matter transmission rather than personal and social transformation. Also, professional teacher organizations tend to clash with reconstructionists favoring local community groups and parents. Rivalry between professional teacher and parent power movements regarding *what* should be taught and *how* it should be taught has already surfaced. The challenge, therefore, is to apply the principle that calls for a "community of persuasion," probably by including teachers in the decision-making process but also by giving the community—parents and others—more of a controlling voice.

QUESTIONS

1. What circumstances would be most likely to give rise to a curriculum along social reconstructionist lines?
2. Paulo Freire speaks of the curriculum obstacles preventing a clear perception of reality (for example, control of learning from the outside, content and method that foster learner dependency, and standardized ways of thinking). Can you provide specific examples of these obstacles in schools which you have known?
3. Consider computer literacy, drug education, and dropout prevention programs known to you. Was their approach social adaptionist or social reconstructionist? Why?
4. Are you optimistic or pessimistic about the ability of curriculum to change existing social structure or institutions? Why?
5. What predictions about the world future appear "good" to you?

Which predictions appear ''bad?'' How should a curriculum be designed in order to prevent the bad future?

6. Whose interests are best served by the curriculum with which you are familiar?

SELECTED REFERENCES

Apple, Michael W. *Education and Power.* Boston: Routledge & Kegan Paul, 1982.

Freire, Paulo. *The Politics of Education.* Amherst, MA: Bergin & Garvey, 1985.

Giroux, Henry. *Ideology, Culture and the Process of Schooling.* Philadelphia: Temple University Press, 1981.

Oakes, Jeannie. *Keeping Track: How Schools Structure Inequality.* New Haven: Yale University Press, 1985.

Shore, Ira, ed. *Freire for the Classroom: A Sourcebook for Liberating Teaching.* Portsmouth, NH: Heinemann, 1987.

3

Technology and the Curriculum

Educational consumers are familiar with technology in the form of computer-based instruction, individualized learning systems, and video and audio cassettes. Many consumers have been exposed to Seymour Papert's program for the promotion of technological literacy. In the program, primary grade children learn to program robots and learn mathematical concepts by giving ''turtle talk'' commands to a computer, such as teaching the turtle to draw a square.

Most persons are less aware, however, that technology is also helpful in the analysis of curriculum problems as well as for the creation, implementation, evaluation, and management of instructional solutions. Technology as a curriculum perspective focuses on the effectiveness of programs, methods, and materials in the achievement of specified ends or purposes. A technological perspective has been applied in many contexts: the development of training programs in industry and the military, the design of instructional systems with matching objectives, activities, and tests, and the development of instructional products or materials. Recently, the technological perspective has been a major factor in the competency testing movement and other responses to public demand for school accountability.

Technology influences curriculum in two ways: application and theory. Applied technology is a plan for the systematic use of various devices and media or a contrived sequence of instruction based on principles from behavioral science. Computer-assisted instruction, systems approaches using objectives, programmed materials, tutors following scripts aimed at teaching a specific skill, and criterion-referenced tests all are examples of applied technology. A defining element of technology is that its systems and products can be replicated. That is, the same results can be attained on repeated occasions, and the system itself is exportable, useful in many situations.

Technology as theory is useful in the development and evaluation of curriculum materials and instructional systems. In the developmental process technologists formulate rules which, if followed, will result in more predictable products.

General systems philosophy is a technological framework for viewing problems of curriculum. It emphasizes the specification of instructional objectives (usually derived by needs assessment, a study that contrasts the student's level of achievement with the learning goals), precisely controlled learning activities or instructional sequences to achieve these objectives, and criteria for performance and evaluation. Developing a general systems philosophy also requires stressing feedback to modify the learner's behavior and to adapt instruction (i.e., measurement of the achievements of the program), recognizing the interaction between components of the instructional system, and paying attention to the complex interactions between the program and the larger environment in which it is to be implemented.

At first glance, technology appears to be concerned with *how* to teach rather than *what* to teach. Technologists think of themselves as finding efficient and effective means to achieve specific ends. A second glance shows that the instructional sequences produced by the technologist's model are primarily concerned with what is or is not learned. In focusing upon a specified objective, however, the technologist is less likely to develop flexible instructional sequences that contribute to a range of desirable outcomes.

This chapter includes a description and analysis of technology as a learning system as well as procedures for using technology as the basis for curriculum development. Knowledge of these should help in understanding the characteristics of the approach and in discerning the strengths and weaknesses in the technological concepts of curriculum.

TECHNOLOGY AND THE IDEAL OF EFFICIENCY

Early in the twentieth century, curriculum specialists such as Franklin Bobbett thought that the methods used by industry for increasing productivity could be applied in education. Decisions about what to teach were to be reached by analysis of what was required in the performance of jobs. Instructional methods were to be based upon research as to which procedures were best for maximizing student achievement toward clearly specified objectives related to performance in a world of industry and business.

In the 1960s, B. F. Skinner promoted efficiency in learning by suggesting a way to teach "more of a given subject, in more subjects, and to more students."[1] His answer was to sequence learning tasks toward specific terminal behaviors, elicit overt responses from learners to these tasks, and reinforce correct responses. Accordingly, curriculum was seen as a sequence of content arranged by steps or objectives with each step to be mastered as a prerequisite to subsequent learning.

Following the work of Skinner, technologists developed these rules for constructing curriculum-programmed lessons and training programs:

1. gain attention of the learner
2. inform the learner of the expected outcome
3. activate relevant capabilities
4. present stimuli inherent to the task
5. elicit correct responses by prompting
6. provide feedback
7. appraise performance
8. provide for transfer of learning
9. ensure retention

EXAMPLES OF TECHNOLOGICAL CURRICULUM

Systems Technology

Systems technology is used as the framework for developing and monitoring state and local district curriculum. This approach emphasizes the specification of outcomes that students must demonstrate, stipulates the criteria for performance and evaluative information, and sets direction for controlling learning experiences for achieving the specified objectives. The California State Board of Education, for example, has used systems technology in projecting state policy initiatives to districts and classrooms. Model curriculum standards are issued for mandated graduation requirements. The standards specify both the content and the behav-

---

[1] B. F. Skinner, *The Technology of Teaching* (New York: Appleton-Century-Crofts, 1968), p. 856.

ior expected from each required course. In addition, the document suggests classroom activities for achieving the standardized lesson strategies and assessment measures.

Statewide tests that match the specified objectives are given to monitor the program. The system is further tightened by ensuring that the criteria for both textbook adoption and staff development are tied to the Board's intents. School principals throughout the state attend training centers to become informed of curriculum objectives and to learn how to translate the standards into classroom practice. Subsequently, principals guide teachers in focusing on what students are to know and do and in developing strategies for achieving the prescribed outcomes.

Instructional Alignment

Instructional alignment is another example of the measured curriculum, involving ''teaching to the test'' or to the outcome signified by the criterion assessment. In his review of instructional alignment, S. Alan Cohen presents evidence that when instructional stimuli match assessment, effects about four times what is ordinarily seen in typical classrooms occur.[2]

In instructional alignment, the critical elements are the congruence between the stimulus conditions of criterion behaviors and the instructional sequence. Tests are created *before* designing the curriculum. Personalized systematic instruction and mastery learning are instances of outcome-driven curriculum.

Personalized Systematic Instruction in Higher Education

Over 90 percent of the nation's colleges and universities use highly sophisticated electronic devices to transmit some portion of their curriculum to students. Television, for example, is an ancillary means to extend conventional pedagogy to undergraduates in many large public universities. Professors' lectures are videotaped and cassettes made available for viewing at the convenience of the student. The practice is not common in small colleges and secondary schools in which social oversight is a teacher's duty. As the use of educational technology becomes even more widespread, the teacher tends to replace the role of imparter of knowledge with that of manager. The content of instruction and its applications

---

[2]S. Alan Cohen, ''Instructional Alignment: Searching for a Magic Bullet,'' *Educational Researcher* 16, no. 8 (November 1987): 16–20.

are set in advance. In contrast to traditional higher education, the boundaries of knowledge are not fluid, and the results obtained are more important than the process. When course content is viewed as finite, it can be packaged in advance, duplicated, and transmitted. Although the view may narrowly define content, it also allows students to work at their own pace.

A popular use of technology as a means to more effective instruction is the personalized system of instruction (PSI). This system is a soft technology involving persons, content, materials, and organizations as opposed to a hard technology, which involves only devices such as television, projectors, and computers. PSI uses the principles of behavioral science that call for frequent active responses from students, immediate knowledge of results, and a clear statement of objectives. It also allows for individualization; different students may use different amounts of time and different approaches for attaining mastery of the instructional tasks.

With PSI, a course or subject is broken into small units of learning, and at the end of each unit learners take tests to determine whether they are ready for new material or should receive additional instruction. Whenever students believe they are ready, they go to a "proctoring room" staffed by advanced students who administer the test, score it, and give feedback to the students. If less than "unit perfection" performance is shown, the proctor becomes a tutor, explaining the missing points and guiding the student in restudy. There is no penalty for failing a unit, but one must study further and try again. Frequent interaction with proctors often develops affect and contributes to understanding.

PSI permits one instructor to serve as many as 1,000 students, or possibly more. Instructors are responsible for conducting one- or two-hour weekly large group sessions for motivating and clarifying. They also have overall responsibility for planning the course, including the procedures and procurement or development of materials and examinations.

Mastery Learning

Mastery learning is a curriculum produced by technologists. Instructional objectives, arranged in an assumed hierarchy of tasks, are the keystone of the system, and lesson materials are built around that arrangement. The objectives are the intended outcomes of instruction. Each pupil must master them before going on to the next step in the learning hierarchy. Mastery is indicated by successful responses to criterion-referenced tests matched to the content and behavior specified in the objective. Objectives in the teaching of mathematics, for example, are grouped by topics such as numeration, place value, and subtraction.

Lesson materials are matched with the objectives and allow the pupil to proceed independently with a minimum of teacher direction. The pattern for involving the pupil with the system has three parts:

1. Finding out what the pupil already knows about the subject. Usually a general placement test is administered to reveal the pupil's general level of achievement. The pupil is also given a pretest to reveal specific deficiencies.
2. Giving the pupil self-instructional materials or other carefully designed learning activities. Such activities focus on one of the specific deficiencies previously identified.
3. Giving the pupil evaluative measurements to determine his or her progress. Such measurements help the teacher decide whether to move the pupil ahead to a new task or to provide additional materials or tutoring.

Materials usually include placement tests, pre- and posttests (criterion-referenced), skill booklets, a record system, games and manipulatives, and cassettes and filmstrips. Paid aides and volunteers (such as parents) assist pupils, check response sheets, and help to keep the materials organized.

GENERAL CHARACTERISTICS OF CLASSROOM TECHNOLOGICAL SYSTEMS

Objectives

Objectives have either a behavioral or an empirical emphasis. They specify learning products or processes in forms that can be observed or measured. There is no inherent reason why technological systems cannot employ affective as well as psychomotor and cognitive objectives. Typically, however, the objectives are detailed, specific, and skill-oriented. Commercially available materials feature objectives that are likely to be appropriate for most children in this country. Those skills that most curriculum developers believe to be useful in learning to read and in solving mathematical problems, for example, are often focuses of instruction. The instructional objectives of technological systems thus tend to reinforce the importance of conventional goals and the traditional divisions of academic subject matter. With the exception of locally designed materials, such as Unipacs, learning centers, and learning activities packages (LAPs), objectives more appropriate for local social conditions are seldom treated. In addition, there are not many opportunities for pupils to generate their own objectives.

Methods

On the one hand, the technologist prepares programs and materials for wide use and tries to make his or her sequence of instruction "teacher proof," with the learner responding independently. Tapes and audiotapes such as those which teach English required for amnesty examinations are a case in point. Many adults favor these self-instructional materials with which they can practice in the privacy of their homes. On the other hand, the technologist's rules for sequencing instruction have been widely promulgated as a model for teaching. Madeline Hunter's designs for lessons closely follow the technologist's rules including the influence of anticipatory set, perceived purpose, task analysis, modeling or guided practice, checks for understanding, and independent practice when it is unlikely that the student will make errors.[3]

Learning is viewed as a process of reacting to stimuli—attending to relevant cues—rather than as a transactional process in which the learner influences the stimuli. The learner is directed to attend to more significant features and is reinforced for appropriate behavior. Goals of instruction are predetermined rather than emergent.

Individualism is restricted to pacing, corrective feedback, and supplementary tasks when deficiencies and misconceptions are noticed. Some students can make their responses more quickly and require fewer exercises to learn a generalization. Individual learners spend time on tasks leading to behaviors already in their repertoires.

Organization

The technologist's curriculum is usually related to subject disciplines such as mathematics, sciences, reading and other language arts, and fine arts, and to applied technical fields. Usually only a few aspects of these fields are selected for treatment at any one time. Decimals in mathemat-

---

[3]Madeline Hunter, "Knowing, Teaching and Supervising," in *What We Know About Teaching* (Washington, DC: 1984), pp. 169–197.

ics, for example, are treated in a separate program, not as mathematics in general. The objectives of instruction are arranged in a fixed continuum or hierarchy of skills; and end-of-program objective such as the ability to multiply would follow enroute objectives of addition and subtraction. End-of-program objectives are precisely and operationally stated, and these objectives are the basis for organizing instruction. The objectives are analyzed in terms of prerequisites. Each prerequisite in turn is then stated as an enroute objective, and these enroute objectives are arranged in an assumed hierarchical order. A learner may follow a series of activities or tasks such as the following:

1. Define a given concept.
2. Recognize instances of the concept.
3. Combine two given concepts into a principle.
4. Combine given principles into a strategy for solving new problems.

Complex subject matter, in short, is sequenced by the simple components. A particular sequence may vary in length from a single lesson to a course of instruction for a year.

Task analysis, breaking down an objective into its basic elements, steps, or rules, is the chief procedure for designing technological curriculum as well as for determining enroute tasks and the order of their acquisition.

Evaluation

Unique to the technologist is the assumption that if the intended learner (the kind of person for whom the program was designed) does not master the specified objectives, the program maker is at fault. Learners are not responsible for their own success or failure. Programs are developed, tried out on a sample of the intended population of learners, and revised according to the findings until the program attains intended results.

Until recently, technologists evaluated their programs only in terms of their own objectives. Unanticipated side effects were seldom sought. Neither was the validity or justification for end-of-program objectives established by considering the full range of criteria that various consumers might apply to both process and product. Technologists examined achievement but sometimes did not consider whether attaining the objective produced desirable or undesirable effects on the community or whether the individualized techniques inadvertently impaired learners' social skills. The technologist, as such, is concerned more about the effectiveness of the process than the validity of the objectives.

Generally, the technological approach is most effective for conventional, easily measurable tasks. Students achieve more with these techniques than they would otherwise. The tightly structured, programmed approach including frequent and immediate feedback to the pupil, combined with a tutorial relationship, individual pacing, and individualized programming is positively associated with accelerated pupil achievement. Ben Bloom claims that the typical result of mastery learning studies in the schools is that about 80 percent of students with mastery learning reach the same level of achievement (A or B+) as approximately the top 20 percent of the class under conventional instruction.[4] Robert Slavin, however, in his review of the literature on achievement effects of mastery learning, found essentially no evidence to support the superior effectiveness of mastery learning on standardized achievement measurements and only modest positive effects on tests designed to match the instructional program.[5]

TECHNOLOGY IN THE DEVELOPMENT OF CURRICULUM MATERIALS

Curriculum development has been a search for some general value—an important idea, problem, or skill—around which content and activities could be organized. The technological curriculum offers these guidelines: (1) the developmental procedures used should be reviewed and validated by other developers: they should be able to be replicated; (2) products developed in accordance with models that can be replicated should produce similar results.

The heart of the technological revolution in curriculum is, however, the belief that curriculum materials themselves, when used by those learners for whom the materials are developed, should produce specified learner competencies. This belief is an advance over the belief that curriculum materials are mere resources that may or may not be useful or influential in a certain situation. The change in concept can be seen in two different ways for judging curriculum materials (Table 3–1).

Other commonly found criteria in the instructional system design model are *developmental consideration*—adaptability, justification of need, cost-effectiveness, instructional environment, *design components*—link to

---

[4]B. S. Bloom, "The Sigma Problem: The Search for Methods of Instruction as Effective as One-to-One Tutoring," *Educational Researcher* 13, no. 6 (1984): 4–16.

[5]Robert E. Slavin, "Mastery Learning Reconsidered," *Review of Educational Research* 57, no. 2 (Summer 1987): 175–213.

TABLE 3–1 Comparison of Criteria for Selection of Instructional Materials

Old Criteria	*New Criteria*
Do authors have professional reputations?	Where and how extensively have materials been tried out?
Are materials based on sound pedagogical principles? Are they consistent with established suggestions for instruction and practice? Will the content broaden the child's view of the world?	Is information available about the number of students who started and completed the materials? Does the information say how much time learners of different ability spent on portions of the material and differential results?
Are selections arranged by level to satisfy the needs and interests of children as they mature? Is the art imaginative and appealing?	Do the materials specify intended-learner characteristics including enumeration of prerequisites? Does the art contribute to affective learning?
Are type faces and sizes, lengths of lines, and space between lines appropriate for the maturity of the children at each level?	Are materials being revised to reflect trial results? How are student responses used in revising the material?
Do materials use high quality paper, clear print, and sturdy binding?	How effectively do students learn specified skills? Do appropriate criterion-referenced tests show student gains?

prior learning, practice, and *organization*—alignment of components, integration of components, small steps. Although research backing for these criteria is limited, technologists use them because they were effective in a previous application and are part of the technological lore.[6]

A nonprofit corporation, Educational Products Information Exchange Institute (EPIE), has attempted to make impartial studies of the availability, use, and effectiveness of educational materials, equipment, and systems. EPIE reports tend to be descriptive. They indicate the effects of the materials on teacher time, costs, and staffing, and state the underlying assumptions or philosophy of the materials. They also reveal the extent to which there has been learner verification of the materials. Surprisingly, although more than 90 percent of student time is spent with some form of instructional text, fewer than 2 percent of all instructional materials rely on learner response as the source of revision.[7]

---

[6]Alenoush Saroyan and George L. Geis, "An Analysis of Guidelines for Expert Reviewers," *Instructional Science* 17 (Fall 1988): 101–128.

[7]P. K. Komoski and A. Woodward, "The Continuing Need for the Learner Verification and Revision of Textual Materials," in *The Technology of Text* ed. D. H. Jonassen (Englewood Cliffs, NJ: Educational Technology, 1985).

TECHNICAL INNOVATIONS

In the 1970s many investigators compared the live teacher with the new innovations of the period: programmed learning, closed circuit television, films and slide tapes. In the end, they concluded that the element *within* a given medium (structure, pacing, presentation) had more influence on the level of learner success than any differences measured between different media. Similarly, today's new technical innovations—computers, interactive videos—do not provide learning benefits in themselves. The creation of good programs for use with these tools is critical.

Computers

In *Mindstorms: Children, Computers, and Powerful Ideas*, Seymour Papert offers a fresh alternative in the technological curriculum. Papert arranges the computer so that young people learn to control, not be dominated by, their technological environment. To him, the computer is a vehicle for Piagetian learning by which children are encouraged to integrate new concepts into their existing repertoires as they manipulate objects defined as figures on an interactive computer display. Thus children "take new knowledge and make it their own by playing with it and building on it."[8]

Using a Logo language program, a triangular shaped "turtle" can be made to appear and move on a television screen. By giving "turtle" talk commands to the computer, the child can learn geometry. In controlling the position and heading of the turtle, for example, children deal automatically with concepts such as *angle* and *variable*. Learning, then, is a result of controlling and being controlled by the computer, a good example of the environment affecting their environments. Children create their own program for geometric designs, learning new mathematical concepts while developing a sense of power over the machine.

Papert's use of computers may seem a free-form curriculum structure, but the structure is imposed by the need for language. Pupils must talk "turtle" in order to operate the machine. Papert's idea is a far cry from using computers as electronic workbooks and drill exercises. His idea is for children to manipulate the computer to create their own vision of the world and thus prepare themselves for the future by learning about learning.

---

[8]Robert McWergney, "The Influence of Computers on Children and Vice Versa," *Curriculum Inquiry* 12, no. 3 (1982): 301–303.

However, the value of the computer as a way to introduce formal thinking procedures is yet to be shown. Experimental studies tend to show negative results from the use of Logo for teaching a problem-solving competence that would transfer from Logo to other domains.[9] Logo programming may have generalizable effects in the teaching of the metacognitive skills of self-monitoring, time management, and reflection. Improvements in Logo knowledge transfer may be achieved by students combining everyday situations and school situations that require the same problem solving approach.

Robert Karplus's model for developing a computer curriculum has three phases. In the first phase, students play with the phenomenon, building insights through a series of experiences in a subject area. In the second phase, students acquire concepts in the content area, and in the third phase, students do something with the mastered content.[10] Examples of third step computer activities are: *language arts*—creative writing and publishing of ideas, *science*—modeling a biological system and predicting outcomes, *arts*—integrating graphic and textual material to explain one's ideas, composing music, or creating new visual forms.

As a laboratory instrument, computers can be used to sense and record variables like temperature, motion, sound, and pit ranges in the environment. The cooperative curriculum project "Kids Network" (sponsored by the National Geographic Society) is a good example of capitalizing on the sensory and recording feature as K-12 students from various parts of the country collect data on acid rain and weather with standardized collection times and procedures. These data are then pooled into a large computer. More than 40,000 teachers have Logo in their classes, although it is used mostly as a means of enrichment rather than as a way of improvement of students' cognitive abilities.[11]

From his historical study of the classroom use of technology since 1960, Larry Cuban predicts that teacher acceptance of the computer for reinventing the curriculum is doubtful. Teachers are slow to adapt any technical innovation when they do not see it as a practical tool for their curriculum goals and situational demands. Instead of having their students search, sort, and create new meanings with computers, teachers

---

[9]Roy D. Pea and K. Sheingold, eds. *Mirrors of Mind: Patterns of Experience in Educational Computing* (Norwood, NJ: Ablex, 1989).

[10]Robert Karplus, in *Personal Computers in Education*, ed. Robert Bork (New York: Harper & Row, 1985).

[11]Henry Jay Becker, "The Importance of a Methodology That Maximizes Falsifiability: Its Application to Research About Logo," *Educational Research* 16, no. 5 (June 1987): 11–18.

will use it to cope with the routine, tedious teaching problems that machines do so patiently—drill, simulation, games.[12]

Interactive Video

Interactive video has capabilities that make it an attractive learning device. A computer-controlled videodisk delivery system can do rapid, random search and access, store up to 54,000 still pictures, play back clear still frames, play back stereo or dual track audio, and permit the learner to respond through the use of such devices as joysticks, keyboard, light pen, touch seven, and graphics pads. Hence, learners can control the pace and content of the instruction, and their performance can be monitored and recorded. Videodisks can create simulation of equipment operation. Interactive video is extensively used in vocational and industrial training. Extensive studies by the military indicate that the medium is as effective or more effective than other delivery media, including classroom instruction. Programs through interactive video do not require an instructor, so training is available on demand. Most courses are instituted as a series of modules which can be taken individually. Although generic coursework for interactive video is relatively inexpensive, these courses seldom meet specific training requirements. Development of one's own program is costly because it typically takes 100 hours to produce a one-hour lesson that is validated and ready for use. Cost-effectiveness is important in technological delivery systems. Hardware and software developmental costs must be balanced against savings in reduced instructional time and materials. Using a videodisk simulator instead of actual equipment saved the military 118.3 million dollars on one course.[13]

As with studies of computer-based instruction, it is difficult to ensure that what is learned with videodisks in training environment will transfer to performance on the job.

ISSUES IN A TECHNOLOGICAL APPROACH TO CURRICULUM DEVELOPMENT

On the one hand, many claim that the technological approach leads to products that are consistent with the learner's predispositions because

---

[12]Larry Cuban, *Teachers and Machines* (New York: Teachers' College Press, 1986).

[13]Henry M. Halff, James D. Hollan, and Edwin L. Hutchins, "Cognitive Science and Military Training," *American Psychologist* 41, no. 10 (1986): 1131–1139.

the developer must be attentive to the learner and not rely on armchair planning. The approach is also said to provide procedures for making curricula that can be replicated and manipulated, helping us to learn which curriculum works and which does not.

On the other hand, people are concerned about the costliness of the technological approach, which has resulted in a greater need for government and corporate financing. Such funding is automatically suspect when people fear governmental influence on what their children learn, and view state and federal influences as antagonistic to local development of the curriculum. Also, the technologist's logical approach, which attempts to help the learner achieve mastery of specified objectives, has been faulted for excluding more potential influences on learning outcomes than it includes. In many ways, the older notion of providing rich environments without specific objectives may have more fruitful results.

Special Problems

An overriding concern about the technological curriculum is the stress on the mechanics of learning, testing, accountability, measurement of objectives, and other empirically verifiable aspects of education. Accordingly, education becomes a commodity to be assessed in terms of the profitability or usefulness to existing social and political interests. The systems approach especially aims at an efficient way to achieve goals set by those with powerful political and economic interests who control the system. Modifications in the systems approach purport to give local administrators and teachers more freedom in molding the systems. Deregulation of some aspects, discretionary budgets, local team approaches to instructional management are encouraged. However, control still comes from the top through the setting of performance goals and state requirements that focus on mastery and criterion-referenced achievement such as exit testing and mandated performance reports.

Three problems plague most technological curricula: their invalid hierarchies of prerequisites and arbitrary standards of mastery, their unsuitability for uncertain situations, and their limited concepts of individualization.

Invalid Hierarchies. Technologists have not fully succeeded in defining essential prerequisites and learning hierarchies for complex subject matter. Analysis of cognitive skills is difficult or impossible within the behavioral framework. A case in point is found in the military, which has followed an Instructional Systems Design in which the curriculum is geared to task requirements of jobs as defined through task analysis. Currently, this approach to curriculum development is being reconsidered by the services.[14]

In addition to its high costs, Instructional Systems Design fails to analyze the mental structures that underlie competence. Problems are exacerbated in the increasing number of courses that address cognitive skills. The technologist's approach is most easily applied to tasks with a high ratio of overt behavioral skills to cognitive skills. Neither have technologists been able to determine the degree of mastery required for programs. Attempts to determine mastery or competency through statistical or psychological means have not been satisfactory. In fact, it is argued that the attempt to set standards of performance for promotion is futile except as a political endeavor.[15] Although technologists have contributed greatly to equity among students by introducing criterion-referenced tests, which assess students by their progress toward a defined task rather than by their achievement relative to a peer, the validity (content and construct) of many of these tests is suspect. Many reasons may account for poor performance on a criterion-referenced test, and successful performance on the test may not predict success in situations that demand transfer.

Inappropriateness for Uncertain Situations. Gary Klein asserts that the usefulness of the technological approach is limited to certain kinds of tasks and to lower levels of proficiency.[16] Its limitation rests on the distinction between procedural and nonprocedural tasks. Procedural tasks can be broken down into steps or rules that, when followed, accomplish the mediocre level of competence. By contrast, the rules or procedures that a person needs to follow to perform nonprocedural tasks, such as producing a work of art, writing a critique, solving a problem, and making a decision, are not clear. It is difficult to break down such tasks into basic steps and rules, and, even if they were broken down, it is not clear whether a student who learned the rules could perform at a satisfactory level.

---

[14]Henry M. Halff, James D. Hollan, and Edwin L. Hutchins, *American Psychologist* 41, no. 10 (October 1986): 1131–1140.

[15]Gene V. Glass and Mary Lee Smith, "Standards of Competence: Propositions on the Nature of Testing Reforms," *Educational Researcher* 17, no. 3 (November 1988): 4–9.

[16]Gary A. Klein, "Curriculum Development Versus Education," *Teachers College Record* 84, no. 4 (Summer 1983): 831–836.

When it is effective, technology is usually aimed at a procedural task. It is a limited tool for nonprocedural tasks and may even hinder proficiency. Forcing proficient people to follow prescribed steps appropriate for novices, for example, would probably impede performance. On nonprocedural tasks, highly proficient persons do not follow abstract rules but use a repertoire of analogies from experience to guide their performance. Experts can perceive a current task as similar to a previous situation and thus use what they know about that situation to predict outcomes, determine what is relevant, and decide what action to take. They do not go through calculations of formal elements. (Imagine someone trying to use Polanyi's rule for riding a bicycle—''At any given angle of unbalance, the rider should turn the front wheel to the degree inversely proportional to the square of the speed.''[17] Furthermore, the question exists about whether complex tasks can be analyzed into simple, discrete elements. Elements may exist only in the context of the overall task and the goals of the person performing it.

Organizational plans of the technologists' curriculum usually make no real contribution to the problem of helping learners transfer what they learn to new subject matters and to the real world. The technologists' curriculum is usually tied to the achievement of traditional or static goals, to those things that schools have long been attempting to do. Its main contribution is to allow schools to do these things more effectively.

Limited Concept of Individualization. The technological curriculum may be best for helping students who would never be expected to gain proficiency—those for whom following rules represents a higher level of performance than they could otherwise achieve—but not for students capable of becoming highly proficient if free from restrictive rules and procedures. Individualization in the technological curriculum seldom allows the learners to generate their own objectives. Also, technologists have not given sufficient attention to learners' predispositions toward specific methods. Students with low aptitude, for example, may respond differently to some technological features than do students with high aptitude. Technologists might take their responses into consideration by developing alternative programs rather than expecting all to learn from the same materials. Tightly structured programs, for example, may be more effective for those with lower aptitude.

---

[17]M. Polanyi, *Personal Knowledge* (Chicago: The University of Chicago Press, 1958).

CONCLUDING COMMENTS

Technology has improved curriculum. Its emphasis on objectives has led curriculum makers to ask what kinds of objectives are most valuable. Some question the tendency of the technologists' curriculum to maintain objectives consistent with conventional fragmented or compartmentalized subject areas. We are likely to have more warranted objectives as a result of such objections.

Technologists' influence on curriculum developers has been great. Without technologists prodding for evidence of results, most developers would have been satisfied to provide what they thought were valid educational environments, never taking responsibility for the consequences. More clearly to be seen is the technologists' contribution to instructional effectiveness, the ordering of instructional sequences, and the monitoring of learners' progress. It is reasonable to suppose that more persons can now produce an effective curriculum by following the technologists' model. Many of these persons may not, however, do any better or as well as the rare creative developer following his or her own intuition.

People who make decisions about how to develop curriculum, such as publishers and school officials, will have to weigh the value of the technologists' model against its heavier development costs (often a threefold time increase over traditional approaches to curriculum development). They may find that the higher costs are balanced by increased learning for more pupils when the the model is implemented.

One weakness in the technologists' model for curriculum development is that it does not give sufficient attention to implementation of the products and the dynamics of innovation. Just developing a more effective product often is not enough. Unless attention is given to changing the wider environment (school organization, teachers' attitudes, community views), the good product may not be used or at least not in a way that will fulfill its promise. Efforts to improve the conditions of implementation, however, are likely to draw resources away from efforts to improve the product itself.

QUESTIONS

1. List probable consequences from the systems approach to curriculum whereby state and local governments a) specify the competencies to be learned as well as the materials to be used, and b) maintain a tight

control by testing students and monitoring the curriculum plan while helping teachers translate the plan into effective teaching practices.

2. Most schools use the computer for drill and practice rather than as a tool for problem solving or the creating of new knowledge. Why?
3. How can you best approach the problem of teaching something of interest to you, given the technology and other resources that exist?
4. The measured curriculum tends to use test scores in making critical decisions about pupils, teachers, programs, and schools. What other information is important?
5. In order to sense the difficulty of making a task analysis, compare your list of basic elements for learning to plan a unit of study with the elements identified by your peers.

SELECTED REFERENCES

Block, James, et al. *Building Effective Mastery Learning Schools*. New York: Longman, 1988.

Gagné, Robert M. *Principles of Instructional Design*. New York: Holt, Rinehart & Winston, 1988.

Kaufman, Roger. *Planning Educational Systems: A Result-Based Approach*. Lancaster, PA: Technonic Publishing Co., 1988.

Nickerson, Raymond and Zodhiate, Philip P. *Technology in Education: Looking Toward 2020*. Hillsdale, NJ: Lawrence Erlbaum, 1988.

Papert, Seymour. *Mindstorms: Children, Computers, and Powerful Ideas*. New York: Basic Books, 1980.

4

The Academic
Subject Curriculum

Depending as it does on public financial support and the political climate of the country, the curriculum vacillates between the goals of equity and social justice at one time and academic excellence at another. In the late 1950s, national anxiety about keeping ahead of the Russians generated a curriculum reform movement that enlisted the talents of the nation's leading scholars in the cause of an academic curriculum. The National Science Foundation funded 53 separate curriculum projects. These new programs updated the content of subject matter so that it reflected what scholars thought was important. Moreover, the programs featured laboratory practices and discovery methods so that subjects would be introduced to the modes of academic inquiry practiced by the specialists in major academic fields.

In the 1970s, the crises of domestic, economic, and social strife became more important than scientific rivalry with the Soviets. Monies were shifted to curriculum projects aimed at new social concerns (multicultural education, career education, functional literacy) and to curriculum developers outside academic fields. Humanistic psychologists also weakened the academicians' hold on the curriculum by stressing subjective and personal knowledge as an alternative to objective knowledge that can be tested through reason and empirical evidence.

Just as suddenly in the 1980s, the emphasis upon social and personal relevance was disparaged. One reason for the change in emphasis was Americans' perception that the Japanese educational system was better equipped to produce workers for the future economy with its requirements for high levels of mathematical, scientific, and technical knowledge. Declining achievement scores, dropping enrollment in academic courses, insufficiently challenging texts, and weakened college entrance and graduation requirements further encouraged the change.

Worried parents, educators, and politicians began to call for academic excellence and quality. How to achieve these goals, however, remains a problem. Is it to be academic subject matter for all or just for those students who will be future scholars and scientists? Can the academic curriculum be made relevant to daily living and current social issues without at the same time diluting it? And can such a curriculum encourage clear thought and critical thinking rather than merely demand the memorization of facts? This chapter will show the answers some are finding for these questions and the ways in which curriculum developers are strengthening the academic curriculum.

APPROACHES TO THE ACADEMIC CURRICULUM

The various academic subjects represent a range of approaches to truth and knowledge. Academicians define knowledge as *justified belief*, as opposed to ignorance, mere opinions, or guesses.

The academic curriculum is in disarray. Although those holding an academic conception believe that the development of a rational mind is the primary goal, they do not agree on how best to achieve this goal. Some look at the radically plural world of knowledge and believe that if students are to find their way about this world and learn how to acquire meaning in human experience, they should participate in the forms of knowledge and acquire a unique mode of thought associated with each.

Others who value inquiry—the discovery of knowledge—recommend teaching the concepts, attitudes, and processes of inquiry of selected disciplines as the way to develop thinking persons.

Still others look to ancient truths as the source of judgment and argue for teaching the great books of the Western world, using a dialect method to eliminate inconsistencies in thinking.

Finally, some believe that the transmission of traditional information is a necessary basis for intelligent participation in the national culture.

The Forms of Knowledge Approach

The forms of knowledge approach addresses the problem of selecting from among the more than 1,000 academic disciplines that could be part of the school curriculum. The problem is not new:

> Good Lord! how long is Art,
> And life, how it goes flying!

> It is so hard to gain the means whereby
> Up to the source one may ascend.
> And ere a man gets half-way to the end,
> Poor devil! he's almost sure to die![1]

It is impossible for a person to delve deeply into many disciplines. How shall those administering the curriculum decide which disciplines to offer? A number of measuring rods are proposed: (1) comprehensiveness with respect to ways at arriving at or justifying truth or knowledge, (2) social utility—the usefulness of the discipline for all citizens, (3) prerequisite knowledge—the importance of certain disciplines as a basis for others or for subsequent education.

In the interest of comprehensiveness, it would be well to sample disciplines that emphasize different avenues for justifying knowledge. Philip Phenix, for example, has illustrated how to achieve comprehensiveness in the fundamental disciples. In *Realms of Meaning*, he describes and analyzes six basic types of meaning, each of which has a distinctive logical structure.[2] Art, with its concern for subjective validation, can balance a discipline like science, which uses objective observations to confirm an expected occurrence. History can be used to illustrate the criteria of coherence and verifiability to show that ideas have to fit together and that new conclusions can be weighed against past events. Mathematics can prepare learners to gain knowledge through reason and logic. It may be possible to find a form that will help students recognize that some forms of knowledge can be validated by intuition and divine revelation. Such a curriculum would preclude the exclusivity of contemporary schools, which tend to emphasize the scientific mode of learning.

Similarly, Paul Hirst believes that the curriculum must develop the mind and that this is best done by mastering the fundamental rational structure of knowledge, meaning, logical relations, and criteria for judg-

---

[1]Goethe's *Faust*, trans. and ed. J. F. L. Raschen (Ithaca: Thrift Press, 1803), pp. 29–31.
[2]Philip H. Phenix, *Realms of Meaning* (New York: McGraw-Hill, 1964).

ing claims to truth. In answer to the classical curriculum question, "What knowledge is of most worth?", Hirst proposes seven or eight forms of cognitive knowledge for understanding the world. Each of these forms is said to meet four criteria: (1) certain concepts are peculiar to the form (for example, gravity, acceleration, and hydrogen are concepts unique to the physical science form); (2) each form has a distinct logical structure by which the concepts can be related; (3) the form, by virtue of its terms and logic, has statements or conclusions that are testable; and (4) the form has methods for exploring experience and testing its statements (for example, in mathematics the "truth" of any proposition is established by its logical consistency with other propositions within a given system, while in physical science, knowledge is validated by data from observation). The forms of knowledge discerned by these criteria are: mathematics, physical sciences, knowledge of persons, literature and the fine arts, morals, religion, and philosophy. This range in forms allows for many different kinds of meaning.

In proposing forms of knowledge rather than stipulating a particular fixed substance of subject matter (particular facts and operations), such as in basic skills programs, Hirst argues for a dynamic curriculum. His forms do not, however, encourage a subjective or relative view of knowledge. To him, knowledge consists of ways to structure experience so that it can be public, shared, and instrumental or useful in daily living.[3]

Criticisms of Hirst's views of knowledge and the curriculum center on whether he has indeed discovered distinct forms and whether he has slighted the idea of subject matter as substance. Jonas Soltis, for instance, worries that a focus on the forms of knowledge will result in an absence of attention to specific knowledge of what has been learned about the world.[4] Soltis believes that learning a form should include learning the substance within it, not just acquiring knowledge of concepts, rules, and criteria for claims to truth. Hirst admits that there is no complete agreement on the descriptions of the forms of knowledge and that mastery of the formal features of a discipline should not be mistaken for mastery of a particular area of knowledge itself.[5] Therefore, he wants pupils to acquire both substantive knowledge that has significance for them and knowledge of the general principles and ways of thinking that are the inherent features of the forms by which knowledge is gained.

[3]Paul H. Hirst, *Knowledge and the Curriculum* (London: Routledge & Kegan Paul, 1974).

[4]Jonas A. Soltis, "A Review of Knowledge and the Curriculum," *Teachers College Record* 80, no. 4 (May 1979): 785–787.

[5]Paul H. Hirst, "A Reply to Jonas Soltis," *Teachers College Record* 80, no. 4 (May 1979): 788–789.

Both Phenix and Hirst place more emphasis on the teacher of representative ideas of a discipline than coverage of facts from that discipline.

Structure in the Disciplines Approach

In his celebrated book, *The Process of Education,* Jerome Bruner proposed that curriculum design be based on the structure of the academic disciplines. He proposed that the curriculum of a subject should be determined by the most fundamental understanding that can be achieved of the underlying principles that give structure to a discipline. The basis for his argument was economy. Such learning permits generalizations, makes knowledge usable in contexts other than that in which it is learned, and facilitates memory by allowing the learner to relate what would otherwise be easily forgotten, unconnected facts. "The school boy learning physics is a physicist, and it is easier for him to learn physics behaving like a physicist than doing something else."[6] Years later, Bruner, caught up in the social movements of the day, urged a deemphasis on the structure of history, physics, mathematics, and the like and called for an emphasis on subject matter as it related to the social needs and problems of the American people.[7])

The concept of *structure in the disciplines* was widely heralded as a basis for curriculum content. This concept refers to rules for pursuing inquiry and for establishing truth in particular disciplines. Three kinds of structure are posited:

1. *Organizational structure*—definitions of how one discipline differs in a fundamental way from another. A discipline's organizational structure also indicates the borders of inquiry for that discipline.
2. *Substantive structure*—the kinds of questions to ask in inquiry, the data needed, and ideas (concepts, principles, theories) to use in interpreting data.
3. *Syntactical structure*—the manner in which those in the respective disciplines gather data, test assertions, and generalize findings.

The particular method used in performing such tasks makes up the syntax of a discipline. Sociologists, for example, generally observe in naturalistic settings, identify indicators believed to correspond to the theoretical framework guiding the inquiry, and often rely on correlational data

[6]Jerome S. Bruner, *The Process of Education* (Cambridge: Harvard University Press, 1960), p. 31.

[7]Jerome S. Bruner, "The Process of Education Revisited," *Phi Delta Kappan* 53, no. 1 (September 1971): 18–22.

to show relationships among factors observed. Experimental psychologists, on the other hand, manipulate their treatment variables in an effort to produce desired consequences. Experimentalists believe they have found knowledge when they are able to produce a predicted result.

The structure of the disciplines concept was widely used in designing curriculum whereby students were to learn how specialists in a number of disciplines discover knowledge. An intellectual emphasis was the basis for most nationwide curriculum development projects of the 1960s. Curriculum builders of this period were primarily subject matter specialists who organized their materials around the primary structural elements of their respective disciplines: problems or concerns, key concepts, principles, and mode of inquiry.

The so-called curriculum reform movement of the 1960s was identified with the shock that came from the Russians' first satellite launching. In the cold war climate, fear moved government to emphasize the teaching of science and mathematics. Scholars in colleges and universities prepared materials focused on single subjects. These programs began as early as kindergarten and were designed on the assumption that all pupils should understand the methods of science and the basic properties of mathematics. This was in contrast to the prevailing practice of teaching scientific facts and a style of treatment in mathematics best characterized as rote and applied. Algebra, in the "reform" course, was treated as a branch of mathematics dealing with the properties of various number systems rather than as a collection of manipulative tricks.

What little debate there was regarding the "new programs" centered on the argument that what was being taught would be needed only by students who were to become professional scientists and mathematicians. The rebuttal offered these arguments:

1. There is need for appreciation from the general culture for well-trained scientists and their fields.
2. It is better to develop a deeper comprehension of the fundamentals than to touch on many facts that are often the outdated conclusions of science. A discipline approach, for example, can help the learner deal with the "knowledge explosion."
3. True understanding of the facts in more fields of learning comes only from an appreciation of various interpretations, and a continuing investigation is far more interesting to the student than a set piece. There is a growing realization that the process of inquiry itself is a form of knowledge to be acquired.
4. A discipline is an internal organization, a subject matter suitable for efficient learning.

In almost every field such as English, social studies, art, health education, there was an updating of content, a reorganization of subject matter, and fresh approaches to method. Typically, the stress was on a separate entity—not science, but biology, chemistry, or physics; not social studies, but history, geography, or economics; not English, but literature, grammar, or composition.

Under the structure in the discipline approach, pupils learn how to acquire or justify facts rather than merely recall them. Until recently as many as 20 percent of the nation's school districts used materials for teaching a "new history," in which each student compiles his or her own version of an historical event. The new history uses an inquiry approach that seeks to teach pupils to judge conflicting evidence and draw their own conclusions. Each student's position is valid if researched, reasoned, and articulated well. New history minimizes the importance of chronology and memorization. Advocates stress that they do not want students to reach absolute conclusions but to learn how to judge evidence, to see the other side, and to recognize the biases of other interpreters. Secondary school students question traditional views of Jefferson, Jackson, and Lincoln. They compare capitalism with socialism. They examine the United States' treatment of the Indians and the historical records of the Spanish-American War as well as Vietnam and other recent events. The approach is not without criticism. Some scholars fret about the loss of chronology and absence of traditional historical content. Others believe the approach develops cynics; they say that students need belief in heroism and virtues to build clear ideals and confidence.

Reaction Against a Structure of Knowledge

Not all went as well as hoped. Teachers who themselves had never produced knowledge, who had not made an original scientific finding or historical interpretation, had difficulty leading students in the ways of discovery. The validity of the concept of structure as a basis for curriculum development was questioned, i.e., that the concept was only an after-the-fact description of the way knowledge can be organized by mature scholars and not the way it was really won and that such structure is not necessarily the best way to organize knowledge for instructional purposes or to start and direct significant inquiry and reflection. Enrollments in advanced physics courses declined. Many students, in both high and low ability groups, did not achieve as well as intended.

No causal relationship was shown, however, between reform projects and lower student interest or achievement. Other factors, such as students' changing social attitudes in an era of social discontent, might have been more influential. The availability of numerous programs created problems of maintaining balance and organization. Many subjects had to be omitted from a school's offerings. Furthermore, the subject specializations were so narrowly focused that it was difficult to combine their concepts into broader fields.

The 1970s saw a decline in the academic approach to curriculum making. The popularity of a disciplined approach to the science curriculum waned with a growing distrust of science. It was argued that scientists should be doing more to solve humanity's problems. Also, those with nonacademic curriculum bents attacked the structure of knowledge approach to curriculum development through an attack on a well-publicized exemplar of this approach: MACOS.

MACOS, the acryonym for *Man: A Course of Study*, was to have been the primer for curriculum in the 1970s.[8] Bruner himself established the initial guide for this curriculum and directed much of its development, which was supported by the National Science Foundation (NSF) and the United States Office of Education in order to reform the teaching of social sciences and humanities. MACOS is a curriculum designed for students in the elementary school and consists of books, films, posters, records, games, and other classroom materials. More important, it sets forth assumptions about humans. Three central questions define the intellectual concerns and reveal the assumptions of MACOS: What is human about human beings? How did they get that way? How can they be made more human? The developers of the course wanted children to explore the major forces that have shaped and continue to shape humanity: language, tool use, social organization, mythology, and prolonged immaturity. Through contrast with other animals, including the baboons, children examine the biological nature of humans. By comparing American society with that of a traditional Eskimo group, they explore the universal aspects of human culture.

The intellectual models used to get ideas across to children are disciplinary. Children are given examples of field notes and encouraged to construct their ideas about animals and humans in the ways ethnologists and anthropologists do. The principal aims of MACOS are intellectual: to give children respect for and confidence in the powers of their own minds and to provide them with a set of workable models that make it simpler to analyze the nature of the social world. Its values include the

---

[8]*Man: A Course of Study* (Washington, DC: Curriculum Development Associates, 1970).

scientific mode of observation, speculation, hypothesis making and testing; understanding of particular social science disciplines; and the joy of discovery.

Attacks on MACOS came from those with different curricular concerns. Humanists criticized Bruner for failing to recognize the potential of MACOS for fostering emotional growth. Social reconstructionists opposed MACOS on the ground that it was created by a scholarly elite. A ruling class should not foster ideas in teachers and students, they said. The topics that children are asked to study are not related to improving the social life of the community in which they live. Congressman John B. Conlan criticized the course on the House floor as depicting "abhorrent and revolting behavior by a nearly extinct Eskimo tribe." Conlan said the material was full of references to adultery, cannibalism, killing of female babies and old people, trial marriage, wife-swapping, and violent murders. Many congressmen and others began to view the National Science Foundation as indoctrinating children and showing preference for certain scientists and curriculum makers. The controversies surrounding MACOS led to restricted NSF funding for educational research and greater surveillance of NSF by Congress. A suit in federal court asked that the state be enjoined from compelling children to participate in MACOS. The plaintiffs charged that this curriculum espoused secular humanism and that the United States Supreme Court had defined this as a religion. They argued that this course violated the First Amendment.

Revival of the Disciplines Approach

A revival of the structure in the disciplines approach is underway. Nearly every national report on education calls for curriculum concentrating on "higher-order" skills in reading, writing, mathematics, problem solving and abstract reasoning. Accordingly, curriculum is supposed to engage students in emergent learning rather than merely reciting known conclusions. The new mathematics curriculum in algebra and geometry, for instance, insists on developing analytic reasoning and the student applying concepts in the solution of unfamiliar problems. Students are expected to formulate hypotheses about problems at hand and then test them against available data.[9]

A recent study of policy for science education recommends that the National Science Foundation (NSF) take the lead again in developing

---

[9]C. Hirsch and M. C. Zweng, eds., *The Secondary School Mathematics Curriculum*, 1985 Yearbook (Reston, VA: National Council of Teachers of Mathematics, 1985).

high quality K–12 science curriculum.[10] Among the arguments for having NSF generate alternative curricula as it did in the 1960s and early 1970s is that new evidence shows that the structure in the disciplines curriculum of those times was much more effective than critics thought. For example, as recently as 1984, a majority of those holding a bachelor's degree in physics had received high school instruction using the NSF sponsored Physical Science Study Committee (PSSC) materials.[11]

Conflicting Views of Knowledge. Proponents of the forms of knowledge and structure of disciplines reject the fixed view of knowledge and instead hold that knowledge is tentative. The creation of knowledge—valid statements, conclusions, and truth—occurs by following the inquiry systems of the specific discipline or cognitive form. Hence, proponents of these approaches reject the practice of students reciting conclusions apart from the methods and theories by which they are established.

Many oppose the forms and disciplines approaches. Humanists claim that all knowledge is personal and subjective. For them, knowledge is the result of a person's unique perceptions of the world. Social reconstructionists, on the other hand, see knowledge not only as a human product but a product of specific social groups whose knowledge reflects their ideologies. Reconstructionists regard attempts at imposing a discipline in the same way they regard imposing an ideology—as a form of social control.

Other opponents are academicians who work in the tradition of the liberal arts and those who believe in the transmission of "essential" information derived from the dominant cultural experience. The latter opponents fault the disciplines and forms approaches for (a) failing to inculcate traditional values and (b) fostering vocationalism, relativism, and pluralism at the expense of a coherent curriculum and common learning.

Liberal Arts and the Academic Core

From its early association with the study of Latin and Greek, the liberal arts have been expanded to the study of language, creative arts, expressive arts, and other subjects believed to have the power to stir the imagination, develop appreciation for beauty, and disclose the nature of

---

[10]James H. Scheur, *The Education Deficit* (Washington, DC: Subcommittee on Education and Health of the Joint Economic Committee, 1989).

[11]George Pallrand and Peter Linderfeld, "The Physics Classroom Revisited—Have We Learned Our Lesson?" *Physics Today* 38 (1985): 46–52.

humankind. The push for excellence fixes on wisdom of the past and cultural heritage.

Liberal Arts in Higher Education.   Higher education is under attack for failing to disseminate the great traditions of philosophy, literature, and the arts. Allan Bloom's popular *The Closing of the American Mind* attributes major moral and social changes to the failure of colleges and universities to teach the traditions from Plato through Rousseau. According to Bloom, students lack a sense of intellectual adventure and, because of their pursuit of careers, believe they have no time or need for the classics of Western culture. To solve the problem, Mr. Bloom suggests something similar to the old Great Books approach to learning, whereby students study classical Western thoughts. Another critic, Lynne Cheney, chairman of the National Endowment for the Humanities, indicts colleges for failing to teach the best that has been thought and said. Cheney alleges that colleges have pandered to new interest groups and mixed the universal ideals of art and morality with history, politics, gender, and race.[12] Cheney might have been thinking of the instance of the Stanford University faculty voting to replace the university's Western cultural requirement with a new year-long program called "Culture, Ideals, and Values," which gives substantial attention to the issues of race, gender, and class and includes the study of works by women and minority-group members.

Since the 1980s, conflict has existed between those who want coherence (a unifying purpose and structure for the undergraduate college curriculum) and those who want to offer students more opportunities to engage in specialized studies of their own choice. In 1982, Harvard University implemented a new undergraduate core curriculum designed to bring a common purpose and coherence to courses of study. This curriculum replaced 80 to 100 highly specific courses, ranging from the historical origins of inequality to lectures on law and social order, with academic requirements in five areas: literature and the arts, history, social analysis and moral reasoning, science and foreign culture. Harvard's students were also required to show proficiency in writing, mathematics, and the use of computers. Knowledge was not to be conveyed by rattling off facts but by helping students understand the modes of thought employed by a range of disciplines in a spectrum of fields.

---

[12]Lynne V. Cheney, *Humanities in America: A Report to the President, the Congress and the American People* (Washington, DC: National Endowment for the Humanities, 1988).

Nearly 95 percent of all institutions of higher education have followed Harvard in completing curriculum review, with a host of these colleges instituting core requirements.[13]

Traditionalists are unhappy with many colleges, charging that their core curricula have been weakened by eliminating courses featuring classical texts of enduring value. However, empirical data show that requirements still emphasize exposure to texts integral to the traditional canon, and many scholars believe that a national core curriculum or list of books would be both a recipe for unimaginative teaching and a restriction on intellectual liberties.[14]

Underlying the problem of what content should be taught in the core curriculum are these questions: (1) What is to be the relationship between works traditionally taught as great and writing reflecting the experiences of other people, either within Western society or from other societies and (2) Should "great books" be used to blaze a trail back to shared values and traditional content, or can contemporary research and contexts be reinvestigated in new ways to think about the classics?

Few schools offer a curriculum based on the proposition that there is a body of eternal and absolute truth, valid under all conditions, or that reason can be enhanced by familiarity with the most profound and grandest of humankind's intellectual works. St. John's College in Maryland is an exception. When students take biology at St. John's College, they are handed a stiff frog and an Aristotelian treatise. In this school an older view of academic education, including science, mathematics, Greek, French, music, and the Great Books seminars, is maintained. In preceptorals, similar to electives, seven or eight students and a tutor work intensively on one of the Great Books or on a limited subject like Freud. In the all-required curriculum, third- and fourth-year students study physics, measurement theory, and chemistry in their science course. Sophomore biology emphasizes anatomy, embryology, and genetics in the framwork of evolution. When they dissect their frogs, students read Aristotle's book *On The Parts of Animals* and ponder his notion of aliveness. They also read Galen, the second-century physician whose works were definitive for more than 1,000 years, while they dissect rabbits. When they progress to the rabbit's circulatory system, they discuss William Harvey's treatise, "On the Motion of the Heart and Blood in Animals," published in 1628.

---

[13]Elaine El Khawes, *Campus Trends*, American Council on Education, Report #75 (August 1987).

[14]George Levine et al., *Speaking for the Humanities* (New York: American Council of Learned Societies, 1989).

Rather than presenting only the most current research to students to memorize and repeat in exams, tutors encourage students to practice scientific inquiry. To do that, they believe, students must confront the great minds. Almost half of the biology sessions are spent in laboratory dissections and experiments that demonstrate genetics and embryological theory. Although students read from a half-dozen contemporary books, they also read and discuss the works of such trailblazers as Claude Bernard, Gregor Johann Mendel, and Karl Ernst Von Baer.

Liberal Arts in the Elementary and Secondary Curriculum. In 1982, Mortimer Adler proposed a common liberal education for all students from ages six through eighteen. His Paideia Proposal has been the basis for many of the school reform movement's curriculum changes. According to this proposal, there should be a single program and common academic core in which students learn their own language, literature, fine arts, mathematics, natural science, history, geography, and social studies. This required curriculum allows only one elective—a second foreign language. Students also take industrial arts, physical education, and hygiene. They are involved in drama, music, and the visual arts, and they learn how to exercise critical and moral judgment. The Paideia Proposal _____ any conventional offerings: vocational education, electives, specialized courses, and tracking. This mandatory curriculum emphasizes three modes of teaching (learning at successive gradations of complexity): didactic instruction for acquiring organized knowledge; coaching, exercises and supervised practice for developing intellectual skills; and Socratic dialogue for understanding ideas and values.

Noteworthy among the central claims of the Paideia Proposal are the following: (1) universal education and universal suffrage are inseparable and (2) education for all (grades 1 through 12) must be liberal, not specialized or occupational.[15]

An interesting description of teaching the classics and implementing the Paideia Proposal is available.[16] Although states differ in their policies toward curriculum reform, a surprising number of state curriculum changes are consistent with the Paideia Proposal. More students are taking courses in the academic subject areas. Even non college bound stu-

---

[15]Edwin H. Delattye, ''The Paideia Proposal and American Education,'' *The Humanities in Precollegiate Education,* 1983 Yearbook of National Society for the Study of Education (1984): pp. 143–154.

[16]Robert D. Brazil, *Engineering of the Paideia Proposal—The First Year* (School Design Group, 1018 West White Street, Champaign, IL, 61821, 1989).

dents take more math, science, and social studies; enrollments have declined in vocational and business education. The high school curriculum has become more concentrated around core subjects with students taking fewer electives and having less time for career preparation.[17] Curriculum for those with special needs is increasingly aligned with the core curriculum, and the teaching of English gets more emphasis than bilingual education.

Cultural Literacy

For nearly forty years, the Council for Basic Education, a conservative political group, has lobbied consistently for the teaching of fundamental intellectual subjects, including history and geography with an emphasis upon facts rather than process. Members of the Council now have new proponents: Diane Ravitch and Charles Finn, Jr., launched a campaign for the national revival of the teaching of history and literature by presenting data that reveal that seventeen-year-olds exhibit "a distressing lack of knowledge about major historical and literary events."[18] The new revivalists want the curriculum to present more than "just the facts." They want factual knowledge linked to the world of culture and to make sense to students. In their emphasis on knowledge of literary works and historical events, they give little attention to whose knowledge is selected and why it must be taught.

California was one of the first states to respond to the cultural literacy revival by including a new history curriculum stressing content and historical chronology. In the early grades, pupils are exposed to fairy tales, myths, legends, and biographies of dramatic historical figures. In every grade, history is tied to literature—both literature of given historical periods and literature about the period under study. Acknowledging the importance of religion in history, the curriculum introduces the basic ideas of major religions and the ethical traditions of each time and place. The curriculum plan calls for study of the fundamental principles of the United States Constitution and the Bill of Rights by examining how these principles were formed. Three goals direct the plan: (1) knowledge from other cultural understandings, incorporating learnings from history and the other humanities, geography, and the social sciences; (b) democratic

---

[17]Susan Fuhrman, William H. Clune, and Richard F. Elmore, "Research on Education Reform: Lessons on Implementation of Policy," *Teachers College Record* 90 (Winter 1988).

[18]Diane Ravitch and Charles E. Finn, Jr., *What Do Our 17 Year Olds Know: A Report on the First National Assessment of History and Literature* (New York: Harper & Row, 1987).

son by examining the reasoning found in Euclid, the Federalists, Darwin, Lincoln, Galileo, and others. In thinking about these works and what they mean for present circumstances, students might become more able thinkers. Similarly, cultural literarists value enduring classics from history and literature as vehicles for appealing to children's imaginations and also the transmission of background information that will ensure that students derive the same meanings from text as do members of the dominant adult culture.

Methods

Exposition and inquiry are techniques commonly used in the academic curriculum, although inquiry may be less prevalent in the curriculum of the fundamentalist. Indeed, the ideals of the academic curriculum are violated by teachers who rely upon textbooks and factual questions instead of seeking problems that involve the students' understanding and higher level cognitive processes. Ideas should be stated and elaborated on so that they may be understood. Main ideas can be ordered, illustrated, and explored. Problems that fall within certain disciplines may be formulated and pursued. Appropriate methods for validating truths in the different disciplines are important to teach. Students should discover that reason and sense perception are used to gain knowledge in the sciences, logic in mathematics, individual form and feeling in art, and coherence in history (a fact must be consistent with other known facts). They should examine statements to ascertain their meaning, their logical grounding, and their factual support. The academician wants students to read the greatest works in order to stretch their minds and to come into contact with great minds from the past as well as those in their own age.

Organization

There are two functions of organization: (a) to relate learning experiences in several subject areas (integration) and (b) to ensure that subsequent experiences build on early ones (sequence).

Integration. The structure of knowledge curriculum with its emphasis upon the concepts and methods for discovery knowledge as a discipline favors a single subject approach to organization—history separated from social studies, biology isolated from physics. Alternative organizational patterns for overcoming narrow specialism and fragmentation include:

1. *Correlations.* Connections are made based on temporal, spatial, and agentic elements; all events occurring at a given time in history are studied in a unit, such as the War for Independence.
2. *Tool Applications.* A skill or concept from one discipline is applied to another; for example, writing skills are used in a science report, mathematics is used in solving a problem in economics.
3. *Unifying Themes.* In the sciences, a unifying theme is either a major idea (concept) that permeates several sciences, a process common to them, or a social problem inviting scientific interpretations.

Sequence.　Within a course, academic subject matter is typically organized in a linear fashion based on some provision for the progressive development of a concept or a method. Organizational principles that guide this development include: simple to complex (one-celled animals before many-celled animals); whole to part (allowing for topographical study showing the overall scheme of the course before studying detailed topics); chronological narration (events arranged in a time sequence); learning hierarchies (learning to place cells in empty matrices before learning to infer the characteristics of the object needed to fill an empty cell).

With respect to sequence within total school programs, it is interesting to recall John Dewey's views that the learner should be reintroduced to certain forms of subject matter at different school levels. He stressed the continuity of subject matter and illustrated how subject matter can be adapted in light of the learner's maturation (Table 4–1).

Including certain subjects as prerequisites is sometimes defended on the ground that there is a logical dependency between fields of knowledge, which supersedes learner interest or relevancy to social problems. There are scientists, for example, who would not make biology the first course in the secondary school curriculum in science; they believe that to learn biology it is necessary to understand the principles of chemistry and that to understand chemistry, it is necessary, in turn, to know the basic concepts of physics. Others believe that a prerequisite discipline should help the learner know what posture to assume, what sources to consult, and what to admit as relevant for a point at issue. Because philosophy leads to an understanding of all fields of knowledge, forms of knowledge advocates suggest philosophy as the initial course in the academic curriculum to prepare learners to see similarities and differences among the disciplines they will meet.

TABLE 4–1 Levels of Schooling and Forms of Subject Matter

School Level	Subject Matter Emphasis
Primary	Varied subject matter through concrete experiences
Upper elementary	Mastery of fundamental tools of inquiry and communication—reading, writing, arithmetic, observation, investigation
Secondary	Differentiation of subject matter—systematic instruction in separate fields Views of how each subject is related to another (encyclopedic survey)
Higher education	Subject matter in accordance with individual capacity and interest

A powerful example of the prerequisite criterion is found in the requirements for college admission. These requirements have set the standard for the high school curriculum for many years. Many schools gear their curriculum to the subject matters demanded by the College Board's Admissions Testing Program, which until recently has been broadly conceived as four years of English, mathematics, science, and foreign language, and three to four years of social studies.

Now the College Board specifically outlines what college entrants are expected to know and to be able to do.[22] This outline of academic preparation is divided into two sections: (a) Basic Academic Competencies and (b) Basic Academic Subjects. The academic competencies are the broad skills of reading, writing, speaking, listening, mathematics, reasoning and studying. Illustrative competencies expected are the following:

Reading—the ability to interpet a writer's meaning inferentially as well as literally

Writing—the ability to vary one's writing style for different readers and purposes

Mathematics—the ability to formulate and solve a problem in mathematical terms

Reasoning—the ability to draw reasonable conclusions from information found in various sources

Studying—the ability to accept constructive criticism and learn from it

---

[22]College Board, *Academic Preparation for College* (New York: College Board, 1983).

Basic academic subjects and illustrative expected outcomes are the following:

English—the ability to read a literary text analytically, seeking relationships between form and content

The arts—the ability to express oneself in one or more of the visual art forms: drawing, painting, photography, weaving, ceramics, and sculpture.

Mathematics—the ability to draw geometrical figures and use geometrical modes of thinking in the solving of problems

Science—the ability to understand the unifying concept of the life and physical sciences, such as cell theory, geological evolution, organic evolution, atomic structure, chemical bonding, and transformation of energy

Social studies—the ability to retain factual knowledge of major political and economic institutions and their historical development

Foreign languages—the ability to cope with typical situations in another culture, such as greeting, leave taking, buying food, and asking directions.

In response to recent trends in high school that put a premium on sophisticated types of reading, mathematics, and writing skills, college entrance tests are being redesigned to emphasize a wide range of mathematical knowledge and more abstract thinking skills.[23] For the first time, students face a test of how well they can deal with scientific concepts, reason with science, instead of recalling factual scientific information.

Evaluation

At the classroom level, the means of evaluation vary according to the objectives of the different subject matters. In humanities, essays are preferred over multiple-choice tests, and there is a preference for answers that reflect logic, coherence, and comprehensiveness rather than a single right or wrong choice. In the arts, the expression is judged by faithfulness to personal subjectivity and to standards for beauty and taste, such as adherence to the principles of unity and balanced contrast. The highest grades in mathematics are given to the students who learn to appreciate the formal axiomatic nature of the field. In science, numerous

[23]Edward B. Fiske, "More Sophisticated Skills Stressed in Changed College Entrance Tests," *New York Times* CXXXVII, no. 47, 739 (January 2, 1989): 1.

criteria are used. Value is placed on the learner's use of given processes and modes of thought as well as knowledge of facts and themes. Logical rigor and experimental adequacy are highly prized. Paideia, for example, recognizes the need for testing but recommends that tests be designed by teachers who will not create examinations that merely involve regurgitation of textbook or course material.

Academic specialists are often ambivalent toward evaluation of their curriculum. They see evaluation as valuable, providing useful information, yet they often worry that it will interfere with the realization of broad teaching objectives. They also believe that evaluation may antagonize the teacher and students, take time that can be spent in other ways, and demand a compulsive attitude toward record keeping, which is not compatible with a spirit of enthusiasm. Furthermore, academic specialists share the fear that short-run evaluation may focus on simple skills rather than on the complex skills of inductive reasoning. Ideally, academicians would survey not one term, but five or ten years of work. They want the child to change, not for a weekly examination, but for life.

Making Subject Matter More Appealing to Growing Minds

The academic curriculum has been indicted for putting the logic and orderliness that appeals to the academic mind over the psychological logic of the learner. The failure of the subject organization to inspire learners is a common challenge. The fact that teachers often are not willing or able to carry out the curriculum plans of the academic scholars with the intended enthusiasm and insight is related to this criticism. Academicians are also said to be guilty of two curriculum fallacies: the fallacy of content and the fallacy of universalism.

Those who commit the *fallacy of content* are preoccupied with the importance of *what* students study rather than *how* they study. They emphasize content that they believe is intellectually rigorous and difficult and that they presume will make the necessary demands on students. As indicated in Chapters 1 and 13, the goal of teaching science as inquiry is rarely observed. Instead, textbook information is emphasized—terminology and definitions. Laboratories tend to be used for demonstrations of information already presented rather than for discovery.

There is concern about the lack of emphasis upon application. Academic studies are treated as if they are important chiefly for future studies, a means of advancing up the academic ladder. Certainly students should have access to the very best concepts, principles, and generalizations which civilization has created, but they should seldom be instructed before they are prepared to engage in examining and testing what they are being taught. The process of learning is more important than the content. It is not *declarative* knowledge (knowledge of facts) that students lack. The deficiency is in *operative* knowledge (understanding of how the facts are known and the capacity to apply this knowledge in new situations).

The *fallacy of universalism* rests on the belief that some content areas have universal value regardless of the characteristics of specific learners. One extreme of this view is found in the Paideia Proposal and in the statements by one of America's best known educators, the late Robert Maynard Hutchins, who said that "Education implies teaching. Teaching implies knowledge as truth. The truth is everywhere the same. Hence, education should be everywhere the same."[24] Another instance of universalism is the presumption that academicians can adapt the disciplinary mode of university scholarship for wide use in elementary and secondary schools by pupils who are anything but budding knowledge specialists.

Partly in response to these criticisms, efforts are being undertaken to improve the academic subject matter curriculum. Newer academic subject matter encourages intuition (clever guessing) as a hand maiden of the recognized analytical thinking of the disciplines. School people are supplementing, adapting, and developing the scholars' curriculum materials, not regarding them as panaceas for given local educational needs. For example, teachers are preparing extra resources for less able pupils, as well as additional ways to stimulate the gifted child. Local facilities are being organized for introducing more creative elements into programs, illustrating the techniques of disciplines in a different environment than that intended by the original planners. Instead of studying biology solely from a textbook, students learn the nature of biology from studies of tidepools and animal husbandry. Home-grown academic programs are flourishing. Indeed, they may survive better than the national transplants.

The curriculum designed by the Biological Science Curriculum Study for kindergarten through high school is a good example of how subject matter, such as genetics, can be made valuable in the personal and public lives of students.[25] In this curriculum, kindergarten and first-grade chil-

---

[24]Robert Maynard Hutchins, *Higher Learning in America* (New Haven: Yale University Press, 1936), p. 66.

[25]Biological Sciences Curriculum Study, "You, Me, and Others," "Genes and Surroundings," "Basic Genetics: A Human Approach," and "Living with Cystic Fibrosis" (Boulder, CO: BSCS, 1982).

dren are provided opportunities that introduce basic scientific concepts and modes of investigation. For example, as the basis for the concept of continuity, children observe the growth and development of seeds, sort organisms of various species into family groups and identify physical resemblances between parents and their offspring in human and nonhuman families.

In grades two through four, pupils have experiences with the idea of variety by comparing body measurements and individual preferences for foods, color, hobbies. They are helped to be made aware of the concept of change by studying their own patterns of daily living, making predictions about certain days and times of day in their routines. The principle of continuity is reinforced for students in the middle grades by their study of families and other organizations and their constructing of family trees.

In grades two through four, pupils have experiences with the idea of variety by comparing body measurements and individual preferences for food, color, and hobbies. They are helped to be made aware of the concept of change by studying their own patterns of daily living, making predictions about certain days and times of day in their routines. The principle of continuity is reinforced for students in the middle grades by their study of families and other organizations and their constructing of family trees.

Fifth and sixth graders begin population studies considering their own class and other classes as prototypes. They conduct scientific experiements with preschoolers to see how little ones think about problems. The principle of continuity is extended as the children examine the transmission of specific traits from generation to generation.

The curriculum for the junior high or middle school learners, ''Genes and Surroundings,'' stresses individuality, continuity, variability (both in time and in relation to others), and adaption. Variability is featured because it is an important developmental concept for the adolescent. The activities in this curriculum require students to apply knowledge about human genetics to their personal growth and to the local physical and social environment.

Basic genetics for the high school and adult learner emphasizes the physical, psychological, and social delineation of health created by new knowledge in genetics. Although students learn as a traditional class would about gene segregation, blood types, pedigrees, and genetic disorders, they also learn the content from a human point of view. In the study of inheritance, for example, human beings are featured in preference to animals. More important, students learn the principles of genetics, not as ends in themselves, but in connection with personal and familial concerns such as genetic counseling, prenatal diagnoses, prenatal care and in connection with social concerns—the ethical issues of such matters as prenatal screening and abortion.

Improvement in the quality of the academic curriculum requires attention to four interdependent parts: learning, application, consequence, and value. Learning, especially what students should learn, receives much attention, and some attention is given to helping students criticize academic assertions and to help design tests for refuting them. More attention is needed in helping students to learn strategies for applying knowledge and predicting consequences: ''What must I do with what I know?'' ''How do I take action?'' ''How do I make desirable outcomes more likely?'' ''Do I know what would happen?'' Last, teachers must develop an academic curriculum that students will value. Currently, few academic programs exploit the need for students to answer questions which they themselves regard as important: ''Where do I fit in?'' ''Do I care?'' ''Do I value the outcome?''

In short, some curriculum makers are attempting to provide learning opportunities that are appealing and well within the learners' capacities to serve as the starting point for organizing subject matter intellectually as the specialist does. They are able to differentiate between those activities which lead to growth and those which do not. These developers have taken a long look ahead. They know the academic forms (facts, principles, and laws) to which the children's present activities belong. Curriculum developers are giving children opportunities for intelligent activity, for seeing how things interact with one another to produce definite effects, not aimless activity.

CONCLUDING COMMENTS

Academic specialists have at different times attempted to develop a curriculum that would equip learners to enter the world of knowledge with the basic concepts and methods for observing, noting relationships, analyzing data, and drawing conclusions. They wanted learners to act like physicists, biologists, or historians so that as citizens they would follow developments in disciplines with understanding and support and, if they continued their studies, become specialists themselves. One weakness in the approach was the failure to give sufficient attention to integrative objectives. Learners were unable to relate one discipline to another and to see how the content of a discipline could be brought to bear on the complex problems of modern life not answerable by a single discipline. Two current movements to overcome this weakness are (1) ''integrated'' studies, in which content from several fields is applied to important social problems and historical topics, and (2) the teaching of the forms of knowledge so that learners acquire a range of perspectives for understanding experience.

A second weakness in the academic conception of curriculum is a tendency to impose on pupils adult views of the subject matter. Academic specialists and cultural literacy advocates have given insufficient attention to the present interests and backgrounds of individual learners. They might use those interests as sources for problems and activities by which learners might acquire the intellectual organization and powerful ideas that constitute academic subject matter.

If the academician's goal is to teach people to think better, there must be more consciousness of the kind of thinking that needs to be done and more engagement of students in genuine problem solving, inventing, and critical appraisals. To encourage science programs, for example, that involve scientific ideas and allow students to use these ideas in their daily life, the National Science Foundation has funded projects for elementary and secondary students that promote questions and problems of local interest. In these projects, students acquire the knowledge they need as they consider and try solutions. One of the projects at the University of Iowa involves more than 300 teachers who have reorganized their school program to solve local problems with applications of science.[26]

QUESTIONS

1. Science and English successfully challenged the classics, Greek and Latin, as useful academic subjects in teaching students to think. What are the possibilities that knowledge of the computer with ability to use it in problem solving may become a leading contender for a basic academic competency?
2. The capacity to discriminate and judge is a central goal of all education. For centuries, languages, literature, history, philosophy, and the arts have been viewed as the sources of knowledge for best attaining this goal. Is this true today? Why? Why not?

[26]''What is S/T/S?'' *Chautauqua Notes* 1, 4. *Science* 1986. (Iowa City: University of Iowa Science Education Center, 1986).

3. The issue of "elitism" versus "populism" shows clearly in curriculum changes from personal and social relevance to academic excellence. Are the goals of relevance and excellence mutually exclusive? Is it possible for the curriculum to reflect the different directions simultaneously? If so, how?

4. The daily lives of most people are going to be complicated and constantly changing. They will be assailed by new laws, new traffic schemes, and new sex roles; these will loom larger in their lives than the works of Shakespeare or the Third Law of Thermodynamics. They will not be able to find textbook answers to their daily problems. Neither will they be able to categorize the problems into subjects like history or physics. And so, more value should be placed on education for ordinary life than on academic education. How would you respond to both the premises of this argument and the conclusion which shows a belief in educating students for life rather than for academic achievement?

5. Judge each of the following definitions of the academic curriculum in terms of feasibility (ease of learning and teaching), utility (extent to which it contributes to learners' basic needs for survival, independence, and respect), and idealism (degree to which it is consistent with the highest ideas about human nature):
   a. Academic subject matter as the intellectual tools—questions, methods, concepts, processes, and attitudes—by which knowledge is currently acquired
   b. Academic subject matter as conclusions (facts, principles, and laws) carefully chosen from those derived by specialists on the basis of their relevancy to the conduct of daily living
   c. Academic subject matter as the finest achievements of our cultural heritage, the works of those great minds that have had an effect on civilization

SELECTED REFERENCES

Bernstein, Jeremy, "Science Education for the Non-Scientist." *The American Scholar* 29, no. 2 (Winter 1982–83): 7–12.

Cultural Literacy and the Ideas of General Education, Ian Westbury and Allan C. Purves, eds. 87th Yearbook of the National Society for the Study of Education, Part 2. Chicago: The University of Chicago Press, 1988.

Eisner, Elliot, ed. *Learning and Teaching the Ways of Knowing*, 84th Yearbook of the National Society for the Study of Education, Part 1. Chicago: The University of Chicago Press, 1985.

Mathematical Science Education Board Curriculum Framework for K-12 Mathematics. Washington, DC: Mathematical Science Education Board, 1987.

Popkewitz, Thomas S., ed. *The Foundations of School Subjects: The Struggle to Form an American Institution.* New York and London: Palmer Press, 1987.

Sharpes, Donald K. *Curriculum Traditions and Practices.* New York: St. Martin's Press, 1988.

Curriculum Development

This part of the book features what curriculum specialists consider the core of curriculum knowledge. Chapter 5 presents modern ways to answer the old question of what to teach. More precisely, the chapter indicates procedures and principles for establishing new curriculum purposes: goals, objectives, and content.

Chapter 6 is a guide to the selection and creation of learning opportunities, such as activities, instructional sequences, interventions, experiences, and lessons, which put students in touch with valued content. Specific factors related to learner satisfaction and success are treated in the context of instructional planning.

Curriculum organization is the topic of Chapter 7. Organization in curriculum refers to the sequence and integration of learning opportunities that enable learners to connect important ideas and have continuity in their instructional experiences. Persons attend to organization because they believe that relating learning opportunities to one another makes a difference both in what is learned and in how easily it is learned. Curriculum organization influences the way students view their studies, their attitudes toward learning, and their ability to learn on their own after leaving school. It makes possible the illumination of essentials, less obvious attributes, and generalizations. Good curriculum planning allows for events to be ordered so that patterns rather than individual entities are seen, and significant concepts and skills are enlarged over time.

5

Deciding What Should Be Taught

The decision about what should be taught in an institution, corporate training program, academic department, classroom, or other instructional situation is a decision about curriculum purposes. Persons differ in their desires to determine what should be taught. On the one hand, there are those who flee from curriculum responsibility. They acquiesce to the decisions of others. For example, teachers sometimes accept without question and justification the static goals of boards, administrators, or textbook writers. Trustees and administrators sometimes avoid making decisions about curriculum and what should transpire in classrooms, excusing themselves on the grounds of academic freedom. Responsibility is sometimes avoided by denying the need for the decision, claiming that the present curriculum is good enough.

A more subtle way to avoid responsibililty is to apply a technological approach, in which determination of curriculum ends is treated as non-problematic. Content is determined by the ratings that respondent groups give to proposed goals; the highest rated goal is designated the priority.

On the other hand, many individuals and groups want to propose what should be taught. They may have special concerns and interests, such as AIDS, drug abuse, ethnic studies, computer literacy. Similarly, prospective employers and those at the next rung in the academic ladder often are eager to say what should be taught in preparation for future jobs and study.

Rather than avoiding responsibility and mandating curriculum purposes without justification, those at all levels of schooling should constantly question the purpose of curriculum. Changing circumstances make even the most enduring of subject matters questionable. Of course, some situations offer instructors little freedom to determine ends; the military instructor ordered to train recruits a certain task, for instance. However, having curriculum goals chosen by the largest number of people involved in an educational enterprise is still the best general principle. Thus, in this chapter basic approaches to setting curriculum purpose are stressed. Although not all the approaches give equal opportunity to discover new directions, the reasons why one of the approaches is more appropriate than another in a situation should be recognized.

ARENAS FOR DECIDING WHAT TO TEACH

Levels of Decision Making

Curriculum planning, including decisions about what to teach and for what purpose, occurs at different levels of remoteness from intended learners. These levels are *societal, institutional, instructional,* and *personal.* Participants at the societal level include boards of education (national, local, or state), federal agencies, publishers, and national curriculum reform committees. At the institutional level, adminstrators and faculty groups are the prominent actors. Parents, as well as students, play a role in institutional decision making about curriculum. The instructional level refers to teachers deciding upon purposes that are appropriate for the learners at hand. Recently, the personal or experiential has been recognized as a fourth decision level in curriculum making. This level is consistent with the view that learners generate their own purposes and meanings from their classroom experiences and are not merely passive recipients of curriculum ends and means.[1]

The scope and basis for curriculum decisions vary according to the level. At levels remote from the learner are policy decisions, which either prescribe procedures to be followed by others in formulating the curriculum or establish the character of curriculum by specifying what must be

---

[1]Louise Tyler, ''The Personal Domain,'' in *Curriculum Inquiry: The Study of Curriculum Practice,* eds. John I. Goodlad and Associates (New York: McGraw-Hill, 1979), pp. 91–208.

taught. Societal level decisions are based ideally on theoretical data and are influenced by the norms and pressure groups in the society. Intermediate between policy and the learner are curriculum decisions, which translate policy into specific terms.

Different techniques and personnel are involved in curriculum making at the different levels. Curriculum making at the national societal level includes development of goals and objectives as well as textbooks and other instructional materials for wide use, for example, federally financed curriculum projects in universities and educational regional laboratories, the curriculum work of nonprofit organizations, and the objectives that accompany school materials produced by publishing houses in cooperation with professional educators. Often curriculum designers at this level do not focus on a wide range of educational goals such as social adjustment, self-expression, manual dexterity, and general social attributes. Instead, they center on domains and objectives that are specific to a single subject, grade level, or course. In this arena, specialized personnel—subject specialists, curriculum specialists, and editors—make most of the decisions about *what* should be taught and *how*. These specialists do, however, attend to professional and public opinion as reflected in the yearbooks published by national subject matter organizations such as the National Council for Social Studies (NCSS), professional journals, and popular media. They also seek the advice of representative teachers, textbook salespersons, and other consultants. Results from marketing efforts and trials of preliminary versions also bring about changes in both the ends and means of their curricula.

Curriculum development at the state societal level involves the production of curriculum guides and frameworks. These materials are prepared by professional staffs in state departments of education assisted by representative teachers, college and university personnel, and curriculum specialists. The purposes and goals set forth in these materials are usually formulated by advisory committees composed of professional educators, representatives from educational agencies, and selected nonprofessionals. In the last decade, the influence of economic and business interests has increasingly dominated the development of curriculum purposes at the societal level. State department personnel also engage in curriculum making in response to state laws pertaining to the teaching of such topics as narcotics, health, and bilingual education.

Beginning in 1977 and continuing into early 1980, legislation in most states mandated minimum competency testing for elementary and secondary students. The mandates concentrated on the skill areas to be tested, the grade levels to be covered, and the elaborate procedures for test selection. State departments of education were given responsibility for the implementation of competency-based education programs. These statewide actions and similar testing programs initiated independently in many local school districts had an implicit but inevitable effect on curriculum. In the 1980s, states increasingly prescribed courses of study, graduation requirements, and academic curriculum offerings. However, by 1990, it was clear that local districts were not merely adapting to state policy but amplifying them around local priorities.

The most common arena for curriculum planning is the school district, although there are signs that curriculum decision making at individual schools is increasing. Districts usually involve specialized personnel in curriculum as well as curriculum generalists, subject matter specialists, consultants, representative teachers, and some nonprofessionals. Ideally, all these persons should be concerned with adapting and designing curriculum to local situations and problems. They should consider the implications of regional economy, history, and arts for learners in the local schools. Curriculum making at the individual school level should involve all classroom teachers and administrators, and representative parents and students. Their activities should focus on goals, materials, organization, and instructional strategies. Within the self-contained or nongraded classroom, the single teacher or the teaching team should develop the curriculum objectives and activities most appropriate for specific pupils, keeping in mind the overall goals of the school. Although many teachers rely on an outside source such as a textbook or course of study to determine the concepts to be taught, they frequently expand on this curriculum, reflecting on student responses.

The relative importance of the levels of decision making varies from country to country, state to state, and school to school. Centralized educational systems such as those in Japan and France give the ministry of education more authority over curriculum ends. Less centralized educational systems such as those found in the United Kingdom have established local organizations to explore aspects of the curriculum and to develop new schemes or projects intended to improve the quality and relevance of what is offered. In the United States, local authority for curriculum decisions has been greatest in New England and among the states of the Midwest. State control has always been more evident in such states as Texas, Florida, New York, and California. Now, however, the central role of the teacher in curriculum planning and development is increasing everywhere, partly because of a growing belief that no curriculum derived from outside agencies is successful without teacher commitment.

Different Curriculum at Different Levels

Persons reading casually about curriculum get inconsistent messages. On the one hand, they read that the curriculum is rapidly changing—a new program in mathematics, health education, more appropriate content for the gifted, and mastery learning for the slow. On the other hand, reports indicate that schools are teaching the same thing in the same way as always—reading, writing, arithmetic in the elementary school and vocational and college preparatory programs in the secondary school.

One explanation for the conflicting reports is that there is a curriculum of rhetoric, official proclamations, and a curriculum of practice behind the classroom door. A curriculum formulated at one level is not necessarily adopted and implemented at another. John Goodlad and his associates, for example, have proposed five different curricula, each operating at a different level.[2]

1. *Ideal curriculum.* From time to time foundations, governments, and special interest groups set up committees to look into aspects of the curriculum and to advise on changes that should be made. Curriculum recommendations proposed by these committees might treat multicultural curriculum, a curriculum for the talented, early childhood curriculum, and computer literacy. These proposals might represent ideals or describe desired directions in curriculum as seen by those with a particular value system or special interest. The proponents of such ideal curricula are competing for power within the society. It should be clear, however, that the impact of an ideal curriculum depends on whether the recommendations are adopted and implemented.
2. *Formal curriculum.* Formal curriculum includes those proposals that are approved by state and local boards. Such a curriculum may be a collection of ideal curricula, a modification of the ideal, or other curriculum policies, guides, syllabi, texts sanctioned by the board as the legal authority for deciding what shall be taught and to what ends.
3. *Perceived curriculum.* The perceived curriculum is what the teachers perceive the curriculum to be. Teachers interpret the formal curriculum in many ways. Often there is little relationship between the formally adopted curriculum and the teachers' perception of what the curriculum means or should mean in practice.

---

[2]John I. Goodlad and Associates, eds., *Curriculum Inquiry*, pp. 344–350.

4. *Operational curriculum.* Operational curriculum is what actually goes on in the classroom. Observations by researchers and others who make records of classroom interaction often reveal discrepancies between what teachers say the curriculum is and what teachers actually do.

5. *Experiential curriculum.* The experiential curriculum consists of what students derive from and think about the operational curriculum. Each student's background of experience interacts with classroom activities contributing to unique meanings from common instruction. This curriculum is identified through student questionnaires, interviews, and inferences from observations of students.

CONTENTS FOR DEVELOPMENT OF CURRICULUM

Range of Activity

Major categories of plans derived from curriculum efforts are curriculum policy, programs of study, courses, instructional units, and lesson plans. *Curriculum policy* is usually a written statement of what should be taught and a guide to curriculum development. Graduation requirements, curriculum mandates, and frameworks outlining the content for a field of knowledge are examples. Curriculum policy making is the authoritative allocation of competing values. Elaboration of the political nature of curriculum decisions is treated in Chapter 11.

Programs of study are designed for broad fields: mathematics, science, language arts, vocational education. Each program allocates content activities, and resources to different grade levels or courses, providing curricular linkage by specifying the common abstractions (skills, concepts, attitudes) to be extended in each course of the program. A *course* is a set of learning opportunities within a field of study for a year, semester, or quarter. Within courses, there are *instructional units,* plans aimed at one or more topics, problems, themes, or activity (foci). The particular focus of a unit is not only an important study in itself, but allows for the integration of learning experiences and gives purpose to the classroom activities. *Lesson plans* indicate teaching strategies and procedures for student engagement.

Curriculum developers also produce more detailed instructional materials: textbooks, taped and filmed programs, and instructional sequences. These materials often require the curriculum developer to detail steps for the teacher or child to follow and to prepare tests and record-keeping systems, as well as procedures for training the teacher on how to use the materials.

Before undertaking the production of any materials, the curriculum developer will consider time and the intended learners. Will the material serve an hour's lesson, a year's work, a six-year program? What are the ages, mental and physical characteristics, and experiential backgrounds of the future users of the materials?

In determining what the individual or target population should learn, curriculum developers take either a restricted or an unrestricted approach. In the restricted approach, the developer looks for possible objectives from within a domain of knowledge and practice. Mathematics, health, intellectual development, and vocational education are typical domains. In an unrestricted approach, the curriculum developer is willing to regard any problem, idea, or situation as having possible implications for what should be taught. The curriculum maker's task of conceiving possible and desirable outcomes does not mean that all proposed ends will be accepted and acted upon. Boards of education, principals, teachers, and pupils all have ways of rejecting the best conceived purposes. However, persons who propose outcomes should be able to justify them. Later in this chapter, we will describe the ways in which developers formulate their purposes and justify them.

Institutional Purposes

Those who plan to develop curriculum within a given institution must attend to the nature of that school, especially to the school's manifest purposes. Why? One reason is that the selection of an appropriate model or set of procedures for the formulation of objectives depends on the central purpose of that school. Vocational and other training schools, for example, are expected to prepare students for specific jobs. Hence, the use of *job analysis*, a technique for deriving objectives that directly contribute to helping students find jobs and keep them, is warranted. This technique seeks to ensure a match between what the student learns and what he or she will do on the job. The method can be amplified, of course, with procedures for collecting data that will help anticipate likely job requirements. Job analysis would be a less appropriate tool to use in the formulation of objectives within an institution whose mission is to further humanistic goals. Such an institution should use a different technical tool to formulate objectives, i.e., a tool more consistent with actualizing learners as individuals.

Illustrations of how institutional purposes match procedures for curriculum development can be seen in the familiar practices of the community college. There is more freedom in the formulation of curriculum goals in community colleges than in traditional schools devoted to the liberal arts because they frequently have a very broad goal, that of community service, an invitation to meet the educational needs of the community. Because of such goals and the state legislature's practice of funding community colleges on the basis of student enrollment, the curriculum problem becomes a search for courses that will attract students. Anything that appeals to aged persons, young mothers, veterans, and immigrants must be considered. The appropriate technical tool for the formulation of objectives in this case is needs assessment, a procedure for uncovering local deficiencies and trends to decide what might be taught, and a way to sample and stimulate interests in various kinds of learning.

Some curriculum leaders do not want curriculum objectives to be shackled to institutional purposes. Indeed, some people believe that curriculum specialists should be trying to change the purposes of institutions. They believe that curriculum developers have been shaped by the bureaucratic nature of the schools, and thus have formulated objectives that serve an industrial model of education with an emphasis on efficiency. They would prefer curriculum workers to advance both futuristic and humanistic ends, helping institutions to focus on getting people to define problems that were not perceived before and to make contact with one another in stronger ways.[3] The role of the curriculum worker is not determined by the constraints of educational institutions; instead, curriculum workers create new institutional forms and environments. The introduction of forms such as nondirective teaching roles, student goal setting, women's studies, service learning, cooperative learning and therapeutic modes of working may broaden the function of a traditional school to include humanistic ends.

Functions of the Curriculum

Before preparing any curriculum plan—whether for a textbook, lesson, course of study, document, product, or program—one should be clear about the functions the proposed curriculum will serve. Those persons responsible for total curriculum offerings of a school can also find

---

[3]Jerry L. Patterson et al., *Productive School Systems for a Non-Rational World* (Alexandria, VA: ASCD, 1986).

a functional concept useful in bringing balance to their programs of study. Four functions are:

1. *Common or General Education.* The function of common education is met through a curriculum that addresses the learner as a responsible human being and citizen, not as a specialist or one with unique gifts or interests. It means, for instance, including as content the ground rules (Bill of Rights) for participating in the civic affairs of the community and developing those minimal competencies essential for the health, welfare, and protection of all. Successful general education enables everyone to support and share in the culture; hence, a curriculum worker must decide what the individual needs in order to communicate with others. The planner must consider what outcomes and experiences all should have in common.

2. *Supplementation.* Individuality is the key to understanding supplementation. Objectives consistent with it deal with both personal deficits and unique potentials. To serve this function, a curriculum might be designed for those whose talents and interests enable them to go much farther than the majority or those whose defects and deficiencies are severe enough to require special attention. Such a curriculum is personal and individual, not common or general.

3. *Exploration.* Opportunities for learners to discover and develop personal interests capture the meaning of exploration. When well executed, it enables learners to find out that they do or do not have either the talent or zeal for certain kinds of activities. Exploring experiences should *not* be organized and taught as if their purposes were to train specialists. Nor should they be conceived as shoddy and superficial. Exploration demands a wide range of contacts within a field, realization of the possibilities for further pursuit, and revelation of one's own aptitudes and interests.

4. *Specialization.* A specializing function is rendered by a curriculum in which the current standards of a trade, profession, or academic discipline prevail. Students are expected to emulate those who are successfully performing as skilled workers or scholars. Entry into such a curriculum requires that students already have considerable expertise and drive.

The balance among the different functions and the curriculum conceptions associated with them varies every few years. With secondary schools, for example, academic specialization was in the ascendancy in the 1960s. In the early 1970s, general education was weakened in favor of exploration; minicourses, optional modules, alternative curriculum, and other electives were used. In the early 1980s, the demand for basic skills by parents and some educators pushed the curriculum back in the direction of general education. Vocational specialization, too, received more attention, particularly training on the job site itself. The beginning of the 1990s finds the core of common learning and academic specialization driving the curriculum.

In higher education, newer curriculum policy favors general liberal education, often said to be an unwelcome chore. Opposition to general education comes from humanists and specialists who (for different reasons) believe it best for teachers and students to select their own areas of interest for study. In their defense of specialization, a scholar's gavel holds that research must be specialized in order to focus effort and delve deeply. To be specialized is not to be trivial, because the best specialized research has broad implications.[4] As a countercharge to the charge of narrowness, the academic specialist says that by understanding one field in depth, the student will learn to appreciate a wider array of intellectual tools and artistic achievement. This notion has not gone unchallenged. Elliot Eisner, for instance, views it with skepticism.

> I am not convinced by the thesis that specialization breeds general understanding, or that it cultivates an appreciation of the variety of ways in which meaning can be secured . . . If attention to a wide range of problems and fields of study is necessary for the type of personal and intellectual range one wished to develop in students, how then can one cultivate, in depth, those idiosyncratic interests and aptitudes which almost all students have?[4]

The curriculum also performs less recognized functions. They are the *consummation function* (whetting the student demand for material things such as a car or the latest microcomputer), the *custodial function* (keeping students from job markets and entertaining them), and the *socializing function* (allowing students to meet members of the opposite sex).

DETERMINING WHAT TO TEACH

The power to frame educational purposes is central in the curriculum field. Those who are not sensitive to the need for this power, who merely accept what others have proposed, are, in one sense, instruments. The following paragraphs describe the ways in which individuals and groups generate and select curriculum ends, content, and experiences. These ends indicate the purposes for which our programs and lessons are un-

---

[4]Elliot W. Eisner, "Persistent Dilemmas in Curriculum Decision Making," in *Confronting Curriculum Reform* (Boston: Little, Brown, 1971),pp. 168–169.

dertaken. They give direction to what would otherwise be blind activities and enable us to prepare plans of action. A curriculum goal is more than a whim or desire. Its formulation is a complex intellectual operation involving observation, study of conditions, collection of relevant information and, most of all, judgment. Curriculum planning demands an intellectual anticipation and evaluation of consequences.

It is important to note the difference in curriculum work by (a) conservative curricularists who seek to justify existing goals, content, and experiences by showing how these answers are relevant to cultural realities and (b) curriculum inquirers who use cultural analyses as a basis for generating alternative goals, contents, and experiences.

In order to plan curriculum based on a justifiable selection from the culture, it is necessary to have a process. Denis Lawton recommends analyzing the kind of society that exists and then mapping out the knowlege and kinds of experiences that are most appropriate for this culture.[5] According to Lawton, it is necessary to identify both cultural invariants and cultural variables. Cultural developers should have access to many dimensions in the dominant cultures and subcultures: social and economic, level, communication, nationality, technology, morality, belief, and aesthetics. Alternative and existing curriculum can be compared for their fit to the realities described.

It is true that many curriculum plans are drawn in response to perceived inadequacies or single issues without comprehensive cultural analysis. Current curriculum reform policies, for example, are responses to business and industrial concerns about American economic growth, and are based upon limited data regarding present and future work.[6] Furthermore, these policies neglect consideration of the educational functions. To the extent that these policies operate at a high level of abstraction and aim at uniformity in curriculum, they will fail. Reform policy succeeds when it accommodates to cultural invariants—regional and individual variability. Policy is best when it initiates local curriculum development in which people in schools fashion solutions to their real problems.[7]

In addition to familiarity with policy and the analyses underlying it, those developing curriculum at the school and classroom levels require

---

[5]Denis Lawton, *Curriculum Studies and Educational Planning* (London: Hodder and Stoughton, 1983).

[6]*Global Competition: The New Reality* (The Report of the President's Commission on Industrial Competition, 1988).

[7]Richard Elmore and Milbray W. McLaughlin, *Steady Work: Policy, Practice, and the Reform of American Education* (Santa Monica, CA: Rand Corporation, 1988).

data from cultural analyses of their particular community. Consideration of the implications of local data for what to teach is central to curriculum development.

RATIONAL AND TECHNICAL MODELS IN CURRICULUM DECISION MAKING

In most rational models, the decision making process follows an orderly pattern. The determination of goals is the first priority. Othe decisions about structure, content, activities, materials, and accountability are tied to the goal. Goals themselves are determined by means of a logical problem solving approach. The following paragraphs feature the most widely known rational models for formulating goals; these models are adaptable for use at societal, institutional, and instructional levels.

Needs Assessment Model

Needs assessment is the process by which educational needs are defined and priorities set. In the context of curriculum, a need is defined as a condition in which a discrepancy exists between an *acceptable* state of learner achievement or attitude and an *observed* learner state.

Needs assessment is one of the most frequently used ways for justifying curriculum goals and objectives. Several reasons underlie the popularity of needs assessment as a tool for formulating desired outcomes. Some people are motivated by efficiency. They want to identify and resolve the most critical needs so that resources can be employed in the most efficient manner. They want to avoid the practice of trying to do a little bit in many problem areas and solving none of them. Other people are concerned about social disorganization, the lack of consensus among the school community. They see needs assessment as a way to effect shared values and mutual support. The discussion of alternative ends by parents, students, teachers, and other citizens is an educational activity in itself. Other people want new value orientations to be reflected in the curriculum and see needs assessment as a vehicle for influence. Cultural pluralists, for example, use needs assessment to ascertain the values of subcultures such as those of Hispanics, blacks, and Asians. They also try to persuade the dominant society to accept these values as worthy goals to be advanced through the curriculum.

Steps in Needs Assessment. A needs assessment requires four steps: formulating a set of tentative goals statements, assigning priority to different goals, determining the acceptability of learner performance in each of the preferred goals, and translating high priority goals into plans.

1. *Formulating a Set of Tentative Goals Statements.* Comprehensive sets of goals that reflect the dominant culture are readily available.[8] Such goals statements are collected from curriculum guides, textbooks, evaluation studies, and basic research studies by psychologists and educators. These goals refer to the conventionally sought outcomes in most schools: fundamental competencies for reading, writing, mathematics, health, citizenship, aesthetics. Goals may be found in four areas: academic, social and civic, vocational, and personal. Goals statements may also include attributes of character such as friendliness, respect, and independence.

   In order to apply needs assessment to a cultural minority, additional goal statements that reflect subculture values are necessary. Cross-cultural investigations reveal fundamental differences among the values of different cultural groups. Many Hispanic parents, for example, believe that learners should make their choices in terms of family interests rather than personal desires. Some Hispanic Americans do not want their children to express personal feelings in the presence of an adult. These goals often contrast sharply with those of many in the dominant culture and with goals of other subcultures. Sometimes, goals statements from minority group members reflect a desire to gain better treatment for their children in majority-dominated schools. Such a goal might be that learners should see school as a friendly and helpful place.

   Goals statements about community values must also be obtained. Those conducting needs assessments must consider more than the conventional goals available from state and federal publications. They must focus on their own perception of what they want their learners to think, feel, or be able to do as a result of school instruction.

   Typical techniques for eliciting data for needs assessment are *concerns conferences* and *sponsor speakups*. Concerns conferences, organized by school administrators and curriculum specialists, are attempts to identify local problems as most people in the community perceive them. At a large convocation community members are prepared for the task of identifying community problems, and later, in small discussion groups, problems are articulated and suggestions

---

[8]Roger A. Kaufman, ''Needs Assessment'' in *Fundamental Curriculum Decisions*, ASCD 1983 Yearbook, ed. Fenwick W. English (Alexandria, VA: ASCD, 1983), pp. 53–67.

made for their solution. Frequently, new educational goals are proposed in order to attempt a solution to the identified problem. In sponsor speakups students are organized into groups so that they work cooperatively to identify the most pressing needs of their school situation. Efforts are made to encourage uninhibited student expression. Although many of these needs may be met by actions that are not curricular in nature, it is important to consider the curriculum goals that might contribute to resolving the perceived difficulties. A perceived problem in health, for example, may involve a different goal for medical health agencies than for a school. The school's curriculum goal might be limited to helping students understand the reason for the health problem and explaining some ways the learner can cope with it. A medical agency might take more direct action, i.e., inoculate the students to prevent disease.

2. *Assigning Priority to Goal Areas.* The second phase consists of gathering preference data, typically from parents, staff, students, and community members. Members of these groups are given goal statements and asked to rank them in terms of importance. Opportunities are provided for the respondents to add to the set of goals presented. Usually they rate the goals on a five-point scale (a rating rather than a ranking allows more goals to be considered). Samples of goals can be given to different persons to effect average group estimates. Later, the combined ratings of all the people sampled will reveal those goals considered very important, important, average, unimportant, and very unimportant.

3. *Determining the Acceptability of Learner Performance in Each of the Preferred Goal Areas.* In the third phase either a subjective or an objective approach can be taken. A subjective approach calls for a group of judges to rate the acceptability of present learner status on each goal. No direct measure of the learners with respect to the goals is undertaken; judges estimate the present status of learners with respect to goal. Their impression might be gained by whatever they have observed or been led to believe by the media and reports from the children and other neighbors. Judges' ratings become indices of need. The objective approach requires actually measuring the status of students relative to each goal. Measures must be congruent with the goals, of course. To this end, instuctional objectives within each goal area are selected. Matching assessment devices are chosen and administered to representative samples of pupils. If the students' level of performance on a measurement is less than the acceptable level, a need is indicated. Levels obtained on each measurement are compared.

Those showing the widest gap indicate a greater priority. However, one must also consider the relative importance of the goal as indicated by preference data.

4. *Translating High Priority Goals into Plans.* In the fourth phase, goals that are preferred and for which a need has been identified become the bases for new curriculum instructional plans. The selection of new target outcomes, goals, and objectives has implications for course offerings and for instructional materials and arrangements because the realization of new goals requires new facilitating means. Learning activities, teaching strategies, and evaluation techniques must be changed. For example, having once identified a need for pupils to learn to read and write in Spanish and acquire minority cultural values as well as positive attitudes toward school, the school may need to develop a bilingual program. Consequently, the staff must acquire new materials in the Spanish language and offer activities consistent with minority values—group cooperation and family involvement. Furthermore, teachers must be helped to use teaching strategies that are effective with the culture, such as learning how to indicate nonverbal acceptance through touching.

Problems in the Needs Assessment Technique. Technical and philosophical problems need to be resolved before needs assessment can fulfill its promise. One technical problem involves making the meaning of the goals clear so that respondents are choosing the same goals. A vague goal, such as citizenship, creative fluency, or application of scientific methods, indicates only a general direction. On the other hand, making a vague goal specific often results in numerous objectives, so many in fact that no single person could rank them according to their value. More than fifty years ago, Boyd H. Bode commented on Franklin Bobbitt's claim that 1200 high school teachers in Los Angeles had given an almost unanimous judgment on a long list of objectives. Bode said, ''If the list really represents common judgment, we are bound to conclude that men and women are more amenable to reason in Los Angeles than anywhere else on the globe. . . . One almost wonders whether the teachers of Los Angeles did not mistake Bobbitt's list of abilities for a petition to be signed.''[9] One answer to the problem of how to discriminate among objectives is to rely on broad-scope but measurable objectives that repre-

---

[9]Boyd H. Bode, ''On Curriculum Construction,'' *Curriculum Theory* 5, no. 1 (1975): 39–59, reprinted from *Modern Educational Theories* (New York: Macmillan, 1927), p. 17.

sent significant competencies rather than to stipulate the many objectives that contribute to the general competency. Another answer is to have different persons rate different goals and objectives, with no single person having to evaluate carefully more than seven, (a digestible number).

It is helpful to ask all who are to rate goals to engage first in common discussion and to ascertain that particular goals or objectives satisfy these three criteria: (1) that the goal is needed for future learning and contributes to fundamental needs, such as making a living and gaining the respect of others, (2) that the goal is teachable, and (3) that it is not likely to be acquired outside the school.

Needs assessment is frequently used by those who have adaptive conceptions of curriculum and see it as a way to ensure that the curriculum is responsive to changing social conditions. It can also be used by social reconstructionists who want not so much to prepare students for changing conditions as to alter the social institutions that are creating undesirable social conditions. Group deliberation and judgment thus become factors in needs assessment. There must be opportunity for sharing facts and logical persuasion, i.e., facts and ideas brought by the participants themselves, not by outsiders, and there must be deliberation involving normative philosophical considerations. The fact that something exists does not mean it is desirable. The reflective curriculum worker inquires about not only what is desired but also whether it is worthwhile, right, and good.

Those who regard needs assessment as nothing more than a scientific information gathering procedure see it as a way to avoid ethical issues by justifying the curriculum merely on the basis of the popularity of certain goals and the magnitude of the discrepancy between where learners *are* and where learners *should be* with respect to these popular goals. Needs assessment has been opposed when it is regarded solely as an information gathering procedure on the grounds that "No scientifically derived information can yield a judgment about 'what should be' because science deals not with normative considerations but with facts."[10]

It remains to be seen whether the dominant groups in schools will attend to the goal priorities of minority groups. Can the curriculum reflect the priorities of all groups within the community or must a consensus be reached? If there is group conflict, how will the conflict be resolved?

---

[10]Maurice L. Monette, "Needs Assessment: A Critique of Philosophical Assumptions, " *Adult Education* 29, no. 2 (1979): 83–95.

The Futuristic Model

There is a growing realization that the world of the future is going to be different from the present, that it will demand new kinds of people, and that the time is short to prepare the citizens of the future. Hence, efforts have been made to develop educational objectives consistent with this realization and specific enough to imply action.

Common Ingredients. Although there are slight differences among authors' conceptions of the model, the following techniques and phases are regarded as important:

1. *The Multidisciplinary Seminar.* Professional educators and specialists from outside education (political scientists, economists, medical psychologists) meet for several days to discuss possible future developments that would affect curriculum planning. Members of this seminar prepare papers examining the research frontiers in their field. The results of literature searches on educational innovations and goals are also presented.
2. *Judgment of Projected Trends.* Major anticipated changes are ordered according to their importance to society and probability of occurrence. The difficulty of bringing about these changes in terms of time, money, and energy is considered. A period of occurrence is estimated. The potential social effects of these changes are classified as good or bad on the basis of carefully examined opinions on which there is a consensus. Participants rate each change from "very desirable" to "very undesirable."
3. *Educational Acceptance for Creating the Future.* After the social consequences of trends have been established and rated, school persons and others suggest how they think the schools should respond. In deciding the educational responsibility to be taken, consideration is given to the certainty of a future occurrence, the social consequences of that occurrence, and the possibility that educators can effect it or can prepare students for it. Educational objectives, thus formed, should support "good" futures and resist "bad" ones. The educators also decide what items in the present curriculum are unlikely to prepare students for the future world and suggest that these items no longer be supported.
4. *Scenario Writing.* A group of writers prepares at least two descriptions. One is a description of what learners will be like if action is taken on the decision in phase 3 and implemented by the school. The second is a description of the necessary related changes in subject matter,

learning activities, curriculum organization, and methods. Attention is also paid to institutional arrangements that will bear on the new curriculum.

A Strategy Planning network, consisting of twenty-three schools and sponsored by the Association for Supervision and Curriculum Development attempts to analyze changes for which the schools should be planning if they are to have a program suitable for all students in the next century. An example of strategy planning within the network is "Project 2001" undertaken by Lake Washington School District, Washington. In this project futurists were commissioned to write reports on the skills schools should teach in 2001, so they asked other members of the community for their views on what schools should be doing.

The Delphi method is used by curriculum workers to obtain a consensus on goals and objectives for the future. By this method one tries to obtain the intuitive insights of experts and then uses these judgments systematically. In vocational education, content is often selected through Delphi as a way to find what is likely to be useful to future graduates of the school. Members of an employers' advisory council to the school are sent a series of questionnaires. The first questionnaire indicates present content offerings and asks participants to indicate their recommended course subject areas in light of anticipated futures and to state the amount of time to be spent on each. In an attempt to gain consensus, more questionnaires are sent, providing information about all the participants responses to the previous ones. Participants are asked to reconsider their first recommendations and to give their reasons. Usually survey participants begin to form a consensus.

Problems With the Futuristic Model. The difficulty that any group of persons faces in trying to predict or invent the future is a problem. However, difficulties are also associated with getting a broad enough base of participation within and outside school systems and with understanding the complex factors that affect school curriculum. different community contexts and different views of the school's role delay consensus. There is no consensus about the goals different educational institutions should be trying to achieve. A related aspect of the problem is that many people do not like to make choices and find it difficult even to make hypothetical choices. Even when groups arrive at a consensus on some preferred alternatives, many dissensions remain unresolved. Educational objectives frequently are not consistent with other objectives or have more than one meaning even for one person. One objective may call for the learner to show initiative; a second objective may call for the learner to follow directions. Respondents experience a tension in deciding between creativity on the one hand and order and tradition on the other.

The Rational Model

Ralph Tyler's rationale is the best-known rational model for answering questions about formulating educational purposes, selecting and organizing education experiences, and determining the extent to which purposes are being attained.[11] It is called an ends-means approach because the setting of purposes or objectives as ends influences the kinds of activity and organization most likely to assist in reaching the goal. Evaluation, too, according to this model is undertaken to see how the learning experience as developed and organized produces the desired results.

Deriving Objectives. Tyler's assumption is that objectives will be more defensible—will have greater significance and greater validity—if certain kinds of facts are taken into account. One source of facts consists of studies of the intended learners. A second source is found in studies of contemporary life outside the school, and a third source is made up of suggestions about objectives from subject matter specialists regarding what knowledge is of most worth for citizens. The following elaborates how objectives are derived from data provided by the different sources.

1. *Learners.* In order to derive objectives from this source, learners should be studied in terms of their deficiencies in knowledge and application of a broad range of values in daily living; their psychological needs for affection, belonging, recognition, and a sense of purpose; and their interests. Essentially, the process of deriving an objective from studies of the learner demands that an inference be drawn about what to teach after looking at the data. Making inferences also involves value judgments. If the data show that learners are chiefly interested in reading comic books, it must be decided whether this is a desirable interest to be extended or a deficiency to be overcome.

   Let us assume that the curriculum worker has discovered this fact: "During adolescence, learners are likely to have the cognitive skills

---

[11]Ralph W. Tyler, *Basic Principles of Curriculum and Instruction* (Chicago: The University of Chicago Press, 1950).

of intuition, generalization, and insight; and their sensibilities toward justice are awakened." The curriculum planner can use this information to infer what to teach, perhaps deciding that learners should acquire knowledge of utopian thought and the methods for effecting a more perfect social order. The curriculum planner might also infer that students should suppress the tendency to believe that wars, tyrannies, and the like are caused by human nature and believe instead that changes in social structure may preclude injustices.

2. *Social Conditions.* Facts about the community—local, national, or world—must be known and taken into account if what is to be taught is to be made relevant to contemporary life. Again, a value judgment must be made in deciding what kinds of facts to collect. Comprehensiveness is sometimes sought: one might collect data on health, economics, politics, religion, family, and conservation. The educational responses to these facts often provoke controversy. After discovering from health data that venereal disease is at an epidemic level, the curriculum worker might make inferences that range from (a) learners should be taught the causes and means for preventing communicable diseases to (b) learners should be taught those moral principles governing conduct which uphold the sanctity of marriage. It is obvious that a curriculum worker's responses in such a case could be controversial.

3. *Subject Matter Specialists.* In rational curriculum making, scientists and scholars, the discoverers of disciplined knowledge, are consulted in order to find out what the specialist's subject can contribute to the education of the intended learners. Suppose that a curriculum planner asked this question: "What in your field might best contribute to the aim that learners generate new questions and that they conceptualize alternatives and their consequences?" He or she would receive different answers from specialists in different fields. A historian might reply, "You should teach the principles for interpreting historical events. Help students to comprehend such schemes as the greatman theory, cultural movements, and economic determinism as explaining factors." A linguist's response might be, "You should teach concepts that show the unitary and meaning-bearing sequences of language structures, such as intonation patterns." An anthropologist might want to stress the processes of inquiry that illuminate culture or might say, "Be sure learners understand the difference between nature and the symbolic devices, institutions, and things constructed by people."

Selecting from Among Education Goals and Objectives.   After formulating tentative purposes, the rationalist applies the following criteria before accepting them as suitable for the selection of learning activities:

1. *Congruency with values and functions.* Objectives must relate to the values and functions adopted by the controlling agency. If authorities for the institution value general education, objectives must further common understanding; if they value specialization, then objectives must be related to the development of specialists in a field.
2. *Comprehensiveness.* Objectives that are more encompassing, that do not deal with a minuscule sort of learner behavior, are more highly valued. Often many such objectives can be coalesced into a single powerful objective.
3. *Consistency.* Objectives should be consistent with one another. One should not have objectives stressing both openness or inquiry and dogmatism or unconditional acceptance.
4. *Attainability.* Objectives should be capable of being reached without great strain. The curriculum maker should consider teacher and community concurrence, costs, and availability of materials.

As guides to instructional planning, educational objectives are then stated in a form that makes clear the content that the learner must use. the *domain* or situation in which the knowledge is to apply, and the kind of *behavior* to be exhibited by the learner. The following objective is an illustration: ''In different writing samples (domain), the learner will be able to recognize (behavior) unstated assumptions (content).''

Learning activites must allow the learner to work with the defined substantive element at a level of behavior consistent with that called for in the objective. Activities designed to teach prerequisites to that terminal task can also be provided, of course.

Problems with the Tyler Model.   The Tyler model represents conciliatory eclecticism. In recommending the three sources to use in formulating objectives, Tyler confronts the decision maker with three warring conceptions of the curriculum. The learner as a source is consistent with the humanistic conception, especially when data regarding the learner's own psyche needs and interests are considered. Society as a source is in keeping with social adaptive and some reconstruction orientations, while the subject matter specialist as a source tends to recognize the academic conception of curriculum.

Little help is given in the way of assigning weight to each source when one must take precedence over another. On the other hand,the model offers the possibility of treating learners, society, and subject matter as part of a comprehensive process rather than as isolated entities.

Not all criteria by which some objectives are excluded are stipulated by the model. Users of the model must identify their own set of philosophical axioms for screening objectives. The fact that objectives must be consistent with one another does not in itself indicate the value of the objectives formulated.

The role of values and bias is not highlighted in the model. Values and bias operate at all points in the rationale—in the selection of specific data within the sources, in drawing inferences from the data, in formulating the objectives, and in selecting from among the objectives.

Three other criticisms remain. The model tends to lock curriculum making into the "top-down" tradition, with those at the top setting the purposes and functions that narrow the school's goals and objectives which in turn control classroom instruction. Those who favor teacher or learner autonomy in the selection of ends and learning opportunities oppose the model. They charge that the predetermined purposes which guide all other aspects, such as learning experiences, are like a production model with its input (students) processes (learning experiences), and output (prespecified objective or product). The second criticism, which the model takes time to implement, is related to the third: the resolving of disagreement over values. The practical difficulties of getting the right data sources and being able to infer appropriate implications for schools require imaginative thinkers.The model does not resolve the political conflict in curriculum policy making even if common values are accepted. Even those characterized as devout members of the same value persuasion may have their disagreement over methods:

> Those who agree that the truths honored in our tradition should be the primary curriculum elements may still disagree over whether certain classics should be taught in English translation, Latin translation, or the original Greek. They may argue whether to include Virgil together with Tacitus and Julius Caesar in a fixed time of study. They may differ over the amounts of time to be allotted to the Bible and other more strictly oriented texts.The resolution of such problems requires a decision procedure in addition to a value base.[12]

---

[12]Michael W. Kirst and Decker F. Walker, "An Analysis of Curriculum Policy Making," *Review of Educational Research Association* 41, no. 5 (December 1971): 485. Copyright 1971, American Educational Research Association, Washington, DC.

Curriculum specialists have tried to improve upon the Tyler model. Usually the improvement consists of reversing the order of procedures by placing the statements of educational values or aims as the first step and then refining these aims in light of information about learners, social conditions, and new knowledge in the subject fields. In working with students of curriculum, I often randomly divide the students into two groups: (a) those who follow the procedures outlined by Tyler, beginning with sources and ending with the application of philosophical and psychological screens and (b) those who follow the revised procedures, making value orientations explicit before looking at data from the sources. I give both groups the same facts or generalizations from each of the three sources and then observe how variations in ordering of the procedures influence the number and kinds of objectives generated. Table 5–1 illustrates the contrast in procedure.

The difference in number and kind of objectives generated by the two procedures is considerable. The Tyler model results in many more objectives and objectives that are more responsive to the range of data available about learners and the community. The difficulty experienced by the revisionist group in getting agreement on educational aims is much greater than the difficulty of establishing a philosophical framework after forming tentative objectives.

The Vocational or Training Model

Training usually implies narrower purposes than educating. Educating allows for objectives that include the wholeness of a student's life as a responsible human being and a citizen. Training tends to look at the student's competence in some occupation. Although these two sides of life are not altogether separable, different procedures are used in deriving training objectives than in formulating educational objectives. The training model for formulating proposed outcomes has essentially two functions: one is to reveal particular manpower needs or occupations that the institutions or programs should serve. A second purpose is to determine the specific competencies that must be taught in order for learners (trainees) to take their place within the target occupations.

Determining Occupational Targets. Procedures for determining needed occupations rely initially on existing studies and plans. Most states release detailed area manpower requirements for more than four hundred key occupational categories, reflecting for each category current employment, anticipated industry growth, and personnel replacement. The an-

**TABLE 5–1 Comparison of Tyler and Revisionist
Procedures for Generating Objectives**

Tyler	Revisionist
1. *Data* Facts about learners indicating that they do not feel responsible for their successes or failures in school. Facts about the community indicating perhaps ideological confusion about traditional ways of doing things and newer technology. Confusion about traditional ways of doing things and newer technology.	1. *Philosophy* State what you think the goals of the schools should be (cognitive development, development of respect for the rights of others, desire for continuing education, ability to enter the world of work) and the aims, functions, and programs most important for the school you have in mind (general, remedial, or vocational).
2. *Tentative Objectives* Suggested objectives in response to the facts and generalizations.	2. *Data* Facts about learners indicating that learners do not feel responsible for their successes or failures in school. Facts about the community indicating perhaps ideological confusion about traditional ways of doing things and newer technology.
3. *Philosophy* State what you think the goals of the schools should be (cognitive development, development of respect for others, desire for continued learning, ability to enter the world of work) or the aims and functions most important for the school and programs you have in mind (general, remedial, or vocational).	3. *Objectives* Objectives are derived by keeping in mind detailed educational aims and functions and responding to facts in light of these aims.
4. *Final Objectives* Accept or reject the tentative objectives on the basis of your educational values, educational aims, and functions of schooling.	

nual *Manpower Report of the President* issued by the United States Department of Labor gives an overall picture of the employment problems facing the nation. Specific organizations such as the military, large industries, and business have projected their own manpower needs, which indicate the types of training that will be necessary. State and regional planners attempt to estimate future employment opportunities and to foresee fluctuations in mobility within the area and in mobility likely to result as firms enter or leave an area. These planners try to coordinate the programs that determine vocational services with those aimed at developing jobs. They take into account job market analysis, program reviews, curriculum resources, and state, local, and national priorities.

It is customary to use advisory councils in connection with planning vocational programs. These councils are composed of parents, students, representatives from labor, and potential trainees. Members help supply more information both on what will happen in a community and what kind of employee employers are seeking. Furthermore, they help inform the community of the forces affecting the job market.

Determining the Objectives for Training Programs or Courses. Job descriptions and task analysis procedures are used to enhance the relevancy of the training program to the job to be performed. A job description is a paragraph or two listing the tasks involved and any unusual conditions under which those tasks are carried out. All classes of tasks are listed. The task analysis begins with a study of the particular job or jobs. The curriculum developer tries to answer these questions: What tasks are required on this job? How frequently are they required? What skills and information is the graduate of the training program expected to bring to each task?

A task is a logically related set of actions required by a job objective. The first step in the task analysis is listing all tasks that might be included in the job. Second, for each of these tasks an estimate is made of the frequency of performance, relative importance, and relative ease of learning. Third, the task is detailed by listing what the person does when performing each task. Note that what is done is not necessarily the same as what is known.

Task identification occurs through interviews, questionnaires, reports of critical incidents, and hardware analysis. Observation shows what the employees *do* while being observed; questionnaires and interviews reveal what they *say* they do. Critical incident techniques also indicate what people say they do. A critical incident report may describe a specific work assignment which an employee carried out very effectively or very ineffectively. Such reports are especially valuable in identifying unforeseen contingencies, difficult tasks, and interpersonal aspects of a job. Reports are sorted into topics such as equipment, problems, or groups of incidents that go together. The features common to these incidents are categorized. Each incident is judged effective or ineffective and characterized by the presence or absence of some skill or knowledge. The records may be further classified by such dimensions as work habit, management effectiveness or ineffectiveness, and method problem. From these data new training objectives are derived for courses. Critical incident reports are completed by representative samples of job holders and supervisory persons who interact with job holders.

The job analysis and a knowledge of the characteristics of the intended learners are all that is necessary for the blueprint of expected student performance. The course objectives can be obtained by subtracting what the student is already able to do from what he or she must be able to do. Course objectives are not the same as task analyses. Objectives specify the abilities that a beginning learner must have after training; task analyses describe the job as performed by a highly skilled person. Subtracting what students are already able to do from what they must be able to do helps one to decide the course objectives. One cannot go directly from a task analysis to the formulation of objectives for a course. It is necessary to decide which skills demanded by the occupation may be better taught on the job and which skills are best taught in the course.

Problems with the Vocational Model.   There are several criticisms of the training model. First, the objectives derived from it usually prepare a learner for work as it *is* rather than as it *should* be. Related to this criticism is the charge that the model is associated with *presentism,* a focus on the current situation rather than on a likely future condition. Most critics admit, however, that the model is ahead of the practice of deriving objectives only from tradition, convention, and the curriculum maker's personal experiences.

A second criticism is that the task analysis procedure is only valid for aspects of jobs that are certain. If we know what an employee must do in a situation, the training model is effective. However, many aspects of jobs are uncertain—what to do in light of unanticipated circumstances, what to do when the situation is altered. Furthermore, not many developers know how to make task analyses for situations demanding political, economic, or moral judgments. Preparing students for instances in which the grounds for decision are not clear or unique requires a different model for curriculum development, a model that is unrealized but probably will take the form of critical inquiry as suggested by Habermas.[13] Briefly, the model will call for opportunities by which learners (a) relate proposed decisions to common norms, (b) question the validity of the common norms in light of satisfying human needs, and (c) use the weight of evidence and reason in arriving at the best solution.

---

[13]Thomas McCarthy, ed.,*The Critical Theory of Jurgen Habermas* (Cambridge: MIT Press, 1981).

Disjointed Incrementalism

Disjointed incrementalism is not really a model; it is a nonmodel. It occurs when curriculum decisions are made without following a systematic procedure. In the nonmodel, decisions about what will be taught occur through a political process. Advocates of a particular curriculum try to justify the ends they already have in mind. Advocates of the liberal arts and fundamental skills appeal to tradition; advocates of cognitive skills appeal to psychological and educational research; advocates of relevant vocational skills appeal to community; advocates of self-improvement appeal to personal judgment. Those who must resolve the conflicting pressures—school boards, advisory councils, textbook publishers, professional educators—tend to use informal methods of decision making. Disjointed incrementalism is a strategy, and it has these rules:

1. Contemplate making only marginal changes in the existing situation.
2. Avoid making radical changes and consider only a few policy alternatives.
3. Consider only a few of the possible consequences for any proposed change.
4. Feel free to introduce objectives consistent with policy as well as to change policy in accord with objectives.
5. Be willing to look for problems *after* data are available from implementation.
6. Work with piecemeal changes rather than making a single comprehensive attack.

Decisions made under disjointed incrementation are not based on much objective data. Hence, political processes are used to resolve conflicts. In Chapter 11, we describe this process in detail.

Problems with Disjointed Incrementalism in Curriculum Making. Disjointed incrementalism in making curriculum decisions about what to teach is not very different from what occurs in other areas of government and industry. It tends to result in a fragmented curriculum that lacks continuity. Many, however, prefer such an irrational model over a more logical and effective model that might be more appropriate in a totalitarian society. The main defect in the procedure is associated with the democratic process: the lack of well-informed citizens who exercise wide participation, assume responsibility for starting social improvements, and show competency in the skills of political action.

Disjointed incrementalism is the approach used most frequently in times of affluence; programs and courses are added rather than hard choices being made about their elimination. It represents a realization that conflict over what to teach is not merely a conflict of ideas but a conflict of persons, groups, and factions. Under disjointed incrementalism, conflicts over goals and objectives are not resolved on the basis of principles, logic, and evidence but by political power. Future fiscal and demographic trends will make disjointed incrementalism more difficult to practice, and so scrutiny of curriculum offerings should increase.

Emergent Approaches in Curriculum Decision Making

Emergent approaches differ from rational models in that they are guided by principles rather than by specified procedures. Furthermore, the process of determining desired outcomes is seen as more important than the goals themselves. Hence, participants in the curriculum making process are the prime benefactors; this makes wide empowerment of persons—teachers, parents, students—important in curriculum development.

Reflective Deliberation. Guiding principles for reflective deliberation are (1) policy and action should be determined locally rather than at a centralized level; (2) policy is not developed prior to action but through it; (3) understanding of participants is as important as the outcomes or list of action priorities; (4) both oral or conventional modes of expression (the mode in which participants operate most easily) and written codification of what is decided (authentic account of the particular ideas) are important.

Steward Bonser and Shirley Grundy have illustrated the principles in their description of a faculty facing the need to develop a school curriculum policy regarding computers.[14] In this case, teachers and an outside consultant go through four phases. In each phase, planning, data production, and reflective deliberation are present. In phase 1, planning consists of focusing upon the approach to be taken for data generation and teachers sharing their understanding about computer education. Data production is in the form of audiorecorded accounts from individual interviews. Reflective deliberation occurs when the transcribed state-

---

[14]Steward A. Bonser and Shirley A. Grundy, "Relfective Deliberation in the Formulation of a School Curriculum Policy," *Journal of Curriculum Studies* 20, no. 1 (January/February 1988): 35–45.

ment is returned to the individual participant for personal reflections and the preparation of a jointly authored statement.

In phase 2, the planning centers on how to code the information contained in each of the jointly authored statements. Data production occurs as participants meet in small groups and identifies each member's issues and concerns documented in another member's statement. In reflective deliberation in this phase, the "owner" of each statement elaborates on points. The consultant summarizes the concerns of the group as a whole for subsequent documentation.

In phase 3, whole group planning takes place with the purpose of classifying concerns from all groups according to those implicated (teachers, pupils, community), teaching and learning tasks and strategies for teaching, managing, and staff development. Data production in phase 3 occurs as members from opposite groups focus on classifying the intergroup data and attempts to get a consensus through group discussion.

The plan for phase 4 calls for the outside consultant to take information from the previous phase and to develop from it a school statement about computer education. Data collection consists of teachers' knowledge, viewpoints, concerns, and issues relevant to the subject. A statement prepared from the data collected is returned to the participants for affirmation. This statement provides the basis for curriculum documents delineating the school's policy for computer education.

Student-Generated Curriculum. Student-generated curriculum is consistent with principles of both humanistic and social reconstructionist conceptions. The curriculum is situated in the students' culture: their literacy, their themes (obstacles, concerns, ideas, values, hopes), their present cognitive and affective levels, their aspirations, and their daily lives. The derived goal will reflect personal background and experience as much as the academic subjects. This approach is not always easy for teachers to use. It will be rejected by those who see their role as transmitting "right" questions to predetermined problems. The measured curriculum, curriculum frameworks, textbooks, and other prescribed curriculum are counterproductive to student creation of knowledge and curriculum.

The teacher's role in this approach requires studying the life and language of the students' generalized themes that can be used in linking student and teacher realities to learning. The themes vary with the context, the students, and the era. When students engage in critical dialogue about their generative themes, they connect their concrete ideas to more abstract ones. Words like *drugs* and *gang* may mean money, security, escape. With understanding teachers, dialogue may extend these themes to their implications for becoming more human and to ways of negating and overcoming, rather than passively accepting the given. Students learn to identify persons who are served by situations involving drugs and gangs and those who are negated and crushed by them.

Tomas Graman has shared his experiences with student-generated curriculum in teaching English as a second language.[15] Graman fosters active dialogue about reality so that the immediate need to confront real problems and resolve them can be met. Instead of emphasizing practical language for tourist or the empty artifical words in language textbooks, Graman has workers (students) analyze their own experiences and build their own words to describe and understand their experiences.

After discussing their generative words—*bonus* (growers' deduction of money from paychecks until all crops are picked) and *short hoe* (a tool that is painful to use), farmworkers (students) began thinking about the practices and conditions of their work. Their analyses, construction of meanings, and choice of words became acts of overcoming what many had considered to be their unfortunate lot in life. Graman generates themes for discussion and writing by having students examine pictures, photographs, and newspaper articles (unedited for second language students) that contain such themes as early linguistic levels. Students read and discuss articles on familiar topics. Students do not merely practice language by answering questions to which students and teacher already know the answers. The goal is to become more critically conscious, not only to acquire language as a tool.

The student-generated curriculum requires examining beliefs and the basis for them, aiming at supporting arguments that reflect intelligent ways to resolve problems.The point is not to learn *what* to think and say, but *how* to think for oneself and express these thoughts in a new language.

A COMMENT ON MODELS FOR CURRICULUM BUILDING

Thus far, we have focused upon models and approaches for determining the purposes that curriculum should fulfill. Other decisions must

---

[15]Tomas Graman, "Education for Humanization: Applying Paul Freire's Pedagogy to Learning a Second Language," *Harvard Educational Review* 58, no. 4 (November 1988): 433–449.

be made about how to achieve stated purposes and how best to evaluate progress toward intended goals. The choice of emphasizing purpose and content as a first step in curriculum development is arbitrary. Alan Purves has been building curriculum for over twenty years. When asked to think about the processes by which he developed and arranged materials to effect learning, he realized that existing models are a fine way to look at curriculum but that they don't tell a person how to proceed any more than a blueprint tells where to begin building a house. Purves knows that curriculum reflects the maker's view of the society, the people who are to be affected, and the nature of what is to be learned. However, he thinks the metaphor of a game is the best way to describe the process by which curriculum is built.

Rules for playing the curriculum game center on these pieces: legal constraints and administrative structure. Who is the decision maker in the school—the principal, the teacher, or some more remote body? How does the proposed curriculum fit with other curricula? Other pieces include teacher attitude and capacity, student interests, principles for sequencing activities, activities themselves, and the constraints of time and resources. Obviously, formulating objectives and anticipating possible outcomes are important pieces. Purves believes that the formulating of objectives and outcomes might take place at the same time as the selection and arrangement of materials, just as evaluation can take place during the course of devising the curriculum.

Curriculum is like a board game. Just having the pieces does not mean that a person knows how to play the game. Some start with a sense of the overall look of the classroom either structured or open. Others begin with a view of how society should be. Purves says, "A number have started with evaluation and built a dog to fit the tail."[16] Some begin with behavioral objectives and others with a set of materials. Others start with a theory about subject matter.

Purves' rules indicate that a player may start with any piece, as long as all the pieces are picked up. His next rule is that all pieces must be perceived in some relationship to one another. Activities should relate to objectives and theories of learning. A final rule is that there are several ways to win the game. One way is to have all the pieces placed in some relationship to one another. Another way to win is to have the finished board approximate a model of rationality with objectives determining

---

[16]Alan C. Purves, "The Thought Fox and Curriculum Building," in *Strategies for Curriculum Development*, eds. Jon Schaffarzick and David Hampson (Berkeley: McCutchan, 1975), p. 120.

learning activities, organization, and evaluation. A person can also win by showing that the intended outcomes were achieved by the learner. If the learner achieves the stated purposes, no matter what else is learned, it is a winning curriculum. It is even possible to have a winning curriculum by virtue of the attractiveness of the materials or their intellectual modernity. Conflicting views of winning make curriculum one of the most controversial games in town.

CONCLUDING COMMENTS

The needs assessment model for determining curriculum has been a popular means of curriculum making. It is seen as a way of restoring community confidence in the school and of advancing the interests of previously ignored groups when it allows clients to determine what they want to learn and not merely to select from a list of meaningless choices. It is closely associated with the adaptive and social reconstructionists' conception of curriculum, but may also be used by those with other philosophical orientations.

As the name implies, the futuristic model emphasizes future conditions more than present status. It is a form of needs assessment in that future needs are anticipated. For this model, the curriculum maker decides what students should be like in light of some desirable future.

Few models are as idealistic and comprehensive as the rational model. It is appealing because it gives attention to the interests of learner, society, and the fields of knowledge. In practice, however, curriculum makers often fail to respond equally to these interests. After specialization is accepted as the overriding function of a school program or course, the outlooks of subject matter specialists carry the most weight. Similarly, when those in an institution prize the general education function, i.e., wanting to develop shared values and to make schooling relevant to social needs, they tend to respond to generalizations about society to the exclusion of other considerations. Almost no curricula have appealed to the learner in order to decide what to teach. However, emergent approaches address this problem.

The vocational training model is most appropriate in institutions claiming to prepare students for jobs. Those using the model must be aware, however, that its use may tend to perpetuate the status quo.

Curriculum ends should not be narrowly conceived. Objectives that are relevant to present and likely future conditions, to the concerns of the learners, and to a wide span of cultural resources are better than those that rely solely on tradition. The final acceptance of educational ends is a value judgment. The decision to accept, however, should be influenced by evidence that shows that the end (the goal of objective or content) will be of value to the learner, that it is attainable, and that it probably will not be achieved without deliberate instruction.

To keep curriculum workers in touch with reality, let us admit that disagreement on the proper base for assessing the worth of the curriculum is likely. Hence, political processes are used for dealing with the value conflicts.

QUESTIONS

1. Consider one of the following curriculum tasks, and indicate the model or approach you would take to determine purposes for the following endeavors:
   a. to generate instructional goals for a school
   b. to determine curriculum goals for a program in science, arts, or health
   c. to select purposes and content for a new course of instruction.
   Give reasons for your answer.
2. In using the needs assessment model, would you want the preferences of special groups—parents, teachers, students—to be given equal or weighted importance? Why or why not?
3. State an aim of importance to you, such as health, conservation of resources, self-worth, vocational skill. How would you refine this aim into an educational objective? What might be taught in order to help learners make progress toward this aim?
4. Read the following generalizations and then infer what should be taught in light of one or more of the generalizations.
   a. Students construe moral issues in terms of power relationships and physical consequences. They see morality as something outside their control.
   b. Adults are strangers who grant neither substance nor interest in one another and do not see a society larger than their private world.
   c. The cry for law and order is a fundamental demand for cognitive order, for normative clarity, and for predictability in human affairs.
   d. The average person will change jobs seven times and find work less a source of satisfaction than in previous years.

5. What do you believe is the function of the school? Is there something the school can do better than any other agency? Indicate how your answer might be used in deciding what and what not to teach.

SELECTED REFERENCES

Brandt, Ronald and Tyler, Ralph W. "Goals and Objectives," in *Fundamental Curriculum Decisions*, ASCD Yearbook, ed. Fenwick W. English. Alexandria, VA: 1983, pp. 40–53.

Glatthorn, Allan A. *Curriculum Renewal.* Alexandria, VA: ASCD, 1987.

Kaufman, Roger. "Assessing Needs," in *Introduction to Performance Technology*, ed. R. Smith. Washington, DC: National Society for Performance and Motivation, 1986.

Sharpes, Donald K. "Curriculum as Craft," in *Curriculum Traditions and Practices.* New York: St. Martin's Press, 1988.

Shor, Ira. *Critical Teaching and Everyday Life.* Chicago: The University of Chicago Press, 1987.

6

Developing and Selecting
Learning Opportunities

One of the three purposes of this chapter is to critique the principles that guide development of classroom learning opportunities, i.e., activities, experiences, lessons, the interactions between learners and conditions arranged by teachers. A second purpose is to describe the different developmental procedures used by social reconstructionists, technologists, humanists, and academicians in some detail. The third purpose is to examine criteria used in selecting instructional materials—textbooks, films, software.

It is important to note that emphasis is increasing on teacher development of learning opportunities. In the early 1980s, teachers were often disenfranchised from curriculum development and expected to use pre-specified activities found in adopted textbooks and district plans; by the 1990s, it was recognized by policy makers that curriculum reform is heavily dependent on context at the local level and requires the active engagement of teachers. Curriculum policies from above came without batteries, necessitating teacher creativity to make them fly.

Today's teachers are expected to create rich and varied experiences tailored to students' strengths and interests. Researchers are beginning to study the minor miracles of stunning teaching, instead of prescribing methods for teachers.[1] In hundreds of ways, teachers modify curriculum

---

[1]Elliot W. Eisner, ''The Primacy of Experience and the Politics of Method,'' *Educational Researcher* 17, no. 5 (June/July 1988): 15–20.

for the needs of the class; that all girls and boys need a particular level of learning opportunity is likely to be incorrect at least 60 percent of the time. Similarly, the problem of matching activities to high and low ability students is considerable. In classes of students of unequal ability, the outcomes are determined only in part by ability; the teacher and pupil expectations for success, effort, and other factors are as important in the selection of content and its organization.

The idea of teachers offering opportunities suited to their own personalities and educational goals may be more powerful than adapting instruction to the personal needs of students. At least it should be tried. Although some evidence exists that students perform better when taught by a method consistent with their preferred learning style, it is not clear whether curriculum should always be matched with learning style. Under some conditions, mismatches may be beneficial; sometimes it is desirable to increase a learner's ability to learn a variety of content under different circumstances. Also, there is danger that in offering a curriculum for students who have particular learning styles, other important variables will be ignored, such as learner variables like ability, cultural background, and motivation; and classroom variables like teacher knowledge, subject matter, and peer influences.

Adaptation of instruction is best undertaken by the teacher's sensitivity to learner responses and the ability to learn from students and to vary instruction according to hypotheses about how learning takes place.

In hundreds of ways, teachers modify curriculum for the needs of a class by preparing handouts, making arrangements for visiting speakers, creating learning games, designing learning packets, planning field trips, arranging original displays, suggesting individual studies, and posing novel questions. Teachers recognize the inadequacies of available instructional materials in matching the requirements for each child. It is as if textbooks, curriculum guides, and other instructional material developed by those outside the classroom are highways, which are satisfactory for general planning but from which the teacher must at times turn off and take a different route to provide something more appropriate for a learner or a group of learners. Usually the development and modification of curriculum by teachers is undertaken for the following reasons:

1. The individual learners require learning opportunities that are closer to their present background and level of attainment. Students may need explanations drawn from familiar instances or more simple or more advanced tasks than have been provided. The development of a lesson in the language of a non-English-speaking child is one example.

2. The individual learners or their community have pressing questions or problems that require the experiences, the facts, or the introduction of new activities and material.

3. Teachers desire to provide opportunities that are motivating. Hence, they create learning opportunities in accordance with motivational principles such as:

   Choice. Learners choose from among activities. A range of opportunities is offered to accommodate the learner's style or mode of learning.

   Utility. Opportunities encourage learners to use what is learned in satisfying unmet physical and psychological needs and to satisfy motives such as curiosity, exploration, and manipulation.

   Link to Other Values. Opportunities place learners in contact with highly valued persons or activities.

   Interests. Opportunities are related to special interests of learners at hand.

   Models. Older peers, parents, and other significant persons are selected as exemplary models.

   Success. Adaptations in conventional materials are made in order to ensure success, including prompting, flexible standards, and provision for learners to recognize their own success.

4. Teachers' interests, capabilities, and style make departures from standard materials desirable or necessary.

PRINCIPLES FOR DEVELOPING LEARNING OPPORTUNITIES

John Amos Comenius (1592–1670) was a prophet of modern curriculum principles who looked at nature for his guide to pedagogy. Among his principles were the following:

The process of education will be easy—(a) if the mind be duly prepared to receive it; (b) if it proceed from the general to the particular; and (c) from what is easy to what is more difficult. . . . ; (d) if the intellect be forced to do nothing to which its natural bent does not incline it, in accordance with its age and with the right method; (e) if everything be taught through the medium of the senses; and (f) and if the use of everything taught be continually kept in view.[2]

---

[2]John Amos Comenius, *The Great Didactic,* trans. M. W. Keatinge (London: Adam & Charles Black, 1896), p. 279.

In modern history of curriculum thought, Ralph Tyler proposed five general principles for developing learning experiences.[3]

Appropriate Practice.   Tyler viewed the principle of appropriate practice as a means-ends context in which objectives (ends) determine learning opportunities (means). This principle states that learning opportunities must give the student practice in what is called for by the objective. If the objective is to develop the skill of problem solving, students must have opportunities to solve problems and not merely to watch how others solve problems.

The degree to which the practice situation and the learner performance must be identical varies. For an objective such as swimming, students should have practice in the water. Hands-on opportunities are important in the learning of procedural tasks; however, conceptual knowledge can be acquired without having conceptual practice identical with the situation called for by the objective. In conceptual learning it is important that the practice situations (simulations, partials, imaginary and symbolic rehearsals) induce the mental representation of the desired concepts and relationships. Indeed military trainees have found it more effective to give students practice with artificial tasks that have no surface resemblance to real world tasks but direct students' attention to difficult and crucial aspects of the real world task.[4] With the use of computers, we can expect more learning opportunities that will free mental resources (memory) that would otherwise be enjoyed in noncrucial tasks.

Satisfaction.   According to the principle of satisfaction, the learning opportunity should be satisfying to learners. As indicated in Chapter 1, cognitive abilities do not guarantee success. A person must like what he or she is good at. Unless students enjoy the process, they won't cross unexplored frontiers. Satisfactions are derived from several sources. The research on flow experience (page 7) suggests that importance of activities that offer continuous challenge, social approval, the meeting of physical needs, and success itself contributes to satisfaction. For young and many old persons, *physical manipulation,* i.e., activities that allow for making things go, pushing buttons, constructing something, or handling objects, is satisfying. Also satisfying is *incongruity,* i.e., the exposure to

[3]Ralph W. Tyler, *Basic Principles of Curriculum and Instruction* (Chicago: The University of Chicago Press, 1949).

[4]Henry Halff et al., "Cognitive Science and Military Training," *American Psychologist* 41, no. 10 (October 1986): 1131–1139.

novel and puzzling situations, to events that are inconsistent and incompatible. An illustration comes to mind: that of Robert Prigo, an expert physics teacher, lowering his body onto a bed of nails, with an assistant placing a second board spiked with nails on Prigo's chest, putting a cinder block on top of that, and, to the crescendo of death scene music, bringing down a sledge hammer that shatters the block, after which Prigo gets up smiling. Prigo first captures student interest before embarking them on pursuit of the theories behind the demonstrations. Interacting with *significant others* such as parents, friends is often satisfying. *Confluence*, i.e., activities that combine thinking, feeling, and physical movement—are generally well received.

Not everyone is satisfied by the same activity. Hence, there are attempts to adapt learning activities to learning styles. Learning styles may have different dimensions. The cognitive dimension refers to different ways in which students mentally perceive and order information; the affective dimension is the effect that students' social and emotional responses have on their learning; the physiological dimension indicates such elements as auditory, visual, tactile preference for learning and how the learner is affected by light, temperature, and room design; and the psychological dimension involves the student's inner strengths such as self-esteem.

Kathleen Butler has a learning style program, "style differentiated instruction," which applies four predominant types of "mind styles" in the planning of learning activities. Figure 6-1 outlines the categories.[5]

Success. The principle of success requires deciding whether the learning activity is within the range of possibility for the student. The student's background experience is the best predictor of success: what the student already knows determines what will be learned from the activity. Hence, teachers design activities that link new content to the student's prior experiences and teach prerequisites to critical tasks.

The theory of Vygotsky—What students can do today with parent or teacher, they can do alone tomorrow—is also applied.[6] First, the teacher controls and guides the student's activity; later, the responsibility is shared by teacher and student; and finally the student has full responsibility.

Sheila Tobias, an expert in mathematics anxiety, has devised a

---

[5]Kathleen A. Butler, "Learning Styles," *Learning* 88 (November/December 1980): 31–34.

[6]L. S. Vygotsky, *The Development of Higher Psychological Processes* (Cambridge, MA: Harvard University Press, 1979).

Styles	Characteristics	Need an Instructional Focus That Supports	Prefer Strategies Such As	Styles Are Matched When Asked To	Types of Products
Concrete Sequential	organized, factual, efficient, task-oriented, detailed	structure & pattern, directions, details, practical problems, realistic situations, hands-on learning	hands-on approaches, workbooks, data-gathering, how-to projects, computers	sort, label, list, collect, chart, make, construct, classify, measure, prepare, build	time-line, graph, diorama, model, exhibit
Abstract Sequential	intellectual, analytical, theoretical, critical, convergent	reason & logic, ideas & information, theory & concepts, analysis & evaluation, independent study	lecture, text, content, mastery, extensive reading, reporting, conceptual problems	outline, report, devise, speculate, infer, hypothesize, summarize, verify, critique	debate, document, theory, lecture, research
Abstract Random	imaginative, emotional, interpretive, holistic, flexible	interpretation, explanation, communication, illustration, peer-teaching	group work, webbing, mapping, media, music, personalized examples, role playing	associate, connect, relate, express, share, present, interpret, perform, imagine, counsel	writing, arts, music, interview, helping projects, journal
Concrete Random	divergent, experiential, inventive, independent, risk taking	open-ended activity, exploration, investigation, experimentation, options	brainstorming, simulations, games, problem solving, experiments, finding alternatives	explore, consider, reorganize, forecast, process, predict, create, recommend	invention, editorial, solutions, games, experiments

FIGURE 6–1 Matching Your Teaching Style to Your Students' Learning Style. From Anthony F. Gregorc: *An Adult's Guide to Style* (Columbia, CT: Gregorc Associates, Inc., 1986). Adapted by Kathleen A. Butler in "Learning Styles," *Learning 88*, Nov/Dec, pp. 31–34.

method of analyzing the teaching of mathematics and science for the purpose of identifying what makes these subjects hard. Her findings were the following: (1) the students lacked a framework and prior knowledge (As one student said, ''I had no way of telling what was important and what was not.''). (2) Demonstrations often led to confusion instead of clarification (''I could follow what was described but I could not grasp what was actually happening in what was described.''). (3) Lectures moved along preordained tracks, making it difficult for students to slow down the train. (4) Students needed more time to think about ideas. (5) Words that were used caused confusion. To the teacher, zero is in the middle of plus and minus; to the student it meant absence or void. (6) Students were interested in *why* questions; the teacher in *how* questions.[7]

In addition to learning style, status variables, including sex, race, and socioeconomic factors, are sometimes considered in planning for success. However, Thomas Good and Deborah Stipek's review of the literature on individual differences in the classroom concludes that status variables do not provide a systematic basis for planning instruction.[8]

Multiple Approaches. Many different activities can be used to attain the same purpose. I have found that when teachers are given the same objective, each teacher develops a unique approach for achieving the objective. One of the most rewarding aspects of teaching is the creativity that is possible. Nevertheless, studies indicate that teachers tend to rely on textbooks and paper and pencil activities, rather than activity centers, projects, simulations, debates, dramas, investigations, media, and mediation. In Kohlberg's terms, teachers stress linguistic and logical mathematical activities rather than musical, spatial kinesthetic, interpersonal, and intrapersonal activities.[9] Although several reasons for the lack of rich and engaging activities are possible, McNeil attributes minimal effort to the organizational context of the school in which management control emphasized order and student discipline (conduct) rather than valuing student creation of knowledge or supporting teaching and learning.

Multiple Outcomes. In one sense there will always be multiple outcomes from a learning activity because each student interprets and ap-

---

[7]Sheila Tobias, ''Insiders and Outsiders,'' *Academic Connection* (Winter 1978): 1–4.

[8]Thomas L. Good and Deborah J. Stipek, ''Individual Differences in the Classroom: A Psychological Perspective,'' in *Individual Differences and the Common Curriculum*, eds. Gary D. Fenstermacher and John I. Goodlad, NSSE Yearbook (Chicago: The University of Chicago Press, 1983), pp. 9–37.

[9]Linda McNeil, *Contradictions of Control: School Structure and School Knowledge* (London: Routledge and Kegan Paul, 1987).

plies ideas from the classroom in his or her own way, depending on prior experience. In another sense, it is economical to arrange learning activities that are likely to contribute to multiple desirable outcomes. A curriculum that provides a study of a historical event in the context of geography, writing, critical thinking, literature, and the like offers an increased possibility of maximum outcomes.

LEARNING OPPORTUNITIES FOR HIGHER ORDER THINKING

In view of the current clamor for teaching higher order thinking to all students, a review of conditions appropriate to these ends is in order. John Goodlad has suggested that a significant change in instructional time allotted to various learning activities must take place if improvement in problem solving and creativity are to occur. He recommends that instead of the current norm of 70 percent of instruction being aimed at declarative and procedural levels of learning, 70 percent should be given to learning opportunities that involve higher order thinking processes.[10]

Walter Doyle defines higher level academic tasks as tasks that require understanding rather than memory, routine, or opinion tasks.[11] Understanding tasks are often not reduced to a predictable algorithm. For example, writing a descriptive paragraph isn't simply following steps but using complex procedures and a high level executive process to generate a product. The student must not only understand the procedures but why they work and where they apply.

In Chapter 12 we discuss the best ways to teach thinking, such as is it better to develop within or without a domain of conventional subject matter. For general purposes, we will consider general guidelines for developing learning activities for problem solving and creative thinking, emphasizing processes for generating meaning rather than routine skills.

Problem Solving

Transfer occurs whenever a previous learning influences the acquisition of a second learning. Meaning (the formation of schemata) is the key to problem solving, including the ability to learn a new task. In ad-

---

[10]John I. Goodlad, *A Place Called the Classroom* (San Francisco: Freeman, 1984).

[11]Walter Doyle, "Academic Work," *Review of Educational Research* 53, no. 2 (Summer 1983): 159–201.

dressing problems for which a solution is not readily available, students must relate various facts and ideas. Without the conceptual structure (schemata) with which to analyze the problem and to deal with its various elements, students will not have success. Hence, the teaching of problem solving centers not only on practice in using basic concepts and schemata for viewing specific phenomena so that students acquire the mechanisms for analyzing the facts and conditions that must be considered, but also on ways to activate relevant analogies. E. L. Wright found that persons who failed at a problem said they could have been more successful if they had taken more time to sort out its crucial elements before adopting a strategy.[12]

Problem solving also depends upon combining knowledge with metacognitive strategies such as having a plan, identifying subproblems, and examining alternative solutions (brainstorming). Students should have learning opportunities that feature generalized procedures for problem solving in situations in which the problems are not clearly stated, all the needed information is not available, and no algorithm or simple correct answer exists. Nevertheless, the acquisition of problem-solving procedures for a specific domain may be more useful than generalized procedures.

Joseph Agassi's approach to teaching problem solving aims at guiding the natural activity of students seeking knowledge for themselves.[13] Hence, the problem is always based on the interest and desire for knowledge of the student. In order to articulate the problem, the activity begins with the expression of discomfort or interest of the student. Analysis of the initial statement of interest helps make explicit the knowledge which the student assumes to be true and the limitations to that knowledge from the student's perspective. The awareness of a limitation may form the starting point for the development of a problem.

Agassi's approach to problem solving has two great strengths: (1) It is unlikely that a problem will be formulated that is beyond the range of the student's abilities or stage of development and (2) the problem will not be trivial because the student explains its importance so that an answer can be pursued. The student adopts prima facie explanations of how the solution may be pursued and may change the plan as the project

---

[12]E. L. Wright, "Effects of Intensive Instruction in Cue Attendance on Solving Formal Operational Tasks," *Science Education* 63 (1979): 381–393.

[13]John Wellersten, "On the Unification of Psychology, Methodology and Pedagogy," *Interchange* 18, no. 4 (1987): 1–14.

goes along. If the plan breaks down, the student should be able to reformulate a clear and specific problem and a plan for solving it.

Similar approaches are found in *strategic teaching*, which aims at student construction of meaning by learning activities that take into account background knowledge, organizing patterns, and metacognitive strategies.[14] Strategic teaching begins with something that activates students' prior knowledge, so that students articulate how they think about a problem. Later, they are helped to confront inconsistencies or contradictions between their assumptions and the phenomena. After students perceive gaps, there should be opportunities to reconstruct new meanings and to acquire alternative conceptions. By way of illustration, students count the number of grid sequences touched by the diagonal of each of several rectangles they have drawn on squared paper, attempting to see how that number relates to the dimensions of the rectangle. Students then debate what is to count as "touching" a grid square. Discussions of students' findings is followed by writing an account of the investigation, indicating whether they have reached a firm "result."

Some clue to the development of problem solving comes from studies of experts who (a) describe a problem in detail before attempting a solution, (b) determine what relevant information should go with the analysis of the problem, and (c) decide which procedures can be used to generate a problem description and analysis.[15]

Creativity

As with problem solving, creativity can be enhanced not only by knowing much about the area in which a person is creative, but by encouraging the transfer of training from one subject to another, the search for common principles, the stressing of analogies, similes, and metaphors, and the seeking of symbolic equivalents in the highest possible number of sensory imaginal modalities such as imaginative play. Obviously, creativity can be nurtured in other ways: by granting student autonomy, avoiding criticism and rejection, encouraging students to solve problems for themselves.

Can you teach children to be creative? E. Paul Torrance analyzed the results of 142 studies in the literature of the effects of attempts to teach

---

[14]Beau Fly Jones et al., *Strategic Teaching and Learning: Cognitive Instruction in the Content Areas* (Alexandria, VA: ASCD, 1987).

[15]José Mestre, "Why Should Mathematics and Science Teachers Be Interested in Cognitive Research Findings?" *College Board Academic Connection* (Summer 1987): 3–5.

creative thinking skills. The overall percentage of successes was 72 percent.[16] Some teachers believe that creative skills should be taught directly in courses that are separate from the rest of the curriculum. Edward de Bono, for example, has developed a set of independent materials aimed at helping students deal with novelty.[17] De Bono poses incomplete problems and encourages students to list the positive, negative, and interesting features of each alternative solution, getting them to see both familiar and unfamiliar problems in novel ways. On the other hand, Vera John-Steiner has uncovered clues to the nurturing of creative minds that can be an integral part of any curriculum.[18] She interviewed more than 100 creative men and women and sifted through the personal papers of distinguished artists and scientists, showing that these persons drew heavily from childhood play—the delight in nature, devices, and books.

Children everywhere have a drive to know, to wonder, and to invent. However, as they grow older, they lose their skill to dip into their own stores of pleasure and fantasy. The sense of wonder over early experience is kept alive only with the help of a caring and knowledgeable adult. Most great contributors single out a parent, teacher, or mentor who helped them have a dialogue across generations as they absorbed the values of their society and made their own fresh discourse, going from the known to the new, from immersion to exploration. A key to their creativity was a sustained concern about something. They recalled their engagement with play, ideas, and the world while they were young. Their childhood preoccupation with ideas, images, and questions gave intensity to their mental life. In Einstein's case, the questions he asked about space and time reached back to his early years and were childlike in their simplicity, but the answers were wrought through his concentration.

Suggestions for learning opportunities aimed at creativity focus on creating a climate for incubation and the freeing of that mind of influence that inhibits discovery. Teachers should treat students' imaginative ideas with respect and show the students that these ideas have value. An attitude of playfulness rather than evaluation is helpful as is a class in which there is freedom from time pressure.

---

[16]E. Paul Torrance, "Can We Teach Children to Think Creatively?" *Journal of Creative Behavior* 6 (1972): 114–143.

[17]Edward de Bono, "The Direct Teaching of Thinking as a Skill," *Phi Delta Kappan* 64 (1973): 703–708.

[18]Vera John-Steiner, *Notebooks of the Mind* (Albuquerque: University of New Mexico Press, 1985).

PROCEDURES FOR DEVELOPING LEARNING ACTIVITIES

Selecting learning opportunities is not the same as developing them. Some persons can apply criteria in deciding among various textbooks and other materials but are not able or willing to produce them. Similarly, the ability to carry out opportunities in the interactive phase with learners calls for additional skills. Development is a creative art and allows for personal expression of the developer's values and style. As indicated in Part I of this book, techniques of development can be categorized by the four major categories of curriculum.

Major Orientations

Social Reconstructionist Guidelines. The social reconstructionist wants the learners to use knowledge and intelligence to help improve the quality of public decision that determines the conditions under which they live. Hence, student learning activities combine knowledge and action in effecting change in the community. The following are ten key steps in the processes of developing a learning opportunity:

1. *Select an idea for a learning opportunity.* The developer might reflect on a topic or problem such as public opinion, elections, media, or conservation, which makes sense to the students and is related to school and course goals. Issues and problems in the community are among the best sources of ideas for learning opportunities. Persistent struggles and value premises also suggest areas for learning. A topic to consider may be apathy toward general welfare or the importance of keeping informed on public issues and informing others.

2. *Explore the idea.* Here, ask, "What can students do about the issue or problem besides studying about it?" A learning opportunity for the reconstructionist requires the students to take responsible action, whether working with community groups, providing information, or taking a stand on issues. Students may provide information to persons about a public issue, try to influence them to a point of view, serve the community, or work with and as adult citizens.

3. *Plan for action.* Surveys, field trips, and interviews are not what the reconstructionist means by action. Although these activities may contribute to the action phase, they don't constitute *taking action* in a political sense. Because the essence of the civic act is carrying knowledge into action, a student activity that omits persuasion, decision making, and so forth, is not viewed as satisfactory. Planning

means thinking of the action or project desired, for example, organizing a public forum and indicating how students will carry it out.

4. *Test the idea or project for realness.* Work in the community, such as helping persons to get out to vote, campaigning for a candidate, talking on issues, is real. Mock trials, mayor for a day, reading, and taking straw votes are not real to the reconstructionist; they are role playing. To the reconstructionist, action must promise to contribute to the solution of the situation and be seen by students as important.

5. *Specify the educational purposes that will also be served by the project.* The purposes might stress competencies such as persuasion, obtaining information, arriving at valid conclusions, predispositions toward recognition of others, acceptance of responsibility, and knowledge of function and structure in institutions.

6. *Limit the scope of the learning opportunity.* The project must be subject to reasonable limits of time and effort. Enough time must be allowed for students to complete the action phase. For most effective results, the project should be focused. One idea is to plan the project around the action of the city council on a particular issue rather than around a broad interest such as government. Include only those activities necessary to achieve the goals of the plan. Decide on the termination date at the outset and keep it in mind daily. The sixth consideration is met when teaching has limited student actions to a specific job, enumerated the students' tasks, and justified the time needed for completing the project.

7. *Involve others in the project.* Involve the school administrator and other persons in the community whose help is desirable to participate.

8. *List the sources of firsthand information needed.* Consider interviews, polls, surveys, filming, and making visits.

9. *Select study materials.* Collect textbooks, pamphlets, films, and other materials on the subject matter of the project, which are pertinent to the educational purposes.

10. *Plan for evaluation.* Design an evaluation plan to determine what gains and losses accrue as a result of the project.

Technological Guidelines. In Chapter 3, the technologists' product development procedures were delineated. Technologists identify four states in developing learning activities:

1. *Specify terminal objectives.* The instructional objective guides all development. The objective must be specific enough to remove ambiguity about what the learner is expected to know and do in particular situ-

ations or classes of situations. A posttest or other procedure for indicating achievement of the desired terminal behavior is often created in order to further designate all dimensions of the learning task.

2. *Make a task analysis.* An effort is made to list all prerequisite skills and knowledge believed necessary before one can perform in accordance with the objective. After this list is prepared, the developer must indicate which of these prerequisites will be taught in the learning opportunity and which will be considered ''entry behaviors'' (requirements that the learner is expected to demonstrate on entrance to the learning opportunity).

3. *Specify the intended population.* At this point, an idea of the anticipated learners can be gained. In addition to entry skills, characteristics such as cultural differences, learning styles, personality, and interests are used to guide the developers.

4. *Formulate rules for development of the materials, activity, or product.* These questions give direction to the developer and determine the characteristics of the learning program of activity.

   a. Concept presentation. Will the concept be taught by means of examples leading to a generalization (inductive) or will a generalization be given followed by examples (deductive)?

   b. Response mode. Will the learner be actively involved in speaking, writing, touching? In addition to overt responding, are there anticipated covert responses? How often will learners be expected to respond overtly?

   c. Elicitation of correct responses. How can learners be helped to make a correct response and learn? Can all answers be confirmed as right or wrong? Can they be confirmed with reiteration of the reasons for correctness? How? Can the learner be prompted to make the right answer by hints, as through visual cues, questions, metaphors, and other verbal means?

   d. Learning sequences. How will enroute objectives be ordered and reviewed? Will all learners be required to follow the same order? Will there be provision for ''branching'' (a point of choice at which students are sent to alternative material depending on their prior responses)?

Early use of the computer featured computer-assisted instruction (CAI), a technological approach to curriculum in which the designer focused on specific objectives, made a task analysis of enroute objectives, and then decided upon a presentation strategy. The designer might consider whether the program will give the learner examples and ask for a generalization (examples to rule), or present a generalization and ask the learner to recognize examples that match the generalization (rule to examples)? Other decisions included *pacing* and *branching* (Will the learner be advanced to more difficult material when responses indicate mystery?); *response format* (multiple choice or constructed?); and *feedback* (Will the learner simply be told whether an answer is right or given additional explanation if there are errors?).

As described in Chapter 3, newer uses of the computer give the student more control over the machine by applying LOGO and the word processor to one's purposes. The development of educational games by teachers and students is another way to gain control of one's learning. Procedures for designing instructional games for the computer are as follows:

1. Define a subject theme area.
2. Create a list of games that lend themselves to the subject: Hangman, puzzles, tic-tac-toe.
3. Stipulate the capabilities of the computer: graphics and animation, counters and timers, number of words or letters that can be displayed at one time, keyboard layout, voice activation, memory available for use.
4. List rules for program construction:
   a. Justification for educational content
   b. Population of problems
   c. Problem generation—problems shall be randomly generated and consist of new instances of the family of problems rather than particular problems whose answers have been confirmed previously.
   d. Feedback—how will correct responses be determined and information regarding performance be presented to the user? How will progress be charted? Will a summary of user's strengths and weaknesses be available?
5. Specify player rules. Will it be a cooperative or competitive game? If competitive, will it be against the machine, peers, or self? Can player select a particular game or level of difficulty?
6. Specify computer decision rules: Does the computer respond to player's input? How does play change after correct responses? How does play terminate?
7. Prepare preliminary story board for each activity generated. Indicate display format and specify sounds.
8. Select the best set of activities within constraints of the computer.
9. Outline the flow of the activity using a flow chart showing message,

prompts, and paths for user's replies. A partial example of such an outline is as follows:

SAME SUM

Players try to find one number that will fit in the corners of the puzzle so that each side adds up to a given total.

1 or 2 players?

1 player—player vs. machine/computer problems
2 players—player vs player/player's problems

2 players

Player 1's SUM			
	5	4	
8			2
1			7
	9	0	

Prompt for player 2 to enter player 1's sum.

Player 1's SUM is 21

Player 2 has entered the sum "21" for player 1. Player 1 must find the one number that will fit in the corners of the puzzle so that each side adds up to a total of 21. Use the same number in all four corners.

	5	4	
8			2
1			7
	9	0	

5	5	4	5
8			2
1			7
5	9	0	5

Player 1 misses sum. Computer emits a razz sound and the puzzle reappears.

6	5	4	6
8			2
1			7
6	9	0	6

If player 1 is correct, a fanfare is sounded.

(1)				0	9	0
(2)				1	4	0

Scoreboard shows cumulative score for rounds.

Humanistic Guidelines. The humanistic curriculum has its roots in both the individual humanism of the Renaissance with its stress on personal culture, individual freedom, and development as the best way toward a full and rich life, and the naturalism of the eighteenth century which was a revolt against the cold aristocracy of intellect. The naturalists worshiped feelings and regarded education not as a preparation for life but as life itself. They believed that the activities which spring naturally from the interests of the pupils, from the needs of life, should make up the curriculum.

In contrast to other curriculum orientations, learning opportunities in the humanistic curriculum are not planned in the framework of a means-ends continuum. Indeed, many humanistic educators believe that *after* an opportunity has been experienced, purposes may be generated. Students may themselves establish plans for reaching a distant goal and have wide freedom in following their own routing. How then does one create a more humanistic experience? The answers from the neo-humanists fall into three categories:

1. Emphasize teaching as transformation of the student, not teaching as transmitting subject matter. Instructional plans, textbooks, courses of study, and other artifacts designed to shape learners in specified ways all are seen as less important than interaction with the student. Interpersonal associations experienced with a teacher influence the student's growth. Humanists give more attention to method and the interactive phases of instruction than on advanced planning. Indeed, the planning of opportunities, activities, and experiences should be a cooperative process by students and teacher in which the student's own purposes are respected.

   This emphasis takes many directions. It may mean that the teacher prepares by developing procedures of reflective teaching, group dynamics, and sensitivity training-methods that may be of value in releasing the creative capacity of learners. It may mean that teachers anticipate what they will bring to students by "knowing" themselves. They try to recognize their prejudices, biases, fears, loves, strengths, and other attributes that bear on the ability to care, feel, and relate to students.

2. Create an environment that does not impede natural growth. The most general guide to developing learning opportunities is focused on the conditions of learning. On the positive side, creating good conditions for learning includes attending to conditions such as the characteristics, interests, and growth patterns of each student; the richness of the environment; opportunities that stress wholeness and putting all senses to work; opportunities to wonder and be puzzled; and opportunities for the learner to feel independent by facing problems alone.

   On the negative side, some warn that such an environment implies that learners do not have to meet standards beyond their abilities, endure great tension, face destructive criticism, think in terms of previous solutions to problems, conform to tradition, regard achievement as the production of a similar rather than a unique product, and be denied choices.

3. Arrange situations in which learners determine what they will learn. The teacher as arranger considers physical conditions, including safe facilities as well as natural objects of beauty, and uses those from which the learner can benefit. The cultural environment, too, is a responsibility of the humanistic teacher. Cultural excellence in music,

painting, and literature, and scientific equipment, musical instruments, and art supplies may constitute an invitation to learning. Arrangement of the social environment also may be planned. Association with others in a variety of shared enterprises may permit self-activated students to respond and, by their own urge toward self-realization, bring the learning process to fulfillment.

Academicians' Guidelines for Instructional Materials. To the academician, learning opportunities are chiefly textbooks, films, teachers' guides, and laboratory apparatus, with the textbook considered as most important. Development of these tools is seen as an effort to convey the authenticity of content and method of given subject fields. Organizing centers are central to academic developers. These centers are topics, questions, or problems that will guide the class activities. Until about the 1930s, for example, textbooks by scholars were descriptive and usually consisted of a mass of disconnected facts and primitive generalizations. Between the 1930s and the 1960s, textbooks were more often written by professional educators than by specialists in the disciplines. Their books were criticized as being too busy with many topics to treat any in depth. The student was given many conclusions but had little opportunity to understand how these findings were achieved and how they were interrelated. About 1960, distinguished scholars began to select and guide the development of textbooks as well as courses and materials. They used five steps:

1. Choose organizing centers. Organizing centers relate text, laboratory apparatus, films, and the content for study of a field over a year-long span. The following criteria guide the selection of centers: Do they stress major achievements, that is, powerful ideas? Do they show ways in which the powerful ideas were conceived and sometimes improved upon? Do they show how the ideas are interrelated?
2. Lay out the ordering of the centers. Usually this step rests on an assumed principle of dependency in which the basic concepts are given so that the student can have the understanding necessary for further study. The presentation is through general concepts rather than specific definitions so that the students make some contact with the subject matter they will deal with later in greater depth.
3. Develop suggested units of instruction. Each unit deals with a particular topic and has its own purposes. Each unit also includes an outline of suggested information to be presented and a bibliography suggesting other sources of information.

4. Recommend specific instructional content and ideas for learning opportunities. The content often includes methods that help students interpret data, examples that lead to important generalizations, background information that encourages generalizations, opportunities that lead students to apply generalizations, demonstrations that show the limits of the generalizations, and lists of useful materials such as maps, apparatus, and collections that might be used.

5. Recommend teaching strategies. Unlike the technologists, academicians do not specify in detail the methods teachers are to follow; each teacher must adapt the material to his or her methods. Academicians, however, prize the method of choice, learning how to inquire by doing it. Hence, they not only suggest different ways for students to discover important principles, they also provide training materials, workshops, and films to help the teacher move from didactic methods to those of discovery. Furthermore, they preface the experimental and theoretical problems presented to students with a variety of step-by-step solutions. However, the communication of method has turned out to be one of the weakest aspects of the academic curriculum. Teachers who have never themselves developed skill in scientific reasoning and problem solving have difficulty teaching methods of inquiry to others. Also, each teacher may have a favorite method and is likely to stress ideas and concepts different from those of other teachers.

The instructor interested in laboratory methods, for example, emphasizes laboratory procedure. Teachers filter the materials through their own perceptions.

It can be inferred from the classic monograph on text material by Lee Cronbach that academicians and others do not know how to achieve a perfect learning opportunity in text materials. Cronbach thought that creative developers might make real progress if they kept these questions in mind:

> Does the text create readiness for the concepts and accomplishments to be taught in subsequent grades? Does the text assist the pupil to understand why certain responses are superior to others for given aims, rather than present them as prescriptions? Does the text make provisions for realistic experience, through narration, proposal of supplementary experiences, and laboratory prescriptions, so that students will be able to connect generalizations to reality? Does the text formulate explicit and transferable generalizations? Are the text explanations readable and comprehensible? Does the text provide for practice in application either by suggesting activities or by pos-

ing sensible problems in symbolic form? Do these problems call for the use of generalizations under realistic conditions and require the student to determine which principles to use as well as how to use them? Does the text provide an opportunity to use concepts from many fields of study in examining the same problems? Does the text help the learners recognize the intended outcomes from the study.[19]

The classroom activity into which the text fits should make it possible for the student to acquire emotional attitudes and skills of group membership. The text should fit as closely as possible the readiness of the students for whom it is intended and help develop their readiness.

CRITERIA FOR SELECTING LEARNING ACTIVITIES

Five kinds of criteria are used for guiding and justiying the selection of learning activities: philosophical, psychological, technological, political, and practical. Each curriculum orientation tends to place priority on different criteria. Humanists, for example, are more interested in the inherent qualities of a learning activity than in data indicating that the activity has had an effect in some specific but limited way. Learning activities are judged as good or bad when they meet our value expectations or philosophical assumptions. If a person holds human variability to be of great worth, then he or she will favor activities that advance learner variability rather than activities that stress common outlooks and capacities. Learning activities are also judged in accordance with psychological criteria. Those who have different viewpoints on whether learning should be painful or pleasant have different viewpoints on their assessments of learning opportunities. The technologists' studies of learning and instruction have resulted in a number of new criteria to use in designing and evaluating learning activities. Technologists claim that their criteria are empirically based principles for effective learning rather than canons established by philosophical beliefs.

Philosophical Criteria

Values are the chief basis for judging proposed learning activities and instructional materials. Typically, these value positions appear as options as indicated in the curriculum maker's dilemma seen in Table 6–1.

---

[19]Lee J. Cronbach, *Text Materials in Modern Education* (Urbana: University of Illinois Press, 1955), pp. 90–91.

TABLE 6–1   Curriculum Maker's Dilemma

Learning Activities Should	*But They Also Should*
Be immediately enjoyable.	Lead to desirable future experiences.
Show the ideal: the just, beautiful, and honorable.	Show life as it is, including corruption, violence, and profanity.
Treat the thought and behavior of the group to which the learner belongs.	Treat the thought and behavior of the groups other than those to which the learner belongs.
Minimize human variability by stressing common outlooks and capacities.	Increase variability by stressing individuality.
Stress cooperation so that individuals share in achieving a common goal.	Stress competition so that the able person excels as an individual.
Allow students to clarify their own positions on moral and controversial issues.	Instruct students in the values of moral and intellectual integrity rather than allowing students to engage in sophistry and personal indulgence.

Psychological Criteria

Psychological beliefs about how learning best takes place often determine the acceptability of a learning activity. However, not all people agree on the specific learning principles to use. Some examples of conflicts are shown in Table 6–2.

Behaviorists judge learning activities on the basis of whether they minimize errors by prompting and reinforcing correct responses. Cognitivists value activities that activate students' backgrounds, prod the students to hypothesize, predict, seek patterns, plan to confirm their predictions, and to monitor and revise their plans, if necessary. Developmentalists emphasize opportunities that match the maturation of the student's biological organism; learning activities should be student-initiated and match student ability and interest.

Technological Criteria

Technologists studying instructional variables and procedures have gained great influence over the kinds of factors used in both judging and developing learning opportunities.[20,21] Persons like Benjamin Bloom have

---

[20]Robert Greer, "Contingencies of the Sciences and Technology of Teaching and Pre-Behavioral Research Practices in Education," *Educational Researcher* 12, no. 1 (January 1983): 3–9.

[21]Geneva D. Haertel et al., "Psychological Models of Educational Performance: A Theoretical Synthesis of Constructs," *Review of Educational Research* 53, no. 1 (Spring 1983): 75–91.

TABLE 6–2 Conflicting Views of How to Enhance Learning

Closed View *Learning Activities Should*	*Open View* *Learning Activities Should*
Be under the direct influence of the teacher who demonstrates the learning activities so that the learner imitates and acquires.	Be removed from direct teacher influence, allowing self-actualization by finding meaning in a situation where the teacher is a resource person.
Be pleasant and comfortable for the student.	Allow for hardship and perplexity so that significant growth can take place.
Teach one thing at a time but teach it to mastery, simplifying the environment and giving enough instances to help the learner abstract desired generalizations.	Bring about several outcomes at once, helping students develop interests and attitudes as well as cognitive growth.
Allow the learner to acquire simple basic patterns before being exposed to higher orders of learning.	Allow the learner to grasp the meaning and organization of the whole before proceeding to study the parts.
Allow the learner to see and imitate the best models of talking, feeling, and acting.	Allow the learner to create and practice new and different ways of talking, feeling, and acting.
Feature repetitive practice on a skill not mastered. Don't let the learner practice error.	Feature novel and varied approaches to an unlearned skill. Recognize that learners can learn from error.

adapted constructs of programmed learning and behavioral and contiguity psychology to instructional development.[22] Hence, psychological and technological criteria are often overlaid; practice and knowledge of results can be both psychological and technological criteria. Technologists accept the revolutionary idea that all students can master a learning task if the right means for helping the student are found. Chief among the means they turn to are careful analysis and sequencing of tasks so that prerequisites are provided. They make sure that learners understand the task and the procedures they are to follow, and adapt instruction to the characteristics of individual learners. One way to adapt to these characteristics is to give more examples, frequent testing with immediate knowledge of results, reteaching if necessary, alternative procedures, and variation in time allowed for learning.

The technologists' criteria are found increasingly in instruments for assessing instructional materials, as indicated in the following list of criteria selected from widely used instruments:[23]

---

[22]Benjamin S. Bloom, *All Our Children Learning* (New York: McGraw-Hill, 1982).

[23]Alenoush Saroyan and George L. Geis, "An Analysis of Guidelines for Expert Reviewers," *Instructional Science* 17, no. 12 (1988): 101–128.

1. The objectives for the activity or material are stated in behavioral terms, including type of behavior, conditions, and level of expected performance.
2. A task analysis (identification of components of a complex behavior) has been made, and a relationship between the tasks and the final objectives has been specified.
3. Learning activities are directly related to the behavior and content of the specified objectives.
4. Evaluation procedures are comparable to these objectives:
   a. There is immediate feedback regarding the adequacy of the learner's responses.
   b. There are criterion-referenced tests that measure stated objectives.
   c. Attention is given to evaluating both process, by which the learner learns, and the product, or what the learner learns.
5. The product or activity has been carefully field-tested. A technical manual might cite sources of available evidence to document claims about effectiveness and efficiency, including reports of unintended outcomes.

Political Criteria

Some pressure groups have been very successful in promoting new criteria for guiding the adoption of instructional materials. Although many of these new criteria reflect the philosophical belief that every human being is important, legal and political actions were necessary before the portrayal of racial, ethnic, and cultural groups, the handicapped, and the sexes began to change nationally. Typical of criteria that reflect the political efforts of minorities are the following legal requirements:

1. Teaching materials must portray both men and women in their full range of leadership, occupation, and domestic roles, without demeaning, stereotyping, or patronizing references to either sex.
2. Material must portray, without significant omissions, the historical role of members of racial, ethnic, and cultural groups, including their contributions and achievements in all areas of life.
3. Materials must portray members of cultural groups without demeaning, stereotyping, or patronizing references concerning their heritage, characteristics, or lifestyle.

As a consequence of these standards, publishers and teachers count the pictures of boys and girls to be sure that both sexes are depicted in a range of roles, rather than traditional masculine and feminine ones. In addition, they are careful not to attach a color to an animal serving as the antagonist in a tale. They also modify the language by making changes in affixes and other structures. The singular *he* is replaced with *they* and *person* substituted for *man*.

At policy levels, curriculum planners attempt to meet the political criteria by designating curriculum domains or areas such as women's studies, American Indian studies and Hispanic studies. Curriculum planners at a policy level also confront the special interests of conservationists, religious and veterans' organizations, automobile-related industries, and other groups. Numerous admonitions to curriculum developers are the direct result of such pressures. They are told to teach the responsibilities of individuals and groups in preserving or creating a healthful environment, including appropriate and scientifically valid solutions to environmental problems, to present the hazards of tobacco, alcohol, and drugs without glamorizing or encouraging their use and to be sure that the curriculum reflects and respects the religious diversity of people.

Practicality as a Criterion

At the policy level, practicality generally takes the form of economy. Planners weigh the cost of providing a certain learning opportunity. In times of a financial pinch, for instance, curriculum planners may consider the cost of initiating an expensive laboratory course to be prohibitive. Instead, they may suggest a science course that features a less expensive instructional process such as a lecture and video demonstration format. Curriculum programs can be expensive in many ways, such as in the outright costs of purchase of materials, the costs of maintaining the materials, the costs of purchasing necessary supplementary materials, and the additional costs of acquiring or training personnel for these programs.

Costs of purchase and installation should be weighed against the expected level of goals or objectives to be achieved. If powerful forces outside the school are working against the attainment of a goal, the purchase of new means for attaining that goal is impractical. In times of economic austerity, curriculum planners must also consider diminishing returns in learning opportunities. There is a level of educational attainment beneath which dollars invested show a return in student progress. Beyond that level, however, gain occurs only at rapidly increasing cost.

At both policy and classroom levels, there are other practical concerns. Safety, durability, and adaptability of the activity must be considered. There also is the factor of *conditions of use:* Does it demand that a teacher interact with pupils or does it free the teacher from direct instruction? Is it appropriate for learners with given abilities and motivational levels?

With respect to the latter, Connie Muller and Melissa Conrad recommend "kid rating" as a method for textbook evaluation. The practice is a learning opportunity for critical thinking as well. A topic, concept, or skill is selected and alternative textbooks are examined by students to determine which book best teaches the task. Using the criteria for considering texts, students seek consensus and why.[24]

CRITICISMS OF CRITERIA FOR SELECTING LEARNING OPPORTUNITIES

Criticisms may be directed both at the criteria themselves and at their use. Simply having criteria does not take care of the problem of who will use them in making decisions; it may make a difference whether they are used by state curriculum committees, individual teachers, or boards of education. Furthermore, little thought has been given to decision rules. Answers are seldom given to these questions: How many criteria must be satisfied before adoption? What should the planners do if two alternative opportunities meet the same number of criteria? Will the decision require agreement among evaluators?

It is often difficult to obtain agreement on the evidence that a particular criterion has been met. Criteria demanding few inferences, such as the specification that objectives be stated in behavioral terms, present little difficulty. Criteria requiring high levels of inference, such as the requirement that materials be appropriate for the learners' motivation levels, allow for more subjective and varied judgments.

Many persons also disagree on the relative merits of the respective criteria. Kenneth Komoski, president of the Educational Products Information Exchange Institute, would put primary emphasis on learner verification—data showing the learning effectiveness of the opportunities. No clear basis exists for claiming the superiority of materials that have provisions for feedback, behavior objectives, task analysis, and criterion-referenced tests; little conclusive evidence exists that these variables are directly related to the attainment of specific goals and objectives.

---

[24]Connie Muller and Melissa Conrad, "Kid Rating: An Indepth Textbook Evaluation Technique," *Educational Leadership* 46, no. 2 (October 1988): 79–80.

Disagreement on the worth of learning opportunities occurs because the value of activities and content depends upon the time, place, and the persons involved. What was deemed worthwhile in the past is not necessarily worthwhile today. For example, the supremacy of calculus in the freshman mathematics curriculum is being challenged by those who would substitute discrete mathematics on the ground that calculus deals with continuous problems whereas discrete mathematics allows for individual values to be treated—something more appropriate for use with computers that manipulate individual symbols and quantities. However, trying to justify an activity or content on the ground that it is instrumental to the pursuit of other ends leaves much to be desired. The instrumental argument is of little consequence if the ultimate justification cannot be sustained. Generally, an activity is justified if it satisfies a range of impulses, rises above mere partisan considerations, meets a social norm, and is highly prized by those who have reflected on the activity and its value.

CONCLUDING COMMENTS

The previous discussions of reviewing learning principles, developing learning activities, and selecting programs and materials should have illuminated the kinds of choices that can be made among the instructional materials and activities available. What has not been made clear is that some consistency should exist between these different guides to instructional planning and both the curriculum domains and teaching modes to be used. Just as failure to match a domain with the right learning opportunities makes an ineffective curriculum, so, too, does a mismatch between goals and teaching modes. Currently, a teaching mode appropriate for teaching basic skills is being widely promoted as an exemplary teaching model. The inappropriateness of this mode for use with social reconstructionist, humanistic, and inquiry goals within an academic curriculum is not considered by those promoting it. M. Frances Klein has long faulted the limited focus of the skills model for teaching and at the same time suggested that the use of activities representing a number of different curriculum orientations within a single classroom might be confusing to learners.[25]

A serious deficiency in curriculum planning is the gap between con-

---

[25]M. Frances Klein, ''Alternative Curriculum Conceptions and Designs,'' *Theory Into Practice* 25, no. 1 (Winter 1986): 31–36.

cepts for designing learning activities and concepts for guiding teacher preparation. Paradigms for teaching are not often related to specific opportunities. Hence, teacher training programs sometimes prepare teachers in methodologies that do not correspond to the curriculum designs those teachers are likely to encounter or use in their particular school settings. Teachers are given methods for conducting inquiry lessons but later find themselves responsible for designing and implementing didactic lessons or managing instructional systems.

An indication that the problem is being addressed is found in the writings of Bruce Joyce and Marsha Weil,[26] and Fenwick English.[27] Joyce and Weil have described models of teaching within four major families that correspond closely to prevailing views of curriculum, thereby relating teaching strategies, curriculum structures, and educational goals. For example, they match the learning opportunity approach of the late Carl Rogers with the domain of personal development, the academic modes of Bruner with information processing and the goal of intellectual development. By clarifying alternative purposes and domains and by using the appropriate sets of criteria for developing the activities and instructional strategies, curriculum workers are engineering a consistent curriculum. In the process, they are encouraging broad conceptions of purposes and extending options in order to attain those purposes. In contrast to Joyce and Weil, English would align the curriculum by *mapping*, a technique for recording instructional and learning time given to tasks, and then by analyzing the recorded data to determine its suitability to the officially adopted curriculum and testing program.

Development of learning opportunities will continue at both policy and classroom levels. It is not known which set of procedures will dominate. There is a question whether the technologists' more expensive procedures, which have guided the developmental projects of regional laboratories, will be adopted by publishers or whether less rigorous operational standards will prevail. We need to study what happens when different procedures are followed. Are different ends promoted by different approaches? Do some procedures pay off in demonstrably superior programs? What is the relative economic and procedural efficiency of the different approaches?

---

[26]Bruce R. Joyce and Marsha Weil, *Models of Teaching*, 3rd ed. (Englewood Cliffs, NJ: Prentice-Hall, 1988).

[27]Fenwick English, ''Contemporary Curriculum Circumstances,'' in *Fundamental Curriculum Decisions* (Alexandria, VA: ASCD, 1983).

QUESTIONS

1. How do technologists, humanists, academicians, and social reconstructionists differ in their models for developing learning opportunities?
2. Consider a learning opportunity that you might like to introduce as an innovation within a school system. What factors would you use in defending the proposed innovation? How would you justify the proposal? Would you use costs as a criterion?
3. Consider something you would like to teach a given learner or learners. Describe a learning opportunity for this learner(s) consistent with the purpose, illustrating the following principles: (a) appropriate practice (opportunity to practice what you want the student to learn), (b) learning satisfaction (provision for the learner to find the opportunity rewarding), and (c) success (assurance that the learner has the background for participating in the opportunity).

SELECTED REFERENCES

Duckworth, Eleanor. *The Having of Wonderful Ideas.* New York: Teachers College Press, 1987.

Gagné, Robert M. *Instructional Technology: Foundations.* Hillsdale, NJ: Laurence Erlbaum Associates, 1987.

Glatthorn, Allan A. *Curriculum Renewal.* Alexandria, VA: ASCD, 1987.

Gow, Dovis, and Casey, Tommye W. "Selecting Learning Activities." In *Fundamental Curriculum Decisions,* ASCD Yearbook. Alexandria, VA: ASCD, 1983, pp. 112–126.

Hennessey, Beth A., and Amable, Teresa M. *What Research Says to Teachers: Creativity and Learning.* National Association of Professional Librarians, P. O. Box 509, West Haven, CT 06516.

Tennyson, Robert D., and Rasch, Mariana. "Linking Cognitive Learning Theory to Instructional Prescriptions." *Instructional Science* 17, no. 4 (1988): 369–385.

7

Designing and Organizing Classroom Learning Opportunities

Chapter 6 focused on learning opportunities that are satisfying and teach students concepts for which they are developmentally ready. This chapter considers the organization of learning opportunities so that the goals of the instructional activity are clear and the different experiences reinforce each other. Hence, curriculum designers try to relate purposes, contents, learning opportunities, and organizing structures to one another.

Learning opportunities can be joined by two kinds of devices: organizing centers and organizing elements. *Organizing centers* indicate the scope of the curriculum. Centers may consist of topics, problems, questions, and projects which are important in their own right but also valuable in motivating students and extending their skills, concepts, and attitudes in pursuing the selected focus. *Organizing elements* are threads or strands of knowledge (concepts, generalizations, skills, and values) which are to be extended in breadth and depth throughout a course or program or indeed throughout all of the school's life. These elements clarify and illuminate less glorious meanings.

Curriculum designers are concerned about the disarray and fragmentation that have overtaken instructional programs. Too often, curriculum takes on the kaleidoscopic quality of television in presenting isolated pieces of information and sensations without cultivating the meaning behind them.

Finally, this chapter describes two major criteria for the organization of learning opportunities: sequence and integration. *Sequence* requires each successive learning opportunity to build upon the preceding one and go more deeply and broadly into the subject matter. *Integration* aims at having students see the links not only between ideas and processes within a single field but also between ideas and processes, in separate fields, and to the world outside of school.

ORGANIZING STRUCTURES

An organizing structure divides time spent in the school into a series of periods for activities. The kind of structure used depends on (a) the level (institutional or classroom) at which curriculum decisions occur, (b) the conception of curriculum (academic, humanistic, technological, social reconstructionist), and (c) the chosen domain or purpose of the curriculum (exploration, general education, specialization). Structure conditions but does not determine social interaction.

Structure at the Institutional Level

Institutions make use of a number of options in structuring curriculum. A *broad fields structure* focuses on fields of study—social studies, language arts, vocational education—whereas *specific subjects structure* concentrates on individual subjects—science, mathematics, business, English. A *core curriculum structure* draws content from a range of subjects or fields by addressing general problems or unifying themes. Amherst College, for example, once organized a program around ''Problems in American Democracy,'' involving the entire faculty and student body. The arts, humanities, and sciences all were related in addressing the problems selected. Finally, a *free-form structure*, common in affluent times and in times when individuality and choice are priorities, offers a potpourri of courses to reflect different students' needs.

At intermediary levels, within departments, structures feature discrete courses such as health care and the law, women's movements, modern dance, and courses that make up a unified program such as first-year science, second-year science, and third-year science.

Whatever structure is chosen, it should be part of an overall design

FIGURE 7–1   Outline of a Curriculum Design

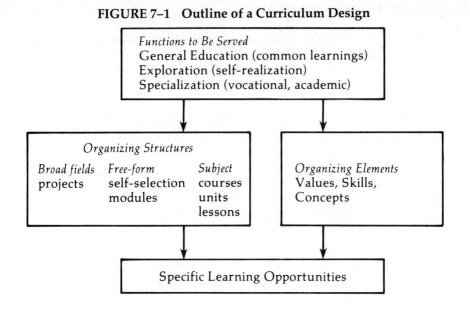

relating purposes (functions, domains, goals, objectives) to organizing elements (concepts, values, skills) and to specific learning opportunities or activties. Such a design is shown in Figure 7–1, in which the designers in the school show that they have a wide range of purposes, domains, and objectives. They provide several organizing structures: broad fields for general education, undifferentiated or open structure for self-realization, and subjects or disciplines for specialization. The organizing elements derived from purposes indicate the kinds of learning opportunities that must be created within the structures.

Structure at the Classroom Level

Open Structure. A popular structure in humanistic classrooms within the elementary school is an *open structure.* Time, space, materials, and human resources are arranged to integrate skills learned in isolation and develop social skills. At Beavers Lane Infant School, for example, the curriculum is divided into three major areas: language, numbers, and drama. The thrust of most activities is to involve children in their own learning. Observers of the school sense a tremendous enthusiasm on the part of both teacher and pupils as they work together in small groups or as a whole class. The following account records observations of such a class during a typical school day.

The Integrated Day—A Number Class

In the number class three children were measuring flour, water, and orange juice in order to make cookies. After measuring the ingredients, they became involved with additional number activities by cutting out squares for each member of the class. After these children finished their project, other children became involved with the same procedure.

At the same time, another child was coloring numbers, another was counting, two other children were painting and finishing their projects, four children were individually taking a number count regarding an upcoming sports event, four others were working with the teacher with counters. There was an abundance of activity, interest, and sustained effort on the part of each of the 31 children in the class-room. Those children who were not involved were questioned by the teacher as to their activity or lack of it. The room was alive with number concepts and activities, but also ample evidence of language and creative activities was present, such as science interest centers, art projects, writing, and verbalization. Other activities included:

Measuring each other to find the tallest, and the shortest boy or girl
Measuring hand spans—number of hand spans needed to fill the inside of a truck
Motor skill development
Questions on who wants to be a nurse, a hairdresser, a fireman, or a policeman
Art
Drawing pictures of their concept of football players on the field
The flower shop—using tissue to make flowers, and selling them, which entails using money
Using the water table to measure water—how many cups in a gallon jug, etc.
Figure 7–2 shows a typical day in a number class.

FIGURE 7–2 Flow of Activities in a Number Class

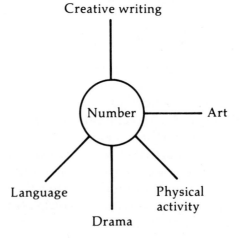

The same type of diagram could be drawn for the language and drama areas. A typical day at Beavers Lane Infant School is arranged according to a schedule which allows each child intensive involvement with all three areas—language, number, and drama. At the same time the schedule allows the teacher opportunity to explore any other area that teacher and child decide upon.

9:00–10:30	language
	number
	drama
10:30–11:00	free play
11:00–12:00	language
	number (change)
	drama
12:00–1:30	lunch
1:30–2:35	number (change)
2:35–3:15	play and activity

Structured Openness

The use of structured openness, an integrated approach, together with vertical grouping (method of organization in which children of different ages are placed in the same class), ensures heterogeneity and expands opportunities for freedom of choice, flexibility, facilitation of PIES (physical, intellectual, emotional, and social) development, and individualization of instruction. Futhermore, progressiveness and personalization of learning experiences are enhanced through this type of school organization. Of course, the integrated day or unstructured day approach, can be achieved only by careful planning to ensure that materials are ready and pupils are prepared for participation.[1]

Lesson Plan. Although structured, prescribed lesson plans can reflect humanistic, academic, or other orientations, teacher education programs have tended to foster the technological view with a prescriptive model of planning. The format is also found in contingency management and competency-based organizational structures. Typically, the plan has these features:

1. Diagnosis. A major objective is identified and there is some provision—a quick quiz or question perhaps—for determining the status of the learners in relation to the objective.
2. Specific Objective. On the basis of the diagnosis, a specific objective for a day's lesson is selected.

---

[1]Alan Wheeler, "Structuring for Open Education," *Educational Leadership* 31, no. 3 (December 1973): 251–53. Reprinted by permission of Alan Wheeler and ASCD. Copyright by ASCD, 1973. All rights reserved.

3. Anticipatory Set. There is a plan for focusing the learner's attention, giving brief practice or relating learning previously achieved, and developing readiness for the instruction to follow.
4. Perceived Purpose. Learners are informed of the objective and told why it is important and relevant to their present and future situations.
5. Learning Opportunities. Activities are selected that promise to help achieve the objective.
6. Modeling. Modeling is a demonstration or visual example of what is to be attained—product or process—and a verbal description of the critical features involved.
7. Check for Understanding. This provision ensures that learners have acquired the essential information or skill.
8. Guided Practice. Activities to test whether students can perform the task successfully are given so that the teacher can decide if students are ready to study on their own.
9. Independent Practice. After learners can perform the task without major errors, they are given an opportunity to practice the new concept, skill, or process with little or no teacher direction either at school or outside of school.

According to Shavelson and Stern, this prescriptive lesson structure is consistently *not* in teachers' planning.[2] A mismatch exists between the demands of classroom instruction and the prescriptive planning model. Teachers must maintain the flow of activity during a lesson so that classes don't become unruly. Teachers, therefore, must give first priority to planning activities that capture the attention of students during the lesson. The focus of teacher planning is on the learners' interest while at the same time attending to the content.

Newer style lesson plans call for the teacher first to engage in self-questioning: What idea am I to teach? What does this idea mean? How does it relate to other ideas with the subject, to ideas in other subjects? How is this idea related to my course goals? Next, the teacher plans ways for relating the idea to the minds and motivations of the students. This may include preparing students for the activity, linking the new idea to something familiar, and the selection of teaching method (inquiry, project, didactic).

---

[2]Richard J. Shavelson and Paula Stern, "Research on Teachers' Pedagogical Thoughts," *Review of Educational Research* 51, no. 1 (1981): 455–498.

The Unit.   Clark and Yinger indicate that the unit structure is cited by teachers as the most important teaching tool, followed by weekly and daily planning.[3] There are two kinds of units: the resource unit and the teaching unit. The difference between the two lies in how closely the recommended practices are tailored for particular learners. The *resource unit* is a guide for teaching a potential and general population of learners. The *teaching unit* is developed for known persons. Both units have the same components: rationale (justification for the unit presented as an overview), goals, objectives, topics, activities, and materials.

The unit's length is usually from two to six weeks, and the body of the document includes activities to introduce the major topics and to prepare for the activities that follow. Problems, demonstrations, and guest speakers are common initiating activities. Developmental activities comprise the major portion of the unit. In these activities, students interact with the content by raising and formulating questions, collecting data, and trying to resolve the initially proposed problem.

In preparing such activities, the designer considers what resources (field site, materials, resource persons) will be necessary as students carry out their investigations and what skills they need to gather information and complete their projects. Culminating activities in the unit give opportunity for students to evaluate and synthesize what has been learned and to summarize and formulate new questions for further study.

Topics for units should reflect the curriculum orientation—subject matter, personal concerns, social problems, and basic skills. These topics are cast as organizing centers and arranged in a sequential order, thereby constituting a course of study.

The following example illustrates the different components in a resource unit for the middle grades entitled "Providing Education."

Organizing Elements: relation of physical environment to quality of life (generalizations)—reading, writing, thinking (literacy skills)
Organizing Centers: the focus of the problem. "What is the function of education?" "How do the differences in living conditions between modern and earlier cultures account for differences in the educational system?"
Activities: Compare a contemporary school with a colonial school, show-

---

[3]C. M. Clark and P. C. Peterson, "Teachers' Thought Processes," *Handbook of Research on Teaching,* ed. M. Wittrock (New York: Macmillan, 1986).

ing the contrast in enrollment, lessons, discipline, and materials. Read and write stories about the school days of pioneer children. Exhibit old textbooks and show how these books differ from current books. Dramatize a day in a colonial school.

Teacher's Materials:

Cubberly, E. P. *History of Education.* Boston: Houghton Mifflin, 1920.

Mayhew, K., and Edwards, A. *The Dewey School.* New York: D. Appleton-Century, 1936.

Children's Materials:

Dunton-Lucy. *School Children the World Over.* New York: Stokes, 1909.

Gordy, W.P. *Colonial Days.* New York: Scribner, 1908.

Wilson, Howard. *Where Our Way of Living Comes From.* New York: American Book, 1937.

Community Resources: Schools (public and private), libraries, museums, interviews with persons from other generations.

The Module. A module is a short course of between twenty and sixty hours, designed in terms of objectives, content, skills required on entry and anticipated at the end of the course, assessment techniques, and suggestions for methodology and resources. Modules are not mere chunks of content; they develop knowledge and skills in a balanced way. The key quality of the module is its relative brevity. This brevity allows students more choices about the composition of their whole course of studies than would be possible if they were committed from the start to a one-year or two-year block of work. Often students can negotiate the specific curriculum they need and want.

Centers and Course Development

An organizing center for a unit gives focus to the learning opportunities in that unit. A series of organizing centers and the accompanying learning opportunities comprise a course. Although each center has educational significance of its own, the instrumental value is paramount. Centers are vehicles for introducing the key content of the course. As in learning opportunities, the center should appeal to prospective learners, give opportunity to practice desired outcomes, and be appropriate in terms of the learners' backgrounds. The center unites many learning opportunities and contributes to multiple outcomes. A field trip to a local archeological dig could be a learning center. Preparation for the trip would teach different skills: studying the historical context, learning how to recover artifacts, and learning how to interpret findings and to recognize special problems. Conducting the trip would require applying the new skills and knowledge, while posttrip evaluation would contribute to reflection and the generalizing of new questions and plans.

The organizing structure of the institution influences the choice of centers. For example, a subject structure would have a concept or topic of importance to an academic subject. For physics, *light* or *motion* might be used as a center. A broad field structure would probably focus on a social problem; a free-form structure would center on personal concerns and interests of learners, such as self-image, isolation from others, and control over one's life.

The arrangement of centers within a course follows some principles of sequence. Humanistic designers often put as an early center one that fosters awareness; next, they put centers that lead to an abstract thought about the matter; finally they put centers that result in the learner taking action. Consider how teachers might arrange centers in a course of literature: fiction (novel, short stories), poetry (popular songs, folk songs, religious songs), drama (comedy, tragedy), journalism (articles, advertisements, editorials). They might start with the center that they think is less complex or which best represents the interests of the learners.

ORGANIZING ELEMENTS

In order for opportunities to be related, some common element must exist between them. Elements are the threads, the warp and woof of the fabric of curriculum organization. They need to be woven together, or organized. If they are not, we will have a situation, as described by Edna St. Vincent Millay:

> Upon this gifted age, in its dark hour,
> Rains from the sky a meteoric shower
> Of facts . . . they lie unquestioned, uncombined.
> Wisdom enough to leech us of our ill
> Is daily spun; but there exists no loom
> To weave it into fabric . . . [4]

---

[4]Excerpt from "Upon this age, that never speaks its mind" by Edna St. Vincent Millay. From COLLECTED SONNETS, Revised and Expanded Edition, Harper & Row, 1988. Copyright © 1939, 1967 by Edna St. Vincent Millay and Norma Millay Ellis. Reprinted by permission.

Common Organizing Elements

Some of the more common elements used as the basis for organization are:

Concepts. Many academic curriculum plans are built around such key concepts as culture, growth, number, space, entropy, metaphor—the ruling ideas in respective fields.

Generalizations. Generalizations are conclusions drawn from careful observations. Two generalizations are ''In stable societies all educative influences operate consistently upon the individual; in heterogeneous societies, there are inconsistencies and contradictions.'' ''A person is both participant (subjective) and observer (objective) in all human behavior.''

Skills. Skills are generally regarded as proficiency plans for curriculum organization. They are commonly used as the basis for building continuity in programs. Elementary schools sometimes organize learning experiences around reading comprehension, fundamental operations in mathematics, and the skills for interpreting data. Metacognitive strategies in problem solving are the latest organizing elements in skill programs.[5] These strategies include sifting out relevant information from irrelevant information, looking for patterns in the information to make it meaningful, perceiving the relationship of old information to the newly acquired information.[6]

Values. Philosophical values are cherished beliefs that are not questioned but taken as absolutes for governing behavior. Two examples are ''respect for the dignity and worth of every human being regardless of race, nationality, occupation, income, or class'' and ''respect for self.'' When organizing a curriculum plan around values, most of the activities must be designed so that they reinforce the particular value selected.

Understanding organizing elements is a distinguishing attribute of the curriculum expert. A child may be immediately aware of learning activities or centers only in their concrete form, but the insightful teacher or curriculum writer is always conscious of their deeper significance. When one asks children what they are learning, they are likely to re-

---

[5]John D. McNeil, *Reading Comprehension: New Strategies for the Classroom,* 2nd ed. (Glenview, IL: Scott, Foresman, 1987).

[6]Thomas J. Shuell, ''Cognitive Conceptions of Learning,'' *Review of Educational Research* 56, no. 4 (1986), 411–436.

spond, "We're learning about Indians" or "We're learning to speak a foreign language." The curriculum person, however, sees, in addition to such direct study, the key abstractions to which the present activity points. The activity dealing with Indians may be pointing toward a generalization about basic needs that all people have always had. Learning to speak a foreign language may be most important for what it illuminates about a person's own language, language in general, language acquisition, and even some more fundamental elements such as communication among people.

Organizing elements are selected in light of the purposes of the curriculum. When the curriculum goals are technical and vocational, skills are an appropriate element to use. When the curriculum goals emphasize moral and ethical domains with an integrative function, values are the preferred element for organization.

Table 7–1 outlines the use of organizing elements in relating an objective to experiences or opportunities.

Elaborating on the outline, consider this following purpose and activities.

Purpose. Given new situations from life, the learner can predict the likely effect of technology on these situations. Characteristics, limitations, and capabilities of modern technology are used by the learner for determining the effect.

Within the first center or unit of instruction (defining technology), students are introduced to a systems approach for reducing complex problems. Students acquire one definition of technology and in the next

TABLE 7–1 Relating Organizing Elements or Organizing Centers

Organizing elements	Organizing centers or units of instruction					
	Defining technology	People	Jobs	Society	Environment	Quality of life
Technology (concept)	X	X	X	X	X	X
Value of persons (value)		X	X	X	X	X
Relationship of natural resources to quality of life (generalization)			X	X	X	X

unit they glimpse the ways in which technology helps people, the limits to its use, and its side effects. The concept of technology is further extended, and the student begins to judge the way in which technology decreases or enhances the value of people. Subsequent units involve students in problems about the application of technology to human uses, to societal needs, to natural and manmade environments. Prior elements are extended and a new element—the relationship of resources to the quality of life—is introduced. Opportunity for students to assess the future effect on and value to persons is given in all subsequent units. The quality of life unit allows for an unusually large number of activities related both to individual and to societal values. As indicated in the matrix, no provision is made for treating values in the first unit; and the relationship of natural resources to quality of life is not dealt with until the third unit.

To illustrate how the element is used in connecting different fields, consider how learners taking a course in technology might be helped if teachers in other courses exchanged elements with the teacher of the course in technology. In their mathematics course, they could acquire other basic concepts for understanding technology and systems such as algorithms, probability, and binary systems. In their English course, they might be able to examine the interaction between technology and society in the mass media. They could appraise American societal values as reflected in newspapers, advertisements, and modern fiction. They could be helped to see how language is related to thought in both persons and machines.

There are two ways to extend the meaning of an organizing element through learning opportunities. The designer can provide for more complex situations to which the element applies, or the complexity of the situation can remain constant but the level of competency expected from the learner becomes more demanding. For example, in early learning opportunities, the learner might be asked only to define and give examples of a concept; in later centers the learners are given the opportunity to apply the concept; and in a final unit they might be asked to evaluate the concept or show its limitations.

PRINCIPLES FOR SEQUENCING CONTENT AND ACTIVITIES

Traditional Principles of Sequence

Principles for sequencing learning opportunities go back hundreds of years. In 1636, Comenius admonished teachers to order activities from the simple to the complex. The principle *simple to complex* means introducing learning activities involving a few factors before activities involving many factors. It also means going from a part to a whole or from general to more detailed. There are other traditional principles of sequence, for example, going from *familiar to unfamiliar*. Activities that involve what the learners know precede completely novel activities. Children study their neighborhood before learning about their state and nation, and about foreign lands. Another principle of sequence is to progress from *concrete to abstract* by presenting opportunities for children to see, touch, taste, hear, or smell a phenomenon before asking them to verbalize and categorize. A useful principle is to teach *dependent factors* first. Addition and subtraction, for example, precede multiplication. The new proposal for teaching physics, chemistry, and biology in that order rests on the argument of dependency.

There are also several ways of sequencing a series of facts or subjects. Ordering by *chronology* means presenting events as they occurred in time. Ordering by *usefulness* means teaching particular school subjects at the time they are needed in everyday life.

In Chapter 14, there is a discussion of the *theory of culture epochs*, which was used as the basis for sequencing studies at the turn of the century. This theory states that the learning processes of children follow the same pattern as the learning process of the human race. The notion is still very much alive. Some modern curriculum writers in the field of music are interested in the ideas of Carl Orff, a German composer who developed new plans and materials for teaching music to children based on the cultural epoch hypothesis. Orff reasoned that primitive peoples used free bodily movement in dance and also simple rhythmic drum patterns; therefore, children should begin with drums suited to their size and skill. Bodily movements should be combined with the beat of the drum, and rhythmic chants should synchronize the spoken rhythm with other movements.

Because primitive peoples first use only one or two pitches before finally progressing to the use of the five-tone scale, the musical experiences planned for children should include songs with only two or three notes, and, at most, five notes from the pentatonic scale. Melodic vocabulary includes other steps only after many opportunities with the simple melodies.[7]

---

[7]Carl Orff and Gunhill Keetman, *Orff-Schulwerk: Musik fur Kinder,* 5 vols. (New York: Associated Music, 1950–53).

Newer Principles of Sequence

Some recent principles for sequencing learning come from psychologists like Robert Gagné,[8] and from the developmental schemes of those like Robert Havighurst, the late Jean Piaget, Erik Erikson, and the late Lawrence Kohlberg.

Gagné's View. As a behaviorist, Gagné orders activities according to types of learning. He believes that children learn an additive series of capabilities; that is, the simpler, more specific capability must come before the more complex and general one. Gagné orders learning activities in this fashion:

1. *Multiple Discrimination.* The student learns to make different responses to stimuli that are similar in appearance. Children in kindergarten, for example, learn to tell the difference between the letters *d* and *b*.
2. *Concept Learning.* The student makes a common response to a class of stimuli. A student may learn to classify or identify different types of literature or to recognize consonant-vowel-consonant spelling patterns.
3. *Principle Learning.* The student acquires a principle, rule, or chain of concepts. The student learns, for example, to predict what word will follow in a given sentence structure according to rules for sequencing English.
4. *Problem Solving.* The student learns to combine two or more principles to produce a solution and in the process acquires the capability to deal with future similar problems with greater facility.

Curriculum ordered in accordance with Gagné's theory uses a cumulative approach to the teaching of reading and mathematics and mastery learning strategies in which learning opportunities are sequenced according to assumed hierarchies. Children at different levels of a hierarchy are given opportunities to learn prerequisite subordinate and superordinate capabilities as appropriate. In skill learning, Gagné's hierarchical sequences are beneficial.

Gagné believes the child comes to school with many capabilities for making multiple discriminations and for building further concepts and

---

[8]Robert Gagné and Leslie J. Briggs, *Principles of Instructional Design,* 2nd ed. (New York: Holt, Rinehart & Winston, 1979).

higher order capabilities. He also realizes that the order of attaining complex behavior is not universal.

Recent theory from cognitive psychology stresses that learning is the making of connections between new information and the learners' existing network of knowledge. Hence, Gagné's concepts of lower and higher order learning seldom makes sense. For example, computational skills do not exist as lower order mathematical problem solving, but are learned in relation to and as part of problem solving.[9]

Gagné's model is also deficient because it does not take into account the unique ways in which children look at a task. Children differ from adults not only in the amount of previously learned subskills, but in the number of subskills they are capable of coordinating at one time and in their ability to avoid applying incorrect subskills or concepts. In making a task analysis or hierarchy, the structure of the task *from the learner's point of view* is important. When such an analysis shows a mismatch between the capacities of the learner and the demands of the task, the sequence should be redesigned either to reduce the hierarchy or to differentiate concepts that are confusing to children.

The Developmentalists' View.   Developmental tasks form an important basis for sequencing curriculum events. Robert J. Havighurst created the concept of a developmental task from (a) the idea that the maturation of the biological organism sets the conditions for learning social tasks, (b) the fact that social and cultural patterns demand that certain things be learned at a given time, and (c) the fact that often a sequential pattern of preferences and dislikes is dictated by the individual personality. He defined a developmental task as ''a task which arises at or about a certain period in the life of the individual's successful achievement of which leads to his/her happiness and to success with other tasks whereas failure leads to unhappiness in the individual, disapproval by society, and difficulty with later tasks.''[10]

Hence, the activities selected for the late childhood curriculum might be those which help to form friendships with peers, learn rules and abstractions for fairness, identify with peers of the same sex, and accept a changing body. Developmental tasks of the adolescent may be forming new relationships with age mates of both sexes, gaining emotional inde-

---

[9]Penelope Peterson et al., ''Using Knowledge of How Students Think About Mathematics,'' *Educational Leadership* 46, no. 4 (December 1980–January 1989): 42–46.

[10]Robert Havighurst, *Developmental Tasks and Education*, 3rd ed. (New York: McKay, 1973).

pendence from parents and other adults, selecting an occupation, and preparing for marriage.

In a simple way most schemes outlining developmental stages and tasks support the commonsense notion that health, safety, and physical survival must be attended to first and then there are opportunities that enable learners to gain the capacity for economic self-maintenance in maturity, which, in turn, bring the ability to maximize cultural values like morality, prestige, wealth, and self-realization.

Erik Erikson has been credited with originating the idea of charting both the desires of the learners and the demands placed on them by cultural expectations.[11] Erikson's chart of life cycle states, from infancy through senescence, has been proposed as a way to organize the curriculum. Children would be given opportunities to deal with the emotional issues which are salient at particular life stages. Children in the latency period (about 8 to 12 years), whose central growth crisis is "industry versus inferiority," want to win recognition by producing and working with facts and things; unless they develop a sense of competency at work, they may despair or consider themselves doomed to inadequacy. Thus, it is important to help students choose concrete tasks involving nature and the physical world that are challenging yet likely to bring success. Modeling and scaffolding, i.e., providing adequate support for learning with gradual transfer of responsibility from teacher to student, may be valuable. Mistakes should be allowed and students should be invited to discuss their difficulties. Erikson has defined crucial tasks for each of the major seven life states. The selection and arrangement of learning activities addressed to these crises might better serve the needs of learners. Although the specific tasks of each age are the same for boys and girls, the content and length of each state differs in each society and from generation to generation in the same society.

The late Lawrence Kohlberg also has created a developmental scheme for ordering learning opportunities, in the area of moral judgment. According to him, learning opportunities must take into account both the learner's existing stage of development and a next higher stage.[12] Kohlberg believed that changes in moral thinking progress step by step through six stages and three levels.

---

[11]Erik H. Erikson, in *Childhood and Society,* 35th anniversary edition (New York: Norton, 1986).

[12]Lawrence Kohlberg, *Recent Research in Moral Development* (New York: Holt, Rinehart & Winston, 1984).

Preconventional Level

Stage 1. Goodness or badness is determined by whether one will be punished for an act (punishment and obedience orientation).

Stage 2. Right action is that which satisfies one's needs (instrumental relativist orientation).

Conventional Level

Stage 3. Good behavior is that which pleases others and is approved by them ("good boy-nice girl" orientation).

Stage 4. Right behavior consists in doing what family, group, and nation expect ("law and order" orientation).

Postconventional Level

Stage 5. Right action means obeying legal standards agreed on by the whole society and, in areas in which there is no agreement, following personal values and opinion. Right action also includes taking action to change the law (social contract, legalistic orientation).

Stage 6. Right action is exercising one's conscience in accordance with universal principles of justice and rights (universal ethical principle orientation).

Developmentalists have the central idea that development—physical, social, intellectual, and emotional—is fairly orderly and internally regulated. This idea has generally had a salutary effect on curriculum. It has kept before us the fact that some things can be more easily learned after minimum levels of maturity. It may be dangerous, however, to give too much credence to the view that capacities are genetically predetermined and unfold automatically. By manipulating environmental factors, we may alter the concept of readiness—the assumption that there is an optimal age for every kind of learning.

The idea of a developmental sequence sometimes leads to a curriculum organization in which children's interests are taken as an adequate index of their developmental needs. However, such a selection process is unreliable because the students' interests would reflect their prior learning opportunities more than their stage of development and would in turn create an inadequate curriculum. The tyranny of fixed age level norms can both lower our sense of what is possible under different learning conditions and keep us from remembering large individual variations.

The late Jean Piaget's ideas on the stages of mental growth are probably the best known among developmentalists. He has postulated the following stages: a *sensory motor stage* (birth to about 2 years), in which the child begins to "symbolize and to represent things by words or gestures''; *representational stages* (about 2 to 4 years), in which the child learns to represent objects by symbolic means and (4 to 7 years) in which the child begins the initial stage of logical thought and can group objects into classes by noting similarities and differences; a *concrete operations stage* (about 7 to 11 years), in which the child learns to solve physical problems by anticipating consequences concretely; and a *formal operations stage* (usually 10 to 15 years), in which the youngster learns to use hypothetical reasoning and to perform controlled experimentation.[13]

An implication of Piaget's stage theory of mental development is that learning opportunities should match or nearly match the child's thought structure. This means analyzing each opportunity in terms of the level of reasoning required and then testing to see whether the intended learner has this level of ability. It is often assumed that learning can be induced when the learning activity requires reasoning that is slightly above the predominant level at which the child is operating. However, about the only way to develop a curriculum that would allow for matching (in most classrooms, children are at different operational levels) is to provide opportunities that have solutions at each level and to let each child choose the level at which he or she wants to experience the activity.

Developmental schemes for sequencing learning opportunities are subject to two criticisms. First, there is a question about the validity of the principle underlying the scheme. Not everyone believes that Piaget has established valid stages of growth. Contrary to Piaget's findings, evidence exists that some young children can think reflectively, recognize fallacies in logic, and make and apply generalizations.[14] Second, it is difficult to relate developmental sequences to the sequences of learning opportunities. The variation in individual needs, interests, and levels of thought makes it necessary to test all intended learners across a wide range of interests and concepts to assess individual developmental profiles. Furthermore, it is difficult to select principles that are effective in teaching a particular subject matter and important in promoting cognitive development. Definitions of cognitive competencies are not precise enough for constructing curriculum, and we lack a means of measurement that characterizes a developmental stage across a range of subject matter.

---

[13]Jean Piaget, *The Psychology of Intelligence* (New York: Harcourt Brace Jovanovich, 1950).

[14]Robert H. Ennis, ''Children's Ability to Handle Piaget's Propositional Logic: A Conceptual Critique,'' *Review of Educational Research* 45, no. 1 (Winter 1975): 1–43.

Categorizing Sequencing Principles

George Posner and Kenneth Strike have devised a scheme for showing how different principles of sequence relate to views of knowledge, views of learning, and views of how content is to be used.[15] Although this scheme serves as an analytical tool for research on sequencing, it lacks prescriptive usefulness because it contains no guidelines as to the type of sequences that are most effective for the various types of content, kinds of learners, and outline variables.[16] By way of example, the category for *relating content to phenomena*—people, events, things—includes:

1. *Space.* Principles of closest to farthest, bottom to top, east to west (for example, in relating such diverse content as parts of a plant, geography, and positions on a football team).
2. *Time.* Principles of cause and effect, chronological—early to most recent events (for example, in relating content of history).
3. *Physical Attributes.* Principles of softness to hardness, smaller to larger, greatest to least brightness, less to more complex structure (for example, in teaching the properties of things in the natural world, science).

The category of sequence principles useful in the *teaching of concepts* includes:

1. *Class Relations.* Principles that call for teaching about a general class before teaching about its members (for example, teaching about mammals before teaching about specific animals in that group).
2. *Sophistication.* Principles by which the less abstract matter is presented first (for example, real numbers before imaginary numbers) and basic ideas before refinements (for example, Newton's laws before Einstein's refinement of these laws).
3. *Logical Prerequisites.* The principle that the arrangement of concepts depends on the relationships among concepts rather than the relationships among their referents (for example, teaching the concept of set before the concept of number).

---

[15]George J. Posner and Kenneth A. Strike, "A Categorization Scheme for Principles of Sequencing Content," *Review of Educational Research* 46, no. 4 (Fall 1976): 665–690.

[16]James Van Patten et al., "A Review of Strategies for Sequencing and Synthesizing Instruction," *Review of Educational Research* 56, no. 4 (Winter 1986): 437–471.

The category of *inquiry-related sequences* includes principles for sequencing learning activities for generating, discovering, or verifying knowledge.

1. *Logic of Inquiry.* Principles of sequencing based on induction (instances before generalizations) and principles based on deduction (hypotheses before evidence is collected).
2. *Empirics.* Principles calling for a general survey of an area before consideration of special problems.

Learning-related content sequences are similar to those mentioned previously as coming from the works of psychologists like Gagné, Piaget, and Erikson. Learning sequences stress ordering of experiences according to familiarity (most familiar to most remote), difficulty (less difficult before more difficult), interest (most interesting first), development (according to developmental stages), and internalization (opportunity to recognize certain features in others before recognizing it in themselves).

The category of *utilization-related sequence* principles includes:

1. *Procedure.* Principle of sequencing steps in the order in which they will be used when carrying out a procedure (for example, teaching golf grip before teaching address of the ball).
2. *Frequency.* Principle of basing sequence on predictions of likely future encounters (for example, teaching the use of chi square and correlation coefficients before factor analysis; teaching a television repairer how to change a tube before teaching how to change a resistor).

You will note how the above categorization system corresponds to different conceptions of the curriculum. Those with an academic conception use the categories of sequence for (a) relating content to phenomenon, (b) development of concepts, and (c) generating and discovering knowledge. Those with a technologist orientation select sequencing principles from the category of learning-related sequences, such as those of Gagné or Bloom, and from the category of utilization, when their interest is in developing curriculum for vocational training. Humanists tend to draw their sequencing principles from the developmental category, such as the sequences for moral development, values acquisition, and stages of growth. Some humanists are trying to apply John Dewey's principles for sequencing of curriculum content by attending to the individual learner's prior experiences—the cumulative result of the learner's use of knowledge gained from one experience to understand more fully the meaning of the next experience.[17] Although social reconstructionists might find the sequencing principle of internalization useful, they give less attention to sequence than to integration of the curriculum. One principle of sequencing sometimes used by reconstructionists, however, is the *principle of graduated responsibility* in ordering learning opportunities for children. This principle is illustrated as follows: *observe→play act→ perform useful service→work as equal partners with adults→carry responsibility for a project on a limited budget of power→exercise full adult responsibility.*

PRINCIPLES FOR INTEGRATING CONTENT

Integration

Curriculum integration is a response to the desire to make curriculum socially relevant and personally meaningful. Proponents of curriculum integration argue that if knowledge is to be important and relevant to students growing up in contemporary society, there must be a departure from traditional forms and organization. Exploration of topics of crucial social and personal concerns, such as relationships between the sexes, life in cities, and war requires introducing content and organizational patterns not found in conventional subject areas. An interdisciplinary approach is required.

Integration of subject matter becomes controversial because it usually means giving up fixed subject matter boundaries and conventional content, emphasizing breadth rather than depth and showing more concern for application of knowledge than for the form of knowledge.

There are several schemes for effecting curriculum integration. In some schemes, academic content is fixed and in others the individual student has much freedom of choice. The teacher is a generalist in some schemes; in others each teacher contributes as a specialist while team teaching. There are also integrated schemes within a discipline, such as integrated science, as opposed to schemes whereby all kinds of subjects—science, art, technology, and so forth—are combined.

Integration is a logical problem when we allow a rigid view of knowledge to dominate curriculum planning. As indicated in Chapter 4, there

---

[17]Chiarelott Leigh et al., ''Basic Principles for Designing Experience Based Curriculum'' (Paper presented at AERA annual meeting, San Francisco, April 1979).

are those with a narrow academic conception of curriculum who view knowledge as fixed. Such persons oppose curriculum reorganization along integrated lines for epistemological reasons. On the other hand, social reconstructionists and humanists, who view knowledge as tentative, favor integration as a way of ensuring that knowledge and curriculum fit changing social and human needs.

We have fewer principles for integrating activities than for sequencing them. When content is integrated, subjects are related to one another, out-of-school experiences, and personal needs and interests.

Integration usually means applying organizational elements to an ever-widening variety of situations. Organizing principles commonly in use call for increasing breadth of application and range of activities and for fitting parts into larger and larger wholes. Sometimes the learner's problems and interests serve as the framework or organizing center within which knowledge from many fields can be brought together. Similarly, opportunities to attack social problems and to conduct projects require concepts and methods from different fields of knowledge. The subject matter is featured then, not as a system of ideas or concepts, but as ideas that have relevance to a practical problem. *The Chicken Book*, a popular nonfiction book, is an excellent example of how an organizing center, the chicken, can be used to bring together a wonderful compendium of history, literature, science, medicine, religion, technology, economics, fact, and lore.[18] One of the authors teaches a course on the fowl dedicated to the idea that what is divided may once more be made whole.

The use of such content elements as key ideas in subject fields, broad concepts, major questions, and methods of inquiry may effectively interrelate courses and out-of-school experiences. In the Carnegie Colloquium on General Education, for instance, the members report new academic alliances as inquiry blends fields of study that traditionally have been isolated.[19] Sociologists, psychologists, biologists, and chemists found themselves seeking answers to the same or closely related questions such as the role of chance in the arrangement of life on the planet.

Typical arrangements for facilitating integration are the following:

1. *Concentration.* Students are not expected to take more than four courses at any one time so that they may gain the depth of prepara-

---

[18]Page Smith and Charles Daniel, *The Chicken Book* (Boston: Little, Brown, 1975).

[19]Carnegie Foundation for the Advancement of Teaching, *Common Learning*, ed. Ernest Boyer (Washington, DC: Carnegie Foundation, 1981).

tion necessary for seeing the ramifications of each subject on the whole curriculum.

2. *Correlation.* Subjects keep their separate identities, but the concepts of one subject are related to the concepts of another. (For example, history and literature are taught concurrently for a given historical period to reinforce each other.)
3. *Integration of a Tool Subject.* Skills learned in one subject are used as tools in another field. (For example, mathematical concepts are used in social science.)
4. *Fields of Study.* Fields or areas of study differ from forms of knowledge and disciplines in that they do not have a distinct rational structure of knowledge. (For example, the fields of geography and health draw on mathematics, the physical sciences, and the human sciences.)
5. *Comprehensive Problem Solving.* Problems such as ecology and conservation are presented, which require a combination of skills and knowledge from such forms of knowledge as science, mathematics, and philosophy to best solve them.

From her observations of teachers engaged in integrative curriculum development, Nathalie Gehrke found teachers using five different definitions of integration:

Simple relational—connections made on temporal, spatial, or agentic elements
Enlightenment—all elements of a particular topic are studied together
Application—connections are made on the use of a skill or knowledge from one domain in another domain
Analogical relational—connection based on how attributes of one thing may be sought in another
Logical relational—connections based on inferential linkages in chains and systems such as ecosystems, social theories

Gehrke also found that in order to create integrative curriculum (production of new connections, not connections already used in the culture), teachers require informal periods of activity in which they can exchange information about individual and common interests, talents, teaching goals, themes, organizing concepts, and their general academic expertise.[20]

---

[20]Nathalie J. Gehrke (Paper presented at the annual meeting of the American Educational Research Association, New Orleans, 1988).

ISSUES IN CURRICULUM ORGANIZATION

Curriculum organization is difficult because the fields of knowledge have not been organized in a way that makes them useful in daily life. Also, those in different disciplines express their findings in different terms with the result that the consumer does not know how to relate the findings. Curriculum efforts to integrate concepts from various disciplines have not been successful.

Practical problems of curriculum integration center on (1) the teachers' loss of identity and security by being isolated as teachers of English, science, history, or other subject fields; (2) the need for flexible scheduling during the school day, along with freedom for student choice of work and movement within the school building and community; (3) the need for material resources that go beyond the normal stock of books and equipment found in separate departments; (4) the difficulty of learning the teaching roles, skills, and attitudes required by the new curriculum; and (5) the need to answer the objection that an integrated curriculum does not prepare students for external examinations based on separate subject matter.

Curriculum integration is an overriding concern. The curriculum reform movement of the 1960s extended the scope of content to include new areas of knowledge, but neglected to evolve a unifying purpose. Pluralistic and humanistic interests as well as governmental programs aimed at social and political causes of the 1970s extended even further the range of electives and the scope of content. Curriculum fragmentation resulted. We are in a wave of curriculum organizational reform in response to the fragmentation. Some of the difficulty involved in responding to this situation and to the lack of shared skills and values can be seen in efforts to build an integrated curriculum.

Designers at the Education Development Center in Newton, Massachusetts, tried to organize learning opportunities around interests that appear to be important to the prospective students, such as child-rearing practices, love and affection, expressions of fear and anger, parent–offspring conflict. Using these interests, the staff sought content from different disciplines (biology, anthropology, psychology, sociology, linguistics) which would help students to meet these interests and at the same time to gain an understanding of their own uniqueness, of their kinship with others of the culture, and of the characteristics that unite the human race.

The curriculum developers found that no academic discipline was adequate to cope with the questions they wanted to raise. They also found that academicians from different fields use different words to discuss similar phenomena and that these words are invested with different meanings. A biologist speaks of "bonding" when examining relationships between male and female or between parent and offspring; a psychologist may use the word "bonding" as well as words like "love" and "attachment" to describe the same relationships. A third problem was that the disciplines not only represented separate languages and analytical tools, but also drew from bodies of data that did not overlap. A final and deeper problem was the difficulty of trying to combine different points of view regarding human nature. There is, for example, much conflict over whether cultural evolution proceeds independently of biological factors or whether biological forces determine the direction of evolution.

Several solutions have been offered as broader approaches to the problem. Philosophers of science have argued that integration can be achieved by using concepts of knowledge about knowledge. One can draw from disciplines the content that represents the field as a whole. The curriculum person can select ideas and instances that exemplify the method of inquiry in these disciplines and offer instruction in *synoptics*—the integrative fields, like history, religion, and philosophy. These disciplines have as their function the making of coherent wholes.

A second proposal is that we live with the fact that scholars in any one discipline are incapable of resolving any complex human problem. In other words, students should try to examine personal and social problems from multiple perspectives, realizing that one of these views alone is entirely unsatisfactory. Perhaps the conclusion that students reach after attending to the different perspectives will be more valuable than any one discipline's answer to the problems.

A third proposal is that we forget about curriculum organization as a way to effect meaning for students. Even when there is a careful attempt to simplify and relate content so that students can follow it, the organization will fit any one student imperfectly. Students individualize their experiences anyway. This position puts the burden on the learners to make sense out of learning opportunities in any order. More positively stated, it challenges students to pose their own questions, seek their own answers, make their own synthesis, and find satisfaction in so doing.

Peter Freyberg and the late Roger Osborne think that curriculum developers have erred in structuring curriculum from the perspective of the teacher.[21] They propose that no matter what curriculum framework

---

[21]Roger Osborne and Peter Freyberg, *Learning in Science* (Portsmouth, NH: Heinemann, 1985).

is employed, learners are going to structure the subject matter in their own way. What is learned can be very different from what is taught. Progress in curriculum development rests on finding out the concepts and cognitive structures that learners bring with them to the learning opportunities. Usually, there are only three or four distinctly different viewpoints regarding a matter. Ascertaining the learners' conceptions and the procedures for dealing with conflicting preconceptions so that students can be helped to accommodate more adequate conceptions is now central. Learning is being viewed less as a process of knowledge accretion than as a process of conceptual change.

Curriculum design has been suspected of preventing learners from comprehending content in any other order and from learning content that is incompatible with adaptive teaching. Underlying most organizational issues, however, are disputes about purpose. Curriculum workers who favor academic specializations value organization as it relates to sequencing for depth, but they are not impressed by integrative arrangements. Those who seek integrated approaches, usually humanists and social reconstructionists, distrust prearranged sequences within a single field.

A final point of view about the problems of integration warns of the political danger of unified and integrated curricula. The integration of separate subjects and the destruction of subject departments in schools often marks a shift of power from the staff in separate fields to the administrator who directs the new master plan. It can be argued that modern societies are better served with power on the periphery and a diversified curriculum (many separate subjects), but with specialists coming together to decide on common objectives.

CONCLUDING COMMENTS

In this chapter emphasis was placed upon two ways to organize learning opportunities: by means of organizing centers and organizing elements. Curriculum design was viewed as a plan showing the relationships among purpose, organizing structures, organizing elements, and specific learning opportunities. Illustrations of curriculum design were presented with special attention to the designing of classroom curriculum structures. Principles for sequencing and integrating content were critiqued. Issues in curriculum organization—particularly concern about the integration of subject matter—were discussed. The problem of linking curriculum planning undertaken at two levels of decision making (institutional and classroom) was also introduced.

Because the planning of a curriculum is a management and political matter as much as a technical one, the connection between the curriculum and these matters is treated more fully in Part III.

QUESTIONS

1. Think of a familiar learning task such as tying shoes, operating an automobile, playing a game, composing a musical or literary piece. Into what units would you divide the task you have in mind? In what order would you teach these steps? What principle of sequence determines your ordering?

2. State an organizing element—a concept, value, or skill—that you would like to build on throughout a number of activities in a course or program of interest to you.

3. Curriculum constructed in accordance with hierarchical theories (that is, curriculum in which there is an attempt to specify prerequisites and to place them in a simple-to-complex order) is sometimes criticized for being boring and ineffective. Critics charge that there are too many unnecessary steps for some learners and that many learners who successfully complete the enroute steps fail at transfer tasks at the end of the programs. What is your response to this criticism?

4. What consequences (good or bad) would be likely from a curriculum in which learning opportunities are ordered on the assumption that there is an optimal age for acquiring particular capacities?

5. Arno Bellack once suggested a program that would include basic instruction in the humanities, natural sciences, and social sciences together with a coordinating seminar in which students dealt with problems "in the round" and in which a special effort is made to show the relationships between the systematized fields of study as materials from these fields are brought to bear on a topic. What are the likely advantages and disadvantages of Bellack's suggestion? What conditions would have to exist in order for the proposed plan to work?

6. Assume that you are a member of a planning committee charged with a new curriculum organization for a school. You have been asked whether the new organization plan should attempt to provide for in-

tegration of subject matter and, if so, how it can best be achieved. What is your reply?

SELECTED REFERENCES

Gibbons, J. A. "A Curriculum Integration." *Curriculum Inquiry* 9, no. 4 (Winter 1979): 321–327.

Posner, George J., and Strike, Kenneth A. "A Categorization Scheme for Principles of Sequencing Content." *Review of Educational Research* 46, no. 4 (Fall 1976): 665–690.

Managing Curriculum

As the decade of the '90s begins, curriculum practitioners at district and school levels are confronted with two dueling movements in curriculum management. On the one hand, system technologists, as described in Chapter 3, are trying to tighten the linkages of school practice to state policies.

William Spady and his network for outcome-based schools represents those trying to move schools in the direction of greater curriculum accountability.[1] His outcome-based approach uses predetermined exit outcomes (knowledge, competencies, personal qualities that students must demonstrate upon leaving school) as the driving force for designing and implementing curriculum. Teachers' planning and practices focus on these outcomes.

Similarly, the State Department of Education in California has given all school districts a "vision" of excellence, specifying a common core curriculum and establishing a program to train school administrators in how to translate the vision into classroom practices. In turn, the administrators give the same "basic training" to teachers in their schools so they can create learning environments to match the "vision."

On the other hand, the local empowerment movement advocates that issues about what to teach should be resolved as close to the school or classroom level as possible, dictated by the needs of students rather than bureaucratic mandates. The empowerment movement has been supported by the work of both (a) John Goodlad, who has long argued for curriculum development at the individual school where the principal and the teacher

---

[1]William G. Spady, Director, The High Success Program on OBS, 14 Whitmont Court, San Carlos, CA 94070.

take responsibility for curriculum dialogue and plans of action along with parents and students[2] and (b) Ted Sizer, who, as chairperson of the Coalition of Essential Schools, believes that every community and every school is necessarily different from any other.[3] Hence, the Coalition Project encourages each school to shape ideas about intellectual development, personalization, and the like in a way that is respectful of the local situation. Coalitions begin with a group of people, including the principal, who are interested in what their school might do to better the intellectual development of all students. Participation grows as the coalition evolves a plan which has to get wide acceptance.

The conflicting positions of technologists and emancipators underlie the issues treated in the chapters of Part III. Chapter 8 focuses upon restructuring as it affects curriculum, giving particular attention to local school responses to reform policies. This chapter features administrative arrangements that affect curriculum choices (middle, alternative, and specialized schools' scheduling, staffing patterns, and tracking) and considers options for developing a coherent curriculum. Newer views of curriculum effectiveness and their implication for management are presented.

Chapter 9 targets on how to generate and implement curriculum innovations and effect change in school settings. Newer ideas in staff development are discussed as related to curriculum policy and practices. Attention is given to shifts in roles of central office staff, principal, and teachers in the light of trends toward professionalization and school-based management.

In Chapter 10, curriculum evaluation is reviewed from both the perspective of traditional evaluation, which attempts to measure effectiveness and pluralistic evaluation favoring broader means and wider participation in the evaluative process.

Chapter 11 explains the formulation of curriculum policy and points out potential sources of conflict among policy makers. A study of the politics of curriculum making may reveal differences in decision making processes at local, state, and federal levels. It also focuses attention on the interest groups making curriculum decisions and the consequences of political solutions to curriculum questions.

---

[2]John Goodlad, Center for Educational Renewal, University of Washington, Seattle, WA 98195.

[3]Ron Brandt, "On Changing Secondary Schools: A Conversation with Ted Sizer," *Educational Leadership* 45, no. 3 (February 1988): 30–36.

8

Administering Curriculum

For decades, school administrators such as superintendents, principals, curriculum directors have been asked to act in accordance with models of curriculum that assume a close tie between decisions and implementation. They are expected to bind their district or school to common purposes and to embrace new models of operation in an environment characterized both by change and by a lack of consensus about policies and procedures.

In this chapter, I take the position that many administrators will respond to curriculum reform and conflicting views regarding the importance of bureaucratic curriculum alignment and local emancipation by *strategic interaction*, seizing and adopting those state policies that meet their needs and making their own policies that reflect local priorities.

THE CONTEXT OF RESTRUCTURING

An agenda for restructuring schools is moving ahead throughout the nation. The Carnegie Forum supports the idea of teachers having a central role in determining what counts as teaching.[1] Several states are practicing school-based decision making and accountability. For example,

---

[1] Carnegie Task Force on Teaching as a Profession, *A Nation Prepared: Teachers for the 21st Century* (Washington, DC: Carnegie Forum on Education and the Economy, 1986).

there are Carnegie Schools, which receive state grants to restructure school organization and governance. The Association for Supervision and Curriculum Development is initiating a consortium of schools involved in restructuring school governance, roles, curriculum, and instruction, and the Rockefeller Foundation has released a report that recommends (a) that school administrators make it possible for teachers to be active participants in curriculum development, giving teachers released time and joint planning periods, (b) that there be team instruction whereby teachers are allowed to share their experiences with colleagues, and (c) that teachers be encouraged to develop their own curriculum programs.[2]

Definitions of curriculum restructuring vary. Federal political leaders have the following marked for reconstruction: greater choice in schools, creation of magnet schools, rewarding of merit schools, availability of child care, improved achievement in mathematics and science, and alternative certification of teachers. The National Government Association advocates (1) providing a greater variety of ways for students to learn such as varied class sizes, cooperative teaching, peer teaching, and better use of instructional technologies; (2) revising teaching methods, deemphasizing lectures and memorization, and more teaching of critical thinking and higher-order skills; (3) making more school-based decisions with accountability for results; (4) giving students more choice in selecting alternative school programs; and (5) experimenting with the length of the school day and year.

Many of the celebrated changes in the Rochester City School District are aimed at restructuring schools as centers of inquiry and reflection, not of unexamined tradition. The Rochester contract provided for school-based planning, empowering all major stakeholders (parents, teachers, administration, and in high schools, students) to decide on such matters as budget, curriculum goals, school dynamics, selection of new teachers on the basis of the school's needs and ethos. Among their considerations were how to allocate time, use space, classify students, divide subject matter, adapt to different types (not level) of intelligence and learning styles. They questioned the assumptions that one building means one school, that children learn best in 47-minute segments, that multiple choice tests are the best indices of student learning and that teaching is telling.[3]

---

[2]*Helping Schools Work* (The Rockefeller Foundation Communications Office, 1133 Avenue of the Americas, New York, New York 10036, 1989.)

[3]Adam Urbanski, "The Rochester Contract: A Status Report," *Educational Leadership* 46, no. 3 (November 1988).

ROLES IN RESTRUCTURING CURRICULUM

The Principal as Director of Learning

System technologists put the principal in the forefront of designing curriculum plans consistent with state and district intents. For example, in California, administrators attend curriculum training centers where they are briefed on state and district curriculum goals and learn how to match classroom activities with the predetermined goals. As they create curriculum plans at the Center, the principals are encouraged to look for ways to expand on what teachers are already doing in the classroom with the idea of seeing how teachers can organize and manage the classrooms envisioned by state and district curriculum makers. The principals shape a mental image of what is to be accomplished with students and how they might look in the various disciplines, including the setting of specific student performance measures consistent with the reformers' intents. District personnel review the performance expectations and make suggestions for modification until they are satisfied that each principal is clear on the operational meaning of state and district goals.

Later, in district-wide training sessions, teachers and administration have their performance expectations for specific grade levels approved, and they develop hypothetical year-long plans in the various subject areas. The plans are critiqued and individual teachers create their classroom plans. The principal and teachers from the same school decide upon the steps they will take to translate their curriculum plans into practice. As the plans are implemented, the principal provides support as the teachers experiment with new ways to modify classroom practice and arranges for groups of teachers to meet regularly for comparing notes and devising new strategies.[4]

The Principal in Shared Leadership

Under emancipation, the principal and teachers have the freedom to generate together their own curriculum visions rather than merely create ways to achieve the purposes set by others. Instead of addressing the problems that state and district think the school has, the staff focuses on the school problems that interest them. One approach is to focus on the school's culture, including beliefs, shared values, traditions, practices,

---

[4]Janet Kierstead, "Is This Just Another Swing of the Pendulum?" in Claremont Reading Conference 51st Yearbook, Malcolm Douglass, ed. (Claremont, CA: California School Leadership Academy, 1987).

expectations, and assumptions. The development of a mission statement and critical analysis of curriculum practice to see where there are consistencies and inconsistencies is a good way to begin curriculum revision.

The idea of a school having an ethos, being distinct from other schools, and subjecting all aspects of school life to this quality is powerful. Quaker schools, for instance, have been singled out as unique in encouraging students to "go beyond their private interests and put their lives in historical, social, and ethical perspective." Among the principles in the Quaker essence is to get students to strive for excellence rather than to be concerned whether they reach it. Other principles are to stress the careful use of language, including "plain speech" and listening.[5]

A second example of shared curriculum leadership is found in the Key school, an Indianapolis elementary school organized around Howard Gardner's theory of multiple intelligences.[6] It is recalled that Gardner attacked the notion that intellect is a single overarching faculty and proposes instead different sets of "core" abilities to process various kinds of information, solve problems, and produce products valued by society. Accordingly, the Key school was designed by the principal and teachers to give all seven intelligences equal emphasis through an interdisciplinary curriculum. In addition to regular academic subjects, each student in grades K–6 receives almost daily instruction in physical education, music, art, Spanish, and computers. The curriculum is tied together by themes that span all grades and all subjects. Themes change every nine weeks. For instance, students might have as a theme the connection between people and their environment. At the end of nine weeks, each student produces a product of his or her own design that illustrates the theme.

Four days a week, students also spend time in their "pods"—multiaged groups which students and parents select based on personal preference, emphasizing work in a particular cognitive area. In the math pentathlon pod students play board games that demand logical, spatial, and mathematical skills. Other pods include an architectural pod, in which students adopt houses in the neighborhood and prepare an architectural walking tour, and an actor's unlimited pod and pods related to music, problem solving, mind and movement, art and physical science. Eight teachers including the principal created the idea for this school and de-

---

[5]Kristen Goldberg, "Quaker Schools: Small for Influential Force," *Education Weekly* 7, no. 7 (April 20, 1988): 1, 7.

[6]Lynn Olson, "Children Flourish Here: 8 Teachers and a Theory Changed a School World," *Education Weekly* 1, no. 18 (January 27, 1988): 18–19.

veloped the curriculum during a year of weekend and evening meetings in their homes.

Instead of beginning with principles and the creating of curriculum to match, teachers and principal may prefer to explore school regularities (grading policy, scheduling, textbooks, field trips, assemblies, and the like) for their consistency with the ideal professed by the school. In such an approach, faculty meets to describe the practice or policy, interpret it, and give accounts of the consequences in terms of the school's idea. Usually, alternatives are introduced which are more in keeping with the idea. Under shared leadership, the principal's role is leadership, not control. One aim of the planning sessions is that all should share their knowledge, observations, and interpretations and that there should be evidence and agreement about the validity of conflicting views. Decisions should be based on a rational consensus of the participants and not on the principal's position or the popularity of certain teachers. Throughout the discussion, participants are consistent with the school's norms and values. However, sometimes the existing norms and values must be subjected to more encompassing principles and ideals; the possibility of creating new norms and values is important for the transformation of the school. The deliberate model of curriculum making as given in Chapter 4 is appropriate in this context.

A role for teachers in participation in curriculum decision making is not new. Gary Peltier has written of a program of curriculum construction in 1922 using teacher participation.[7] The account brings forth most of the arguments for the practice. As a result of participation, teachers become better informed about the aims of education, better able to interpret programs to others, and more accepting of new methods. The courses of study of participating teachers tended to reflect newer views of subject matter, social needs, and attention to the learners.

Department Heads in Curriculum Management

In secondary schools, principals have looked to department heads for curriculum leadership. Indeed, a recent survey reports that 73 percent of principals perceived department heads as functioning successfully in curriculum development.[8] Heads of departments often provide

---

[7]Gary Peltier, "Teacher Preparation in Curriculum Revision: A Historical Case Study," *History of Education Quarterly* 7, no. 2 (Summer 1967): 1209–1217.

[8]Janice Adkisson, *High School Trends Study* (Alexandria, VA: ASCD, 1986).

the structure and sense of purpose for inquiry, discussion, and decision making while enabling genuine participation by colleagues. Departmental curriculum decisions treat such issues as intentions or expected outcomes, content selection and sequencing, criteria for new materials and activities, teaching approaches, monitoring of implementation, and evaluation. A recommended technique by which a department ensures that overall terms permeate planning is "the network of ideas." Figure 8–1 is an adaptation of a map developed by a group of math teachers in response to the goal for students knowing something about the historical development of mathematical concepts.

ADMINISTRATIVE ARRANGEMENTS

In organizing the curriculum, administrators and staff decide how students are grouped, how much time is devoted to each subject and how it will be taught. Since the functions of schooling change, each of these factors requires frequent alteration. In the decade of the 1980s, state-mandated reforms had a chilling effect on a wide range of school arrangements. Mandatory academic requirements resulted in reduced vocational offerings, fewer options for students, reduced flexibility in scheduling.[9] The reform requirement substantially reduced the number of courses that students took in home economics, industrial arts, physical education, business, psychology, and the performing arts. Most reform reports recommended increasing instructional time, adding days to the school year, and lengthening the school day. Achievement replaced effort as the basis for promotion. Students spent more time retaking courses they failed. Most schools continued offering low and middle achieving students "dull" factual repetitive material through tracking. Although more math and science courses were required for low and middle achievers, these courses were focused on a low level of skills at the basic levels. In some cases, low quality academic courses replaced higher quality vocational ones.

The second reform wave of the 1990s promises to encourage greater freedom to school curriculum arrangements. In 1988, the National Association of State Boards of Education recommended the abolition of the Carnegie unit.[10] The Carnegie unit is a measure used for accrediting high

---

[9]William H. Clune et al., *School Responses to Curriculum Mandates* (New Brunswick, NJ: Center for Policy Research in Education, Eagleton Institute of Politics, Rutgers, 1989).

[10]*Rethinking Curriculum: A Call for Fundamental Reform* (Alexandria, VA: National Association of State Boards of Education, 1989).

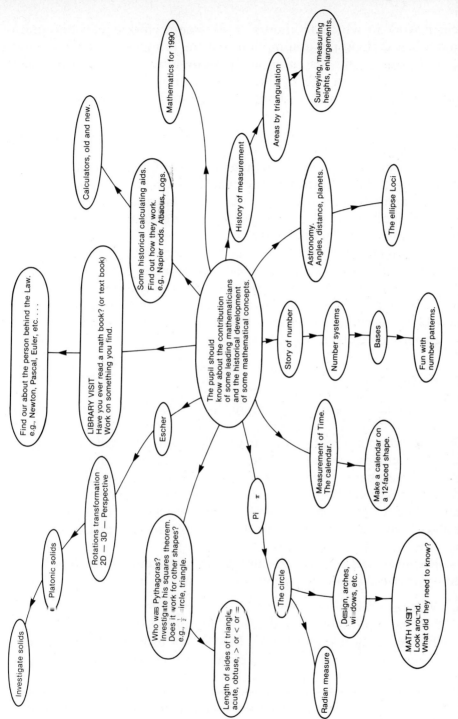

FIGURE 8–1 Cognitive Map for Implementing Goal. From *Managing Mathematics* (The Mathematical Association and Stanley Thornes Publishers, 1988).

school work in which 120 hours of classroom work equals one unit of credit, based upon the assumption that the school year would be from 36 to 40 weeks and the class period from 40 to 60 minutes in length. Since its adoption in 1909 by the College Entrance Examination Board, it has become a fixed part of almost every secondary school program. The Carnegie unit has resulted in uniforming standards, crystallizing the curriculum, limiting freedom for experimentation, and defining education as an accumulation of units.

The National Association of State Boards of Education would replace the Carnegie unit with student achievement in the core areas of language arts, mathematics and science, citizenship, fine arts, health and foreign languages and would give emphasis to the acquisition of central concepts rather than superficial knowledge.

Similarly, the National Education Association's Learning Laboratory's initiative is a project for freeing local communities "to turn their school systems upside down or inside out," to open school doors to four-year-olds and end the arbitrary division of class periods into 50-minute chunks. Increasingly, states are "trading off" greater flexibility in return for greater accountability.

Stratifying Students

The practice of grouping students by apparent ability both along curriculum paths and within classes is under attack. Some schools are charged with perpetuating discrimination against minority students and poverty families by directing them toward lower educational tracks. Most school people reject the notion that curriculum inequality is intentional and regard tracking as a way to meet the special needs of a diverse student body. As a result of her study of tracking, Jeannie Oakes recommends "what we now provide for the most advantaged children, we need to provide for all children."[11]

Recent efforts to organize curriculum to accommodate to individual differences and ensure the same quality of instruction are:

a. Creating a core curriculum to which all students will be exposed even if different students take different approaches to the same material. The San Diego Unified School District, for example, is introducing a common core curriculum to replace all remedial and lower level sci-

---

[11]Jeannie Oakes, *Keeping Track: How Schools Structure Inequality* (New Haven, CT: Yale University Press, 1985).

ence and math courses. This program aims for qualifying all graduating high school students for four-year college entrance requirements. Also, accelerated school projects in San Francisco's inner city schools are offering the active, exciting, and fast-paced curriculum associated with gifted children to "kids who don't have anything going for them."

b. Encouraging within-classroom instruction to feature cooperative learning in small groups with students at different levels studying together and helping one another. Permanent groups based on assumed ability or achievement should not be formed in classrooms.

Empirical findings about the effects of stratification are numerous. Adam Gamoran and Mark Berends' review of studies of stratification reveals patterns of instructional differences favoring high track classes and suggests that tracking polarizes students into pro- and anti-school factions.[12] Grouping does affect achievement. Teachers reputed to be more skilled and successful are more often located in high track classes, which may produce cycles of low expectations, poor morale, and failure for both teachers and students in low tracks. Similarly, Robert Slavin's analysis of ability groupings in elementary schools leads him to conclude that ability grouping does not enhance student achievement in the elementary school.[13]

Attempts to reform tracking and ability grouping may be met with opposition from parents of gifted children concerned that their children will be held back by slower learners and lose advantages such as enriched rooms, better teachers, and more attention. Some parents are looking for schools of choice as a way to maintain tracking arrangements.

Staffing Patterns and Scheduling

A team of teachers can accept responsibility for 100 students for a two-hour block of time each day. This allows the staff to assume different roles such as planning, lecturing, leading discussions, and counseling. A teacher in a team may be involved with a large class for a lecture, with a seminar-sized group of fifteen, or with students engaged in individual

---

[12]Adam Gamoran and Mark Berends, "The Effects of Stratification in Secondary Schools: Synthesis of Survey and Ethnographic Research," *Review of Educational Research* 57, no. 4 (Winter 1987): 415–435.

[13]Robert E. Slavin, "Ability Grouping and Student Achievement in Elementary Schools: A Best Evidence Synthesis," *Review of Educational Research* 57, no. 3 (1987): 293–336.

study. Teaching teams determine in advance the specific pupils they need to teach, the size of the groups, the length of teaching time, and the materials to use. Team leaders provide information for preparation of a master schedule for student guidance. Often, in a daily twenty-minute period, pupils determine their own daily program from the choices available on the master schedule.

One brand of interdisciplinary teaming is found in some middle schools in which four-person teams are composed of one specialist from among the areas of language arts, mathematics, social science, art, and science. Each specialist serves as the resource person for a subject area, doing much of the planning and teaching of that subject. Each teacher on the team, however, teaches all four of the academic subjects. The advantage of this arrangement is that correlation of subject matter areas is easier and teachers are better able to attend to individual students.

Team teaching is not supposed to be a labor-saving device, like cooperative or rotating turn teaching. It is intended to bring about clear joint acceptance of objectives and better conditions for achieving them. Teams of teachers and groups of students can be together, for example, for about three hours each day in what is called a *fluid block*. Two hours are devoted to interdisciplinary activities, and the additional hour is given to one or more open labs in a variety of subcourse content. With twelve teachers operating across three teams for at least two of the three different hours, as many as twenty-four different minicourses can be offered during a nine-week period. Students from each of the three fluid blocks are able to schedule the minicourse of their choice. The fluid block team also schedules large-group, small-group, and individual student activities, always with an option for student placement in the open labs, which operate concurrently on an individual basis. The balance of the school day is given to elective courses such as physics and computers, or to a vocational block in any of a number of different areas (Table 8–1).

Each student is assigned to a specific team or faculty member for the entire day, thus meeting accountability concerns. The organization of the team, advisement, and individualized labs offer several ways to meet student needs.

Modification in the standard schedule through double periods is not dependent upon team teaching. Arranging for Tuesday–Thursday and Wednesday–Friday classes, which meet for one hour and forty-five minutes, for example, has the advantage of giving a teacher more time to spend with each student and giving the students opportunity to reflect upon their laboratory observations and experiments, not merely to carry them out.

TABLE 8–1 A Team Teaching Outline

Hour	Type of Course	Individualized Labs
1	Fluid block: 100–120	Music
2	Students in course	Mathematics
3	(Minicourses or planning)	Drivers education
		Art
		Drama
		Computer
		Other
4	Elective	or 3-hour vocational block
5	Elective	
6	Elective	

Supplementary Personnel

Student tutors, adult volunteers, and inexpensive paraprofessionals allow teachers to serve more pupils effectively and efficiently. Cross-age tutoring, whereby older students tutor younger ones is beneficial to both and has become very popular across the country. No other innovation has been so consistently perceived as successful. Ideally, tutoring is a regular class assignment and not a voluntary activity. Instructional modules are selected that will induce academic growth of the tutor as well as the tutees. Ninth-graders, for example, may teach fractions to fourth-graders if the ninth-grade teacher believes the tutors need to learn and practice fractions and the fourth-grade teacher would like his or her students to learn fractions.

Scheduling of one-to-one tutoring can occur when two classes get together regularly on two or three occasions per week. A room set up with pairs of enclosed desks (carrels) is most desirable, but regular classrooms, cafeterias, or libraries will suffice. The sending teacher prepares the tutors in special training sessions. In these sessions, tutors learn exactly what they are to teach. They may also practice their methods and prepare materials such as flash cards and tests for their tutees.

The tutoring sessions themselves should be supervised by the teachers concerned. Tutors should be free to ask for assistance, and the teacher can check whether the work is being taught correctly.

Nongrading

Nongrading occurs when content and experience are offered on the basis of learner interest and ability and are not restricted to a given grade level. The lack of grade levels permits students to progress at different rates and lets them take advanced or additional courses. A student may wish to take correspondence courses, for example, or participate in advanced placement programs, taking college level courses for credit while in the secondary school. Also, instead of offering world history, United States history, and problems of democracy to tenth-, eleventh-, and twelfth-graders, respectively, schools may offer one of these courses each year to all students. We will see more emphasis on proficiency than on age or grade level as a basis for school progress.

Facilities

Building, grounds, supplies, and equipment should correspond to both the educational purposes and the means by which teachers and students achieve these purposes. Facilities for independent study means students must have a place to work and a place to use the special materials of the subject matter they are learning. There may be a need for places in which to view films, read, practice music, and work with metals and clay.

Classroom walls should not define the limits of the learning environment. Facilities should encourage communication, and there should be variations in lighting—less in small group discussion space than in independent study rooms. The budget for supplies and equipment should be increased as the cost of school building increases. Unlike industry, which wisely puts only 25 percent of total capital outlay into structure, schools have put 75 percent of capital outlay into the building shell and only 25 percent into instructional tools. Although modernization procedures are less costly than building new structures, the politics of education usually means that school persons are vulnerable to the pressures of real estate and building contractors for expensive sites and buildings that are not necessary. Dade County schools have an interesting innovation in that some of their elementary schools are in quarters provided by businesses. Schools get their classrooms without capital outlay and businesses get a perk for their employees.

The Middle School

A major institutional change with implications for curriculum organization is found in the rise of the American middle school. This type of school has grown from a smattering of schools in the 1950s to more than

8,000 in 1990 and is the predominant form of organization. This school is characterized by service to the eleven- to fourteen-year-old age group. Typically, middle schools are centered on the child rather than on the subject matter. The schools usually offer the design components of a sub-school within a larger middle school and an interdisciplinary teaching team. The team operates as a small four- or five-teacher school. The same group of students in the subschool may stay together for a period of three or four years. Another team of teachers offers a related unified arts program to students from all subschools. The unified arts program gives all students experiences in such subjects as art, shop, homemaking, music, physical education, as well as focusing on career opportunities. Exploratory experiences on a nongraded basis are also provided to enrich the students and supplement their needs.

A recent survey has found that middle schools are more likely to provide program characteristics needed by early adolescents.[14] However, simply placing grades 6–8 or 5–8 in a single building does not ensure that students will receive help with problems common to the age group: (1) emotional, social, and academic concerns; (2) making a smooth transition from the child-centered elementary school to more academically oriented institutions; (3) discovering interests and career options; and (4) integrating subject matter. Organizational responses to these problems include teacher adviser programs, transition and articulation activities, interdisciplinary teaching and block schedules, and a wide range of teaching strategies.

Alternative, Magnet, and Specialized Schools

Modular scheduling, team teaching, flexible group instruction, and similar plans did not prove to be ideal solutions in the past or lead to more effective curriculum. Some call these innovations superficial tinkering and are demanding a much more basic reform.

Active groups began to take daring steps toward the reorganization of schooling in the 1970s. Convinced that public schools were instruments of a racist and oppressive society, some community activists opened storefront schools that emphasized both basic skills and black culture. They also tried to enroll school dropouts from the street and

---

[14]Gordon Cawelt, "Middle Schools: A Better Match with Early Adolescent Needs," *Curriculum Update* (Alexandria, VA: ASCD, November 1988).

prepare them for college. These "freedom schools" were financially supported by foundations and dedicated persons. Such schools encouraged a close, non-authoritarian teacher–pupil relationship and an open concept of learning. Not surprisingly, content focused on the ills of the capitalistic society.

By 1971, there were over 200 free schools; however, with the calmer atmosphere of the early 1970s and the loss of available monies during the economic slump, the free school movement lost much of its original impetus. Although alternative schools had no uniform philosophies, they continued to increase in number. By 1989, there were 10,000 alternative schools in 5,000 districts across the country.

It is impossible to generalize accurately about alternative schools. By definition, each one is different. Much of the movement is directed toward making schools effective for students who have been school dropouts. Some alternative programs are organized to allow students to work in a congenial atmosphere consistent with their work style. Most people in alternative schools today are not working as social revolutionaries but either as humanists, who want pupils to have a choice in subject matter to be studied and in styles of learning, or as academic strivers who want early development of talent in prestigious subject matter and careers.

Alternative schools have made us conscious of whether we should allow students to select freely a formal or an informal school, a structured or an individualized curriculum. An alternative school—either a separate institution or a unit within a comprehensive school—is an organizational answer to the old problem of fitting the curriculum to the enormous range of talents and traits that students bring to school and to the diverse expectations that they and their parents have for schooling.

Today's alternative school movement has broadened the definition of an elective from a choice of subject to a choice in ways of working. Generally, people in the movement recognize the need for structure, sequence, and discipline but assert that, for many students, a choice about the degree of structure in a learner's school life is as crucial as a choice of studying either Spanish or stenography.

In some alternative schools, students seldom enter a classroom. They pursue their individual interests outside the school. They may study the stars at an observatory, work with computers at a local firm, learn to make bread at the corner bakery, and discuss medicine with a physician—all for academic credit. Sometimes students travel from place to place in the city, learning from a variety of paid and unpaid teachers. A student may take physics at a university, Elementary Functions and World Cultures from the school staff, Contemporary American Literature and French II from students at another university, Museum Methods from the school staff, and Understanding the Stock Market from a stock broker.

Recently an *options* system has been introduced in which the choice of school curriculum (methods, activities, and environment) is offered to individual students and their families. Instead of a single alternative to an existing program, there are many options. In Minneapolis, for instance, students may attend the school selected by themselves and their parents. In most large cities, there are "magnet" schools which are consistent with the concept of options. These schools offer an especially strong curriculum in some areas, such as science or business education, as a way to further court-ordered integration by attracting students from different ethnic and socioeconomic populations.

An early purpose of magnet schools was to draw children from beyond the immediate neighborhood to foster integration. Now, however, magnet schools are sprouting because they bring together spirited students who want to link education to their visions of careers. Criticism of magnet schools comes from administrators of neighborhood schools who do not like the siphoning off of the brightest children and from those who believe that such schools isolate children, promoting elitism rather than a democratic society.

Other changes are occurring in response to the international competition in mathematics and science. Some "exemplary" schools specialize in mathematics and science—1,000 at the elementary level and 1,000 at the secondary level—in the most ambitious of organizational plans on the national level. State networkings, such as the Louisiana School for Math, Science, and the Arts at Natchitoches where the most talented juniors from the state's 66 school districts are brought together for an elite education, are becoming more common.

Unlike the early 1960s, public schools currently available to students, parents, and teachers offer incredible variety. Some schools emphasize different instructional approaches (open schools, Montessori schools, continuous progress schools, behavior modification schools); some feature distinctive curriculum (centers for world studies, environmental study centers, vocational centers); and others focus on special students (maturity schools, bilingual schools, schools for the gifted and the dropouts). Yet, throughout the country, schools are putting much emphasis on basic skills and college preparation.

DIRECTIONS IN THE REFORM OF SCHOOL ORGANIZATIONS

Options in the Schools

Two directions of organizational reform have emerged out of the ferment over social policy dilemmas and the innovations both from those who would make the school more humane and from those who would make it more productive. Various commissions and study groups bent on studying secondary schools in order to restore them to full strength and vitality agree on two directions.

First, reduce barriers between adolescents and opportunities in the community. Work or volunteer experience outside the school building is seen as desirable in increasing students' independence and helping them to encounter a broader range of people and experiences. Students' time should be well planned, and off-campus programs should be organized to allow for reflection. The study groups also realized that tracking can occur outside as well as inside the school. A combination of action and reflection is believed necessary for adolescents to mature in an integrative manner.

Second, create smaller schools or subschools with more specialized courses of study. Students who are unlikely to get training beyond high school should leave school with enough skill to procure a job. Rather than each school offering training in fifteen or twenty skills, different schools each might offer three or five trades in depth. To facilitate such specialization, the school, satellite, or cluster within schools should be smaller, with each unit focusing on fewer but more specific areas and skills. Basic academic subjects would still be offered in all schools, but students would select a magnet school on the basis of the training it offers.

The reorganization of junior and senior high schools into houses is one possibility. Each house has its own curriculum. The students in each house are at all grade levels; that is, each student spends his or her entire junior and senior high school career affiliated with one house through several grade levels. Teachers have the opportunity to adjust to the student's present attainment, and all students have the opportunity to reach mastery in the general curriculum; slower students would not be tracked into different courses. Furthermore, the longer association of the students and their teachers is likely to reduce both student alienation and teacher frustration.

Teachers within smaller schools, with some of their students on alternating work and study programs outside the school, would have more time to spend with fewer students. They also would perform more varied roles like that of advisor, work supervisor, and role model. The reports from the various commissions and panels trying to reform secondary education emphasize options in high school organization and the need for instruction in informal settings. These reports are not truly plans for curriculum development because they fail to attend to the questions of what should be taught and how. If we return to our metaphor of curriculum as a game, as found in Chapter 5, we might say that the authors of these reports fail to pick up all the curriculum pieces. Like so many administrators and policy makers, they assume that if the structure and organization are changed or if the setting and scene of schooling are moved, then appropriate and effective education will result. This is not so. The learning in the various settings must be coordinated with that of the school, and it should not be assumed that all work settings are appropriate for learning. The task of improving the learning of students in specific tasks has yet to be done. Unfinished, too, is the development of a conceptual framework for the creation of learning activities and the training and deployment of personnel.

ADMINISTRATION FOR INSTRUCTIONAL EFFECTIVENESS

The last decade has seen substantial growth in our understanding of the various conditions that account for achievement in individual schools. Unfortunately, achievement has too often been defined as performance on standardized tests of reading and mathematical skills, not creativity nor critical thinking. Studies suggest that coordination and management of the instructional program and a sense of shared values among students and staff are important to instructional effectiveness.

Coordinating the Curriculum

As with other administrative issues, the administrator can take either a systems approach or a school cultural approach to curriculum coordination.

Systems Approach to Curriculum Coordination. The different aspects of the curriculum in effective schools (effective as defined by achievement tests) are carefully coordinated or "tightly coupled." School goals, classroom objectives and activities, and measures of pupil performance are all aligned. Curriculum alignment has become the most popular way to improve test scores. Alignment consists of three steps: First, the essential skills to be taught are defined and the lists of skills are distributed to teachers. Second, test items for the essential skills are developed. In these tests the item format is the same as those found in the textbooks so that the *skill* is being measured, not the ability to handle a new format. A system for easily scoring the tests is developed and presented to teachers, principal, and district administrators. The teachers and the principal receive reports on student achievement for each grade level in the school. Teachers also receive a separate report for individual students.

Third, teachers must be certain to focus their teaching on the desired skills. To this end, teachers work in grade-level groups, discussing each skill and making sure they agree on the meaning of each objective in terms of classroom instruction. Although all the skills are included in the curriculum, a small number of skills might receive special attention when prior results show the need for emphasis. After priorities are set, groups of teachers plan instruction for the year, ensuring that adequate time and appropriate materials and methods are available. During the year, teachers monitor the program and meet to discuss how well plans are being carried out. Near the end of the year, teachers assess their accomplishments in teaching the skills, discuss problems, and develop plans for improvement.

Tight-coupling requires instructional goals which are clear, public, and acceptable. Such a program must minimize differences in the treatment of students' allocated time to certain content, and expose all students to the same curriculum. It also means that the work of outside specialists (resource teachers, reading teachers, counselors) must support the efforts of the classroom teacher.

School Cultural Approach to Curriculum Coordination. Administrators in schools with strong culture have a vision of quality schooling that does not equate high test scores with a good school. Their definition of a good school includes ethnic and racial pluralism, parent participation, shared governance, rich programs, personal attention to students and supportive environments. One of the significant functions of culture is that it governs how members think, feel, and behave.[15] In schools with strong

---

[15]Terrance E. Deal, "The Culture of Schools," in *Leadership: Examining the Elusive,* eds. L. T. Shelve and M. B. Schoenhelt (Alexandria, VA: ASCD, 1987).

culture, the staff is cohesive in their beliefs and integrated in their efforts to achieve common goals.

Principals of secondary schools require more time to get a consensus on goal setting and problem solving than those in elementary schools. Secondary school teachers often view themselves as working, independently functioning departments which have little to do with overall curriculum goals. An answer to the problem is found in previously described empowerment and emancipation approaches to curriculum development, including matching practices to a predominant moral ideal (ethos). The development and promulgation of a school's "mission" statement of what it is about may help.

Shared Values

Effective schools have a strong sense of community with shared goals and high expectations for student and staff performance.[16] In a successful school more members of the teaching staff discuss their teaching. The teachers are organized as a team, making collective decisions about instructional matters for a common population of students. Shared values also follow from the teachers' acceptance of the need for continuous improvement through analysis, evaluation, and experimentation. A school with shared values is often characterized by (a) talk among teachers about *manipulative variables*—methods of teaching, materials—and *external variables*—pupil background, community attitudes; (b) frequent observations by teachers of each other's teaching; and (c) teachers working together planning, designing, and preparing teaching materials.

Effective Principals

Principals can contribute to the development of collegiality and continuous improvement. They can express clearly the expectation that all staff members are to be knowledgeable about teaching and are to participate in activities for instructional improvement. Principals should themselves participate in instructional improvement activities and support such efforts by providing encouragement, time, and materials. For example, effective principals protect teachers who are trying curriculum innovations from competing demands and possible criticism.

Principals in successful schools are optimistic about the ability of stu-

---

[16]Patricia Ashton et al., "A Study of Teachers' Sense of Efficacy," NIE Report 400-79-0075 (Gainesville, FL: University of Florida, 1982).

dents to meet goals. They are able to work well with others, manage conflict, and cope with ambiguity. Compared with less effective principals, they take more responsibility for instruction, discussing teaching problems, and protecting teachers from distractions.[17] As indicated in the research by Linda McNeil, good principals put more emphasis on learning than on order.

Effective Classroom Practices

As the curriculum goals shift to the teaching of higher order thinking, the definition of effective teaching changed. Instead of the effective teacher universally moving through materials at a good pace and engaging mostly in direct instruction such as structuring lessons, giving detailed explanations, providing examples and demanding practice, professionalization of teaching is in the wind.[18] Under professionalism, teachers are free from the demands to teach a prescribed curriculum using stylized methods to prepare students for standardized tests. Instead teachers are compelled to teach students (1) to read for knowledge and enjoyment not simply for acquiring testable reading skills, (2) to think mathematically rather than simply to work problems, (3) to question and analyze, not merely to give right answers, and (4) to think and write creatively.

Effective Research and Curriculum Policy

Caution must be exercised before translating research on effectiveness to curriculum policy. In the first place, most of the findings are correlational, not causal. The fact that principals who concern themselves with instruction and students who try to accomplish clear learning goals are associated with high test scores may mask the underlying reasons for success. What is it in the school environment or training of a principal that makes it likely that the same principal will be concerned with instruction in one school and not in a different school? How can teachers engage uninterested students in learning? The answers to such

---

[17]Arthur W. Steller, *Effective Schools Research: Practice and Promise* (Bloomington, IN: Phi Delta Kappa Educational Foundation, 1988).

[18]Arthur E. Wise, "Professional Teaching: A New Paradigm for the Management of Education," in *Schooling for Tomorrow,* eds. Thomas J. Sergiovanni and John H. Moore (Boston: Allyn and Bacon, 1989).

questions are more important than the mere association of an instructional variable with learning.

Furthermore, many of the associations are misleading. The use of time in school, for example, often has been discussed in connection with teaching. However, there is evidence that the amount of time spent on a task by itself is meaningless.[19] We need to know how much time is needed and to consider time spent in relation to decisions on content, mode of instruction, and students' willingness and ability to pay attention. In a well-organized school, trying to improve a time-on-task rate of 65 percent is probably constructive. However, in a school where the average attendance is less than 70 percent and the school day is characterized by disorder, more pressing issues than time on task should receive attention.

A serious limitation to the effectiveness studies is that they have ignored achievement in important areas—creativity, desire for further learning, ability to deal with uncertainty. Standardized achievement tests (most of which are skills for reading and math) focus on known tasks for which there are known procedures for teaching. Those interested in good education must also attend to the problem of teaching complex concepts and a range of subject matters for which the teaching strategies are not known. Indeed, there are indicators that the focus upon mastery of isolated skills such as decoding in reading is detrimental to the attainment of higher level cognitive processes—comprehension and critical reading.[20] The heavy emphasis upon answering correctly may reduce curiosity and critical thinking in students. Investigators have found strong resistance from students as teachers make an effort to shift from routine or procedural tasks (teacher directed) to understanding tasks (student directed).[21]

Several implications follow from the findings of the effectiveness studies. The use of achievement test scores, profiles of school practices, needs assessment and other tight-coupling mechanisms may help the staff to identify a curriculum problem. Sources for proposed solutions should include the effectiveness literature and the best thinking of the

[19]Center for Social Organization of Schools, *Time on Task: A Research Review* (Baltimore: Center for the Social Organization of Schools, 1983).

[20]W. C. Becker and R. A. Gersten, ''A Follow-up of Follow-Through: The Later Effects of the Direct Instruction Model on Children in Fifth and Sixth Grades,'' *American Educational Research Journal* 19 (Spring 1982): 75–92.

[21]R. S. Brause and J. S. Mayher, ''Teachers, Students, and Classroom Organizations,'' *Research in the Teaching of English* 16, no. 2 (1982): 131–148.

staff itself. If a school is not successful in a certain area, the first place to look for reasons might be the amount of time each teacher is allocating to that content area. After a solution is proposed, a plan outlining staff responsibilities and procedures for evaluating progress should be developed and put into effect.

Central administrators have several mechanisms for coordinating the curriculum. Districtwide testing programs can focus the curriculum on important goals. The practice of focusing on a limited set of goals and aligning these goals with objectives, content, materials, and tests is a powerful tool. However, efforts to coordinate the system from above are insufficient. Enlistment of the faculty in each school will be necessary because different circumstances exist at each site and because staffs need to develop shared values within each school. Principal and teachers must work together to plan, design, and prepare curriculum materials in order for a school to be effective. Rather than imposing school improvement plans from above, administrators should allow individual school faculties sufficient latitude to adapt new policies and practices to their situations, their unique problems. Along with autonomy, the development of group norms requires time for the staff to talk with each other, observe each other, and engage in planning and preparation. There is need both for trust and for the type of communication framework specified in Chapter 9.

As school superintendent, Larry Cuban successfully coordinated the curriculum at his school. However, he also recognized that the concentration on academic achievement and the coordination of the organization with this goal had undesirable consequences.[22] There was a press toward standardization, a uniform curriculum, and adoption of the same materials for each class in a grade level. (Fewer materials were appropriate for the range of individual differences in each of these grade levels.) Teachers tended to assume that there was a single best way of teaching (usually involving lecturing, recitation, and whole-group instruction). Teaching seemed to be focused on tests rather than on teaching students to think. Teachers were forgetting about responsibility for dealing with such serious matters as being sensitive to the welfare of others.

Tightly coupled procedures narrowly focused on standardized tests are a limited answer to the achievement of the broader and more complex goals of education. Major improvement in academic work depends

---

[22]Larry Cuban, ''Effective Schools: A Friendly but Cautionary Note,'' *Phi Delta Kappan* 64, no. 10 (June 1983): 695–697.

on learning (a) to teach higher order tasks that may not lend themselves to direct instruction, (b) to present difficult material so that slower students can learn it, (c) to ensure that subject matter is meaningful to teachers and students, not just material to be memorized for tests.

CONCLUDING COMMENTS

More coherent school programs are needed. Reform by addition—costly innovations and courses for special interest groups—is not as effective as improving the curriculum by setting priorities, focusing on certain subject matter, and abolishing the tracking system in favor of a common core of knowledge. Guidelines have been presented in this chapter for establishing common purposes and making hard choices about what *not* to teach.

As the purposes of schooling change, so must organizational arrangements. When personal interests and social concerns are foremost, the curriculum features flexible scheduling, electives, and minicourses. As the mode turns to challenging students in basic subjects, fewer electives are offered and the requirements for mathematics, science, and English are strengthened. Remedialism and pluralism, however, have not disappeared. Administrators often arrange through networks, magnet schools, and schools within schools to help students with special needs even in the midst of widespread standardization.

Finally, effective schools are characterized by shared values among staff and students. Curriculum development activities within local schools should be conducted and supported in the interest of developing a common vision of what the school is attempting to do for students.

QUESTIONS

1. There is much interest in ensuring that all students have equal access to powerful subject matter. Consider a school known to you. What are the criteria for student access to courses? What do students see as barriers to taking particular courses? On what basis are they assigned to courses? How do they select courses? Is there tracking and, if so, what effect does it have on instruction, content, self-image, aspiration, and preparation for advanced course work?

2. Which of the following are most important in developing a coherent curriculum for a school?
   a. Periodic analysis of course content, difficulty, and achievement
   b. Students and teachers seeing connections and continuity in their course work
   c. Consistency in course content across teachers in terms of texts, topics, assignments, and entrance and exit criteria
3. Consider an educational situation familiar to you and describe whether the following mechanisms were used in order to focus the curriculum: a schoolwide, jointly developed mission statement by which curriculum goals, materials, and methods as well as policies of student promotion and student achievement are reviewed.
4. Shared educational values among administrators, parents, teachers, and students are important to the success of the school. Describe some ways to foster shared values in a local school.
5. How will tests, textbooks, school and classroom organization have to change if understanding, innovation, and creativity are to become the educational target rather than rote tasks?

SELECTED REFERENCES

English, Fenwick W. *Curriculum Management for Schools, Colleges, Business.* Springfield, IL: Charles C Thomas, 1987.

Lieberman, Anne, ed. *Building a Professional Culture in Schools.* New York: Teachers College Press, 1987.

Metz, Mary H. *Different by Design: The Context and Character of three Magnet Schools.* New York: Routledge & Kegan Paul, 1986.

Walbey, Herbert, and Keefe, James W., eds. *Rethinking Reform: The Principal's Dilemma.* Reston, VA: National Association of Secondary Principals, 1986.

Implementing Curriculum Change

The purpose of this chapter is to introduce several approaches for bringing about curriculum change. The strengths and weaknesses of the approaches are also presented. This chapter provides a perspective on such serious issues as whether curriculum change should start with the teacher, with the administrator, with education committees, or professional reformers at local, state, and federal levels. It emphasizes the importance of considering a wide range of conditions in implementing curriculum change, of matching innovation with the realities of the school, teachers' perspectives and abilities, and the prevailing social climate.

One might think that teachers would welcome the opportunity to formulate a curriculum for their classrooms. However, teachers are often reluctant to develop a curriculum and put it into practice for several reasons. They are constrained by lack of time and heavy teaching loads, and they might perceive a resistance to change from parents, peers, or a principal. Even if others are not actually opposed to teachers implementing a new curriculum, the anticipation of resistance might be enough to preclude innovation. Most curriculum innovations do not affect a single classroom, but an entire school or school district. Without the means for developing shared norms and goals, teachers are more interested in planning for their own classroom rather than for the entire school or school district. Hence, it is difficult to effect a school system's curriculum revision through teacher initiation.

Administrators, on the other hand, often feel helpless in initiating a new curriculum, finding it difficult to persuade staff and others to respond enthusiastically and to carry out the proposed changes. It is not easy to control the classroom from outside it. Even when administrators have money to stimulate curriculum improvement, the results are frequently insignificant.

Those who develop curriculum at the state or national level also run into problems. Their first challenge is getting the curriculum adopted. They must clear the political hurdles of textbook committees, curriculum commissions, boards of education, and other groups so that the curriculum can be made available to teachers. Their next, and even larger, challenge is ensuring that their curricula are properly put into effect in the schools. Teachers do not always have clear-cut ideas about the requirements for enacting the curriculum innovations of others. At best, the innovations are only partially implemented. The novel features often are blunted in the effort to twist the innovation into familiar ways of doing things. Top-down planning generally fails because it does not generate the staff commitment necessary for success and the planning does not take into account the special knowledge and suggestions of those who will be responsible for implementing the curriculum.

What understanding and practical suggestions are available to help those who would implement curriculum changes? Some believe that theories of educational change give fresh interpretations of how to achieve it, whereas others distrust solutions, models, and designs for change because they believe these strategies do not correspond with the reality in the schools. Rather than taking a single position on the argument over the need for theories of change or prescriptions for it, we are presenting both.

CONCEPTUALIZATIONS OF THE CHANGE PROCESS

Kinds of Changes and Difficulties in Implementing Them

Scientists who interpret the change process have found it useful to look at five kinds of change.

1 *Substitution.* One element may be substituted for another already present, for example, substituting a new textbook for an old one. This kind of change is readily made.

2. *Alteration.* Alteration occurs when a change is introduced into existing material in the hope that it will appear minor and thus be readily adopted. The curriculum person who modifies the activities accompanying a popular textbook in the interest of student initiative and independence may hamper other classroom objectives.

3. *Perturbations.* These irritating changes are disruptive, but teachers can adjust to them within a fairly short time. Most teachers, for instance, can quite easily make allowances for a change in scheduling of classes and the length of time allowed for teaching.

4. *Restructuring changes.* These changes lead to modification of the system itself. Decentralization and new concepts of the teaching role are examples of restructuring. When students and parents begin to participate in selecting objectives and designing learning opportunities, there is a change in the system.

5. *Value orientation changes.* These are shifts in the fundamental value orientations of participants. When a school begins to be staffed with new teachers who value student personal growth or social reconstruction more than academic achievement, value orientations are changed.

Curriculum workers will find these conceptualizations useful in making decisions regarding the requirements for implementing particular innovations. Before introducing a change, they should classify it and recognize the probable difficulty and consequences. Such anticipation will facilitate planning of the resources necessary to effect the change. Indeed, in some cases, one may decide that the change should not be undertaken.

SOCIOLOGICAL FINDINGS ABOUT CHANGE

Sociologists study stability and changes in organizations. They have found that both formal and informal channels of communication are features of curriculum change. They tell us that most curriculum innovations in a school are borrowed rather than invented. The borrowing may take the form of direct imitation or the importation of new personnel. The former is exemplified by those who visit another school or district to see an innovation, such as a new writing program, and subsequently start a similar one, perhaps avoiding many of the errors and costs associated with the initial development. Observation of results in classroom situations and the exchange of opinions with fellow teachers are also important in getting teachers to change, particularly when the validity of information is in doubt. Importing occurs when a group of persons from a subculture, for example, minority group members not previously represented, become members of the staff.

For teachers, there is little financial incentive for accepting an innovation. Indeed, disadvantages are often associated with such acceptance. The teacher may have to work longer hours in order to make the change and may attract criticism from those who are opposed to it. It is much more comfortable and a lot safer to be conventional most of the time. It is remarkable that many teachers are as open to innovation as they are, considering the basic reward system which discourages risk taking, experimentation, and responsiveness to some pupils.

School administrators are viewed by sociologists as persons in the middle, with little possibility of being primary advocates for major curriculum change. In the formal organization, school administrators must maintain equilibrium among different forces. They cannot alienate significant segments of the public and remain in charge. Thus, institutional change cannot rest mainly with the administrator. Saying that administrators may not be major advocates is not saying that they may not be key figures in innovation. On the contrary, when they are aware of and sympathetic to a change, the innovation tends to prosper. When administrators are uninformed, apathetic, or hostile, an innovation tends to remain outside the school. Implementation of new curriculum is directly related to immediate administrator support. Teachers alone cannot innovate and implement curriculum. Department and grade level faculty, possibly under the direction of a chairperson or team leader and operating with the backing of the principal, often are influential.

One problem in effecting change is the conflict between the school organization and its external environment. Often, tension arises between those who seek to maintain the values of the school staff and those who would respond to the conflicting values of a changing community. A somewhat different situation arises when some want the curriculum to be more responsive to local concerns than to larger relevant social issues. Though there is vigorous interest in local autonomy over curriculum matters, wider sociocultural problems also receive attention and can be a further source of conflict.

Major curriculum decisions are being made at the national level concerning, for example, bilingual education, early childhood education, and special education. Few persons would deny that we should be sensitive to national interests and to the larger society. Professional reformers supported by federal and foundation funding have raised the consciousness of local communities and influenced curriculum change in the interests of the non-English-speaking, the handicapped, and other students. Yet the concept of the school as a community operation is not dead. Most of us sympathize with those who want to see local lay participation in curriculum planning. The school has been one of the few institutions in which a scattered public could recognize itself and express its interests. Because citizens feel remote from many civic, national, and international affairs, it is desirable to preserve those neighborly vehicles by which the individual can influence a crucial public matter. Furthermore, such participation makes possible the innovations and creations that are essential in implementing general plans. The task, therefore, is to find a way to interest the community in curriculum change without jeopardizing the right of pupils to acquire the knowledge, skills, and attitudes necessary for participation in a larger world.

Groups and individuals in the community can also aid in devising supplementary learning situations. They can plan opportunities out of school in which pupils can apply the intellectual skills being taught and can attack those conditions shown to be detrimental to the instructional program. There is a danger that in collaborating with the community, administrators will make incidental functions dominant and respond to pressures that attenuate the systematic organization of learning.

Conditions Conducive to Change

Curriculum change is most likely to occur when one or more of the following conditions exists:

1. A prevailing social change is in the same direction as the proposed change. For instance, when the nation is in technological competition, it is easier to introduce programs in computer literacy than programs for personal enrichment.
2. Imbalance exists in the traditional power structure. The use of "student power" in the late '60s was connected with the availability of new high school and college courses appealing to student interests.
3. A crisis develops. The fact that something has changed in America and that far more children are at risk, including the growing number of young people who hunger for close relationships, is likely to move the curriculum away from a single-minded interest in achievement standards.
4. Faculty and administrators see the change as beneficial to their own interests. A laboratory-developed, effective school program, which was meant to be adapted to the characteristics of each site, had high

impact because it was seen as practical and motivating to teachers and administrators. More important, "it seemed to make good common sense."

5. A change in the physical arrangements of the institution—a new facility, for example—offers the opportunity to rethink curriculum offerings. Seymour Sarason believes that education will never be interesting or intellectually stimulating until schooling takes place in contexts in which knowledge is derived and used in the outside world.[1]

Although any one of the five conditions may be sufficient for introducing a curriculum change, the simultaneous existence of several of the conditions signals a propitious time for introducing change.

STRATEGIES FOR CHANGE

The level at which a proposed change originates—federal, state, district, school, classroom—determines the strategy for change. Top-down strategies are associated with mandates from the federal and state governments: desegregation, programs for the handicapped and non-English-speaking persons, competency testing, and required course offerings. The implementation of districtwide curriculum policies about goals, content, materials, and testing also use these strategies. Top-down strategies range from merely issuing the decree and requiring accountability reports or visits to help with the school's requirements for staff development, materials, and other support in implementing the mandate.

Bottom-up strategies are found when the local school is the origin of change, the faculty itself examines the school's problems, considers alternatives, and takes action to better the situation.

Top-Down Strategies

Top-down strategies are technological. Improvement is sought by training teachers in new techniques and holding them accountable for following these techniques. A change in some part of the technology of the school, such as a testing program, computers, and mastery learning, is the most likely element open to immediate influence from outside the school. However, unless other elements of the school, i.e., the teachers'

---

[1]Seymour Sarason, *Schooling in America* (New York: The Free Press, 1983).

STRATEGIES FOR CHANGE □ 223

own views of what education should be or the norms of the school, are compatible with the innovation, a technological change is likely to be circumvented or temporary. A researcher was once puzzled trying to understand a school's curriculum plan. Although there seemed to be careful monitoring of pupil progress, well-stated goals, and reams of paper showing compliance with the mandated program, his own observation of the daily life in the school revealed qualities very different from those in the accountability plan. Only when teachers privately commented, ''Oh, you're talking about our official plan—the one we prepared for funding and accreditation—not our real one,'' did he understand. Often the return to a previous equilibrium follows an attempt to change some part of the technology of the school.

Research and Development

The research and development (R and D) model has been popular among those concerned with implementing curriculum throughout a region or nation. The strategy takes programs, research, and projects from universities, regional laboratories, and other institutions and disseminates them as an innovative packages of materials or products. Effective diffusion requires that the consumers be aware of potential benefits and usefulness of the innovation. Influential persons in the schools must be convinced that the innovation will strengthen the school.

The strategy makes use of an aide who first performs the role of salesperson and later of trainer, teaching key school personnel about the program so that they can train others: the *multiplier effect*. The innovator, together with school leaders, monitors and assists with problems that arise during initial installation.

Criticism of the adoption model centers on its lack of attention to political factors that might interfere with acceptance. A teachers' union, for example, might oppose the change because of increased paperwork. Mammoth curriculum innovations often leave their advocators frustrated. The planned treatments become distorted, lacking in standardization when used by teachers and pupils with different backgrounds. Variation among schools often wipe out any noticeable effect of the innovation, making it difficult to say with certainty that the change is valuable.

Multiple Element Strategies

Efforts to improve the R and D model have been made by giving more attention to political, social, and economic factors. Accordingly, researcher and developer conduct participatory activity *with* the school community rather than provide answers *for* the school community.

The newer top-down strategies try to overcome the limitation of ''single element change by acting upon three organizational elements—social norms, teacher perceptions, and the technology to be introduced.'' Susan Loucks and Ann Lieberman, who have long been engaged in curriculum implementation, use three key concepts in addressing teacher perception and the technology[2]:

Developmentalism. Developmentalism refers to the way teachers change as they confront new ideas. It means giving different kinds of help to teachers at different stages in the change process. As teachers implement new curriculum, they change in their feelings about the new ideas. At first, they are self-oriented: ''Can I do it?'' ''What will I have to do differently?'' Later they are task-oriented: ''It takes so long to prepare.'' And still later, after mastering the new procedure, they focus on the impact of the curriculum: ''Is this new curriculum working well with all my students?'' ''Are there ways I can make it better?''

One implication of developmentalism in effecting change is to follow a sequence in ordering training activities. First, focus on personal concerns, clarifying expectations and planning for individual input and consultation. Second, attend to management concerns, modeling and giving hands-on training, and answering questions, and third, reflect on the impact of the innovation and how to improve upon it.

Participation. Participation is related to the need for understanding how teachers see their work. When teachers participate in decision making during the process of implementation, there is a greater probability of success. Trust between those encouraging the innovation—superintendent, principal—is a necessary starting point. Peer demonstrations, observation of others, and team planning are all forms of participation that contribute to a mutual adaptation to a change.

Support. Different kinds of support are needed at various times in the implementation process. Material support is of primary importance initially. Human support—ensuring that parents, administrators, peers, students view the change favorably—is very important at all stages. Time

---

[2]Susan F. Loucks and Ann Lieberman, ''Curriculum Implementation,'' in *Fundamental Curriculum Decisions*, ASCD Yearbook, ed. F. W. English. (Alexandria, VA: ASCD, 1983), pp. 126–141.

for teachers to plan, confer, demonstrate, critique, and revise is also critical. Three to five years must be allowed for the implementation of a complex innovation. One year may be needed to learn which innovation is appropriate and to assess what changes it would bring in a particular school. Teachers need to learn whose help is required and what skills are to be acquired. Curriculum change requires organizational changes, particularly in the staff and students. The shift in roles is often difficult for both. For example, I once visited a classroom where a teacher was trying to implement a curriculum that required interaction among pupils. The furniture had been arranged to accommodate the small group work demanded by the new materials. The teacher, however, had not recognized the need for changing from a didactic role to a resource role. Consequently, the teacher was frustrated in ability to control the attention of pupils working in groups with the new materials.

Bottom-Up Strategies

Bottom-up strategies of change start locally. The change agents may attempt to get a school staff to look at its problems and to consider options as a means of bringing about innovation in the curriculum or they may start with individual teacher-innovators who contact other teachers, forming teacher-to-teacher networks of change. Examples of bottom-up strategies follow:

The Integrative Development Strategy. The strategy in the integrative development model is to handle the immediate concerns of teachers and then move out of the classroom, perhaps even to reorganize the school system. An assumption underlying this approach is that a climate for eliminating clouded vision and fears must accompany change. The model encourages involvement by starting with the concerns teachers face. The first step in the strategy is to help teachers identify their problems. The problems selected, however, should be within the competence of the teacher. The second step is to study the cause of the difficulties. Using the analysis of the teachers' data, the curriculum leader introduces the teachers to new insights and abilities. The integration of theory with the analysis of problems stimulates bolder departures and the transition of general ideas into practice.

A sequential process begins as faculties cope with change. First, people talk about the possibility of bringing about change. Expectations rise and there is uneasiness as teachers feel the pressure to act. Second, some teachers begin to take action. Third, justification for the new departure brings: "Why was I doing this?" "Is the new system better than what I did before?" Fourth, problems with the innovation arise and teachers question the basic assumptions of the program: "What is the relevancy of the program for my students?" "Is the program consistent with educational goals?"

Difficulties with the approach include a lack of time and expertise on the innovator's part both to handle human relations and to relate the theory to the specific problems each situation develops in adapting the innovations. Changes in teacher attitudes and skills take time. An experimental attitude is especially slow to develop at first. Also, there are teachers who feel insecure about engaging in group problem solving. To lessen such problems, productive groups should be composed of persons with good social skills and expertise in several areas: the curriculum, the principles of learning, the realities of the classroom, pertinent subject matter, inquiry skills, and interpersonal relations.

Teacher as as Agent of Change. The teacher as an agent of change was proposed long ago by Hilda Taba.[3] She wanted curriculum making to start by teachers planning specific units of instruction. The results of experimentation with these units would provide a basis for a general design to be created later.

A recent demonstration of the value of a teacher as an agent of change is found in IMPACT II, an experimental teacher-to-teacher network. The Exxon Education Foundation created a program by which teachers who wanted to refine classroom innovations could receive "developer" grants of $300. Other teachers who would try out the developer's innovations could apply for "replicator" grants of $200. About 500 grants were made. Each developer chose a particular innovation to refine; the only restriction was that the project must focus on classroom instruction. Informal interchanges were made among teachers through the network. Teachers met other teachers and had opportunities to be trained and to train others and to visit other schools and be visited. Publishing their ideas, receiving college credit, and gaining recognition were important factors in the success of the program. The evaluation of this program was positive. There were significant changes in the instructional procedures after participation in the program; the work of the teachers was disseminated and attitudes toward teaching improved.

---

[3]Hilda Taba, *Curriculum Development—Theory and Practice* (New York: Harcourt, Brace and World, 1962).

Middle-Up Strategy

Top-down strategies for curriculum improvement rely on extrinsic rewards such as recognition, career advancement, and the threat of sanctions for noncompliance. Bottom-up strategies presuppose an individual or group disposition to change. Critics of the bottom-up approach argue that the culture of schools is inherently conservative and an unlikely source for transforming ideas. When left to their own devices, school staffs often choose innovations of low quality.[4] Karen Louis and Robert Dently propose a middle road. Their strategy assumes the school to be the appropriate unit of change as opposed to strategies that try to introduce identical changes in all schools and strategies that focus on meeting the needs of individual teachers. In contrast, the middle-up strategy is school-focused in the sense that local conditions influence the change. The main elements of the middle-up strategy are:

1. to help staff attend to new information from the outside, capitalizing on incentives for change,
2. to encourage teachers to consider ways to apply the new information with the idea that their cognitive understandings are changed and developed during the process, making information usable,
3. to arrange for the spread of the new ideas by giving opportunities for the staff to share their understandings,
4. to stimulate diffusion of new ideas by giving information to people both within the school and outside the school.

Suggestions for Successful Implementation Through Staff Development

Newer views on staff development, along with modified organizational and role expectations, are among the best answers to curriculum implementation. Curriculum innovations that rely heavily on technology tend to be short-lived. Unlike business or industry, which seeks to eliminate the need for human services, education is a labor-intensive field, which requires teachers more than machines. Hence, a key to educational change must include staff development.

Staff development is now a central focus in successful curriculum

---

[4]Karen S. Louis and Robert A. Dentley, ''Knowledge Use and School Improvement,'' in *Curriculum Inquiry* 18, no. 1 (1988): 33–62.

implementation. As a result of recent studies, staff development is taking the following directions.

Intensive *staff development* rather than single one-day workshops is an important strategy. Staff development is seen as part of curriculum planning tied to a school site. The principal serves as the instructional leader, strengthening the school curriculum by clearly encouraging teachers to take responsibility for their professional growth. *Staff training* activities are specific, such as instruction in carrying out a new reading program or introducing new mathematical material. This contrasts with many old in-service programs in which training activities were isolated from the teachers' day-to-day responsibilities, thus having little impact. There are also *support activities.* So that staff training can result in more than transient effects, the contributions of staff training must be reinforced and extended through (a) classroom assistance by resource personnel and outside consultants (provided these resource persons are perceived by teachers as being helpful) and (b) project meetings whereby teachers learn to adapt the new curriculum to the realities of the particular school and classroom. In addition to feedback between users and consultants, peer discussions seem to be vital for working through the problems of innovation.

Curriculum innovation may require a change in the principal's role. Teachers follow a new curriculum more closely when the principal plays an active role in the implementation; a new curriculum does not flourish when the principal remains in an office, verbalizes support, and lets the teachers struggle with the problems.

Active involvement of the teachers in the developmental process (in developing guides and materials) is more important in persuading teachers to implement plans than their participation on the curriculum committees that decide on the plan. The roles of students and parents as decision makers in relation to the degree of implementation have been largely unstudied.

Central policy makers should emphasize programs with wide support and provide a base for the local development of the specific forms of implementation. Social experimentation should be encouraged during implementation to develop variants that are more appropriate in particular circumstances.

We should recognize that although professional reformers are rewarded for proposing controversial, innovative curriculum changes, school practitioners are usually rewarded for innovations that promote social stability. Therefore, professional reformers are likely to be frustrated in their efforts to persuade schools to implement controversial curricula.

In order to illuminate the problems that come with curriculum implementation, one need only reflect on these considerations: What is the desirable number of new curriculum installations for any one year? What should be the timing of installations and requisite experience of the staff? Must there be agreement on humanistic, technological, and subject matter orientations? What relationships between administrators and teachers are necessary? In what way does a school district's history of innovation efforts influence the decision to innovate?

Networking for School Renewal

Collaborative networks for developing new programs and new curricula are increasing. Networks are mechanisms for linking practitioners, researchers, and policy makers sharing information and giving mutual support for change. One of the first networks was the Metropolitan School Study Counsel of Teachers' College Columbia University, which involved Teachers' College with thirty-seven school districts. The course set yearly goals and activities and arranged workshops and meetings relevant to improvement of the curriculum.

John Goodlad has promoted nationally a Network for Educational Renewal involving universities and their nearby school districts to confront long-established practices that must be changed; a network for school improvement has been formed in the vast Pacific region coordinated by the Northwest Laboratory; and various large school districts have their own networks that bring together schools and the district for purposes of improvement.

Beatrice Ward has identified four characteristics of such collaborations[5]:

1. Variety. All participating agencies are potential locales for improvement. The expertise that can be brought by each agency is given to problems of mutual concern.
2. Problem focus. Efforts are focused on resolving problems that are

---

[5]Beatrice A. Ward, "Collaboration: A Vehicle for Educational Improvement and Professional Development," in *Strengthening the Role of the University in School Improvement* (Urbana, IL: University of Illinois, 1985).

seen as persistent and important by all participants, not merely problems that are of interest to researchers.

3. Responsibility. Collaborators assume responsibility for carrying out the required research, development, and evaluation.
4. Context relevance. The collaboration focuses upon change in the schools and classrooms of the participants. However, accounts of networking indicate that they fail more often than they succeed, and that they require continuous investment of time and energy on the part of each member.

In his reflection on a successful partnership between a university and a number of school districts, community colleges and educational offices, Paul Heckman concluded that inquiry in each school is necessary but that the process is enhanced by the knowledge of researchers. Heckman's conditions for school renewal are[6]:

1. Norms and support mechanisms must exist outside a single school; hence, the justification for a network.
2. Renewal and change effort should focus on the school rather than on nonschool problems.
3. The conventional wisdom of the schools must be challenged. The network is not merely to promote change but to stimulate thinking about fundamental problems.
4. Each solution to a problem affects other aspects of the school. A change in curriculum activity requires a change in method of evaluation.
5. Teachers need help in eliciting their beliefs, in uncovering their tacit knowledge, and in considering alternative viewpoints.
6. Collaborative renewal gives university researchers access to knowledge from school contexts and allows teachers to draw upon disciplines in resolving practical problems. Presumably participants will ground their discussion in a variety of knowledge-seeking procedures, not only those procedures claiming to be scientific.

Introducing New Materials into the Classroom

Ronald Lippitt long ago gave us a model that has proven to be effective in introducing new materials and activities.[7] Lippitt is one of the few

---

[6]Paul Heckman, ''Understanding School Cultures,'' in *The Ecology of School Renewal*, NSSE Yearbook (Chicago: The University of Chicago Press, 1987), pp. 63–79.

[7]Ronald Lippitt, ''Processes of Curriculum Change,'' in *Curriculum Change: Direction and Process* (Washington, DC: ASCD, 1966), pp. 43–59.

to show the importance of involving pupils in the change and to specify the aspects that lead to greater teacher acceptance and use of innovations. If the following guidelines for curriculum committees were followed, our schools would be using more effective curriculum materials.

Student Use of New Material. The decisions students make about their involvement with a new curriculum are the most crucial in the process of curriculum change. Such decisions are determined by *internal supports.* If students perceive the learning opportunity as relevant to their values, interests, and curiosities and if they receive feedback from their responses, they are more likely to learn from the material and experience the excitement of active search and discovery. Other determinants of student involvement are *external supports.* The innovator must take into account peer norms about student participation and cooperation in working with the teacher. Teachers also need to be aware of student norms and to be willing to share leadership with student leaders if students are to become involved. Also, the extent of collaboration of parents and other adults in the community influences student involvement with the changed curriculum.

Teacher Use of New Material. In order to get teachers to use the new curriculum, it is recommended that the curriculum leader first involve the teacher in the review, evaluation, and exploration of the new materials. This means asking teachers to apply criteria for the evaluation of learning opportunities and objectives. Second, the teacher should have freedom to explore the new skills needed for using the curriculum material, to learn new concepts and new techniques, and to collaborate with colleagues in sharing practices and learning together. Third, the curriculum changes must equip teachers with the tools for observing their classes' responses and student involvement in adapting the curriculum.

Adoption of New Material. A curriculum committee's adoption decision should include involvement of appropriate decision makers in a review of the alternatives. There should be a review of the criteria to be used in making the decision and a plan to test alternatives, to judge feasibility, and to learn about the learners' responses to the material and method. Learners should be involved in evaluating the new materials. It is important that adoption committees analyze the needs for staff development that would follow if the materials were adopted.

The Search for Curriculum Innovations. In searching for new ideas, curriculum planners should start with the *home school,* recognizing the creative curricula hidden within the school community. Next, planners should consider *neighboring school systems* and break down the barriers that keep neighbors from sharing. Finally, curriculum workers should obtain information regarding promising innovations. Clearing house procedures for identifying creative innovations should be used to obtain information. The National Bank of Validated Programs available through the U.S. Department of Education, The National Diffusion Network, and the report of the Council for Educational Research and Development are examples of such sources. Also, innovators should be asked about their latest experiments, discoveries, failures, problems, and skills needed to carry out changes in curriculum.

Distribution of New Curriculum. Diffusion of curriculum rests heavily on the staff development available for the teachers. Teachers must have the opportunity to learn the skills for using the new curriculum. They should also have the opportunity to get excited about new materials and to adapt them.

Development of New Materials. New material may be developed through the work of a team in a school system, the creative efforts of a single teacher, or the project staff of a research and development center. Curriculum development requires identifying priority objectives and core units of knowledge, and relating content to experience, interests, and competence of learners. Teachers should be helped to understand and use the resources skillfully and to evaluate the materials so that the curriculum may continue to improve.

CONCLUDING COMMENTS

A number of issues have been raised. One issue arises in the approach to innovative curriculum: Should it be from the teacher-student viewpoint, the developer's orientation toward the product, or the professional reformers? Recommendations that call for the involvement of students, parents, and community members in school curriculum development, staff problem-solving approaches, and the teacher as an agent of change favor one side of the issue. The manipulation of organization, social structure, competency-based approaches, and R and D adoption models favor the other side. Reformers and R and D developers want teachers to implement a focused curriculum in predetermined ways, although teachers may advise and indicate the factors that must be attended to in order to achieve objectives of a specific plan. Those with a teacher-student perspective assume that users should at least have a hand in deciding which innovations to implement and how to implement them.

Tension develops between those external to the school who would impose innovations that foster greater rationality in the curriculum and those who see merit in individual teachers acting responsibly, making their curriculum decisions in the best interests of their students. One answer is to use strategies of change that attempt to match curriculum innovations to the school and have the faculties adapt the innovation to their local conditions. Another answer might be to help teachers create a new social climate that will support the change.

A second issue relates to the value of theories in guiding the implementation process. Disenchantment with a single model of change probably rests on the fact that most settings for curriculum implementation are for specific situations. In one case, the social environment or policy may be crucial in effecting the change. In another, group dynamics or individual personalities may be more important. If such differences exist, then broadly conceived models of change and histories of innovations should be in the curriculum specialist's repertoire.

Finally, the frequent triviality and faddish nature of curriculum changes effected from both outside and inside the school indicate the continuous need to consider the value of proposed innovations. Decision makers should be sure that a proposed curriculum can best serve a specified group of learners or aid general education; contribute to interpretive or applied purposes; be relevant to the world the students will live in when they finish school; and relate to the other domains of knowledge that are supposed to be provided by the school experience.

QUESTIONS

1. Preparing effective curriculum materials is costly. Without broad dissemination, the impact of the materials is minimal. How can broad dissemination best occur?
2. Give examples for each of the following kinds of curriculum changes: substitution, alteration, restructuring of the system, value orientation.
3. Consider the relative strengths and weaknesses of the R and D adop-

tion model and the integrative development model of curriculum change. Can you indicate how both models can be used together or when one or the other model might be more useful?

4. What kinds of curriculum changes do you think can best occur at national, state, district, school, and classroom levels?

5. Consider the curriculum in a situation familiar to you. How would you like to see this curriculum changed? How would you try to bring about the desired change?

6. Describe a situation in which one or more of the following conditions exists: a social climate conducive to change, an imbalance in the power structure, a crisis, an element of self-interest, or a facilities modification. Be specific about the condition. What kind of curriculum change could be successfully implemented in view of the condition(s) described?

SELECTED REFERENCES

Dalton, T. H. *The Challenge of Curriculum Innovation: A Study Ideology and Practice.* Philadelphia: Falmer Press, 1988.

The Ecology of School Renewal, 86th Yearbook of NSSE, Part 1, ed. John Goodlad. Chicago: The University of Chicago Press, 1987.

Griffin, Gary A. "Leadership for Curriculum Improvement," NSSE Yearbook. Chicago: The University of Chicago Press, 1989.

Lieberman, Ann. *Rethinking School Improvements: Research Craft and Concept.* New York: Teachers College Press, 1986.

Lieberman, Ann, ed. *Building a Professional Culture in Schools.* New York: Teachers College Press, 1988.

10

Evaluating the Curriculum

Curriculum evaluation generates a host of responses. Some fear the power and control it might give central authorities. Local communities have been dismayed by those in government who seem to offer autonomy, yet still demand that the school system be evaluated by standardized tests. Others are reassured by the evaluations. People often expect that evaluation will solve many pressing problems—the public who demands accountability, the decision maker who chooses curriculum alternatives, the developer who needs to know where and how to improve the curriculum product, and the teacher who is concerned about the effect of learning opportunities on individual students all look to evaluation for their answers.

The field of evaluation is full of different views about its purposes and how it is to be carried out. Humanists argue that measurable outcomes form an insufficient basis for determining the quality of learning opportunities. They believe it is simplistic to measure higher mental functioning, knowledge of self, and other life-long pursuits at the end of the school year. Curiously, they have no difficulty in evaluating the classroom environment. For them, the learning experience is important in itself, not just a rehearsal whose value will be known only on future performance. On the other hand, technologists perceive evaluation as a set of verified guidelines for practice. They believe that if curriculum workers use these procedures, essential decisions regarding what and how to teach will be more warranted.

David Hamilton has summarized the ideas and events in curriculum evaluation during the past 150 years, illuminating its relatively unchanging features.[1] According to him, curriculum evaluation falls within the sphere of practical morality. As such, it responds to both the ethical question, "What should we do?" and the empirical question, "What can we do?" He recognizes, too, that the importance of evaluation is heightened by social change and politics. Governments make evaluation compulsory, and curriculum evaluation can be seen as part of the struggle by different interest groups—educationalists, teachers, administrators, industrialists—to gain control over the forces that shape the practice of schooling. When more than one person is involved in the selection of criteria for use in an evaluation, agreement cannot be assumed.

Recently, debate has begun over the conduct of curriculum evaluation and over the particular evaluation model to be used. Technologists use *consensus* models and regard evaluation as a technical accomplishment—the demonstration of a connection between what is and what all agree ought to be. They require a consensus on educational goals and on the rules of evidence. If all agree on the ends, the selection and evaluation of appropriate means are only technical problems for them. In reality, technologists have been most active in determining achievement in basic skills and academic knowledge.

Social reconstructionists and humanists have a *pluralistic* view of evaluation. This view holds that evaluators should be sensitive to the different values of program participants and should shift the judgment away from the evaluator to the participants. As evaluators, pluralists tend to base their evaluations more on program activity than on program intent and to accept anecdotal accounts and other naturalistic data rather than numerical data and experimental designs. For them, evaluation is an unfinished blueprint that can point out problems, not solutions. They are more concerned with the fairness of the evaluation than with its effectiveness as measured by changes in test scores, for example. Hence, those with a pluralistic bent advocate handing over control of an evaluation to those who have to live with the consequences and having it conducted *by* the participants rather than *for* the participants.

This chapter shows how to match specific evaluation procedures with specific curriculum decisions, such as how to improve a course, how to decide which program should continue, and how to assess the long-term effects of the curriculum. A major issue raised is whether cur-

---

[1]David Hamilton, "Making Sense of Curriculum Evaluation: Continuities and Discontinuities in an Educational Idea," in *Review of Research in Education*, ed. Lee S. Schulman (Itasca, IL: F. E. Peacock Publishers, 1979), pp. 318–349.

riculum evaluation is best served by classic research models and experts in measurement or by adaptable procedures in which students and teachers judge their own curriculum.

In addition to offering information about a number of evaluation techniques, the chapter covers common errors that prejudice evaluative studies and make it difficult to judge the relative effects of different programs. After studying the material, students should be able to take a personal stand regarding controversial technical issues on the role and form of objectives used in evaluation, the value of criterion-referenced and norm-referenced tests, and evaluation and invasion of privacy.

MODELS FOR EVALUATION

Consensus Models

In a general sense, curriculum evaluation to a technologist is an attempt to throw light on two questions: (1) Do planned learning opportunities, programs, courses, and activities as developed and organized actually produce desired results? and (2) How can the curriculum offerings best be improved? These general questions and the procedures for answering them translate a little differently at macro levels (for example, evaluating the citywide results from several alternative reading programs) than at micro levels (evaluating the effect of a teacher's instructional plans for achieving course objectives). Classroom teachers often have an additional set of evaluation questions to guide them in making decisions about individuals:

1. *Placement.* At which level of learning should the learner be placed in order to challenge but not frustrate?
2. *Mastery.* Has the learner acquired enough competency to succeed in the next level?
3. *Diagnosis.* What particular difficulty is this learner experiencing?

Decisions and Evaluative Techniques. If evaluation is to provide information useful to decision makers, evaluative models should be chosen in light of the kind of decisions to be made. In this connection, a useful distinction can be made between formative and summative evaluation. Formative evaluation is undertaken to improve an existing program. Hence the evaluation must provide frequent detailed and specfic information to guide the program developers. Summative evaluation is done to assess the effect of a completed program. It provides information to use in deciding whether to continue, discontinue, or disseminate the program. Summative evaluation is frequently undertaken in order to decide which one of several competing programs or materials is best.

Guidelines for conducting formative evaluation have been given by Lee J. Cronbach in a classic article treating *course improvement* through evaluation. The following prescriptions are among the most important:

1. Seek data regarding changes produced in pupils by the course.
2. Look for multidimensional outcomes and map out the effects of the course along these dimensions separately.
3. Identify aspects of the course in which revisions are desirable.
4. Collect evidence midway in curriculum development, while the course is still fluid.
5. Try to find out how the course produces its effect and what factors influence its effectiveness. You may find that the teacher's attitude toward the learning opportunity is more important than the opportunity itself.
6. During trial stages, use the teacher's informal reports of observed pupil behavior in aspects of the course.
7. Make more systematic observations, but only after the more obvious flaws in the early stages have been dealt with.
8. Make a process study of events taking place in the classroom, and use proficiency and attitude measures to reveal changes in pupils.
9. Observe several results of the new program ranging far beyond the content of the curriculum itself—attitudes, general understanding, aptitude for further learning, and so forth.[2]

Formative evaluation does not require all pupils to answer the same questions. Rather, as many questions as possible should be given, each to a different sample of pupils. Follow-up studies to elicit opinions regarding the ultimate educational contributions of the course are of minor value in improving the course because they are too far removed in time.

Summative evaluation has several purposes. One purpose is to select from several competing curriculum programs or projects those which should continue and those which are ineffective. To this end, an experimental design is highly desirable. James Popham has illustrated such designs.[3] There is the *pretest/posttest control group design*. As the design's

---

[2]Lee J. Cronbach, ''Course Improvement Through Evaluation,'' *Teachers College Record* 64, no. 3 (May 1963): 672–683.

[3]W. James Popham, *Educational Evaluation*, ed. 2 (Englewood Cliffs, NJ: Prentice-Hall, 1988).

name suggests, students are pretested on whatever dimensions are sought from the programs. Then, after receiving instruction, students in each of the competing programs are tested for their status on a common set of objectives for which each program claims superiority. The posttest must not be biased in favor of one program's objectives. Objectives important to others, but not those of the designers of a particular program, can also be assessed.

The students are assigned to the programs randomly so that each student has an equal chance to be assigned to any one of them. Differences in the performance of students may be attributed to differences in the programs. However, evaluators may not always know whether the respective programs were carried out as planned. It is desirable to try each of the programs in many settings, because the experimental unit for analysis is likely to be schools or classrooms, not pupils. Only in experiments in which the pupils in the same classrooms receive different programs can the pupil be the unit of analysis.

Evaluators should not allow ideas about what must happen in a perfect evaluation to discourage them; they should remember that no evaluations have been perfect. When faced with frustrations such as student absenteeism or the failure to give tests, they should remember that the curriculum evaluator is only responsible for providing the best information possible under existing circumstances.

Purposes of Evaluation. One purpose of evaluation is to decide on the value of a curricular intervention within a course. An *interrupted time series design* is useful for this purpose. In this design, a series of measurements are taken both before and after the introduction of the intervention. Unobtrusive records—absences, disciplinary referrals, requests for transfer—are frequently used with this design, although test scores and other data can also serve. A significant difference in pupil performance during and after the intervention may be taken as evidence that the intervention had a positive effect.

Another important purpose of evaluation is to decide on the long-term value of curriculum offerings. Longitudinal or follow-up studies are undertaken to indicate whether desired objectives are being realized and to reveal shortcomings. One of the better known longitudinal studies was conducted on a national level in Project Talent. This project was initiated in 1960 with the testing of 400,000 secondary school students. Such data as student interests, ability scores, and characteristics of a student's school, including courses offered, were collected. Fifteen years later, a representative sample of these persons was interviewed, and they reported on their satisfaction with their current status on different life activities. One overall generalization from the findings was that educational programs should be improved and modified to enable persons to achieve greater satisfaction in intellectual development and personal understanding.[4] Another example of the findings from Project Talent studies is that, whereas in 1960, 47 percent of the graduating boys and 38 percent of the girls said their courses were not helpful in preparing them for occupations, eleven years later 46 percent of the men and 40 percent of the women felt that high school had been adequate at best.

National Assessment of Educational Progress (NAEP) is an information system designed to furnish information regarding the educational achievements of children, youth, and young adults and to indicate both the progress we are making and the problems we face. Unlike Project Talent, NAEP does not follow individual progress but samples different age groups. The project assesses a variety of curriculum areas. Information on factors that affect student performance is also provided. Test results are reported by age and grade level. Parents, school board members, legislators, and school officials all find the information useful.

An illustration of how the NAEP illuminates problems is the 1989 finding that students have improved their verbal and mathematical skills in the past 20 years, but most cannot apply them to complex intellectual tasks. In reading, 61 percent of seventeen-year-olds cannot find, understand, summarize, or explain complicated information. In math, 49 percent of seventeen-year-olds cannot compute with decimals, fractions, and percentages, recognize geometric figures, or solve simple equations, whereas 94 percent cannot solve multistep problems or use basic algebra. In science, 93 percent cannot infer relationships and draw conclusions using detailed scientific knowledge. The report calls for less emphasis on memorization and more on the promotion of thinking. "Teachers will need to act more as guides, and students more as doers and thinkers."[5] Because NAEP influences school curriculum, the National Academy at Harvard University warns that schools should not teach to the NAEP tests and that textbooks on curriculum should not be adjusted to reflect them. To use such tests for comparing different states can be misleading because state populations differ.

---

[4]John C. Flanagan, *Perspectives on Improving Education* (Los Alamitos, CA: Southwest Regional Laboratory for Educational Research and Development, 1979).

[5]*Crossroads in American Education* (Princeton, NJ: *National Assessment of Educational Progress*, 1989).

Evaluating a Curriculum Project. Technologists evaluate a curriculum project by assessing (a) the merits of its goals, (b) the quality of its plans, (c) the extent to which the plans can be carried out, and (d) the value of the outcomes. Illustrative of such models is the CIPP (Context, Input, Process, Product) model developed by Dan Stufflebeam and others.[6] In the *context* phase of evaluation, the evaluator focuses upon defining the environment, describing the desired and actual conditions and identifying the problems (needs assessment). *Input* refers to the selection of strategies to achieve the educational objectives. Once a strategy has been selected, a *process* evaluation provides feedback to the implementer about faults in the design and the implementation. Finally, a *product* evaluation is undertaken to reveal the effects of the selected strategy on the curriculum.

In his analytical review of evaluation, David Nevo summarized in question and answer form the nature of consensual models and approaches:

1. What is evaluation? Educational evaluation is a systematic description of educational objects (projects, programs, materials, curriculum, and institutions) and an assessment of their worth.
2. What is the function of evaluation? Evaluation can serve four different functions: (a) formative (for improvement), (b) summative (for selecting and accountability), (c) sociopolitical (to motivate and gain public support), and (d) administrative (to exercise authority).
3. What kinds of information should be collected? Evaluators should collect information about the goals of the object, its strategies and plans, the process of implementation, and the outcome and impacts.
4. What criteria should be used to judge the merits of an object? In judging the worth of an educational object, consider whether or not the object (a) responds to identified needs of clients; (b) achieves national goals, ideals, or social values; (c) meets agreed upon standards; (d) does better than alternative objects; and (e) achieves important stated goals.
5. What is the *process* of doing an evaluation? The process should include three activities: (a) focusing on the problems, (b) collecting and analyzing empirical data, and (c) communicating findings to evaluate audience.
6. Who should do evaluations? Individuals or teams who have (a) com-

---

[6]William J. Webster, "CIPP in Local Evaluation," in *Applied Strategies for Curriculum Evaluation,* ed. Ronald Brandt (Alexandria, VA: ASCD, 1981), pp. 48–57.

petency in research methods and other data analysis techniques, (b) an understanding of the social context and the unique substance of the evaluation object, (c) an ability to maintain correct human relations and rapport with those involved, and (d) a conceptual framework to integrate the above mentioned capabilities.

7. By what standards should an evaluation be judged? Evaluation should strike for a balance in meeting standards of (a) utility (useful and practical), (b) accuracy (technically adequate), (c) possibility (realistic and prudent), (d) propriety (conducted legally and ethically).[7]

Pluralistic Models

Evaluation models with the pluralistic concern of humanists and social reconstructionists have had as yet a relatively limited impact. Pluralistic procedures are less frequently used than the research and technological procedures applied by teachers in course improvement, by school managers in rational decision making, by government evaluators in auditing new social programs in the schools, and by statewide evaluators in monitoring the curriculum for accountability purposes.

Pluralistic evaluation models tend to be used only when research and technological models are less attractive for reasons of politics, cost, or practicality. These newer models are chiefly used with curriculum that is out of the mainstream and is associated with aesthetic education, multicultural projects, and alternative schools. Pluralistic models are also increasing in supplementary experimental designs.

Responsive Evaluation. Robert E. Stake was one of the first evaluators to propose the pluralist argument that the evaluator should make known the criteria or standards that are being employed and who holds them. As a pluralist, Stake believes that sensitivity to the perceived needs of those concerned with the evaluation is essential. Accordingly, he urges initial evaluations to discover what clients and participants actually want from the program evaluation. These concerns should be discovered prior to designing the evaluation project. Stake places less emphasis on precisely specified objectives than do technologists, because he wishes to describe all intentions, even those not expressed in terms of student

---

[7]David Nevo, ''The Conceptualization of Educational Evaluation,'' *Review of Educational Research* 53, no. 11 (Spring 1983): 117–128.

learning. The key emphasis in his model is on description and judgment. For him, an evaluator should report the ways different people see the curriculum. Hence, the evaluator's principal activities include discovering what those concerned want to know, making observations, and gathering multiple judgments about the observed antecedents, transactions, and outcomes. A variety of persons—outside experts, journalists, psychologists—as well as teachers and students may participate in the conduct of the evaluation.

The Connoisseurship Model.   Elliot W. Eisner has argued for an evaluation process that will capture a richer slice of educational life than test scores do.[8] One of his procedures is educational criticism in which an evaluator asks such questions as ''What has happened during the school year in a given school? What were the key events? How did they come into being? How did students and teachers participate? What were the consequences? How could the events be strengthened? What do such events enable children to learn?''

Other vehicles for disclosing the richness of programs, according to Eisner, are films, videotapes, photography, and taped student and teacher interviews. These tools useful in portraying aspects of school life are valuable channels for communication when supplemented by critical narrative.

Connoisseurship is involved in noting what is and is not said, how it is said, its tone, and other factors that indicate meaning.

Another procedure recommended by Eisner is the analysis of work produced by children, including a critique to help evaluators understand what has been accomplished and to reveal some of the realities of classroom performance.

The fundamental thesis of the connoisseur approach is that the problem of communicating to some of the public, such as parent, board, state agencies, about what has happened in school (the good and the bad) can be usefully conceived as an artistic problem. In such an approach an evaluator fashions an expressive picture of educational practice and its consequences.

Connoisseurship and criticism are ways of seeing rather than ways of measuring and have been criticized as abstruse technology which re-

---

[8]Elliot W. Eisner, *The Educational Imagination on the Design and Evaluation of School Programs* (New York: Macmillan, 1985).

quires special training in acquiring "interpretive maps" and ways to understand the meaning of what has been said. Judgments are established externally by the nature of artistic virtues and tradition. This approach, though informative and highly adaptive to unique local conditions, is subjective and thus potentially controversial.

Evaluation as Critical Inquiry. Kenneth Sirotnik is a pluralist who believes that evaluation requires multiple perspectives on what constitutes knowledge by people in the school. For him, evaluation is rigorous *self-examination*, a process of critical inquiry. Critical inquiry is a dialectic using such questions as

What goes on in the name of X (any curriculum practice)?
How did it come to be that way?
Whose interests are and are not served by the way things are?
What information and knowledge do we have or need to get it?
After getting the required information, is this the way we want it?
What are we going to do about all this? (action required)[9]

The conduct of critical inquiry in schools is advanced by district encouragement and the support of such networks as are described in Chapter 9.

Critical inquiry allows for the collection of varied but pertinent information including the meanings generated by those in the school. Data are not limited to quality indicators and test scores that lend scientific credibility to superficial accountability systems. In evaluation through critical inquiry, moral questions are raised about the goals given by state and district and the human cost of achieving them, throwing light on why these goals are being achieved at a high or low level. For Sirotnik and others, evaluation is a valuing activity in which evaluators (members of the school community) make explicit their operant values, beliefs, interests, and ideologies as they critically examine school practices enlightened by experimental data.

---

[9]Kenneth Sirotnik, "Evaluation in the Ecology of Schooling," in *The Ecology of School Renewal*, NSSE Yearbook (Chicago: The University of Chicago Press, 1987), pp. 41–63.

CONTROVERSIAL TECHNICAL ISSUES IN CURRICULUM EVALUATION

Curriculum specialists, teachers, and administrators often disagree on which techniques to use in evaluation. Many disputes about procedures occur because each party has different purposes and needs in mind. They argue over the merits of procedures and instruments such as formats for stating objectives or specifying goals, norm- and criterion-referenced tests, sampling, and technical hazards. Their controversies will not be resolved by taking an uncompromising attitude but by showing the circumstances in which one approach is better than another.

The Form of Objectives

During the last fifteen years, no issue in curriculum has received more attention than the value of and proper manner for stating objectives. Part of the problem is philosophical. An extreme position is that an objective must specify the exact overt behavior that a learner is to display at the end of an instructional sequence. This overt response is seen as important in itself. A more moderate position is that the objective must specify behavior or a product that indicates whether the objective has been attained. This position allows for covert responses on the part of the learner, but demands that some overt behavior be specified to indicate whether the desired change in the learner has occurred. Another position is that there should be no stated objectives at all. It is said that objectives represent external goals and manipulation and that they insignificantly indicate a learner's actual experiences from a situation.

Part of the problem is that these groups try to judge the form and value of objectives without understanding their purposes. There are many uses for objectives: They can communicate general direction at a policy level, provide a concrete guide for selecting and planning learning opportunities, and set the criteria for evaluation of the learners' performance. To illustrate, there are at least four degrees of specificity for an objective. Very general statements are useful when trying to get a consensus on direction at a policy level. For this purpose, it is often sufficient to use *general goal statements:* "to learn to respect and get along with people by developing appreciation and respect for the worth of individuals," "to respect and understand minority opinions," "to accept majority decisions."

More specific objectives are useful when planning the learning opportunities for courses or when analyzing instructional materials. These objectives are called *educational objectives* and are illustrated in several taxonomies of educational objectives.[10-12] These taxonomies treat affective, cognitive, and psychomotor domains. The *Taxonomy of Educational Objectives: Handbook I,* for example, treats cognitive objectives and classifies them using six major categories and several subcategories. Categories range from simple recall of information to critical evaluative behaviors. One such category is application. *Application* is defined as using abstractions in particular and concrete situations. The abstractions may be general ideas, rules of procedures, or generalized methods. They may also be technical principles, ideas, and theories that must be remembered and applied. The taxonomy also gives sample objectives. The level of specificity of an educational objective can be seen in this example: "The ability to predict the probable effect of a change in a factor on a biological situation previously at equilibrium." The objective can be further amplified by an illustration of the kind of test or test item that would be appropriate.

The taxonomies have greatly influenced curriculum making. More attention is now given to affective, cognitive, and psychomotor domains. Also, curriculum workers are now more sensitive to the level of performance expected from instruction. They are, for instance, more concerned now that objectives and test items treat higher cognitive processes like comprehension, application, and analysis rather than dealing only with recall of information.

There is an even more specific form for an objective—*instructional objective.* This form is useful when teaching a specific concept. It is often called a Mager-like instructional objective after the person who advocated its use.[13] These objectives specify the behavior to be exhibited by the student, a standard or criterion of acceptable performance, and the kind of situation in which the behavior is to be elicited. An instructional objective might be, "Given a linear algebraic equation with one unknown (the situation or condition), the learner must be able to solve the

---

[10]Benjamin S. Bloom, ed., *Taxonomy of Educational Objectives: Handbook I: Cognitive Domain* (New York: David McKay Company, 1956).

[11]David R. Krathwohl et al., *Taxonomy of Educational Objectives: Handbook II: Affective Domain* (New York: David McKay Company, 1956).

[12]Anita Harrow, *A Taxonomy of the Psychomotor Domain: A Guide for Developing Behavioral Objectives* (New York: David McKay Company, 1972).

[13]Robert F. Mager, *Preparing Instructional Objectives* (Palo Alto, CA: Fearon Publishers, 1961).

equation (behavior and criterion) without the aid of references, tables, or calculating devices (additional conditions)."

Objectives seem valuable in providing guidance for the evaluation of instructional materials and student performance. Other functions of objectives, such as giving direction in teaching and aiding learning, arouse much difference of opinion. It is charged that a teacher who uses specific objectives may not give enough attention to the immediate concerns of learners. The research on this issue, however, is inconclusive. Some studies on the effect of objectives on learning, for example, have shown positive effects, but an equal number have not shown any significant differences. Objectives sometimes help and are almost never harmful. They seem to assist students in determining what is expected of them and in discriminating between relevant and irrelevant content. Charles Clark thinks objectives are all right, provided that students themselves generate or choose the objective(s).[14] A question remains about the number of objectives that should be provided to the student. If the list of objectives is extensive and detailed, both student and teacher are overwhelmed. On the importance of stating objectives, a reviewer cites the philosopher George Santayana, "The fanatic is one who re-doubles his efforts when he has forgotten his aim."

Measurement of Intended Outcomes Versus Goal-Free Evaluation

In the past Ralph Tyler told evaluators that it was impossible to decide whether a particular test would be appropriate for appraising a certain program until the objectives of the program had been defined and until the kinds of situations that would give an opportunity for this behavior to be expressed were identified. Tyler recommended checking each proposed evaluation device against the objectives and constructing or devising methods for collecting evidence about the student's attainment of these objectives.

More recently, Michael Scriven moved beyond Tyler's concern for data about intended outcomes to a concern for all relevant effects. His approach is called *goal free evaluation*. This evaluation does not assess a situation merely in terms of goal preferences. It is evaluation of *actual* effects against a profile of demonstrated needs. It is offered as a protec-

---

[14]Charles Clark, "The Necessity of Curriculum Objective," *Journal of Curriculum Studies* 20, no. 4 (August 1988): 339–349.

tion against the narrow vision of those close to the program, against harmful side effects, missed new priorities, and overlooked achievement. To the extent that Scriven's approach is used, more evaluative measures will have to be used. Selection of these measures will be difficult, for there are thousands of such devices. Practicality will probably dictate the use of measures that assess most intended outcomes and a limited number of possible effects.

David Fetterman is also opposed to use of evaluations of programs based on their goals.[15] He believes that such evaluations are misleading. Goals are often part of the political rhetoric. They are often vague and therefore misrepresent the program. Focus upon procedures, formulative evaluation, and ethnographic techniques may contribute to more accurate understanding of a program, revealing both the manifest and latent purposes of the program.

Among the anthropological tools that evaluators use are *phenomology*—attending to viewpoints of their students; *holism*—considering the larger picture rather than details and looking for patterns; *nonjudgmentalism*—making biases explicit; and *centexturalization*—placing acquired information in its own environment so that it is represented accurately.

Norm-Referenced Tests and Criterion-Referenced Tests

Standardized achievement tests are norm-referenced and designed to compare the performances of individuals with the performance of a normative group. The purposes of these tests initially were to find the most able persons and to sort out those who were most likely to succeed or fail some future learning situation. Only those test items that discriminate between the best and the worst are kept. The assumption that everyone can learn equally well is rejected in norm-referenced testing. These tests tend to correlate very highly with intelligence tests. In order to obtain items with high response variance, writers of norm-referenced tests are likely to exclude the items that measure widely known concepts and skills of schooling.

Although norm-referenced tests identify persons of different ability, they are of questionable value in curriculum evaluation. They may not

---

[15]David M. Fetterman, "Qualitative Approaches to Evaluating Education," *Educational Researcher* 17, no. 8 (November 1988): 17–24.

accurately measure what educational programs are designed to teach or reveal particular problems that are keeping pupils from achieving. Teachers can sometimes improve scores on such tests, but usually such improvement results from tricks such as (1) telling children to respond to all items so that the possibility of getting more right answers is increased,* (2) testing at a time of the year different from that of the previous testing to show apparent but not real gains, (3) capitalizing on regression effects that make the poorest scores look better on the second testing, and (4) teaching pupils how to respond to the test items themselves and to the test format.

Criterion-referenced tests are meant to ascertain a learner's status with respect to a learning task, rather than to a norm. These tests tell what learners can and cannot do in specified situations. The tasks selected can be those which the curriculum emphasizes. The items used in the test match the set of learner behaviors called for in the objective and should not be eliminated, as in the norm-referenced tests, merely because most students answer them correctly. Hence, these tests can be sensitive measures of what has been taught.

Criterion-referenced tests are also useful in showing whether a student has mastered specific material. Consequently, they are popular in instructional settings using continuous progress plans or other individualized teaching approaches. The tests indicate which instructional treatments are needed by individual learners and also indicate when learners are ready to proceed to other tasks.

Criterion-referenced tests are sometimes faulted because they have been based on objectives that are too narrow. The multiplicity of tests necessary to accompany many objectives has been a management problem for teachers. Trends indicate that particular courses in the future will use perhaps eight to ten very important final tests based on objectives that are applicable to many situations, rather than the large numbers of such tests as is now common. Tests that have items dependent on particular materials or programs will also diminish. Other ways of improving these tests are to include a complete description of the set of learner behaviors that the test is to assess and to increase the number of items for each competency measured in order to have an acceptable standard of reliability.

---

*A child needs to get only three to seven more items right to show one-year improvement on typical achievement tests.

Tests and Invasion of Privacy

The American Civil Liberties Union has taken up the cause of students who charge that tests are an invasion of privacy. Students have complained about the use of instruments, usually self-report devices, that probe their attitudes in such areas as self-esteem, interest in school, and human relations. Evaluators want such data in order to assess the effects of schooling. Protests against the use of tests to guide the learning process in academic areas are less frequent. ACLU lawyers argue that authorities have not made it clear that pupils may refuse to take tests that they believe to be invading their privacy. Pupils should also be told that the questions asked in a test might require self-incriminating responses which could later be used against them.

This issue is related to a larger problem, that of the effect of tests on students. Do they affect motivation and self-esteem by producing anxiety and encouraging cheating? Do they create labels and determine adult social status? Marjorie C. Kirkland completed an extensive review of the research treating such questions. Her review throws light on test effects. She shows, for example, that how persons think of themselves and what they believe about a test influences their test behavior. Other examples from Kirkland's review show that students' attitudes about tests in general are negative. The more interested persons are in their test results, the more they perceive positive consequences of tests. Systematic reporting of test results helps students to understand their interests, aptitudes, and achievements.[16] Anyone reading Kirkland's review will conclude that tests are powerful and that their consequences are far-ranging.

Peter Airasian found that testing eroded local school control and shaped curricular goals in response to varied social groups; quality replaced equality.[17] He evaluates tests in light of the likely social and legal implications of their use. For example, instead of following the old maxim "don't teach to the test," Airasian believes that not to teach to a test may be a disservice to students in light of the consequences of failing a test.

Tests have often been criticized as inaccurate and biased against women and minority groups. Indeed a federal judge recently ruled that

---

[16]Marjorie C. Kirkland, "The Effects of Tests on Students and School," *Review of Educational Research* 41, no. 4 (October 1971): 303–351.

[17]Peter W. Airasian, "State Mandated Testing and Educational Reform: Context and Consequences," *American Journal of Education* 95, no. 3 (May 1987): 393–420.

the awarding of a New York State Scholarship based on Scholastic Aptitude Test scores discriminates against female students.[18]

TECHNIQUES FOR COLLECTING DATA

Newton S. Metfessel and William B. Michael's list of multiple criterion measures for evaluating school programs is an old but useful survey of ways to collect evidence.[19] One class of indicators of change in learners includes informal devices, short answer techniques, interviews, peer nominations, sociograms, questionnaires, self-evaluation measures, projective devices, and semantic differential scales. The authors also describe the many ways of assessing the effect of programs without influencing the outcomes. These methods are called *unobtrusive measures;* they include attending to absences, anecdotal records, appointments, assignments, stories written, awards, use of books, case histories, disciplinary actions, dropouts, and voluntary activities.

Creative indicators can be devised if persons think beyond the use of formal tests. Other useful indicators are (1) the learners' products, such as compositions, paintings, constructions, (2) the learners' self-reports on preferences and interests, and (3) the learners' solutions to problems, their conduct in discussions, and their participation in physical games and dances. With these methods, the teacher or evaluator should use an accompanying checklist stipulating the behavior to be exhibited by the pupil and the qualities to be found in the pupil's product.

Michael Patton has written on ways the evaluator can get closer to the people and situations being evaluated in order to understand the curriculum as the students experiencing it do.[20] His suggestions for observation and interviewing are extensive and consistent with pluralistic notions. Patton stresses the importance of understanding the point of view and experiences of others. For example, he believes that evaluators, with their own personalities and interests, are naturally attuned to some people more than others. To resist these attractions may hinder the observer from acting naturally and being integrated into the program. The

---

[18]Mark Walsh, "Judge Finds Bias in Scholarships Based on Scores," *Education Weekly* 8, no. 2 (February 15, 1985): 1–20.

[19]Newton S. Metfessel and William B. Michael, "A Paradigm Involving Multiple Criterion Measures for the Evaluation of the Effectiveness of School Programs," *Educational and Psychological Measurement* 27, no. 4 (1967): 931–934.

[20]Michael Q. Patton, *Creative Evaluation* (Beverly Hills, CA: Sage Publications, 1987).

evaluator as observer must decide about personal relationships and group interest, without losing perspective on the experience of other students with whom the evaluator is less directly involved. Similarly, in interviewing, Patton is opposed to having participants fit their knowledge, experiences, and feelings into the evaluator's categories. Instead, the evaluator must provide a framework for the respondents' understanding of the program. Not asking ''How satisfied are you with this program?'' but asking ''What do you think of this program?''

Measuring Affect

Although it is a controversial activity, the assessment of affect is gaining interest. Special techniques are used for this task, because it is believed that persons are more likely to ''fake'' their attitudinal responses. Hence, mild deception is often used so that learners will not know the purpose of the inquiry or that they are being observed. A student may be asked, for example, to respond to several hypothetical situations, only one of which is of interest to the examiner. The examiner may ask, ''Where would you take a visitor friend from out of town—to the market, the movie, the school, the library, the bank?'' If ''school'' is the answer, it is presumed that the respondent tends to value that institution. Another, less direct approach, is to use high inference and theoretical instruments. The examiner might ask, ''Would you play the part of a degenerate in a play?'' or ''Which of the following names (one of which is the respondent's own) do you like?'' (The inference is that students with high self-concepts will play any role and will like their names.) Situations are sometimes contrived, and students' reactions are interpreted to indicate particular attitudes. Student observers may collect unobtrusive data and report their observations later, for example. Audio recordings are sometimes made of student small group discussions and analyzed later.

Sometimes, too, students are offered ways to respond anonymously. In evaluating the affective consequences of a curriculum, students need not be identified. One only has to know what effect the curriculum is having on students as a group. Furthermore, the measures or scores obtained with most high inference instruments are not reliable enough for making predictions about individual students.

In an effort to improve the credibility of their findings, evaluators may use *triangulation* (the use of three different measures in concert). If a similar attitude is found by all three measures, they have more confidence in the findings. Locally developed instruments also are thought to be more valid when two or more persons score students' responses the same and when several samples of student behavior are consistent.

Sampling

Sampling is the practice of inferring an educational status on the basis of responses from representative persons or representative tasks. James Popham has said, "Sampling should make a Scotsman's values vibrate. It is *so* terribly thrifty."[21] Sampling is controversial mainly because it is sometimes imposed in inappropriate situations. When students are to be graded on their relative attainment of common objectives, it is not proper to assess only certain students nor is it valid to test some students on one set of objectives and others on another set.

Administrators rightfully use sampling when they estimate the typical reactions of students from a few instances of their behavior. It is not necessary to collect all the compositions that students have written in order to judge their writing ability. Samples will suffice—perhaps one at the beginning of the year and one at the end—to show change, if any, as a result of instruction. Similarly, to determine a student's knowledge in one subject, it is not necessary to ask the student to respond to all the items that are involved in this knowledge. A sample of what is involved is enough to draw an inference about the student's status. To find out whether the student can name all the letters of the alphabet, one can present only five letters at random from the alphabet and ask the student to name them. The responses indicate ability to respond to the total population of letters. If all five are named correctly, there is a high probability that the child could name all of the letters. If the child cannot name one or more of the letters, obviously the objective has not been reached. Controversy arises over sampling because teachers have concerns that do not lend themselves to sampling. If sampling indicates that a child cannot name all of the letters of the alphabet, then the teacher wants to know specifically which ones must be taught. Sampling is unlikely to reveal this information.

Controversy may also arise between legislators and others who want achievement records of students and evaluators who prefer to use a technique like *matrix sampling* to determine the effects of a program. In this sampling technique randomly selected students respond to randomly selected test items measuring different objectives. Thus, different students

---

[21]W. James Popham, *Educational Evaluation,* 2nd ed. (Englewood Cliffs, NJ: Prentice-Hall, 1988).

take different tests. The advantages of the technique are many: reduced testing time required of the student, attainment of information concerning learners' knowledge with respect to many objectives, and reduced apprehension on the student's part because examinees are not compared. The disadvantage is that sampling does not tell us the status of an individual on all the objectives. But again, this is not necessary to get an indication of abilities within groups of students.

Technical Hazards

Donald Horst and colleagues of the RMC Research Corporation have identified twelve hazards in conducting evaluations. Each hazard makes it difficult to know whether students do better in a particular program than they would have done without it.

1. *The use of grade-equivalent scores.* One should not use grade-equivalent scores in evaluating programs. The concept is misleading; a grade-equivalent score of 7 by fifth-graders on a math test does not mean that they know sixth- and seventh-grade math. Such scores do not comprise an equal interval scale and, therefore, it is difficult to obtain an average score. The procedures for obtaining these scores make them too low in the fall and too high in the spring.

2. *The use of gain scores.* Gain scores have been used to adjust for differences found in the pretest scores of treatment and comparison groups. Using them in this way is a mistake, because raw gain scores (posttest scores minus pretest scores) excessively inflate the posttest performance measure of an initially inferior group. Students who initially have the lowest scores have the greatest opportunity to show gain.

3. *The use of norm-group comparisons with inappropriate test dates.* A distorted picture of a program's effect occurs when pupils in the new program are not tested within a few weeks of the norm group's tests. Standardized test developers might collect performance scores in May in order to obtain a norm for the test. If the school's staff, however, administers the test during a different month, the discrepancy might be due to the date of testing rather than to the program.

4. *The use of inappropriate test levels.* Standardized norm-referenced tests are divided into levels that cover different grades. The test level may be too easy or too difficult, and thereby fail to provide a valid measurement of achievement. The test might differentiate sufficiently among groups at either end of the scale. Such effects may also occur

with the use of criterion-referenced tests. Hence, tests should be chosen on the basis of the pupils' achievement level, not their grade in school.

5. *The lack of pre- and posttest scores for each treatment participant.* The group of students ultimately posttested is not usually composed of exactly the same students as the pretest group. Eliminating the scores of dropouts from the posttest may raise the posttest scores considerably. Conclusion of a program's report should be based on the performance of students who have both pre- and posttest scores. The reason for dropping out also should be reported.

6. *The use of noncomparable treatment and comparison groups.* Students should be randomly assigned to groups. If they are not, students in a special program may do better or worse than those in other programs, because they were different to start with.

7. *Using pretest scores to select program participants.* Groups with low pretest scores appear to learn more from a special program than they actually do because of a phenomenon called *regression toward the mean*. Gains of high-scoring students may be obscured.

8. *Assembling a mismatched comparison group.* The correct procedure for matching groups is to match pairs of pupils and then randomly assign one member of each pair to a treatment or comparison group. If, for example, one wants to control for age, one should choose pairs of pupils of the same age. Each member of the pair must have an equal opportunity to be assigned to a given treatment. Do not consciously try to place one member in a certain group.

9. *Careless administration of tests.* Pupils from both treatment and comparison groups should complete pre- and posttests together. Problems arise when there is inconsistent administration of tests to the two groups. If, for example, there is a disorderly situation in one setting and a different teacher present, the results may differ.

10. *The assumption that an achievement gain is due to the treatment alone.* The Hawthorne effects—unrecognized "treatments," such as novelty—may be responsible for gain. Plausible rival hypotheses should be examined as a likely explanation.

11. *The use of noncomparable pretests and posttests.* Although conversion tables allow one to correct scores on one test to their equivalent on other tests, it is best to use the same level of the same test for both pre- and posttesting. Often it is possible to use the identical test as both pre- and posttest. Obviously, this does not suffice if teachers teach to the test and if there are practice effects from taking the test.

12. *The use of inappropriate formulas to estimate posttest scores.* Formulas that

calculate expected posttest scores from IQ or an average of grade-equivalent scores are inaccurate. The actual posttest scores of treatment and comparison groups provide a better basis for evaluating treatment effects.[22]

CONCLUDING COMMENTS

Evaluation is useless if conclusions are not drawn from the data and acted on in modifying the curriculum. Looking at test scores and filing them away mocks the evaluative process, although admittedly, evaluation sometimes serves other purposes. Results are sometimes used to gain support of parents and others.

Consensus evaluation also may be undertaken because it is a necessary basis for requesting monies or reassuring a public that the school is doing its job. The principal purpose for using the data, however, should be improvement of the curriculum. Hence, some schools now have curriculum groups that study the findings and then make plans both for the whole school and for individual teachers.

Scores or descriptive terms summarize learner performance and give study groups the opportunity to see the strengths and weaknesses of their programs. Analyses of different populations of pupils reveal how well the curriculum is serving major cultural subgroups, such as the physically handicapped, or how different groups compare with each other. Teachers attempt to ascertain from the data what individual students need. Diagnosing needs becomes a basis for giving personal help. Study groups also discuss the reasons for a curriculum's strengths and weaknesses. Members try to explain the results of particular learning opportunities, the time spent on an objective, the arrangement of activities and topics, the kinds and frequency of responses from learners, the grouping patterns, the use of space, and interactions with adults. Explanations are verified by determining whether all the data lead to the same conclusion. Plans are made to modify the curriculum in light of deficiencies noted and the cause of the deficiencies.

The results from consensus evaluation should be used in at least two ways. First, they can be used to strengthen ends. Results can be the basis for deciding on new instructional objectives aimed at meeting revealed

---

[22]Donald P. Horst et al., *A Practical Guide to Measuring Project Impact on Student Achievement*, Monograph Series on Education, no. 1 (Washington, DC: U.S. Office of Education, 1975).

needs. If evaluation of a program or particular learning opportunity results in the selection of more important objectives than were originally held, the evaluation was valuable. Dewey said it well: ''There is no such thing as a final set of objectives, even for the time being or temporarily. Each day of teaching ought to enable a teacher to revise and better in some respect the objectives arrived at in a previous work.''[23]

Results can also be used to revise means. They can serve as a guide to the need for new learning opportunities and arrangements that might remedy deficiencies in the curriculum. That is, evaluation pinpoints needs and guides a person in the selection of new material, procedures, and organizational patterns. These innovations in turn must be tried out and their results appraised. In short, evaluation is only one part of a continuing cycle.

Pluralistic evaluation, especially critical inquiry, is consistent with the rise of professionalism and the school as the center for evaluative focus. Accordingly, responsibility, learning, and change become more important than scoreboard accountability. Such evaluation includes teachers, students, administrators, parents, community members, and possibly a researcher from the university. As they focus upon curriculum matters like content, goals, learning opportunities, and grouping, participants create a new awareness, knowledge, and values, at least if they engage in inquiry for action and try to answer Sirotnik's generic questions. Conditions for critical inquiry include trust among participants, understanding (comprehension) of one another, and sharing of feelings, observations, and interpretations. In the evaluative process, any statement can be challenged. Evaluation of the statement rests solely on the strength of the evidence and supporting arguments. All curriculum practices are subject to questions and to examination of their consequences. ''Deep'' critical evaluation even allows for evaluation of the school's normative structure in which local values are assessed in light of larger values for human life.

QUESTIONS

1. How would you respond if faced with the choice of obtaining important data about the learner through deception or obtaining less important data in a straightforward manner?

[23]John Dewey, *The Sources of a Science of Education* (New York: Horace Liveright, 1929).

2. What kind of student progress is best revealed by (a) products of learners, (b) self-reports, and (c) observations of pupil behavior?

3. Compare the purpose and construction of norm-referenced and criterion-referenced tests.

4. Think of a learning opportunity that you might select for learners (a particular educational game, lesson, field trip, experiment, textbook article, or story). Then indicate what you would do in order to find out whether this opportunity produced both intended outcomes and unanticipated consequences.

5. Whose criteria should be used in an evaluation situation known to you: experts, participants, or those affected by its consequences? Explain your answer.

6. Discuss the strengths and weaknesses of each of the following evaluative purposes and accompanying approaches:

Purpose	Approach
To measure student progress	Determine gain by testing
To resolve crises and increase perception of school as legitimate	Blue ribbon committee
To generate more defensible goals and practice	Critical inquiry
To make rational curriculum decisions	A history of options and the costs of each

SELECTED REFERENCES

Alkin, Marvin C. *A Guide for Evaluation Decision Making.* Beverly Hills, CA: Sage Publications, 1985.

Cronbach, L.J., et al. *Toward Reform of Program Evaluation: Aims, Methods, and Institutional Arrangements.* San Francisco: Jossey-Bass, 1980.

Eisner, Elliot W. *On the Design and Evaluation of School Programs.* ed. 2. New York: MacMillan, 1985.

Fellman, David M., and Pitman, Mary Anne, eds. *Education Evaluation in Theory, Practice and Politics.* Beverly Hills, CA: Sage Publications, 1986.

Grundy, Shirley. *Curriculum: Practice or Praxis.* London: Palmer Press, 1987.

Popham, W. James. *Educational Evaluation.* ed. 2. Englewood Cliffs, NJ: Prentice-Hall, 1988.

11

The Politics
of Curriculum Making

With the 1990s, every policy maker is making new policy. The federal government is concerned with curriculum on a scale not seen since the 1970s, with new programs for the gifted, expansion of Chapter I to include high school dropout prevention programs and programs to educate disadvantaged preschoolers and illiterates. States as well as local districts are increasing curriculum regulation and aligning curriculum texts, tests, and teacher evaluation. In contrast to older views of local responses to policy interventions (resistance, compliance, and adaptation), we are witnessing strategic interaction whereby district leaders and principals seize policy opportunity, expanding upon state policies to meet local priorities. The rising demands for teacher professionalization and more parental and student discretion in curriculum matters make it necessary to rethink the balance of curriculum control.

This chapter addresses the question of who should control the curriculum. It treats the influence of textbook publishers, testing organizations, and other special groups. The roles of teachers, students, board members, and administrators are included in this analysis of curriculum policy making. This chapter also delineates the underlying struggle between complex political and professional reform apparatus at the national and state levels and educational systems at other levels attempting to preserve local values and interests.

CURRICULUM POLICY

Curriculum policy is seldom rational or based on research. Decisions are not often based on careful analysis of content in the disciplines and on societal needs, or on studies of the learning process and concerns of learners.

The Politics Involved

Curriculum decision making is a political process. Different pressure groups are proposing competing values about what to teach. For example, a state board must decide whether to give in to efforts to have the biblical version of human origin, the creation theory, become part of the content in the school or to follow the pressure of those who want only the Darwinian evolutionary theory to be taught. Members of state and local public agencies legally responsible for these decisions regularly are accepting and rejecting different values in some way. They may bargain and permit new values to enter the program on a piecemeal basis. They may give lip service to the new values, indicating their importance in general terms but not providing concrete ways for their fulfillment. They may reject a proposed curriculum because it does not meet their view of a school's functions. The decision to accept or reject a proposal often depends on the decision maker's own view as to whether the school should emphasize individual growth and enrichment, transmission of subject matter, or preparation for life in the community.

Some idea of the complexity of curriculum policy making can be gained from this paragraph by Kirst and Walker:

> A mapping of the leverage points for curriculum policy-making in local schools would be exceedingly complex. It would involve three levels of government, and numerous private organization foundations, accrediting associations, national testing agencies, textbook-software companies, and interest groups (such as the NAACP, the PTA and the Heritage Foundation). Moreover, there would be a configuration of leverage points within a particular local school system including teachers, department heads, the assistant superintendent for instruction, the superintendent, and the school board. Cutting across all levels of government would be the pervasive influence of various celebrities, commentators, interest groups, and the journalists who use the mass media to disseminate their views on curriculum. It would be very useful if we were able to quantify the amount of influence of each of these groups of individuals and show input-output interactions for just one

school system. Unfortunately this is considerably beyond the state of the art.[1]

Decisions About What Will Be Taught

Several definitions of curriculum would alter most analyses of curriculum making. To say that the curriculum is what the learner actually experiences from schools—the outlooks, predispositions, skills, and attitudes—implies that the learner personally has a major role in determining the curriculum. Individual learners can decide at least to some extent what they will learn. To say that curriculum encompasses everything that influences learning in the schools increases the range of curriculum makers by including peers, custodians, visitors, and cafeteria workers. Furthermore, the definition means that anyone whose actions affect the school experience, either fortuitously or on purpose, is engaging in curriculum making.

For this analysis, we will treat curriculum decisions as conscious policy choices that affect what is learned. These decisions pertain to the nature of programs, preinstructional plans, materials, or activities that delineate organized educational programs of the school or classroom. They are made with the intent of controlling the purposes, subject matter, method, and order of instruction. Curriculum policy making is indeed anticipatory. However, plans and materials are not always used as intended. Also, learner differences make it difficult to ensure that all will derive the same meaning from a common experience or opportunity.

Not everyone who influences the curriculum does so in the same way. A school superintendent who persuades his or her board to install a prekindergarten program is influencing the curriculum. Testing agencies that determine what will be measured on standardized tests, thereby guiding the instructional program, are also making curriculum decisions. When deciding to substitute projects that would make use of the skills learned in social studies to improve life in the community for textbook exercises, the teacher is engaging in curriculum policy making because each of these learning opportunities probably will lead to different outcomes. The authoritative decision to advance one goal over another is policy making.

---

[1]Michael W. Kirst and Decker F. Walker, "An Analysis of Curriculum Policy Making," *Review of Educational Research* 41, no. 5 (1971): 488. Copyright 1971, American Educational Research Association, Washington, DC.

CONCEPTS FOR INTERPRETING THE PROCESS
OF POLITICAL DECISION MAKING

Certain ideas and issues provide a framework for understanding the politics of curriculum decision making. Some of these come from studies by sociologists and some from insightful educators observing how curriculum decisions are being made.

The Professionalization of Reform

The professionalization of reform is the notion that efforts to change the American social system (including schools) have in recent years been undertaken by persons whose profession is to reform. National curriculum reform has been spearheaded by persons like the late Mario Fantini, Edward F. Zigler, and Ernest L. Boyer. Professional reformers tend to measure their success by the number of changes they begin.

Examples of professional reformers in action are found in: (1) J. Hottois and N. A. Milner's study citing evidence that the initiative for introducing sex education came from educators, although the educators themselves claimed that sex education was added in response to public demands for it; (2) D. Nelkin's complaint that, in connection with the nationwide introduction of the curriculum *Man: A Course of Study,* ''an elite corps of unrelated professional academics and their government friends run things in the school''[2,3]; (3) Norman Drachler's account of how a United States commissioner of education established the Right to Read Program with overtones of a political manifesto, including demands for accountability, minority teachers, cultural pluralism in the curriculum, bilingual education, voucher plans, and competency-based teacher certification; and (4) description of the Reverend Jesse Jackson's Push for Excellence Program with funding from such sources as the Ford Foundation and the federal government.[4,5]

In his analysis of professional reformers, William Boyd sees them as

---

[2]J. Hottois and N. A. Milner, *The Sex Education Controversy* (Lexington, MA: Heath, 1975).

[3]D. Nelkin, ''The Science-Textbook Controversies,'' *Scientific American* 234, no. 4 (April 1976): 36.

[4]Norman Drachler, ''Education and Politics in Large Cities, 1950–70,'' in *The Politics of Education,* NSSE Yearbook (Chicago: The University of Chicago Press, 1977): pp. 188–219.

[5]Barbara Sizemore, ''Push Politics and the Education of America's Youth,'' *Phi Delta Kappan* 60, no. 1 (1979): 364–370.

a controversial new force in educational policy making. He describes them as pursuing their visions of equal opportunity and a more just society convinced of their expertise and its prerogatives, armed with ''solutions looking for problems,'' assisted by an educational research establishment with its built-in incentive to discover failure, which justifies even more research, supplied by federal and foundation funding, and stimulated by the civil rights discovery of new classes of disadvantaged students and forms of discrimination, such as the non-English-speaking, handicapped, and victims of sex discrimination.[6]

Forces of Stability

In contrast to professional reformers, many communities, school boards, school administrators, and teachers are more interested in maintaining the social values of the current curriculum and the structure of the schools. To them, carrying out the curriculum changes proposed by professional reformers is too costly to coordinate, too difficult to guide, and too controversial to avoid conflict. The power of the forces for stability may be eroding, yet Lawrence Iannaccone and Peter Cistone testified to the strengths of constraint in innovation by saying, ''Two decades of effort in the area of race, equality, and curricular revision with more federal input than impact speak loudly enough for those who will listen. Schools today are more like the schools of twenty years ago than like anything else.[7]

Similarly, Larry Cuban has revealed how little instruction changes at the classroom level in spite of changes at the rhetorical level.[8] The pronouncements made in writing and speeches and those given in official statements are not necessarily translated into action. Reform policies that are acted upon tend to be policies with which principals and teachers feel comfortable.

The pressures from key figures in the Excellence Movement of the 1980s for more academically oriented high schools, for instance, were well received by teachers prepared and disposed to teaching for the re-

---

[6]William L. Boyd, ''The Politics of Curriculum Change and Stability,'' *Educational Researcher* 8, no. 2 (February 1979): 15.

[7]Lawrence Iannaccone and Peter J. Cistone, *The Politics of Education* (Eugene, OR: ERIC Clearinghouse on Educational Management, University of Oregon, 1974), p. 64.

[8]Larry Cuban, *How Teachers Taught: Consistency and Change in American Classrooms, 1890–1980* (New York: Longman, 1984).

production of academic subjects.[9] It is recalled that the Excellence Movement was initiated with the U.S. Department of Education Report *A Nation at Risk: The Imperatives for Educational Reform*. Shortly after this report numerous commission reports and state level actions created a new political agenda.

The more frequently acted upon curriculum reforms of the Excellence Movement were the adding of courses in computer literacy, adopting textbooks with no stereotypes, adopting special textbooks for disadvantaged or gifted students, increasing requirements in math, science, and English, offering foreign languages to elementary students, and increasing homework.[10]

Constraints on Policy

Constraints on policy for curriculum innovation occur through *non-decision making, conflict avoidance,* the *threat of controversy,* and *loose coupling.*

Non-Decision Making. This term refers to the ability of powerful interests to control the decision-making agenda, preventing the discussion of "undesirable issues." Wilson Riles, while California State Superintendent of Public Instruction, along with leaders from the California educational establishment, avoided public exposure of a campaign to place a school voucher initiative on the 1980 ballot. A low profile strategy was laid out at a meeting of educational groups at which they also agreed to step up propaganda efforts to improve the public image of public education. Riles turned down numerous invitations to debate the voucher question, saying, "If we were to get into a knock-down drag out fight, it would get attention. If they (voucher advocates) are going to get publicity, they are going to have to do it on their own." Non-decision making is a formidable barrier to change by keeping potential issues from being discussed or recognized.

Conflict Avoidance. Conflict avoidance refers to educators' unwillingness to introduce curriculum changes that conflict with community values and are likely to arouse controversy and opposition. William Boyd

---

[9]Susan Fuhrman and William H. Clune, "Research on Education Reform; Lessons on the Implementation of Policy," *Teachers College Record* 90, no. 2 (1988): 237–257.

[10]William W. Wayson, *Up From Excellence: The Impact of the Excellence Movement on Schools* (Bloomington, IN: Phi Delta Kappa Educational Foundation, 1988).

found that the degree of latitude for local educators in effecting curriculum change depends on the community.[11] In general, rural school districts and those in the "sunbelt" of the United States are more restrictive about the content of courses such as social studies, literature, and biology. Prevailing controversies center on evolution, obscenity, sex education, and religious views. Methods of teaching reading or mathematics are also sometimes a matter of public controversy, especially in conservative communities.

The Politics of Controversy. A technique used by those with a minority viewpoint to control the majority is called the politics of controversy. Using a squeaky wheel tactic, those opposed to a curriculum innovation create a controversy in the hope that school authorities will back off from it. Textbook publishers, for example, are known to be sensitive about introducing into their materials content that is likely to be controversial. Thus, the threat of controversy results in nonpublication and weak pablum in the curriculum.

Loose Coupling. The goals set by reformers (the ideal curriculum) may not be faithfully followed by local school boards (the formal curriculum) and certainly are not likely to be attained by the procedures of teachers in the classroom (the actual curriculum). Awareness of loose coupling, or the inability of policymakers to implement their curriculum plans, has resulted in what Arthur Wise calls "hyper-rationalization."[12] Because teachers have failed to attain the goals, they must be made accountable for the goals. For example, classroom methods and procedures for treating handicapped children are now specified in detail by federal and state agencies and by the courts. Compliance is sought through program evaluation, site visits, reviews of classroom records, and learner verification, i.e. pupils both displaying desired competencies and reporting to authorities about teachers' practices. Policy makers in federal or state governments now mandate measurable goals (narrow, selective, and minimal) and demand frequent testing of student achievement with respect to these goals. Additional control over the curriculum occurs through special staff development of experienced teachers and competency-based education for novices—both types of training programs consistent with the curriculum goals of the centralized planners.

---

[11]William Boyd, "The Politics of Curriculum Change," p. 15.

[12]Arthur E. Wise, "The Hyper-rationalization of American Education," *Educational Leadership* 35, no. 5 (February 1978): 354–362.

PARTICIPANTS IN DETERMINING CURRICULUM POLICY

School-Based Participants

Teachers. Michael Kirst has shown that the teacher is a crucial maker of curriculum policy.[13] Even in such a seemingly clear-cut subject as elementary arithmetic, the teacher is not simply an implementor of policy. Teachers decide whether to spend time on drill or problem solving. Similarly, John Schwille and others have pointed out that teachers have considerable freedom to use their own notions of what schooling ought to be even when subjected to the external pressures of state textbooks and district curriculum guides.[14] In deciding which student will get what kind of curriculum content, the teacher takes on a political role.

At the classroom or instructional level, most teachers have the opportunity to define instructional objectives within an overall framework that indicates what is to be taught. Often they can also design and order learning activities to achieve these ends. They make important curriculum decisions when they decide to group activities around particular organizing centers such as a problem, a project, an area of inquiry, a subject topic, or a unit. However, a teacher's freedom in curriculum development varies. Many years ago, Virgil Herrick proposed three different degrees of teacher responsibility for making curriculum decisions. At position 1, teachers do little more than to follow the textbook and school policies. At position 2, teachers take responsibility for decisions regarding learning activities, the time to be spent on particular subjects and how to evaluate students. Teachers at position 3 go beyond textbooks, selecting concepts to be taught, designing learning activities, and creating smooth transitions between steps.

Reformers now propose a framework with "four positions" for analyzing the degree of responsibility taken by teachers in curriculum decision making (Table 11–1).

A radical proposal for curriculum decision making was made by Hilda Taba in 1962. She called for a deliberate inversion of the common procedure. Instead of starting with a general design in which curriculum began at the societal level and rippled down through institutions to the

---

[13]Michael W. Kirst, "Policy Implications of Individual Differences and the Common Curriculum," in *Individual Differences and the Common Curriculum*, NSSE Yearbook (Chicago: The University of Chicago Press, 1983), pp. 282–299.

[14]John Schwille et al., "Teachers as Policy Brokers," in *Teaching Policy*, ed. Lee Shulman (New York: Longman, 1982).

TABLE 11–1 Positions of Teacher Responsibility for Curriculum Decisions

Area of Decision	Position 1	Position 2	Position 3	Position 4
Concept to be taught	Textbook	Prespecified objectives	Subject matter units	Social analysis
Activities and materials	Text, lecture	Student participation, modeling, practice	Cooperative projects Both directed and inquiry lessons	Students construct knowledge Project is in the real world
Evaluation	End of chapter, final exam	Test and essay	Observation Product test	End-of-year project
Continuities and next steps	Textbook	Sequenced objectives	Units seldom related	Students decide what they want to learn next

classroom, Taba proposed that curriculum making start at the teaching level with the planning of specific units of instruction. The results of experimenting with these units then would provide a basis for a general design to be created later. Taba's strategy was calculated to infuse theory into the operation of the practitioner from the outset.[15] The concept of teacher participation as given in Chapter 9 is a similar notion. However, school or districtwide coordination of curriculum by teachers is unlikely because of their focused interest in their own classrooms.

Teachers are likely to influence curriculum policy in the larger political arena through their unions. Teacher organizations are beginning to look at curriculum issues. Accountability procedures, differentiated staffing, schools of choice, and other innovations affecting teachers force them to take positions on what shall be taught. Until recently, however, demands from such organizations focused primarily on staff benefits such as pay, class size, and extra assignments. But today teachers are expected to use this organized power in the interests of curriculum to exercise authority over such matters as textbook selection. In many school districts in the United States, teacher participation in the selection of textbooks is part of the negotiated contract.[16] Teachers want to estab-

---

[15]Hilda Taba, *Curriculum Development: Theory and Practice* (New York: Harcourt Brace and World, 1962), p. 529.

[16]Sherry Keith, *Politics of Textbook Selection* (Palo Alto, CA: Stanford University Press, 1981).

lish the minimum knowledge that students enrolled in particular courses should derive from the courses and to determine the concepts and values to be taught in a particular course.

Teachers also want the authority to choose the appropriate method for teaching the course. In general, teachers desire to have a modest amount of influence over school policies and practices, particularly those affecting their classrooms. They like to be consulted and to have the opportunity to initiate change as it affects their own classroom, but not to have a large responsibility for the entire school.[17,18]

Teachers are beginning to influence some curriculum decisions through collective bargaining. For example, innovative programs are being traded for smaller classes and guaranteed jobs for experienced teachers. Van Geel wonders whether boards of education should be forced to "pay off" a private group (the teachers' unions) to keep control of what they were established to do.[19] Collective bargaining has raised the issue of whether public interests in curriculum—the interests of students, parents, and others—might be trampled on if disproportionate powers are given at the bargaining table to board and teacher groups.

In 1989, the bilingual program in the Los Angeles City Schools was threatened when local teachers' groups opposed bonus payments planned to attract bilingual teachers to poverty areas. Teachers' organizations also have had much influence at the state and federal levels. Teacher political action committees are active in nearly all states raising funds for politicians friendly to teachers' causes.

Nevertheless, teacher associates played a secondary role to business interests in recent school state reforms. Despite the centrality of reforms dealing with curriculum, teachers' associations accommodated to reform rather than shaped it. Although they were able to block parts of reform that they particularly disliked, teacher associations offered no virulent resistance. When the reform carried increased educational funding and had the support of business elites, teacher associations suppressed their antagonism.[20]

---

[17]Gerald Grant et al., "The Teacher's Predicament," *Teachers College Record* 84, no. 3 (Spring 1983): 593–609.

[18]Susan Mones Johnson, "Teacher Unions in Schools: Authority and Accommodation," *Harvard Educational Review* 53, no. 3 (August 1983): 309–326.

[19]T. Van Geel, *Authority to Control the School Program* (Lexington, MA: Heath, 1976), pp. 178–179.

[20]Lorraine M. McDonnell and Anthony Pascal, "Teacher Unions and Educational Reform" (Santa Monica, CA: Rand Corporation, 1988). Prepared for the Center for Policy Research in Education.

Principals. Despite the formal job description as curriculum leader, the principal tends to be little more than a middleman between the central office, parents, and the staff in implementing curriculum. Principals often are burdened with such a multitude of managerial activities that it is extremely difficult for them to devote the time and effort required for innovation on a substantial scale. Principals can be actively engaged in curriculum making only in schools in which their planning responsibilities can be carried out without heavy managerial responsibilities.

The role of the principal in curriculum making is not settled. Some people think that the principal should initiate curriculum change. Others believe that principals can be more effective and influential by implementing curriculum decisions already made. One would expect principals working in centralized school systems to be more likely to accept the latter role. To date, however, they have not. Although the principal now has the power to make some decisions that were formerly made at the central office, accountability is still directed upward, not toward the community. Decentralization has probably made some principals more responsible to their communities and more attentive to system-wide goals and to ways of tailoring local school objectives to meet these goals. Esra Staples, for instance, found that under decentralization the principal's influence was the greatest in selecting materials, altering programs in content areas, and determining the school goals.[21]

Mainly, curriculum development has not improved in decentralized school systems because teachers and principals lack the technical skills for curriculum making. Decision making has been placed at the local level with very little guidance for the principal. Meanwhile, we continue to hear the platitude that the "greatest amount of power to change and improve the curriculum lies in the hands of local administrators." Older studies in support of this belief are found in the work of Henry Brickell and of Paul Mort and F. G. Cornell, who reported that administrators were the vital force in the initiation of change and that neutrality on the part of principals prevented changes.[22,23] The reason for this conflicting assessment of the school principal is that older studies were referring to the legal authority of the principalship as a power in effecting change.

---

[21]Esra I. Staples, *Impact of Decentralization on Curriculum: Selected Viewpoints* (Washington, DC: ASCD, 1975).

[22]Henry Brickett, *Organizing New York for Education Change* (Albany: New York State Department of Education, 1961).

[23]Paul Mort and F. G. Cornell, *American Schools in Transition* (New York: Teachers College, Columbia University, 1941).

The newer view attends to the principal's lack of expertise, which impedes his or her ability to make wise decisions about curriculum. Also, as curriculum has become increasingly legalized because of the growing body of legislation, regulation, and judicial doctrine, principals have had their authority to initiate curriculum diminished.

Superintendents. The superintendent influences curriculum policy by responding to matters before the board of education, initiating programs for the in-service education of teachers, making district personnel aware of changes occurring in other schools, and moderating outside demands for change. The superintendent must take the curriculum demands from state and federal governments and make them acceptable to the local population. Existing studies of the superintendent are outdated. The data we have, however, indicate that school board members tend to feel that superintendents are poor in curriculum planning. Superintendents also rate themselves weakest in curriculum and instruction, as opposed to performance in finance or plant management. Nevertheless, the superintendent is the key figure in curriculum innovation and educational decision making.[24] In large cities, assistant superintendents for curriculum and instruction attempt to influence the curriculum through their work with committees of teachers and their preparation of guidelines, bulletins, and staff development sessions.

The superintendent, like the principal, is losing control over the curriculum to the centralizing forces of state and federal legislators and to the courts. On the basis of his review of research over the past two decades, William Boyd concluded, on the other hand, that one of the most effective means for local control of the curriculum was held by communities with superintendents whose values were consonant with those predominant in the district.[25] Superintendents were fired when they strayed from community values. Recent developments in the state took much control out of the hands of local superintendents. In addition, new structural layers—specialists in different areas—dilute the influence of the superintendent and local school board. The salaries of these specialists come from state categorical funds which help to insulate them from the superintendent's influence.

---

[24]Gordon M. MacKenzie, Harmon Zeigler et al., ''Communication and Decision-Making in American Public Education,'' in *The Politics of Education,* NSSE Yearbook, ed. Jay Scribner (Chicago: The University of Chicago Press, 1977).

[25]William L. Boyd, ''The Changing Politics of Curriculum Policy Making for American Schools,'' *Review of Educational Research* 48, no. 4 (Fall 1978): 622.

Students.   Students seldom have formal influence over course content. There are, of course, schools in which provisions are made for some genuine self-government by students. Student officers can be elected and appointed to policy boards. They may even approve faculty appointments and determine course offerings and academic requirements. The extent of control given students is usually a function of the maturity that they have attained and the nature of the particular community. Student policy making is generally derivative rather than absolute, a privilege granted by higher powers and subject to revocation by them. Often student government is an administrator's or teacher's means of securing student cooperation.

Informally, however, students have much influence over what is taught. Often they can vote with their feet by refusing to enroll in courses that feature the curriculum of academic specialists. The failure of students to respond to the Physical Science Study Committee's "physics" was an argument for curriculum change. Alternative schools and underground newspapers are other examples of student power. The late 1960s saw both college and high school students rebelling against their role as captive audience and asking for both a social curriculum that would confront the facts of war, racism, oppression, and a personal curriculum to help them discover themselves.

With the advent of the 1990s, one increasingly reads of students protesting assignments involving animal rights (biology and the dissection of frogs) and attempts to teach attitudes (sensitivity games in social studies). An example of student sophistication in politics involves the California "Cash for Caps" program, which rewards schools that increase their scores on the state's achievement tests. Seniors in a particular school threatened poor performance on the test unless school officials agreed to remove speed bumps from the school's parking lot and to permit the senior class to have a field trip to the beach. When administrators failed to meet the demand, students carried out their threat, losing the district $70,000.

Community Participants

Local School Board.   Political analysis shows local boards of education playing a diminishing role in actual decision making. Members of these boards often rubber stamp the professionals' recommendations. Board members usually lack the technical competence they need to decide on specific programs. Hence, they vote on intuition or the advice of others. Also, growing state and federal pressure has weakened local jurisdiction, and in large districts at least, the less specific policies are not carried out according to the board's mandates. Usually the smaller the community, the more likely the public is to believe that school board members are primarily concerned with the welfare of children. Residents of large urban centers tend to see board members as persons seeking prestige and power.

Lee K. Davies described how the actions of legislators, judges, and lay groups took away the control from local school boards.[26] She finds the courts the focus of the current struggle for control. Special interest groups prefer to go to court if board policies are not to their satisfaction rather than to discuss board policy at public board meetings. Law suits are especially popular with those who cannot prevail in ordinary political decision making.[27] Similarly, legislation is viewed as a last resort for the citizen who is in opposition to the local board. The instances of Massachusetts legislation on the local policy for the assignment of pupils to special classes and of Florida legislation in opposition to a district's policy regarding sex education are examples of legislation which began with parents seeking a change.

Briefly, state and local professionals seem to be determining the curriculum, and the board is serving as an advisor. The realities of implementing federal and state directives and court orders tend to make board members more dependent on experts, especially those with legal expertise.

The Public. The role of the local lay community in formulating curriculum is minimal. The public knows little about course content and is not involved with general curriculum issues. Vandalism, drugs, and discipline tend to be seen as problems, not as curriculum issues. Until very recently, local communities left curriculum planning to professionals. Only occasionally did the public get involved in curriculum. These occasions are viewed as episodic issues which emerge under special conditions and shortly subside. Thus it is not textbooks that cause concern, but a particular textbook under a special set of circumstances.

Community participation in local curriculum making was thought to increase because of the establishment of such innovations as local school

---

[26]Lee K. Davies, "The School Board's Struggle to Survive," *Educational Leadership* 34, no. 2 (November 1976): 95–99.

[27]Michael A. Robell and Arthur R. Block, *Educational Policy Making and the Courts* (Chicago: The University of Chicago Press, 1982).

advisory bodies charged with representing community needs and interests and local school site management. To date, however, studies of such councils have shown that most participation has come from parents of successful learners and that not much has been improved by virtue of the school councils. This may have been due either to the school boards' lack of specificity in stating what they mean by participation or to the reluctance of educators to share in decision making.

In contrast to many cities that have moved toward centralization, Chicago is experimenting with decentralization, establishing local school councils in each of Chicago's 595 buildings. Each council consists of six parent representatives, two teachers chosen by their peers, two representatives chosen by the community at large, and the building principal. Each council draws up a school improvement plan and assumes much of the responsibility for budgetary planning and oversight.[28]

Jon Schaffarzick found that citizen participation in curriculum policy making tends to be minimal, perfunctory, reactive, and superficial.[29] Citizens take part very early when general goals are being established or very late when most of the preparation for change has been completed. Citizens can, however, be influential when they become activated. When significant conflicts arise between citizens and school board, lay groups usually win. Most active parent groups represent special interests in the curriculum, working for such programs as those in behalf of the handicapped or those that will strengthen the fields of athletics, art, and music. Together with the professional educator associated with those particular programs, they engage in campaigns to protect and enhance their interests.

Most citizen groups active in school affairs are not parents, however, but members of noneducational organizations, such as business associations and property owners' groups. They are more interested in school policies bearing on taxes and the prestige of the school in connection with property values than in decisions about course content.

State Agencies

During the 1980s, the states increased their role in educational policy at the expense of local school districts. This growth was a result of an

---

[28]Chris Pipho, "Sorting out Local Control," *Phi Delta Kappan* 70, no. 6 (February 1989): 430–431.

[29]Jon Schaffarzick, "Teacher and Lay Participation in Local Curriculum Change Considerations" (Paper presented at the American Educational Research Association Annual Meeting, San Francisco, CA, 1976).

increase in the states' fiscal capacity to regulate education and the activities of interstate policy issue networks that influence federal funding and educational directives.[30]

States exercise leverage on the curriculum in many ways. State legislatures frequently prescribe what shall be taught. Driver training and courses on the dangers of alcohol and narcotics have long been mandated. Insurance, oil, and automobile interests, too, have influence in such matters as driver education legislation. Professional organizations, like those of vocational, special interest groups long ago cemented links within state departments of education.

The most noteworthy evidence of state control of curriculum is in the national minimum competency movement and academic reform by state legislation. This competency movement is concerned with assessing the basic academic skills of students at the high school and grammar school levels, and, ultimately, with establishing competency standards which all students must meet. By 1980, most states had either adopted legislation on the testing of such skills or had enacted regulations through their state boards of education. Academic reform legislation chiefly in setting tougher standards—more mathematics, science, English and foreign language—was common in 1984.

Unlike the federal government and its chief reliance on fiscal control, states use many controls in shaping the process and quality of the curriculum. Required texts, mandated testing, and requirements for teacher certification and competency are some of their means of control. The monitoring mechanisms are also more informal than those of the federal government—informal conciliation, district self-review, and management by media.

The roles of state departments of education and state boards of education vary from state to state. In New England, the local schools have had much freedom from state control, whereas in most southern states, textbooks and courses of instruction are mandated by the state. The manner of control has also differed. Some states, like New York, have long exercised control through required tests and examinations. Others, like Texas and California, exercise their leverage through state adoption of textbooks and instructional systems. In Texas, for example, the state commissioner nominates the members of the State Textbook Committee, and the State Board of Education has final authority in the selection of texts. State education department personnel specify the criteria for se-

---

[30]Michael W. Kirst, *The State's Role in Educational Policy: Innovation* (Palo Alto, CA: Stanford University Press, 1981).

lecting the books, including the topics to be covered. Books that have been selected are distributed to schools at state expense. Districts that want to use other texts must do so with local money.

Some states use accreditation procedures to maintain a particular curriculum. Accreditation may be done by the state department of education itself, by an association of professional educators (such as the National Association of School Principals), or by a private regional accrediting organization (such as the North Central Association of Colleges and Secondary Schools). Usually these agencies require site visits and evidence of a school's adherence to each of their detailed standards. One of their standards might read, "English courses are organized by themes or experiences with a minimum of emphasis on type or chronology." A standard for social studies might read, "Social studies offerings assist pupils in understanding ideologies that differ from democracy."

Testing Agencies

Testing agencies have helped make a "national" curriculum. Standardized tests for college adminssion have defined what students going to college must know in the way of understanding and reasoning. (See the *College Board Specification of Outcomes*, Chapter 4) Furthermore, national standardized reading and math tests given in the elementary schools determine much of the specific content of the curriculum. The Educational Testing Service, with an annual budget of more than fifty-two million dollars, dominates the testing industry and administers a broad range of vocational and college placement tests. Its Scholastic Aptitude Test has been considered the most important test the company has although ETS's acquisition of the National Assessment Contract might rival in importance. About one and one half million students take the SAT test each year. The test publishers say they try to hold a middle ground; they try not to freeze the secondary school curriculum and not to adopt innovations too quickly. Their practice of involving professionals from secondary schools and colleges in the preparation and review of the tests is intended to keep the achievement tests abreast of important trends

Publishers

Book publishers are the gatekeepers of ideas and knowledge. Most teaching in our schools is from textbooks or other curriculum material, such as guides, workbooks, and laboratory apparatus. Nearly 75 percent of students' classroom time and 90 percent of their homework is spent with instructional materials.[31] Student achievement—what students acquire from instruction—mirrors to a substantial extent the content in the textbook. Students are more likely to learn what they find in their textbooks than in something else. After an item of content has been included in a text as important for children to use, Walker and Schaffarzick say,

> . . . the multiple resources of the curriculum in use and the variety of active student learning processes combine to produce a level of achievement that is usually greater than any additional increment that might be produced by any further refinement of the curriculum or any improvement in teaching style or method or medium of instruction or organizational change in the school or classroom.[32]

Sometimes the textbook publisher is only a disseminator, and the actual product is developed by professionals in regional laboratories, universities, and nonprofit organizations paid by agencies of the federal government, private foundations, and professional and scientific associations. At other times, the publisher contracts directly with teachers to develop the company's products. There is pressure on publishers from state curriculum commissions and groups demanding emphasis on certain content. The list of topics to be avoided in textbooks is getting longer every day: the supernatural, war, sex, suicide, and sadness have been added to junk food, treatment of animals, and racial, gender, and age stereotyping. Publishers also use their sales organizations for information and guidance in the revision and production of texts. ''Strangely enough this network of salespeople is the only reasonably dependable comprehensive mechanism for compiling the preferences and prejudices of schools on curriculum matters.''[33] Even so, textbook content is generally one decade behind the scholarly fields with respect to knowledge and interpretation.

The Courts

The involvement of the courts in curriculum matters has become a critical issue. Some curriculum specialists are disturbed by what they see

---

[31]Sherry Keith, *Politics of Textbook Selection.*

[32]Decker Walker and Jon Schaffarzick, ''Comparing Curriculum,'' *Review of Educational Research* 44, no. 1 (1974): 101.

[33]Kirst and Walker, ''An Analysis of Curriculum Policy Making,'' p. 497.

as a trend in the courts to exceed their authority in curriculum matters.[34] Recent court decisions have mandated specific tests, methods, and materials that schools must use. Some courts have even mandated achievement goals in desegregation cases which, in effect, have made them the evaluators of school curriculum and programs. For example, in San Diego, a judge ordered a controversial approach to teaching reading involving mastery learning. In Tucson, a specific teaching method was mandated for use with minority pupils; and in Detroit, a judge ordered school officials to submit an instructional plan for use by all teachers in the system.

The explosion of school lawsuits is over, according to new studies. At the federal level, the number of opinions is expected to decline in the decade of the 1990s in all categories except special education. In state courts there has been a refocusing of court attention from area to area, such as from dress codes in the 1970s to drug and alcohol abuse in the 1980s. "Each issue seems to have a life of its own and then fades in importance."[35]

Authority to control public school curriculum resides as a matter of state law primarily with state education officials. However, Gail Sorenson has suggested two practical and legal ways to deal with challenges to curriculum content such as occur in censorship matters[36]:

1. Consider the fundamental First Amendment principle of nonsuppression of ideas. "Our Constitution does not permit the official suppression of ideas."
2. Recognize that materials used in public schools must be educationally suitable. That is, the decision to accept or reject material must not be on the basis of ideas expressed but on whether the material fosters or hinders the intellectual, emotional, and social development of students.

The Federal Government

In the 1960s and 1970s, the federal government became a very powerful influence on the kinds of materials used in schools. Mainly through

---

[34]Nicholas G. Crisculo, "Seven Critical Issues Facing Today's Schools," *Catalyst for Change* 12, no. 2 (Winter 1983): 28–30.

[35]Henry Lufflen, Jr., "Explosion in School Lawsuits Is Over, Studies Find," *Education Weekly*, (November 30, 1988): 7.

[36]Gail Paulus Sorenson, "Constitutional Considerations in Content-Based Curriculum Decision-Making" (Paper presented at the Annual Meeting of the AERA, April 11–15, 1983).

the National Science Foundation (NSF) and the United States Office of Education (USOE), it dwarfed all previous curriculum development efforts by states, districts, and private enterprise. Federally supported regional laboratories, academic scholars, and nonprofit organizations produced curriculum materials that have been used in most of our schools. Generally, this material modified the content of existing subject matter—mathematics, science, English, and reading. Also, by specifying the use of standardized tests for evaluating the projects they finance, federal agencies fostered national objectives.

Initially the government seemed to be interested in increasing the number of curriculum options available to schools. Later, however, there were deliberate efforts to ensure that schools used the new curriculum through evaluation requirements and special monies given to disseminate materials developed with federal funds. The government became more interested in producing change than in merely making change possible.

The 1977 federal policy established equalization of educational opportunity for minorities, women, non-English-speaking persons, the poor, and the geographically isolated as the focus of federal curriculum development (instructional improvement) efforts. Nevertheless, there was little consensus about the proper role of government in curriculum development, particularly in the areas in which values are so prominent: social studies, moral education, and sex education. The educational community feared that federal sponsorship of development, demonstration, dissemination, and teacher training activities was an illegitimate attempt to weaken state and local control over the school curriculum.

In the 1980s under President Reagan, there was a shift in federal curriculum policy. New organizational structure was created to implement President Reagan's call for a return to traditional values, recognition of the primary rights and responsibilities of parents in the education of their children, and a focus on private and parochial as well as public schools.[37]

Exemplary curriculum programs that had been disseminated to local educational agencies were discontinued because they seemed to allow for changes in attitude and critical outlook toward existing social structures and might have fostered moral relativism.[38]

---

[37]Marvin Pasch and Bert I. Green, ''A Case Study in Curriculum Decision Making and Federal Education Policy,'' *Educational Leadership* (October 1984): 43–47.

[38]Onalee McGraw, ''Reclaiming Traditional Values in Education: The Implication for Educational Research,'' *Educational Leadership* 42, no. 2 (October 1984): 39–42.

Secretary of Education Bennett introduced the phrase "three C's" to describe his curriculum emphasis: *content*—concentration on the basics of literature and history and the new basics of science, math, and computer skills; *choice*—parental control over where their children attend school and parental influence on what is to be taught, by whom, and how; *character*—thoughtfulness, kindness, honesty, respect for the law, knowing right from wrong, respect for parents and teachers, diligence, self-sacrifice, hard work, self-discipline, and love of country.

The flow of federal involvement in curriculum policy was reversed by the Education and Consolidation and Improvement Act, which replaced federal funding of categorical programs with a system of block grants and program responsibilities to states and local agencies. Although a new emphasis was placed on national needs in areas such as math and science, programs for big-city schools, especially for minorities and low income groups were cut back. Funding for bilingual education, for example, declined by 54 percent between 1980 and 1988.

Congressional initiatives in curriculum are made less likely by the fact that state governors have gained visibility and power in educational policy making and are not influenced as in the past by "education senators and representatives."[39]

There are signs that Congress will attempt to restore the federal government's role in improving elementary and secondary education. The Hawkins-Stafford School Improvement Amendment of 1988, for example, proposes programs for magnet schools, a new foreign language program, and programs for training science and math teachers. The new law states that Chapter I, the largest federal program, should expand its services from one-half, as at present, to all eligible (poor) children by 1993. Also, the law calls for a program "Even Start" that will educate disadvantaged preschoolers and their illiterate parents simultaneously. Two new funds are created for grants to local districts: One fund is for innovative programs and the other is for encouraging teachers to create new ways of dealing with educational problems. However, there is a catch to the law. Every school receiving Chapter I aid will have to show that test scores or other measurements of achievement have increased for educationally disadvantaged children participating in the program. The new law forbids states from telling local school districts what they can or cannot do or to determine the grade level to be served, the content

[39]David L. Clark and Terry A. Astuto, "The Significance and Permanence of Changes in Federal Education Policy," *Educational Research* 15, no. 8 (October 1986): pp. 4–13.

of instructional materials, the basic skills to be addressed, or the qualifications of teachers. States have to convene panels of local practitioners to review any proposed state regulations before they are issued.[40]

Foundations

Foundations are a major source of funds and influence on the curriculum. The Ford, Rockefeller, Carnegie, and Kettering foundations have been very active in curriculum development. An indication of the direction and effect of their influence is found in *A Foundation Goes to School*.[41] This report tells of deliberate efforts to change the habits of school systems and to modify the curriculum by underwriting the production of locally made curriculum materials. The foundations' effort was only partially successful, mostly in suburban school districts. The effort to package curriculum stalled because individual teachers wanted to create their own materials. Yet, in many instances, overproduction of inadequate curriculum units at the local level occurred because of failure to estimate the difficulties of curriculum construction.

In terms of both cost and learning, the adoption of professionally developed curricula produced far more substantive change than in-house curriculum development. Without systematic teacher preparation, the use of new curricula tended to be superficial, sporadic, and ephemeral. The most lasting application seemed to occur in middle-sized suburbs, which were small enough to avoid the divisive debate between powerful interest groups but large enough to require that innovative movements be identified with more than individual or simple localized concerns.

In recent years, the Heritage Foundation, composed of conservative activists, has gained curriculum power. The foundation claims that almost two-thirds of the nearly 2,000 recommendations had been or were transformed into policy by the end of President Reagan's first year in office. This foundation issued an influential document *Mandate for Leadership II*.[42] Among the recommendations in this document were those calling for (a) more parental control over their children's education, (b) constitutional amendments to permit school prayer, and (c) an end to federal

---

[40]Jack F. Jennings, "Working in Mysterious Ways: The Federal Government and Education," *Phi Delta Kappan* 70, no. 1 (September 1988): 62–66.

[41]Ford Foundation, *A Foundation Goes to School* (New York: Ford Foundation, 1972).

[42]Stuart M. Butler, Michael Sanera, and Bruce Weinsrad, *Mandate for Leadership II: Continuing the Conservative Revolution* (Washington, DC: Heritage Foundation, 1984).

intervention in state and local school matters related to the educational opportunities of black Americans, handicapped persons, women, and new immigrant populations. The document designated the federal role in schools to that of pressing for improved academic performance and traditional values as defined by conservatives. The foundation's techniques for managing policy changes include staffing federal agencies with "credible" personnel who support conservative ideological views of what education is for and who should be educated. Accordingly, the President is to use appointments over budgetary control to weaken equity programs that enjoy congressional support. Federal influence over state and local practices is to be exercised by controlling information and focusing public opinion on getting the desired action from state and local officials.

Pressure Groups

Kirst and Walker have differentiated between two separate policy-making processes: normal policy making and crisis policy making. Groups such as the John Birch Society, Chamber of Commerce, National Association of Manufacturers, and AFL-CIO are regarded as relatively weak in normal policy making but very powerful in crisis policy making.[43]

International academic competitiveness, drug abuse, war, depression, violence, energy, and natural disaster are examples of crises that draw the response of different groups. Then there are organizations like the Council for Basic Education, which lobbies consistently for the teaching of fundamental, intellectual subjects, and the American Education Association which is against sex education and atheistic ideas. The political workings of the National Association for the Education of Young Children illustrate a single cause approach.[44] Also, some causes invite the combined pressures of many different groups. Virtually every organization working for the advancement of Afro-Americans, whether militant or moderate, has demanded a more adequate treatment of blacks in books and courses dealing with the history of the United States. Similarly, in protecting against the secular offerings of public schools, members of conservative religious groups challenge the notion that schools teach the truth and that there is such a thing as objective knowledge.

---

[43]Kirst and Walker, "An Analysis of Curriculum Policy Making," p. 498.

[44]Barbara Miller, "Expanding Our Child Advocacy Efforts: NAEYC Forms a Public Network on Children," *Young Children* 38, no. 6 (September 1983): 71–74.

Special interest groups follow a common strategy in influencing curriculum content: (a) they offer their own evaluation criteria for judging instructional materials, in contrast to the criteria given by the state; (b) they politically address the school board rather than go through the bureaucratic structure of the school, and (c) they rely on moral arguments and their own moral positions.

CONFLICTS IN CURRICULUM CONTROL

The control of curriculum in the United States is a shared responsibility. Authority is dispensed throughout three levels of government—local, state, and federal—and curriculum mandates are issued from all three branches of government—legislative, executive, and judicial. These mandates include (a) federal court actions such as those pertaining to meeting the language needs of non-English speaking persons and of children with specific handicaps; (b) federal legislation giving funds to school districts if they agree to meet certain conditions for their use. (Examples of such funding are those for disadvantaged children, for science, mathematical, and environmental education, ethnic studies, vocational education, career education, gifted education, and consumer education); (c) state courts in their decisions relating to school financing, planning, and implementation of educational programs (these have triggered mandates that increase state control of programs formerly delegated to local school authorities); (d) court decisions giving participation privileges to parents and students as well as increased use of legal contracts (collective bargaining) which result in mandates directly or indirectly affecting curriculum, preempting the control by local boards and educators.

Shared control has produced conflict. Federal mandates often combine both educational and social or political goals, as in grant programs for special groups. While these mandates draw attention to the poor, the minorities, and the handicapped, they also conflict with traditional views of how best to develop understanding, skills, and attitudes among learners. For example, children sometimes are required to travel to distant schools, losing instructional time in order to satisfy arbitrary racial composition percentages.

Contradictory mandates from different levels of authority sometimes occur. For example, the federal requirement demands quotas in vocational education, quotas which often conflict with state guidelines on whom is to be eligible for such programs. Mandates for the federal and state governments on behalf of certain special interests have resulted in competition with other special interests and with regular programs, resulting in program fragmentation in the local school. Conflict is triggered by the failure of federal and state authorities to consider the ability of local authorities to carry out the mandates. Although financial incentives are given for starting some curriculum programs, these mandates assume that other agencies will provide the necessary funds, or that the local school can implement the mandate without additional resources.

Conflicts over noncompliance are associated with shared control. Intentional and unintentional deviation from the goals and guidelines of a mandate create tensions. Even when there is surface compliance, the intents of the mandate may not be fulfilled. As Richard Elmore and Milbray McLaughlin point out, "We have some perfectly legal but perfectly horrible Title I programs in our state."[45]

As the discussion in Chapter 9 of top-down strategies indicated, mandates cannot create commitment. The motivation of local participants to comply with mandated objectives and their willingness to achieve the project's goals are essential if the project is to succeed. More regulations governing implementation is not the answer. The difficulties arising from increased bureaucratic red tape actually hinder attaining the intent of the mandates. It is true, however, that fiscal audits and compliance reviews are influential in shaping administrative behavior.[46]

Recent studies of shared control, thought, are not all pessimistic. Michael Knapp and others, for example, have found that over time, local problem solving and accommodation reduce the conflicts of an external mandate.[47] Most of the burden of particular laws, for instance, diminishes after the first year or two. Although intergovernmental conflicts exist, they are neither massive nor common across all programs.

Suggestions for improving shared curriculum control include an idealistic proposal to limit the authority of each agency so that there is no conflict in power.[48] Other more feasible suggestions call for employing

---

[45]Richard F. Elmore and Milbray W. McLaughlin, "The Federal Role in Education," *Education and Urban Society* 15, no. 3 (May 1983): 316.

[46]Mary T. Moore et al., "Interaction of Federal and State Programs," *Education and Urban Society* 11, no. 4 (August 1983): 452–478.

[47]Michael S. Knapp et al., "Cumulative Effects at the Local Level," *Education and Urban Society* 15, no. 4 (August 1983): 479–499.

[48]Edmund C. Short, "Authority and Governance in Curriculum Development: A Policy Analysis in the United States Context," *Educational Evaluation and Policy Analysis* 5, no. 2 (Summer 1983): 195–205.

implementation strategies emphasizing local technical assistance and capacity building rather than depending upon regulatory or compliance oriented strategies. At least, implementation rather than compliance strategies should be used after a mandatory program has been established. Flexibility for local decision making in designing, managing, and delivering services is a key factor in the quality of education provided under mandates. Similarly, federal mandates should encourage flexibility in responding to the wide variance among states and local communities.

CONCLUDING COMMENTS

The debate over the proper division of responsibility among federal, state, and local government shows no sign of being settled. Issues such as a federal mathematics and science program, tax credits, and school prayer keep the focus on the federal role. The tendency of states to require more of everything—legislated excellence—is strong. The need for local commitment on every undertaking gives support for adaptive policies of implementation and local initiative. Intergovernmental relations will remain numerous and complex.

Many groups and individuals are interested in having a say about what should be taught. No single source believes that it has enough influence or power. Each tends to feel that another element is in charge. In reality, it is a standoff. The curriculum decision of a board of education, a federal agency, a state department of education, or a legislature can be changed in spirit and in fact by principals and teachers. Although students are often thought to be without much power in deciding what will be taught in schools, they have a great deal to say about what is learned.

The political link of special interest groups within professional education to those in government is not too different from the more exposed business and government ties. Most curriculum decisions, however, reflect conflicts among persons and groups. Like most political solutions, the curriculum comes about through compromise, bargaining, and other forms of accommodation. School organizations are not equal in their ability to balance conflicting pressures. Those schools that conduct more community meetings about curriculum issues have to satisfy fewer demands of special interest groups. Public meetings offer opportunity for citizen defense of challenged school policies. The formulation of curriculum policy does not follow a tidy rational procedure resting on the evidence from research. Curriculum, it seems, will continue to be developed by those who have little idea of its effect in the classroom.

QUESTIONS

1. Would you choose a "moral, principled, legal" model of curriculum making, in which curriculum decisions are made by authorities on the basis of logic and with the guidance of experts? Or, would you prefer a model that depends on agreement between different political interests and seeks no more than an imperfect justice because there is no other kind?
2. Should professional curriculum workers, supervisors, teachers, and principals exert more influence in the control of curriculum? Why? Why not? Consider in your answer such matters as whether educators have the unity as well as the necessary intellectual and moral authority.
3. Which forces appear to have the greatest effect on what is taught in a situation familiar to you?
4. What will be the likely outcome of the collision courses among the forces pushing for more power to teachers, the forces favoring strong state control, and the forces restoring the federal government's role in curriculum making?
5. Democratic policies aim at the curriculum reducing inequality; capitalists see the curriculum as a community commodity giving selective advantage in the individual competition for market rewards. Under what conditions will the respective views dominate?
6. Who should control our schools?

SELECTED REFERENCES

Berger, Landon E., and Apple, Michael W. *The Curriculum: Problems, Politics, and Possibilities.* Albany, NY: State University of New York Press, 1988.

Schaffarzick, Jon, and Sykes, Gary, eds. *Value Conflict and Curriculum Issues.* Berkeley: McCutchan, 1982.

Tyack, David, Thomas, James, and Benavol, Aaron. *Law and the Shaping of Public Education.* Madison: University of Wisconsin Press, 1987.

Wayson, William W. *Up From Excellence: The Impact of the Excellence Movement in Schools.* Bloomington, IN: Phi Delta Kappa Educational Foundation, 1988.

Wirt, Frederick M., and Kirst, Michael W. *Schools in Conflicts: The Politics of Education,* 2nd ed. Berkeley, CA: McCutchan, 1988.

Issues and Trends

In the next two chapters we will examine curriculum in a wider context. Chapter 12 deals with some of the most pressing issues confronting those who would develop programs for American schools, such as how best to develop high level thinking, the competitiveness of American curriculum, vocational education, the hidden curriculum, moral education, and cultural pluralism. Underlying these issues is the question of how to reconcile two components of the American ideal: the democratic element which promotes equality and the shaping of power and the element of competitive individualism within a market economy which promotes inequality and status attainment.

Chapter 13 describes changes in the school's presentation of academic subject matters. These subject matter trends reflect the culture of the moment. They also stand as early warnings of developments that have not been generally recognized. Underlying the issues and trends is the tension between furthering the ideals of social justice and equal opportunity through the curriculum and maintaining the pursuit of excellence.

12

Current Issues
Demanding Responses

Six crucial curriculum issues—development of thinking, competition in education with other nations, vocational education, the hidden curriculum, moral education, and cultural pluralism—are examined in this chapter. These matters are crucial because the resolution of any of these issues alters the curriculum in very different ways. However, no definite set of solutions to the issues is given. Instead, a range of views on each problem is offered so that the readers can discover for themselves the grounds for choosing one position over another. The purpose is not to argue for one view but to consider all the factors that apply to each situation and each potential resolution.

Although each issue is important in its own right, you may regard those discussed here as just a sample of the many issues demanding curriculum responses. It is recommended that the descriptions of these issues be used as opportunities to apply the curriculum orientations acquired thus far. In this way you will not only be thinking about the particular issues, but also developing ability to think about these and other issues as a curriculum specialist would. You may wish to examine the issues from the perspective of different curriculum conceptions or note how traditional curriculum questions are being answered by the proponents involved. For example, using a knowledge of curriculum conceptions, you might try to analyze vocational education critically from the academic conception, the hidden curriculum from the perspective of a social reconstructionist, or different views of moral education from the humanistic perspective. You may wish to treat the issue of cultural pluralism by comparing the likely responses of those with academic, technological, and social reconstructionist views of curriculum. If you choose to use traditional questions for examining the issues, you might ask "Does the emphasis upon high level thinking skills advance the idea of a common curriculum for all? How is the subject matter of moral education related to method? Are principles of sequence applicable to the hidden curriculum?"

CURRICULUM FOR THINKING

The curriculum has long been associated with the aim of developing mental power. One view is that thinking—the intellectual power of memorization and reasoning—can best be developed through the right kind of subject matter. Another is that no subject is inherently intellectual. As Dewey says, "Any subject, from Greek to cooking, and from drawing to mathematics, is intellectual, if intellectual at all, not in its fixed inner structure, but in its functions—in its power to start and direct significant inquiry and reflection."[1] Exponents of the doctrine of formal discipline have long argued that the study of Latin and other difficult subjects would develop the ingredients to learn and think in any domain.

In 1894, the Committee of Ten held that the chief purpose of education was to "train the mind," and, although the members differed among themselves as to which subjects were best for this purpose—languages and the classics or math and the sciences—they compromised by saying that all the principal subjects might accomplish this purpose if consecutively taught so that they would enhance the process of observation, memory, expression, and reasoning.

Shortly after the committee's report, there were attacks on the doctrine of formal discipline, including the idea that instruction is abstract and that rule systems can affect reasoning about everyday life. William James presented a withering critique of faculty psychology, the idea that mental abilities consist of faculties such as memory and reasoning and that the mind could be improved by mere exercise as muscles are. Subsequently, Edward Thorndike's research found little transfer across tasks.

---

[1] John Dewey, *How We Think* (Boston: D. C. Heath & Co. 1933): pp. 46–47.

For example, from estimating areas of rectangles of one size and shape to estimating areas of rectangles of another size and shape, he concluded that learning is specific rather than a matter of mental discipline. Transfer can occur but not because of the disciplinary value of classical study, but only if the old and new activities share a common element such as content or method.[2]

Contemporary psychologists added to doubt about mental discipline, holding that learning how to solve one problem produces no improvement in solving other problems with an identical formal structure.[3]

In the late 1980s, the goal of teaching thinking, reasoning, and problem solving has been pursued with new vigor. This renewal follows changes in society that make it necessary for people to think for themselves and to solve novel problems. Assessments suggesting that students may be failing to develop effective thinking is another reason.

New theories for the teaching of thinking stress that knowledge is not important as a "mental discipline" but as a way to conceptualize situations, to identify patterns, and to organize the information so that new problems in the subject area can be solved. Also, today's psychology emphasizes teaching students the kinds of problems for which the subject matter is useful and the condition under which the formal knowledge applies. Psychological findings that reasoning can be taught and that different subject matters teach different kinds of reasoning support the view that thinking can be improved through the curriculum.

David Lehman and other psychologists have found that some of the inferential rules that people use to solve everyday problems are improved by formal training.[4] Although the rule systems of mathematics and formal logic contribute little to everyday reasoning, pragmatic rule systems do. Examples of pragmatic rule systems include (a) *the law of large numbers* (extreme values for a sample are less likely to be excessive when a new sample is observed); (b) *casual schemas* (identify what is necessary and sufficient, what is necessary but not sufficient, and what is neither necessary nor sufficient); and (c) *contractual schemas* (before taking action A, one must satisfy preconditions, and the occurrence of one event obligates another).

Different kinds of education produce different effects on reasoning

---

[2]Edward Thorndike, *The Principle of Teaching* (New York: A. G. Seiler, 1906).

[3]S. R. Reed et al., "Usefulness of Analogous Solutions for Solving Algebra Word Problems," *Journal of Experimental Psychology: Learning, Memory, Cognition* 11 (1985): 105–125.

[4]Darrin R. Lehman et al., "The Effects of Graduate Training on Reasoning," *American Psychologist* 43, no. 6 (June 1988): 431–442.

about various life events. Lehman and his associates investigated the effect of studying psychology and medicine (probabilistic science), chemistry (nonprobabilistic science), and law (a nonscience) finding that the probabilistic training produced large effects on statistical and methodological reasoning, that both probabilistic and law training produced effects on the ability to reason about logic of the conditional, and that chemistry had no effect on the types of reasoning studied. Also, Raymond Nickerson found that teaching the strategies of reasoning to elementary school children can improve their performance on IQ tests. Among the strategies taught were how to use dimensions, to analyze and organize, how to extrapolate different types of sequences, how to see the structure of simple propositions and analyze complex arguments, and how to evaluate consistency.[5]

The renaissance of the doctrine of formal discipline confronts students of the curriculum with questions about which dimensions of thinking should be targeted, which curriculum programs have beneficial effects, and whether it is better to teach thinking as part of traditional content courses or as "stand alone" programs for thinking.

The Focus of a Thinking Curriculum

Social Reconstructionists' Goals of Thinking. Social reconstructionists favor critical thinking and want students to show a healthy skepticism about the world, their community, and their schooling. The liberatory curriculum and critical inquiry described in Chapter 2 illustrated the preferred approach. Another is to teach directly such topics as the need for definition, logic, and the weight of evidence, the nature of evidence, deductive and inductive inferencing, and propaganda analysis.

Robert Ennis has proposed a critical thinking curriculum aimed at helping students analyze arguments, look for valid evidence, and reach sound conclusions.[6]

There are both weak sense and strong sense conceptions of critical thinking. Thinking in the *weak sense* means to construct arguments in defense of one's own point of view. *Strong sense* thinkers are able to critique their own thinking and to reconstruct the strongest arguments for points of view opposed to their own.[7]

---

[5]Raymond Nickerson et al., *The Teaching of Thinking* (Hillsdale, NJ: Erlbaum, 1985).
[6]Robert E. Ennis, "A Taxonomy of Critical Thinking Disposition and Abilities," in *Teaching Thinking Skills: Theory and Practices,* eds. J. Baron and R. Sternberg (New York: Freeman, 1987).
[7]R. W. Paul, "Critical Thinking and the Critical Person," in *Review of Research in Education,* ed. Ernest Z. Rothkopf (Washington, DC: American Educational Research Association, 1989), p. 22.

Humanistic Goals for Thinking. Humanists value creative thinking—the ability to form new combinations of ideas to fulfill individual needs. A great deal has been said regarding teaching strategies and conditions conducive to creative thinking. The importance of psychological safety, freedom, and stimulation is well known. Vera John Steiner's account of how creative people engage in thinking is an excellent source of understanding the origins and elaboration of creative thought.[8]

Various curriculum projects offer exercises in exploring the unfamiliar and creating something new. Usually creative programs call for *fluency* (through such techniques as brainstorming), *flexibility* (changing the focus of thought), *exploring* (confronting paradoxes), *elaborating* (adding new material to existing ideas), and *risk taking* (trying out a new idea). William Gordon's *Synectics* has been useful in developing curriculum for creativity in science, social studies, and writing.[9]

Unresolved are questions whether any formal curriculum would work for Mozart or any other creative genius and whether divergent thinking exercises and programs for learning to use various analogies are as important as equipping minds with the information, principles, concepts, and theories with which to think about something in a new way.

Academicians' Goals for Thinking. Academicians prize the paradigmatic or logico-scientific mode of thinking. This mode is based on categorization, conceptualization, and the operations for establishing and relating categories. In trying to develop academic minds, three kinds of knowledge are taught: (a) basic operations such as classifying, generalizing, deducing; (b) problem-solving strategies; and (c) domain-specific information:

1. *Curriculum for Teaching Basic Operations.* Programs for teaching basic operations are numerous. *Science—a Process Approach* is a successful curriculum focusing on eight basic processes of science.[10] This curriculum represents an integrated approach to teaching intellectual skills in the context of learning science. In contrast, *Instrumental Enrichment* is almost free of specific subject matter.[11] This curriculum offers a three-year series of experiments involving classification, orientation

[8]Vera John-Steiner, *Notebook of the Mind: Explorations of Thinking* (Albuquerque: University of New Mexico Press, 1985).

[9]Arthur E. Costa et al., "Synectics: Making the Familiar Strange," in *Developing Minds: A Resource Book for Teaching Thinking,* ed. Arthur Costa (Washington, DC: ASCD, 1985).

[10]H. J. Klausmeir, *Learning and Teaching Concepts* (New York: Academic Press, 1980).

[11]Reuven Feurstein et al., *Instrumental Enrichment* (Baltimore: University Park Press, 1980).

in space, logical reasoning, and the like through paper and pencil exercises followed by discussions about how the respective thinking processes might be applied in and out of school.

Students of curriculum must weigh the advantages for teaching both processes in the contest of content-rich material which provides a link for relating the thinking skills to a given domain and the advantage of separate programs that explicate processes without presuming any specialized background knowledge on the part of students and which removes the conceptual distraction often found in content-rich exercises.

2. *Curriculum for Teaching Problem Solving.* Curriculum for the teaching of problem solving is based upon studies of how experts elaborate and reconstruct problems and how they look for solutions by reasoning from analogies. Typically, students learn the heuristics of diagramming, breaking a problem into subproblems, finding analogous problems and working backward. An example of a problem-solving curriculum is *The Productive Thinking Program*, which has been used successfully in middle school. With this curriculum, students show gains in both the quantity and quality of their ideas (fluency) and improvement in intellectual independence and self-confidence.[12]

Edward de Bono has constructed a curriculum, *Cognitive Research Trust* (CORT), which aims at having students take a broader view of formally posed problems without being restrained by conventions in their thinking.[13] Lessons in this program focus on the perceptual aspect of thinking. Inasmuch as de Bono wants to develop the habits of mind and thinking techniques that can be applied in any subject area, his curriculum emphasizes generalizable strategies rather than specific subject matter.

The emphasis upon metacognitive knowledge as an aid to problem solving sets the current thinking skills movement apart from earlier similar movements. Metacognition training involves teaching students how to manage their own cognitive resources and to monitor their own intellectual performance. Students are taught to use such strategies as how to access task-relevant information, to recognize when something requires clarification, and to make hypotheses and predictions, revising them as the basis of new information.[14]

---

[12]M.V. Corrington, "Strategic Thinking and Fear of Failure," in *Thinking and Learning 1*, eds. J. W. Segal et al. (Hillsdale, NJ: Erlbaum, 1985), pp. 389–411.

[13]*CORT Thinking Program.* Pergamon, Inc. Maxwell House, Fairview Park, Elmsford, NY 10523.

[14]M. Scardamalia and C. Bereiter, "Fostering the Development of Self-Regulation in Children's Knowledge Processing," in *Thinking and Learning Skills: Research and Open Questions 2*, eds. S. F. Chapman et al. (Hillsdale, NJ: Erlbaum, 1985), pp. 563–577.

Evaluation of programs for the direct teaching of problem solving gives mixed results. Usually students acquire the strategies taught but fail to use these heuristics in other contexts and courses. As with the teaching of the basic processes, results as measured by performance or standardized tests are proportional to the similarity of standardized tests and program practice items, suggesting that the results are attributed more to familiarity with tasks than to changed cognitive functions.

3. *Domain-Specific Knowledge.* Whereas experts tend to organize their knowledge on the basis of abstractions that reflect deep understanding of a subject, novices are more likely to organize their conceptions of the problem around literal objects and relationships explicitly mentioned. Students often acquire knowledge but do not apply it. Hence, the current focus in curriculum for thinking is not upon the acquisition and coverage of subject matter, but on how the subject can be taught so that students think about the content in fresh ways and acquire intellectual tools that can be useful in other contexts.

In brief, the challenge is to develop curriculum that will deemphasize student reproduction of knowledge, which tends to remain inert, and to treat knowledge as a stimulation to inquiry and reflection. There should be opportunities to expose one's own and others' beliefs and opinions to criticism and to know how and when to use the formal and informal tools of thought.

CURRICULUM COMPETITION: AN INTERNATIONAL COMPARISON

Is the curriculum in United States schools lagging behind those in other countries? If so, why, and what should be done about it? These questions are controversial. Some view Japanese, Soviet, and Chinese increases in educational productivity—particularly in science and mathematics—in contrast to declining test scores in the United States as a grave national concern. Others say that the data on the comparisons are questionable and that illustrations of the weaknesses of the American educational system create the false impression that American education should imitate the practices of competing nations.

Invidious Comparisons

Herbert Walberg has summarized the case for those who see America falling behind educationally and who believe that educational decline will have severe consequences on the nation's ability to compete in the world market.[15]

Walberg cites four examples that evidence the decline. First, H. W. Stevenson shows that American students fall farther behind Asian students in mathematics the longer they stay in school and that by the fifth grade, the worst Japanese classes exceed the best American classes. Second, Isaak Wirszup claims that in contrast to the approximately half million students who take a year of calculus in the United States, five million Soviet secondary students complete a two-year course in the subject. According to Wirszup, all Soviet youth are required to complete five years of physics, four years of chemistry, and up to four years of biology by the end of secondary school. Third, Paul Hurd reports that during a visit by the United States science delegation to the People's Republic of China, he observed a massive effort by China to upgrade the science curriculum. In China, local curricula have been replaced by a uniform program emphasizing application and experiments. The academically talented are sought and encouraged to attend key schools. If one measures scientific literacy by an index of the number of years that students must study science and mathematics multiplied by the number of students, the People's Republic probably ranks first in the world.[16-18] Finally, Walberg refers to test data from the International Association for the Evaluation of Educational Achievement that permit reliable international comparisons of achievement. These data showed that Japanese students excelled the grand mean when compared with students in 14 other industrialized countries, whereas American students scored near the grand mean. Japanese students scored higher than students in other countries both on items that require functional information as well as on items that test understanding, application, and higher scientific thought, such as hypothesis formulation. Walberg attributes the high Japanese scores to the requirement of the Japanese Ministry of Education that 25 percent of classroom time in lower secondary schools be devoted to science and mathematics. (Nearly all Japanese students are exposed to this much science and mathematics through the ninth grade.) In their three

---

[15]Herbert J. Walberg, "Scientific Literacy and Economic Productivity in International Perspective," *Daedalus* 112, no. 2 (Spring 1983): 1–29.

[16]H. W. Stevenson, *Achievement in Mathematics* (Palo Alto: Stanford Center for Advanced Studies in Behavioral Sciences, 1983.)

[17]Izaak Wirszup, "The Soviet Challenge," *Educational Leadership* 38, no. 5 (February 1981): 358–366.

[18]Paul de Hurd, *Science Education in the People's Republic of China* (Washington, DC: National Science Foundation, 1981).

years of high school, nearly all college-bound Japanese students (about one third of the total) take three natural sciences courses and four mathematics courses through differential calculus.

Two recent studies of mathematics and science achievement in fifteen to twenty-five different countries played up the "Olympic Game" aspect of mean national achievement scores.[19] However, for comparable populations in a school among the industrialized nations, the range of means is really not large nor consistent across school subjects and age groups. Schools on the average provide for their students as well in one developed country as in another.[20]

The Educational Testing Service conducted an international assessment of mathematics (Table 12–1) and sciences achieved among thirteen-year-olds in five countries and five Canadian provinces. This study is noteworthy for its use of questions adapted for cultural differences derived from the National Assessment of Education Project (NAEP).[21]

With respect to science achievement, the ETS study found diversity among the achievement of thirteen-year-olds across populations. Table 12–2 depicts the percentage of students from each population who have acquired the science knowledge and skills reflected at defined levels of achievement.

The fact that 95 percent of British Columbia's thirteen-year-olds can apply simple scientific principles at a given level whereas less than 80 percent of those in the United States sample demonstrated this level of competence, provokes discussion.

School curriculum, time devoted to science, types of classroom activities are all considerations for study. Other variables such as socio-economic conditions, level of parents' education, and the societal value placed on the study of science also must be considered.

Caution in making too much of the findings of the NAEP study is voiced by Richard Wolfe. Wolfe believes that the findings are exaggerated because the measurements of each skill are composites of different items, and fail to show the means of the test items across countries. Some parts of the test are more difficult for students in some populations. The international comparisons are very much determined by how the topics

[19]International Association for the Evaluation of Educational Achievement, *Science Achievement in Seventeen Countries* (Oxford, England: Pergamon Press, 1988).

[20]International Association for the Evaluation of Achievement, *The Underachieving Curriculum: Assessing US School Mathematics from an International Perspective* (Champaign, IL: Stipes Publishing Company, 1987).

[21]Archie E. Lapointe et al., *A World of Differences* (Princeton, NJ: ETS, January 1989).

**TABLE 12–1 Percentages Performing at or Above Each Level
of the Mathematics Scale, Age 13*†**

Country or Province	Add and Subtract	Simple Problems	Two-Step Problems	Understand Concepts	Interpret Data
Level 300	Level 300	Level 400	Level 500	Level 600	Level 700
Korea	100	95	78	40	5
Quebec (French)	100	97	73	22	2
British Columbia	100	95	69	24	2
Quebec (English)	100	97	67	20	1
New Brunswick (English)	100	95	65	18	1
Ontario (English)	99	92	58	16	1
New Brunswick (French)	100	95	58	12	<1
Spain	99	91	57	14	1
United Kingdom	98	87	55	18	2
Ireland	98	86	55	14	<1
Ontario (French)	99	85	40	7	0
United States	97	78	40	9	1

*Jackknifed standard errors for percentages range from less than .1 to 2.4.
†From Archie E. Lapointe et al., *A World of Difference* (Princeton, NJ: Educational Testing Service, January 1989).

**TABLE 12–2 Percentages Performing at or Above Each Level
of the Science Scale, Age 13*†**

Country or Province	Know Everyday Facts	Apply Simple Principles	Analyze Experiments	Apply Intermediate Principles	Integrate Experimental Evidence
	Level 300	Level 400	Level 500	Level 600	Level 700
British Columbia	100	95	72	31	4
Korea	100	93	73	33	2
United Kingdom	98	89	59	21	2
Quebec (English)	99	92	57	15	1
Ontario (English)	99	91	56	17	2
Quebec (French)	100	91	56	15	
New Brunswick (English)	99	90	55	15	1
Spain	99	88	53	12	1
United States	96	78	42	12	1
Ireland	96	76	37	9	1
Ontario (French)	98	79	35	6	<1
New Brunswick (French)	98	78	35	7	<1

*Jackknifed standard errors for percentages range from less than .1 to 2.6.
†From Archie E. Lapointe et al., *A World of Difference* (Princeton, NJ: Educational Testing Service, January 1989).

were sampled from the small number of items and ''If the problem of achievement varies between countries, how can there be a single comparative scale''?[22] Also, across countries, students are given different topics to learn.

Validity of Invidious Comparisons

Walberg himself raises doubts about the magnitude of the gap between American educational standards and those of other nations. He points out that the general ability of United States high school seniors intending to major in science and mathematics in college has risen. Moreover, as the ranking in the International Mathematics Olympics shows, the best American mathematics students compare well with any mathematics students in the world.[23] Scholars who have directly observed Soviet classes have found that many Soviet schools do not have the textbooks and science materials required by the curriculum, that the preparation of teachers is inadequate, that students are not exposed to computers and programming, and that students lack motivation and often do not understand the lesson.

Iris Rotberg of the National Institute of Education has questions about Isaak Wirszup, one of Walberg's sources.[24] She charges that the comparisons between Russian and American schools are exaggerated, that Wirszup failed to compare the actual hours spent in instruction so that a report of one year of study in the USSR may actually represent less than one semester of study, depending upon how many hours are given to the task during the year.

As for the data from the International Association for the Evaluation of Education Achievement (IEA), Torsten Husen, the chairman of these cross-national comparative studies has pointed out their limitations.[25] Meaningful comparisons among countries in terms of standardized test achievements are difficult to make. Countries in which the government dictates the curriculum with clear-cut expectations and accompanying

---

[22]Richard Wolfe, *Reaching to ''A World of Differences''* (Toronto: Ontario Institute for Studies in Education, in press).

[23]Thomas Romberg and Charles L. Lambert, ''Soviet Mathematics Education: A Response,'' *Educational Leadership* 38, no. 5 (February 1981): 365–367.

[24]Iris C. Rotberg, ''Some Observations on the Reported Gap Between American and Soviet Educational Standards,'' *American Education* 19, no 1 (January/February 1983): 3.

[25]Torsten Husen, ''Are Standards in United States Schools Really Lagging Behind Those in Other Countries?'' *Phi Delta Kappan* 64, no. 7 (March 1983): 455–461.

examination exercises for practice should do well on the corresponding achievement tests. One might expect an unfair comparison between the United States, which has a comprehensive curriculum (programs ranging from highly academic to vocational ones), with countries such as France, England, and Germany, in which the curriculum focuses upon college preparation. However, the IEA surveys showed that in both mathematics and science, the top 10% of all students at the end of secondary education (the elite) performed at nearly the same level whether they attended comprehensive or selective systems of secondary education. Opportunity to learn is the single most important factor accounting for differences in achievement. For example, in looking at the results of achievement in French as a foreign language, the United States (in which only two years of high school French is required) recorded a dismal score; whereas Rumania, which requires six years of French, was at the top. Husen concludes that low standards are not the most serious problem in schooling. The most serious problem for all industrialized nations is the rise of a new educational underclass—those who from the very beginning tend to be failures in school. The key question is how to give an advanced education, one formerly available only to a small social and intellectual elite, to the educationally underprivileged—those who do not have the advantage of a background which stresses education.

Christopher Hurn also believes that most of the implications of American inferiority drawn from the comparisons are inappropriate.[26] He criticizes studies that compare systems that have profound differences in objectives, values, and organization. Such studies lead to the false implication that effective reform lies in borrowing practices from abroad. Instead, Americans must realize that their weaknesses are bound up with their strengths. It may be unrealistic to expect single-minded concentration in one area, such as mathematics, science, or languages, with American values of egalitarianism, utilitarianism, and individualism. These latter values create a lack of selectivity, a suspicion of the liberal arts, and a desire for educational choices. The American utilitarian emphasis on the needs of students and society has influenced both how traditional subject matter is taught and even whether it is taught. The Council for Basic Education also recognizes utilitarianism as an American passion which has competed with the liberal arts education. For thirty years, the Council advocated unsuccessfully that all students have a liberal

---

[26]Christopher J. Hurn, "The Problem with Comparisons," *Educational Leadership* 41, no. 2 (October 1983): 7–12.

arts education rather than a vocational education, and that other ways be provided for the different needs of different students. Furthermore, the decentralization of education in America does not create incentives for vigorous concentration on mathematics, science, and language. Finally, the imposition of narrow national standards for academic excellence runs counter to competing curriculum goals which attempt to foster informed citizens, a diversity of useful skills, self-actualization, and moral values.

VOCATIONAL EDUCATION

Four issues face curriculum planners in vocational education. The first issue is *purpose*. Should vocational education aim at broad intellectual development and guidance, helping individuals make decisions about careers, or should it aim at preparing students with marketable skills? The second issue is *access*. Should vocational education be open to the slow, as well as to the gifted? Is the notion of courses limited to either male or female (home economics for girls and auto shop for boys) obsolete? The third issue is *content*. How well does the content of vocational educational programs match the present and future needs of the economy? The fourth issue is *organization*. Should vocational education be restructured in order to close the gap between the vocational programs of the school and the requirements of work?

Contrasting Purposes for Vocational Education

Americans have long been divided on the relative value of the liberal arts, which seem to have little practical value, and vocational studies, which promise to be immediately useful. During the first 100 years of American secondary education, for example, an elite group attended the Latin Grammar School which featured the classics, while commoners chose ''adventure schools'' which, for a fee, taught a directly useful skill of a technical or applied variety, such as bookkeeping, navigation, surveying.

Many who oppose vocational education reflect a traditional European view of education for different classes of students in which the most prestigious subjects are nonutilitarian.

The nonutilitarian view continues to resurface. A. Graham Down of the Council for Basic Education, for example, expresses this viewpoint with new arguments: ''The idea that a school should prepare students for an entry level job is dear to many hearts, particularly if the vocational training is for somebody else's children. But in today's world, the rudimentary skills needed for success in a first job soon become inadequate. Both change and technology demand highly intellectual skills and adaptability. As Cardinal Newman once put it, 'a liberal education is the only practical form of vocational education.'"[27]

Early Rationale. The justification for vocational education does not rest on usefulness alone. The leading advocate for the comprehensive high school in the late 1950s, James B. Conant, regarded vocational education as an incentive, ensuring student participation in the general educational program. He believed that for certain kinds of people vocational education provided the only motivation to keep them in school where they would benefit from education for citizenship.[28]

Early advocates of vocational education offered manual training as complementary to academic studies and necessary for the balanced education for all students. Manual training was a more meaningful way of learning by doing. Similarly, proponents of modern career education are less interested in teaching specific skills than in erasing the differences between vocational and academic education, relating English, reading, writing, and mathematics to practical applications in careers.

Current Thinking. The current rationale for vocational education rests on three arguments—national interest, equity, and human development. Federal aid to vocational education began with the desire to conserve and develop resources, to promote a more productive agriculture, to prevent waste of human labor, and to meet an increasing demand for trained workers.[29] Presently, the government is interested in the shortages of scientists and engineers that could threaten the ability of the United States to compete in the international marketplace. Thus, we can expect the national concern for scientific literacy and technical competence to become a priority in vocational education.

Equity in vocational education suggests that it should help the young, the refugees, and the hard-to-employ to find a place in the economy. This goal includes training students in specific skills, in general occupational skills, and in the ways of the working world. Students enroll-

---

[27]A. Graham Down, "Inequality, Testing, Utilitarianism: The Three Killers of Excellence," *Education Week* 3, no. 6 (October 1983): 20, 21.

[28]Robert L. Hampel, *American High Schools Since 1940* (Boston: Houghton Mifflin, 1984).

[29]U.S. Congress, House Committee on National Aid to Vocational Education, 63rd Congress, Second Session, 1914, pp. 410–493.

ing in specialized programs do so to increase their chances of obtaining and keeping a job. In their view of vocational preparation, employers have conflicting ideas. Some feel that the school should prepare students with the vocational skills for entry-level employment. Others think that the school should emphasize reading, writing, computation, and social skills, leaving specific skill preparation to employers.

Human development in vocational education underscores the intrinsic value of work. Students gain a sense of how things work—televisions, cars, businesses. Thus, the social environment is made more understandable and the learner acquires a feeling of control. Aesthetic values—the satisfaction of creative expression through the construction of a product—is another dimension in human development through work. Vocational education as exploration of different occupational areas—arts, industry, business—is a means for both creating interest and expanding it. Vocational exploration helps learners discover a broad range of possible careers and find which one suits them. Experiential vocational education, in which students engage in projects such as constructing a house, raising livestock, conducting community service, and programming a computer, points to the highest of educational ideals—knowledge of the relationship between effort and consequences, team work, and sensitivity to community needs.

Access to Vocational Education

Vocational education has been accused of maintaining class divisions; in other words, working-class children are kept in school but do not receive an academic education. While the poor learn the attitudes and skills for work, middle- and upper-class children have access to the more prestigious academic curriculum. Jeannie Oakes, in her study of the relation between race and vocational education, found restrictions in access to such education for certain students, not only to academic programs, but even to higher status vocational programs.[30] Oakes analyzed vocational programs in twenty-five secondary schools. She found that on the average white schools and those with a substantial nonwhite population give about equal emphasis to vocational education. However, the characteristics of the program vary according to racial and ethnic composition. Students at the white schools have more extensive busi-

---

[30]Jeannie Oakes, "Beneath the Bottom Line; a Critique of Vocational Education Research," *Journal of Vocational Research* 11, no. 2 (1986): 33–50.

ness and industrial arts programs than those attending nonwhite or mixed schools, whereas students in the latter schools have greater access to military training and home economics.

Within categories of programs, differences also are found in opportunity. In business programs, for example, courses in management and finance are offered predominantly at white schools. Only in the white schools are students offered courses in banking, taxation, the stock market, data processing, and business law; typing, shorthand, bookkeeping, and office procedures are available in both nonwhite and white schools. Students at white schools could attend courses in marine technology, aviation, and power mechanics; students in nonwhite schools were offered cosmetology, building construction, institutional cooking and sewing, printing, commercial photography. Nonwhite students were more likely to be enrolled in courses teaching basic skills. The courses were long and often conducted off campus.

Clearly the curriculum planners play a part in restricting the access of certain students to future opportunity. Less clear is whether the restriction is a conspiracy or whether it results from well-intentioned efforts to offer "realistic" career choices in a stratified culture.

Discrimination appears also in vocational education according to ability. The new focus in vocational education is upon the gifted. Whether existing programs will be redirected or new ones created for these students is not known. Some schools are offering new courses stressing high technology and carrying academic prerequisites. Others are grouping gifted students within traditional courses but modifying the content. The course in automechanics may, for instance, feature the teaching of mechanical engineering principles.

In addition, schools have discouraged members of both sexes from entering programs that traditionally are the realms of the opposite sex. Courses for skills traditionally thought to be male prepare students for jobs that pay more. The vocational preparation of girls in rural areas presents a particular challenge. As a group, rural women tend to focus their attention on the family, yet they have strong career goals. The rural labor market offers very few choices to most women. Those girls who depart from "sex appropriate" programs such as consumer and homemaking education may experience conflicts in the community and uncertain employment. One answer is a curriculum composed of courses that are sexually neutral and attract both males and females, such as programs in food service, graphics, commercial horticulture and data processing. These fields lessen the conflict between community approval and self-esteem.

Content of Vocational Education

A central question in vocational education is determining the best response to the needs of students who go directly into the job market. For a substantial number, preparation in high school is all they get. For those who think the best preparation is training in the basic skills of reading, writing, mathematics, and science, the problem is already solved. Others, however, urge substituting the familiar automotive, wood, and metal shops with new and broader courses on communication, construction, transportation, and manufacturing. These new programs feature the processes and systems of each area and allow for the application of mathematics and science. The programs are designed to train students in general skills and knowledge about tools and materials.

The advocacy of increased mathematics and science in vocational education rests on the belief that future job opportunities will be in high technology. In California the number of technically related jobs is expanding at twice the rate of total job growth. Many predict that 90 percent of the jobs that exist today will be obsolete in the year 2000. The demand for technical personnel in the military services is a long-standing problem.

Daniel Hull and Leno Pedrotti have suggested a means of designing a curriculum for high-tech occupations.[31] They recommend (a) a common core consisting of basic units in mathematics, the physical sciences, communications, and human relations; (b) a technical core of units in electricity, electronics, mechanics, thermics, computers, fluids; and (c) a sequence on specialization in lasers/electro optics, instrumentation and control, robotics, and microelectronics. Obviously, industry must play a part in assisting schools with the personnel and expensive equipment required for such a program.

Curriculum developers in the vocational field of industrial arts are responding to the newer demands by starting curricula with such goals as relating industrial arts to science and technology. In the curiculum, students design models using principles from these disciplines. Here, too, a broad base of knowledge and an understanding of basic processes are required.

Not everyone believes that vocational education must focus on high technology. Some recent studies indicate that only 7 percent of the new

---

[31]Daniel M. Hull and Leno S. Pedrotti, "Meeting the High-Tech Challenge," *Vocational Education* 58 no. 4 (May 1983): 28–31.

jobs created between now and 2001 will be in high technology.[32] The major demand for workers in the next decade will not be for computer scientists and engineers, but for janitors, nurse's aides, sales clerks, cashiers, nurses, fast-food preparers, secretaries, truck drivers, and kitchen helpers.[33] However, an unpredictable economy means that vocational education will have to adapt to a diversity of skills rather than focus on training students for a career in a single field. Students will require a broad base of technical knowledge and the ability to communicate. Specific training should follow high school and at regular intervals throughout a person's career.

Although employment nationwide is likely to be in service industries, such as health care, trade, education rather than in manufacturing, farming, mining, and construction, curriculum developers must balance the demand for response to national needs with the requirements of the local communities which many vocational programs are designed to serve.

Restructuring Vocational Education

Reorganization represents an effort to close the gap between the vocational programs of schools and the requirements of work, as in the "cluster of skills" approach whereby students are trained in several occupational areas. A course in automechanics might be replaced by a course in industrial mechanics, which would include hydraulics, electronics, and internal combustion engineering. Similarly, day care programs might be renamed human service programs with courses in caring for children, the handicapped, and the elderly.

A second kind of reorganization is to add programs to meet expanding industries. "Quick start" programs, which offer customized training for a growing industry, are popular in states that desire to strengthen school ties with the private sector and influence local economic development. The internalization of the business curriculum to include important export courses and international marketing and distribution is a response to a changing world economy.

Partnerships between industry and the public schools represent a

[32]Henry M. Levin and Russell W. Rumberger, *The Educational Implications of High Technology* (Palo Alto, CA: Stanford Institute for Research on Educational Finance and Governance, 1983).

[33]*Workforce 2000: Work and Workers for the 20th Century* (Indianapolis, IN: Hudson Institute, 1987).

third type of reorganization. Usually partnerships concentrate on a particular problem or population. For example, a group of Texas business executives have launched a program to do something about the disproportionately small number of minority students in engineering. About 70 mathematicians and scientists from business and industry serve as tutors and role models, lecturing and conducting tours for students. About 6,000 students have been enrolled in the program, and an 80 percent increase in minority students going to engineering colleges has been seen.

Internships without pay, which give students on-the-job experience are a form of partnership, popular for talented students. In one executive internship, students spend one semester working a four-day week for a sponsoring organization in their field of interest. Each student functions as a special assistant to the sponsor, attending meetings and conferences and becoming involved in everything from answering telephones and typing to devising computer programs and preparing reports and studies.

The responsibility of business and industry to provide its own training and development is increasing. American firms allocate more than 30 billion dollars a year for education and training, nearly as much as the annual expenditures on the nation's publicly financed colleges and universities. The American Telephone and Telegraph Company estimates that on any given day, 30,000 of the company's 1,040,000 employees are in its classes. Also, recent federal legislation for job training raises the possibility that schools will have a reduced role in training and be replaced by private employer programs.

Trends in Vocational Education

Vocational education in schools is focusing on the development of attitudes toward work, basic communication skills, and knowledge of mathematics and science. National and local interests influence decisions about the particular occupations or fields that vocational education should serve. Congress, through the Carl D. Perkins Vocational Education Act, is influencing curriculum by demanding that recipients of vocational education funds teach job-specific skills. Yet, increasingly, vocational education is viewed as instrumental, as a means by which students from underprivileged classes are able to have success in learning the content formerly available only to those in academic programs. Today's programs go beyond teaching simple vocational tasks and include problem solving and team work. Specialization in a specific occupation tends to be seen as the responsibility of employers and the more than 8,000 private technical and modern adventure schools.

THE HIDDEN CURRICULUM

The term *hidden curriculum* refers to unofficial instructional influences, which may either support or weaken the attainment of manifest goals. Hidden curriculum indicates that some of the outcomes of schooling are not formally recognized. (Some curriculum specialists consider unintentional, frequently negative outcomes, an aspect of the hidden curriculum.) With few exceptions, the hidden curriculum is portrayed as a powerful detrimental force which undermines the professed commitment of schools to intellectual development and a democratic community. The hidden curriculum gives rise to several important questions. From whom is it hidden? Students? Teachers? Whose interests are served by it? What do we do with it when we find it? Should we leave it unstudied, hidden, a natural aspect of school experiences? These questions need to be addressed, but first we should understand what is meant by the hidden curriculum.

The Informal System Within the School

Gordon's Study. C. Wayne Gordon was one of the first to reveal an informal system that affected what was learned—a hidden curriculum. In *The Social System of the High School,* Gordon advanced the idea that the behavior of the individual high school student is related to his or her status and role in the school.[34] Furthermore, the informal system is a subsystem within the community and the still larger complex of American society. In Gordon's study, students were involved in three subsystems: (1) a formal system of curriculum, textbooks, classrooms, (2) a semiformal system of clubs and activities, and (3) an informal system of unrecognized cliques, factions, and other groups. Unrecognized groups controlled much of adolescent behavior both in school achievement and in social conduct such as dating. There was, in fact, a network of personal and social relations. Status in this adolescent system ranged from the ''big wheel'' at the top to the ''isolate'' at the bottom. It was a powerful system, which presented a constant source of conflict to the teachers.

---

[34]C. Wayne Gordon, *The Social System of the High School* (Glencoe, IL: Free Press, 1957).

Teachers sometimes indicated the conflict by such comments as, ''Jones and his gang terrify me.''

Teachers and School Society.   Teachers must recognize the expectations set by the informal system, which determines the prestige of the students and integrates them with the formal system and its demands that students learn specific kinds of subject matter. However, any teacher's ability to adapt to this conflict is determined in part by the extent to which the principal supports the formal expectations of the system. The principal must back up the teacher when there are disturbances or disorders, for example. Also, in order to deal with the hidden curriculum of the informal system, teachers require insight into the informal system. They should be able to identify the roles in the informal groups (boss, brain, clown), the motivations of different cliques, and the individuals within these cliques. Armed with this knowledge, the teacher can make different responses in relation to that system. The teacher may decide, for example, to advance goals that are not part of the formal system by showing more interest in students whose values are not those of the formal system. Or, the teacher may consciously decide to maintain objective or fair relations with all students and thereby run the risk of having conflicts with potent informal student groups. The teacher may also decide to bestow affective and other rewards selectively.

Robert Dreeben has written about the social setting of the school, indicating that there is more to school than experiences derived from formal structural arrangements.[35] He believes that the school has produced outcomes different from those expected because of the strategies that learners discover in dealing with the school's regimen. Different atmospheres may produce cheats, conformists, rebels, and recluses. Pupils derive their principles of conduct from their experiences in school. The principles acquired vary with the particular setting. Hence, a school staff should concern itself with socialization and other effects that follow from specific elements of their hidden curriculum. The staff should ask, ''What kind of character is being built by our practices of grading, grouping, eligibility, promotion, and detention?''

The Sociology of Knowledge

A different view of the hidden curriculum comes from those who study the sociology of knowledge. The sociology of knowledge refers to

---

[35]Robert Dreeben, ''Schooling and Authority: Comments on the Unstudied Curriculum,'' in *The Unstudied Curriculum,* Norman Overly, ed. (Washington, DC: ASCD, 1970).

the notion that the school is not an open marketplace for ideas but that particular kinds of knowledge are selected and incorporated into the curriculum.

M.F.D. Young, in England, and Michael Apple, in the United States, are prominent for their contention that specific social groups are unduly generating and distributing particular content and that this content affects the thinking and feelings of students in support of existing social institutions. Accordingly, curriculum materials bear ideological messages to which most of us are unconscious. Jean Anyon, for example, examined the knowledge in history textbooks and inferred that after reading these books, students could be led to believe (a) that governmental reform and labor–management cooperation are successful methods of social recourse, whereas confrontation and strikes are failures; (b) that the poor are responsible for their own poverty and that poverty is a consequence of the failure of individuals not a failure of society to distribute economic resources universally; and (c) that no working class exists in the United States—workers are middle class. The author argues that just as the school curriculum has supported patterns of power and domination, so can it be used to foster autonomy and social change.[36]

The sociology of knowledge extends our definitions of the hidden curriculum by the assumption that hidden messages are in curriculum materials, which show the world as certain social groups want the world to be seen by students.

Latent Curriculum Functions. The hidden curriculum may consist of secondary messages lying behind the manifest curriculum. Many school offerings have latent functions that serve special interest groups outside the school more than they serve the students themselves. Some courses, for example, have the unrecognized purpose of creating student consumer demand for goods and services. Driver training programs, which use late model cars increase learners' desires to buy cars, especially cars of a recent vintage. Similarly, home economics courses frequently are kept well equipped with the latest appliances, influencing young persons to purchase such items when establishing their own homes.

More understanding is needed about how the hidden curriculum works in a subtly discriminating way to discredit the dreams, experience, and knowledge of students from specific gender, class, and racial group-

---

[36]Jean Anyon, ''Ideology and United States History Textbooks,'' *Harvard Educational Review* 49, no. 3 (August 1979): 361–386.

ings. *The Shopping Mall High School* reveals the power of interest groups both within and outside the schools to arrange curriculum for "preferred customers" to the detriment of others.[37]

Burboles attributes power relationships in schools to those inherently in society: between classes, between sexes, and between various racial, ethnic, and religious groups.[38]

Hidden Curriculum and Moral Growth

The hidden curriculum can be a vehicle for moral growth. It can reflect an atmosphere of justice, giving all a chance to share in planning and executing activities and in gaining the rewards of their accomplishments as part of fair play. This curriculum, more than the formal curriculum, determines to a significant degree the participants' sense of self-worth and self-esteem.

The hidden curriculum is a determining factor in integration. For white and black children to feel like part of the mainstream, curriculum developers attend to the hidden curriculum by manipulating both formal and informal systems through conscious and well-intentioned guidance of pupil interactions. The staff creates specific programs and strategies for interactions across race, not leaving friendships, communications, and cultural understanding to chance. An effective way to encourage interracial relations is to provide situations in which children can discover similarities in interests and attitudes among other students or work together for a common good.

Suggestions for making the hidden curriculum more consistent with the ideals of the formal curriculum have been proposed. Henry Giroux recommends such actions as doing away with those properties of the hidden curriculum that are associated with alienation: rigid time schedule, tracking, testing, content fragmentation, and competition.[39]

In like manner, Catherine Cornbleth notes that formal curriculum fosters conformity to national ideals and social conventions, whereas the implicit curriculum maintains social, economic, and cultural inequali-

---

[37]A. Powell, E. Farrar, and D. Cohen, *The Shopping Mall School* (Boston: Houghton Mifflin, 1985).

[38]N. C. Burboles, "A Theory of Power in Education," *Educational Theory* 36, no. 21 (1986): 95–114.

[39]Henry A. Giroux, "Developing Educational Programs: Overcoming the Hidden Curriculum," *The Clearing House* 52, no. 4 (December 1978): 148–152.

ties.[40] In order to make hidden curriculum consistent with these ideals, curriculum developers must examine the consequences of specific properties within these three categories:

Organizational—time, facilities, materials

Interpersonal—teacher–student, teacher–administrator, teacher–parent, student–students

Institutional—policies, routine procedures, rituals, social structure, extracurricular activities available to the student and the community.

Curriculum specialists are expected to find out whether or not these structures and other practices in schools are consistent with the ideals of human potentiality and social justice. Moreover, they must not only make the hidden curriculum visible, they must try to alter it to enhance the satisfaction of human needs and spirit.

MORAL EDUCATION

Americans are questioning issues of right and wrong and examining their values. Conflicts of conscience arise in such issues as sex, race, drugs, and politics. People are increasingly aware that without a moral base, no governmental, technological, or material approach to these issues will suffice. Hence, curriculum developers, too, are animated by moral concern. The question, however, of how best to take advantage of this moment is not a simple one. A number of possible approaches can be used to guide our conceptions of a moral curriculum.

Philip Phenix has defined the basic question in moral education as one about the values, standards, or norms, and the sources and justification for these norms.[41] He sees four approaches that can be taken: the *nihilistic* position (morality is meaningless), *automatic* position (each must create his or her own values), *heteronomic* position (the laws of God should rule human conduct), and the *telenomic* position (morality must continually be discovered).

The Nihilistic Position. The nihilistic position is a denial that there are any standards of right or wrong. Nihilists hold that all human en-

---

[40]Catherine Cornbleth, "Beyond Hidden Curriculum," *Journal of Curriculum Studies* 16, no. 16 (1984): 29–36.

[41]Philip H. Phenix, "The Moral Imperative in Contemporary American Education," *Perspectives on Education* 11, no. 2 (Winter 1969): 6–14.

deavor is meaningless and without purpose. This position contradicts the notion of education as a purposeful improving activity.

The Autonomic Position. The view that norms or values are defined by each person is the cornerstone of the autonomic position. The individual invests existence with meaning. Advocates of this view believe that values are man-made and that all standards are relative to the persons and societies that make them. The implications of this position for curriculum are many. Inasmuch as human beings make their own values, their schools should *not* teach people how they *ought* to behave. All one can teach is how a particular person or group has decided to behave. Students then learn to adjust to a variety of values to maintain a harmonious society. As Phenix says, ''It is not a question of learning what is right or wrong, but what is socially expedient.'' This position transforms ethical issues into political ones without reference to moral ends. It is not a question of what is good or right but of who has the power to prevail. Also, it causes the curriculum to be judged in terms of its effectiveness in promoting autonomous interests and demands.

The Heteronomic Position. The heteronomic position asserts that known standards and values can be taught and can provide clear norms of judgment for human conduct. People do not make values, they discover them. These moral laws are sometimes seen as originating from a divine source. Sometimes they are regarded as rationally and intuitively deduced demands, apprehended by moral sensibility. Curriculum persons who hold the heteronomic position urge the adoption of strong religious or ethical programs to restore lost values to the young. They also have a pedagogical commitment to transmit established standards of belief and conduct.

Phenix himself believes that each of the previously mentioned positions fails to provide a basis for moral education. The nihilistic position cuts the nerve of moral inquiry and negates moral conscience. The autonomic position substitutes political strategy for morality and allows no objective basis for judging the worth of human creations. The heteronomic position is characterized by ethnocentrism and is untenable in light of the staggering multiplicity of norms by which people have lived.

The Telenomic Position. The telenomic theory holds that morality is grounded on a comprehensive purpose or *telos*, which is objective and normative, but forever transcends concrete institutional embodiment or ideology. It rests on the belief that persons should engage in a progressive discovery of what they ought to do—a dedication to an objective order of values. The moral enterprise is seen as a venture of faith, but not a blind adherence to a set of precepts that cannot be rationally justified. People preserve what is right through the imperfect institutions of society. They know, however, that these institutions are subject to criticism and held up to an ideal order that can never be attained. A curriculum in accordance with the telenomic outlook would foster moral inquiry as a life-long practice. This person would want to do right, not merely be satisfied in getting his or her own way. A person who holds the telenomic position would also see that what is right is a complicated matter, that personal judgments are made on the basis of his or her experience, and that these judgments are extremely partial and unreliable. Hence, a person needs to associate with others who can correct his or her misunderstandings and introduce other perspectives. The learner also would perceive that every value determination is subject to further scrutiny and revision in light of new understandings.

In the domain of moral education, the schools should develop skills in moral deliberation through focus on personal and social problems, offering relevant perspectives from a variety of specialized dimensions. For example, sex education would be considered with the knowledge of biologists, physicians (conception, abortion, pathologies), psychologists (affect, motivation, sublimation), social scientists (family, patterns of sexual behavior in diverse cultures), humanists (literary meaning of sex, historical perspectives), and philosophers and theologians (creation, nature, the destiny of the person, the meaning of human relations, the sanctity of the person, the significance of loyalty). In the end, persons would respond in conscience to the issue. What matters from an educational standpoint is that the decision emerges from a well-informed mind, not from haphazard impulses or personal history.

Kohlberg's Theory of Moral Development

Much of the current writing regarding moral education in schools features the work of two men, Sidney Simon and the late Lawrence Kohlberg, who are having an effect on practice. Their approaches, however, are not as comprehensive as Phenix's, which deals with all dimensions of moral behavior, not merely the intellectual. As indicated in Chapter 7, Kohlberg has attempted to define stages of moral development ranging from the learner's response to cultural values of good and bad to the making of decisions on the basis of universal principles of justice.[42] He regards his stages as stages of moral reasoning. Thus, his assessment of the learner's status is made by analyzing the learner responses to hypothetical problems or moral dilemmas. Kohlberg admits that a person can reason in terms of principles and not live up to these principles. He defends his work by claiming that the narrow focus on moral judgment is the most important factor in moral behavior. Other factors, which admittedly influence moral behavior, are not distinctly moral because there can be no moral behavior without informed moral judgment.

In trying to stimulate moral development, Kohlberg and his followers expose the learner to the next higher stage of moral reasoning, present contradictions to the child's current moral structure, and allow a dialogue in which conflicting moral views are openly compared. Furthermore, their curriculum in English and social studies centers on moral discussions and communication, on relating the government and justice in the school to that of the American society and other societies.[43]

The chief criticism of Kohlberg's view of moral education is that he has omitted important dimensions of moral education. He does not allow for utilitarian ideas of morality in which principles of justice can be problematic. He does not emphasize enough the need for conventional morality among all citizens in order for a society to function. He fails to appreciate that moral rules often have to be learned in spite of the temptation to ignore them. He has not attended to the affective dimensions of morality such as guilt, remorse, and concern for others, and he offers no suggestions for developing other factors, such as will, which are necessary in moral conduct.

Value Clarification

Louis Raths and Sidney Simon have another approach to moral education called *value clarification*. In value clarification the teachers draw out the child's opinion about issues in which values conflict, rather than impose their opinions.[44] Value clarificationists think that the exploration

---

[42]Lawrence Kohlberg, *Hypothetical Dilemmas for Use in the Classroom* (Cambridge: Moral Education Research Foundation, Harvard University, 1978).

[43]David Purpel and Kevin Ryan, eds., *Moral Education . . . It Comes with the Territory* (Berkeley, CA: McCutchan, 1976).

[44]Louis E. Raths, Merrill Harmin, and Sidney B. Simon, *Values and Teaching*, ed. 2 (Columbus, OH: Merrill, 1978).

of personal preferences helps people to (1) be more purposeful because they must rank their priorities; (2) be more productive because they analyze where their activities are taking them; (3) be more critical because they learn to see through others' foolishness; and (4) be better able to handle relations with others. The approach is limited, however; it does not go much beyond helping one become more aware of one's own values. Value clarification assumes there is no single correct answer. Learners discuss moral dilemmas to reveal different values. One criticism of value clarification centers on its reliance on peer pressure (the bias of many of the questions used in the process), its premature demand for public affirmation and action, and its moral relativism.

In response to these critics, both Kohlbergians and value clarificationists claim that there is moral content to their programs. Value clarificationists say they value rationality, creativity, justice, freedom, equality, and self-esteem. Kohlberg says he believes in "core moral precepts" and that the stage-by-stage progression and group resolution of moral conflicts are more effective in arriving at the precepts than direct instruction.

Andrew Oldenquist has raised another serious criticism of both approaches.[45] He believes that neither has been able to show that the values and the morality they wish to teach are rationally justifiable. The value clarificationists do not believe in rational justification, and Kohlberg does not actually show teachers how to do moral reasoning. Oldenquist says that both the value clarification and cognitive development approaches lead to indoctrination, not moral neutrality. They indoctrinate by pretending to be neutral in moral discussions while subtly inculcating their own values and moral outlook without reasons or argument. Oldenquist wants students to acquire a morality composed of (1) personal virtues such as courage, temperance, and a willingness to work for what one wants but lacks, and (2) moral attitudes such as honesty and the abandonment of violence and theft, which are required for a safe and satisfying society. His justification for these moral goals is straightforward; in order to accomplish these moral goals, he looks to teachers who are themselves morally earnest, self-confident about moral education, and capable of engaging in moral reasoning.

Dispute over the assertion that moral development follows a universal pattern centers on how moral growth varies from culture to culture and whether boys and girls have different approaches to morality.

---

[45]Andrew Oldenquist, "Moral Education Without Moral Education," *Harvard Educational Review* 49, no. 2 (May 1979): 240–247.

Nevertheless, William Damon maintains that there is a consensus among experts that morality develops over time, that both reason and emotions play a role in shaping morality, that children learn about morality through their own experiences, and that there are widely accepted values in most cultures, such as respect for truth, justice, and human welfare.[46]

Character Education. The focus of character education differs from other forms of moral education in that it endorses a specific content of moral virtues (honesty, kindness, courage) to be learned, whereas other approaches emphasize reason and value selection. Proponents of character education do not agree on the values to be taught or the meaning of given values; "Does 'honesty' only involve no lying or does it also require volunteering the truth when the situation calls for it?"[47]

A second area of controversy surrounding character education is the allegation that it indoctrinates students. The student is conditioned to behave in specific ways without a self-conscious understanding of why and without the option of accepting or rejecting the beliefs.

Curriculum materials aimed at teaching character education directly are in thousands of classrooms.[48] These programs are said to have positive effects on school behavior and academic achievement, although it is questionable whether the results are enduring.[49] There is also an increase in the indirect approach, i.e., using literature and history to provide moral lessons whereby the student is expected to acquire the virtuous qualities ingrained in the characters of the great men and women read about.

In short, although there is much agreement that programs of moral education would strengthen the curriculum, there is great division as to what such a program should be. People disagree on the relationship between a moral judgment and actual conduct. Some people are not satisfied with pupils merely learning to recognize the right thing to do; they want pupils to do the right thing. A number of different expectations can be held for a curriculum in moral education. Curriculum makers

---

[46]William Damon, *The Moral Child: Nurturing Children's Natural Moral Growth* (New York: The Free Press, 1988).

[47]Ivor Pritchard, *Character Education: Analysis of Research Projects and Problems* (Washington, DC: Office of Educational Research and Improvement, U.S. Department of Education, April 1988).

[48]Frank Goble and David Brooks, *The Case for Character Education* (Ottawa: Green Hill, 1983).

[49]Thomas Jefferson Research Center, *The Character Education Curriculum—Evidence of Success* (Pasadena, CA: Thomas Jefferson Research Center, 1986).

must decide whether they want learners to act for a reason, to respect other people's interests, to be logically consistent, to identify their own and others' feelings, or to act in accordance with the law. In developing moral curriculum, it is a good rule to stress the principle of respecting persons and considering the harm or benefit that the adoption of particular moral rules might have.

CULTURAL PLURALISM

Boards of education historically have resisted a differentiated curriculum for Italians, blacks, Hispanics, and other ethnic, racial, and religious groups. Indications of a reversal in the "melting pot" concept appeared in the early 1970s. At this time, ethnic minority studies appeared in many schools. These were usually studies established in response to black, Mexican-American, Puerto Rican, or Asian demands for content sensitive to their cultural experiences. American history was updated and interpreted from different points of view, which revealed the mistreatment of minority groups by the dominant white culture, the contributions of the minority groups and their leaders, and the social problems they face. These studies were offered as supplementary units and as enrichment within existing courses such as literature or history.

Such ethnic studies soon lost their popularity for various reasons: rivalry among minority group members regarding the content of these studies, fear that the studies were increasing the minorities' isolation, and the failure of our institutions to recognize the studies as intellectually valid. Eventually, efforts were made to refocus the studies. The refocusing led to new content treating intricate cultural patterns of different minority groups and the factors that account for their cultural distinctness in order to help students learn how and why minorities think, behave, and perceive as they do. Curricula included plans to teach the black, Mexican-American, and Asian student reading, social studies, mathematics, and other subjects in terms of each child's cultural perspective. Also, multicultural studies were seen as valuable for all students. Acquisition of different perspectives on personal and social problems was thought to be helpful in understanding the conflicts in values that paralyze our nation. It was recommended, too, that students become aware of the many ways in which all human groups are alike, both biologically and culturally.

Cultural pluralism now embraces many aims. Among them are mutual appreciation and understanding of various cultures in the society;

cooperation of the diverse groups in the society's institutions; coexistence of different lifestyles, language, religious beliefs, and family structures; and freedom for each subculture to work out its social future.

Approaches to Multicultural Education

Christine Sleeter and Carl Grant have developed a taxonomy that is useful in making critical examination of five different approaches to multicultural curriculum.[50]

Teaching the Culturally Different. This approach attempts to assimilate students of color into the mainstream by offering transitional bridges within the existing curriculum. Students are taught English as well as the knowledge and attitudes needed for participation in the dominant society, and they are encouraged to develop knowledge of their own cultural backgrounds.

The instructional method is the chief bridge with teachers who are trying to adapt method to the learning or communication style presumed to be preferred by those in the minority culture. Aside from programs for teaching English, the approach offers few well-developed curricula. Although the idea of building upon the experiences that students bring with them is sound, the approach is deficient because it focuses only on the culturally different. The burden of social inequality is placed on these students, and not on the general population or on whites. In this approach, the answer to social inequalities is to try to equip people of color with knowledge and skills so that they can compete more successfully with whites. It does not teach whites about racism, classism, or other cultural beliefs.

Human Relations. The aim of the human relations approach is to provide good human relations among students of different races. The use of nonstereotypical materials and opportunities for students of different cultures to communicate and to work together on common projects is thought to minimize intergroup conflict and prejudice. This approach is faulted for (a) not drawing upon research in cross-cultural differences that would enrich the approach and (b) not examining the social structure that inhibits positive human relations—institutional discrimination, poverty, and powerlessness.

---

[50]Christine E. Sleeter and Carl A. Grant, "An Analysis of Multicultural Education in the United States," *Harvard Educational Review* 57, no. 4 (November 1987): 421–444.

Ethnic Studies. The aim of ethnic studies is to develop acceptance and appreciation for the rich cultural diversity in America. This approach focuses on prescription more than goals or theory.

The great division in those taking black studies, Hispanic studies, American-Indian studies, Asian-American studies, and women's studies is between (a) those who teach about the particular culture without addressing issues of social stratification and social action and (b) those who aim at social change by studying a single ethnic group, sensitizing students to the group's victimization as well as its accomplishments and attempting to mobilize student participation to improve social conditions for the group. A weakness in this approach is the tendency to ignore multiple forms of human diversity. In attempting to deal with racism in the curriculum, for example, ethnic courses of study may still be sexist and classist, replacing white middle class men with the group's own men (not women).

Cultural Diversity. The cultural diversity approach emphasizes truly multicultural education, entailing such goals as respect for diversity, alternative life choices, social justice, and equity distribution of power among all ethnic groups. The curriculum may include information about the culture of American racial groups, about culture as an anthropological concept, the experiences and issues related to racial minorities, and cultural pluralism as a goal for society.

Reasons are given for the undesirability of cultural assimilation and the notion of cultural deprivation. The promotion of the culture of minority groups is more common than examination of social stratification emphasizing the goal of valuing cultural differences rather than the goal of advancing social justice. More guides and materials are available in elementary level schools than in secondary schools. Little provision has been made for integrating multicultural education into the secondary school curriculum.

Social Reconstructionist. The social reconstructionist approach aims at preparing young people to take social action against structural inequality. The causes of oppression and inequality are emphasized, as well as ways in which these social problems might be eliminated. The categories of gender and social class receive more attention in this approach than from the other approaches. Treatment of policy issues such as bilingual education policy and federal policy on ethnicity and schools is recommended. This approach is the least developed. There are few curricula for teaching this approach, although teaching guides are available for helping students deal with social inequalities engendered by racism, sexism, and classism.

Bilingual Education

The current overriding issue of cultural pluralism centers on bilingual education. Advocates of bilingual education claim that (1) it reduces academic retardation by allowing non-English-speaking students to learn in their native languages immediately; (2) it reinforces the relationship of the school and the home; (3) it offers the minority student an atmosphere conducive to the development of personal identification, self-worth, and achievement; (4) it has a positive influence on children's cognitive and linguistic abilities; and (5) it preserves and enriches the cultural and human resources of a people. Those who oppose bilingual education fear that encouraging the use of languages other than English and foreign cultural values will divide American society, furthering political separation along ethnic lines and hindering the assimilation of minority students into the mainstream of American life.

In the United States, bilingual education is most closely associated with the teaching of Hispanics, although there are bilingual programs for Asians, Haitians, Iranians, and ninety other minorities in United States schools.

A much discussed question is whether the bilingual program should regard the use of another language as *transitional*—a temporary means of instruction in English—or whether the bilingual program should be *maintained*, extending the child's language development in the native language and the child's acquisition of the culture associated with it.

After the abortive attempt of the then Secretary of Education, Shirley Hufstedter, to institutionalize bilingual education in Department of Education regulations, maintenance objectives lost favor. A few schools offered advanced content in Spanish to older, educated students from Latin-American countries. More people began to feel that the development among Hispanics of their native language and culture should occur through the foreign language program which had been isolated from the bilingual movement.

From among the 3.6 million students judged in need of special linguistic assistance to cope with the school curriculum, only 315,000 participate in some kind of bilingual program. The most common curriculum responses are:

1. *Submersion*—When there are fewer than ten non-English-speaking students, students are placed within English-speaking classrooms to

learn both English and the subject matter of the course through instruction in English, with perhaps the assistance of an aide who speaks the first language of the student or with taped lessons in the first language corresponding to the English lessons.

2. *Pull-out Programs*—Non- or limited-English-speaking pupils are separated from English speakers for a time in order to receive either English as a second language (ESL) lessons or lessons teaching children to read in their first language.

3. *Transition Programs*—The non- and limited-English speakers receive intensive lessons in reading in their first language and at the same time receive ESL lessons. In many transition programs, the first language is the medium of instruction for teaching the pupils to read English.

The matter of whether bilingual/bicultural education programs should be only for non-English-speaking students or for those with limited English is also pressing. Some advocate that the monolingual English-speaking student should be included in such programs.

Briefly, minority group pressure for equity in education was greatly accelerated by federal legislation in the 1970s for bilingual and multicultural studies. However, the prevailing political, cultural, and economic climate has placed them under attack. There are a variety of extant curriculum approaches to multicultural education: special programs for culturally different students, programs in which all students learn about cultural differences, programs aimed at preserving and extending cultural pluralism into American society, and programs aimed at producing learners who can operate successfully in two different cultures. In general, the schooling among ethnic groups reflects the fact that the United States is a multicultural society of competing social groups vying for limited political and economic resources.

CONCLUDING COMMENTS

The comparative study of curriculum issues in teaching thinking, vocational education, and multicultural education points out the serious problems that schools everywhere face—how to design instruction that will enable underprivileged students to have success with content formerly available only to an elite population. At this point both the democratic proponents of equality and participatory politics and the capitalistic proponents of individual excellence favor intellectual achievement of everyone—the former because such achievement promises access to power, the latter because they view the intellectual development of workers as a key to international market competition.

Concern about an underachieving curriculum and the restructuring of vocational education reflects the economic and libertory perspectives. The hidden curriculum also mirrors the large society's market-based reality by treating elite and working-class cultures within the school.

The moral curriculum raises old curriculum questions: What is the meaning of morality? Should morality be taught? Can it be taught? Is it possible to teach in an amoral manner? Cultural pluralism is important because it fits in with a growing interest in the rights of children and because it gives us a chance to redefine the purpose of schools.

Most curriculum issues involve two fundamental concerns. Dedicated persons have sensed that aspects of the curriculum are not consistent with the premise that every human being is important, regardless of racial, national, social, economic, and mental status. Exploitation of learners by the hidden curriculum, the denial of minority values in the curriculum, a stratified and narrowly defined vocational curriculum are a few examples. Also, more persons are aware that the opportunity for wide participation in the cultural resources of the society is a fundamental right. Hence, a broader vocational education, an emphasis on thinking, and multicultural education are offered as new resources for the creation of knowledge as well as access to wider cultural capital.

QUESTIONS

1. Can we teach students to use critical thinking in challenging their self-interests?
2. How can the curriculum best help students realize their potential as thinkers?
3. What cultural values in the United States make it unlikely that the curriculum of the United States will follow the Japanese pattern?
4. Should trade, proprietary schools, or industry itself rather than the public schools be responsible for specialized training? Why or why not?
5. It is often assumed that vocational education can contribute to the learning of mathematics and science. How could vocational education be planned in order to enhance academic development?
6. Describe aspects of a hidden curriculum in a school familiar to you. How should the staff respond to this situation?

7. What are the likely consequences of using each of the following approaches to moral education?
   a. Cognitive—Students are encouraged to use moral reasoning.
   b. Commitment—Personal and social action projects help students put their values into practice.
   c. Inculcation—Students observe good models and are reinforced for certain desirable social human behavior.
   d. Clarification—Through such exercises as thinking about things in their lives which they would like to celebrate, students are led to define their values.
8. Which approach to multicultural education promises the most to strengthen the local community and nation? Why?
9. Identify one or more common elements among these issues: hidden curriculum, moral education, cultural pluralism?

SELECTED REFERENCES

Comparative Curriculum

McKnight, C. C. et al. *The Underachieving Curriculum: Assessing U.S. School Mathematics from an International Perspective.* Champaign, IL: Stipes, 1987.

Torsten, Husen. "Are Standards in U.S. Schools Really Lagging Behind Those in Other Countries?" *Phi Delta Kappan* 64, no. 7 (March 1983): 445–462.

Walberg, H. J. "Scientific Literacy and Economic Productivity." *Daedalus* 112, no. 2 (Spring 1983).

Thinking

Baron, J. and Sternberg, R. S., eds. *Teaching Thinking Skills and Practice.* New York: Freeman Press, 1986.

Costa, Art, ed. *Developing Minds: A Resource for Teaching Thinking.* Alexandria, VA: Association for Supervision and Curriculum Development, 1985.

Marzano, Robert J. et al. *Dimensions of Thinking: A Framework Curriculum and Instruction.* Alexandria, VA: Association for Supervision and Curriculum Development, 1988.

Vocational Education

Kantor, H. and Tyack, D. G., eds. *Work, Youth, and Schooling.* Stanford: Stanford University Press, 1982.

Lazerson, Marvin, and Grubb, W. Norton, eds. *American Education and Vocationalism.* New York: Teachers College Press, 1974.

Workforce 2000: Work and Workers for the 21st Century. Indianapolis, IN: Hudson Institute, 1987.

Hidden Curriculum

Bullough, K. V., et al. Human Interests in the Curriculum: *Teaching and Learning in a Technological Society.* New York; Teachers College Press, 1984.

Cornbleth, Catherine. "Beyond Hidden Curriculum." *Journal of Curriculum Studies* 16, no. 1 (1984): 29–36.

Gordon, David. "Education as Text: The Varieties of Educational Hiddenness." *Curriculum Inquiry* 18, no. 4 (Winter 1988): 425–449.

Moral Education

Damon, William. *The Moral Child: Nurturing Children in Natural Moral Growth.* New York: Free Press, 1988.

Enright, Robert D. et al. "Moral Development Interventions in Early Adolescence." *Theory Into Practice* 22, no. 2 (Spring 1983): 134–145.

Phenix, Philip. *Education and the Common Good: A Moral Philosophy of the Curriculum.* New York: Harper & Row, 1961.

Pritchard, Ivor. *Moral Education and Character.* Washington, DC: U.S. Department of Education, Office of Educational Research and Improvement, 1988.

Purpel, David E. *Spiritual Crises in Education: A Curriculum for Justice and Compassion.* Granby, MA: Bergin and Garvey Publishers, 1989.

Raths, Louis E., Harmin, Merrill, and Simon, Sidney B. *Values and Teaching,* 2nd ed. Columbus, OH: Merrill, 1978.

Cultural Pluralism

Ambert, Alba, and Melendez, Sara E. *Bilingual Education: A Sourcebook.* New York: Teachers College Press, 1986.

Bennett, C. I. *Comprehensive Multicultural Education.* Boston: Allyn & Bacon, 1986.

Chu-Chang, Mae. *Asian and Pacific American Perspectives on Bilingual Education.* New York: Teachers College Press, 1983.

Gollnick, D. M., and Chinn, P. *Multicultural Education.* 2nd ed. Columbus, OH: Merrill, 1986.

Tiedt, P., and Tiedt, I. *Multicultural Teaching: A Handbook of Activities, Information, and Resources.* Boston: Allyn & Bacon, 1986.

13

Directions in the Subject Fields

The material in this chapter is arranged chronologically, though more in the sense of trends than as a detailed recital of events. The chapter is intended to reveal the nature of the various subject fields in the past, describe the directions they are now taking, and indicate the forces that should and should not shape them in the future.

It is pointed out that swings in emphasis within the subject fields reflect a difference of opinion about the nature of knowledge. Some view knowledge of subject matter as a tool for resolving problems; others think of it as a series of disciplines for developing the intellect; and some think that subject matter knowledge means access to one's own accrued and personally organized resources. Furthermore, it will be seen how political compromises made by policy makers in the subject fields to accommodate those of different curriculum orientations have resulted in conflicting purposes and incoherent programs.

Discrepancies in subject fields can be viewed in a positive manner. The conflicts are evidence that there are no universal principles that fix curriculum in one direction. Instead, the contradictions can be seen as opportunities for creating dialogue, for considering new possibilities, and for creating our own vision of the fields.

MATHEMATICS

Mathematics in Our Schools

Before the 1950s, schools commonly taught mathematics around one central theme: student mastery of basic computational skills. This practical yet simplistic approach to mathematics instruction did not suit the nation's increasing need for theoretical mathematicians and scientists. By the early 1960s, a new trend in mathematics instruction had emerged—student acquisition of mathematics as a discipline. Two influences helped set this trend in motion.

The first influence reflected the above-mentioned need for competent and creative scientists. The other influence on the mathematics curriculum was the belief that everyone could profit by acquiring knowledge of mathematics as a discipline. Briefly stated, the belief was that subject matter fields should introduce students to the general concepts, principles, and laws that members of a discipline use in problem solving.

The new math consisted of the fundamental assumptions and conceptual theories on which every scientific enterprise is based. Unfortunately, it was deprecated for being abstract, just as the old math was criticized for being boring. For the average student, sophisticated conceptual theories had little practical relevancy. Instruction in topics such as set theory and use of bases other than the generally used base 10 replaced practice in the basic skills needed for everyday problem solving. Developers of the new math paid too little attention to the practical uses of mathematics in the student's present and future life. Hence, many specialists in mathematics argued that the school should stress a knowledge of mathematics as an end in itself, as a satisfying intellectual task. On the other hand, in order for knowledge to be meaningful, it must be applied. The main question regarding the mathematics curriculum is whether it can be useful both for development of the intellect and for the necessities of a technological era and still avoid a meaningless idealism on the one hand and a strict vocationalism on the other.

Both modern and traditional mathematics are found in today's schools. The move toward traditional mathematics results from the emphasis on basics such as computational skills, whereas the move toward modern mathematics results from a concern for bright students. A survey of the status of mathematics in secondary schools indicates that traditional mathematics courses—courses that feature drill and practice, computation, and memorization—are taken by slower students and students not planning on college, not by students who tend to major in mathematics.[1] The latter still take modern mathematics, algebra, geometry, and optional fourth-year courses which place strong emphasis on

---

[1]*Everybody Counts: A Report to the Nation on the Future of Mathematics Education* (Washington, DC: National Research Council, 1989).

structure, definitions, properties, sets, proofs, and other abstract concepts.

Trends in Mathematics

To facilitate the application of knowledge, three new directions have been suggested for future trends in mathematics. The first trend is an integration of mathematics with other subject matter. Opponents of the new math from its inception have proposed that mathematics be studied not as a separate theoretical discipline, but as an integrated part of liberal education. Integration of subject matter facilitates the application of mathematical skills to a variety of situations. The importance of mathematical skills in all subjects from homemaking to physics should be stressed.

Increased use of educational technology is a second means by which mathematics can be made more relevant. The United States Department of Education has funded programs to develop a television series on mathematics designed to show how it may be applied to all occupations and problem-solving situations. The series supplements the teacher, who continues with regular computational skills. It is staged with characters using basic mathematical skills to solve problems relating to measurement, quantity, estimation, and so forth. Technology in the larger sense is also having an effect on the mathematics curriculum. The mathematics educators recommend that calculators and computers be introduced into the mathematics classroom as early as possible.[2] Young children are expected to understand negative numbers and exponents. The use of calculators in all classes requires emphasis on the language of calculators—on decimals, fractions, and algebraic symbols. Less emphasis should be placed on pencil and paper arithmetic and more opportunity given for mental arithmetic, estimation, and approximation. The availability of calculators allows expansion of the traditional program to include numbers of greater magnitude. Teachers are able to spend more time on concrete representations of concepts because they can check instantly for student understanding. Patterns can be detected more easily.

Community participation in curriculum planning and implementation is a third way of increasing the relevancy of instruction in mathematics. In the elementary school, use of parents as tutors, teacher's aides,

---

[2]Patricia F. Campell and James T. Fry, ''New Goals for School Mathematics,'' in *Content of the Curriculum,* ed. Ronald Brandt (Alexandria, VA: ASCD, 1989).

and resource persons not only helps to reduce cost, but also provides a balance between classroom and community perspectives. In the secondary school, visiting mathematics lecturers from industry and opportunities for work experience can narrow the gap between classroom theory and practical application.

Concerns about curriculum content and about ways to develop ideas appropriate to the child's level persist. In their attempts to teach computation, some people ignore concepts and processes for developing proficiency, defining the curriculum as a series of isolated skills to be taught by drill. Also, the role of application and problem solving is far from clear. Incidentalists argue that systematic instruction in abstractions should be replaced by general problem-solving experiences from the real world. Mathematics, they believe, should be taught in relation to other areas such as cooking, building, and sewing. Others advocate experience in mathematical areas that closely resemble the physical world, such as measurement and geometry.

The immediate solution for these issues and concerns seems to be in the direction of a balanced curriculum. Content will be broadened beyond the teaching of whole number ideas in the primary grades. Ideas of symmetry and congruence will be explored. Shapes will be discussed and classified, and measurement and graphing will be popular. Metrics, of course, is necessary. Informal experiences with important mathematical ideas may contribute to greater success in future learning and to application in daily life. A balanced point of view also implies the use of different instructional procedures. No single mathematics program is suitable for all children. Briefly, the balanced curriculum means overcoming an undue focus on skills, mathematical content, and application. Evaluations confirmed that the "back to basics" movement produced improvement in precisely those mathematic abilities that are least important in a rapidly changing, technological society. Computational facility improved, but children failed to solve problems in mathematics.[3] Teachers who follow the policies of the National Council of Teachers of Mathematics stress the interdependence of the following three factors. First, techniques must be designed to help learners focus on specific elements and solve problems on their own. Second, a variety of strategies or ways to solve problems should be encouraged. Third, children should be given opportunities to relate events to mathematical models by estimating, applying estimated abilities in other situations, developing criteria for

[3]Curtis L. McKnight et al., *The Underachieving Curriculum* (Champaign, IL: Stipes, 1987).

comparing lengths, noting the regularities of the coordinate system in the real world, and modifying or imposing order on a real situation and then summarizing it in mathematical form.[4]

In higher education, the supremacy of calculus in the freshman and sophomore mathematics curriculum is being challenged in part because the computer has changed the mathematical needs of students. Colleges and universities are initiating experimental courses in discrete mathematics, which deal with individual values and quantities. Whether discrete mathematics courses will be offered as an alternative to the traditional curriculum or integrated with it remains to be seen.

Magdalene Lampert is a leader in the transformation of the mathematics curriculum. Lampert aims at getting students to know mathematics as it is practiced in the discipline rather than in conventional school learning. Her curriculum calls for students to evaluate their own assumptions and those of others about what is mathematically true; reasoning and mathematical argument become the source of an idea's legitimacy, not the teacher or the textbook.[5]

In contrast, there are mathematicians who do not believe that discourse is what students should be learning in school. Edward Effros, professor of mathematics at UCLA, opposes the deemphasizing of rote learning, collaborative learning, and other new proposals. He holds that the reason why adults do not apply basic mathematical skills is that they cannot handle addition, multiplication, and fractions automatically by hand. He faults computer teaching methods which predigest material for students and deflect them from vital concepts, transforming students into spectators rather than creators.[6]

Three ideas that are driving changes in the mathematics curriculum are the following:

1. Recognition that the American math curriculum has a great deal of repetition and review, with the result that topics are covered with little intensity. There is a loss of the notion of "a spiral curriculum," in which key concepts are revisited at deeper and more complex levels. Instead there is repeating the same information about a difficult concept.

---

[4]National Council of Teachers of Mathematics, *An Agenda for Action: Recommendations for School Mathematics of the 1980s* (Reston, VA: National Council of Teachers of Mathematics, 1983).

[5]Magdalene Lampert, "Knowing, Doing, and Teaching Mathematics," *Cognition and Instruction* 3, no. 4 (1986): 305–342.

[6]Edward G. Effros, "Give US Math Students More Rote Learning," *NY Times* XVIII, no. 47 (February, 14, 1989): A14.

2. Awareness that the sudden shift in focus from arithmetic to algebra is confusing to students. For example, in arithmetic, students are taught that an equation is an action statement: "Do this to these numbers, and you will get an answer." But in algebra, the notion of equivalence is often the central focus: "You can make the same change to each side of the equal sign, and the equivalence does not change."
3. Similarly, awareness that the deep and persistent misconceptions of students about mathematical operations and concepts have insidious consequences. In concluding that mathematics is a collection of procedures that have to be learned, many students do not construct the powerful meanings for the concepts and the ability to use them in real-world situations.

Two national efforts to transform the mathematics curriculum are those by the National Council of Teachers of Mathematics (NCTM) and the National Academy of Sciences (NAS). NCTM's Curriculum Standards Committee has set five general goals for K–12 math education: becoming a mathematical problem solver, communicating mathematically, valuing mathematics, developing confidence in math, and reasoning mathematically.[7]

The Mathematics Science Education Board of NAS is exploring the math curriculum for the year 2000.[8] Also, the National Science Foundation (NSF) is supporting six projects aimed at finding ways to revamp the elementary curriculum by integrating calculators and computers, introducing statistical thinking, and introducing algebra early.

SCIENCE

Evolution of Science Teaching

All branches of the scientific enterprise depend on the principles and laws of mathematics as a foundation for both theory and methodology. Because of this dependency, curriculum trends in the sciences often parallel those applied to mathematics. Science subject matter in the early 1960s was shaped by the same forces that influenced mathematics, namely, the proposal to teach subjects as disciplines and the push

---

[7]*Curriculum and Evaluation Standards for School Mathematics* (Reston, VA: National Council of Teachers of Mathematics, 1989).

[8]Mathematical Science Education Board, National Research Council, 2101 Constitution Avenue, NW, Washington, DC 20037.

toward specialization. These forces particularly affected the sciences because it was felt that advancements in a technological society required the training of highly skilled scientists and technicians.

Science subject matter at this time was conceptually and theoretically sophisticated. Students were introduced to the principles of science by the discovery process of simple experimentation. This instructional approach replaced the more traditional process of memorizing theorems and laws. It was hoped that this approach would endow students with the inquiry mode of thought used by specialists in the scientific disciplines. Science projects in the early 1960s were heavily funded and resulted in a number of new programs. Children were encouraged to participate in scientific research on a very theoretical level. Science fairs enabled more advanced students to gain recognition as practicing members of the science discipline.

During the late 1960s, the discipline approach to science instruction was criticized for dwelling too long on theory and ignoring the need for practical application. Science in schools had been too specialized to be successfully applied to anything other than scientific research. For students uninterested in pursing science as a career, the new subject matter had little practical relevancy. The average student could not identify the role of science in the common affairs and problems of people. Also, Americans were becoming increasingly concerned about societal implications of the scientific enterprise. Prior demands for research relating to space exploration and national defense had distracted scientists' attention from the problems of air pollution, overpopulation, and depletion of natural resources. Scientists had neglected to study the relationship of research to the individual's place in the universe. As a result of this neglect, a new trend to humanize the sciences emerged in the 1970s. Accordingly, some multidisciplinary approaches to instruction appeared. Basic laws of science were applied to a variety of situations in subjects other than science. Science teachers sometimes worked in teams with teachers from other disciplines and helped students relate principles of science to current social, political, and economic problems. Students majoring in social science studied the relationship of scientific discoveries to industrial and technological revolutions. The role of the scientific enterprise in international policy making was sometimes studied in political science courses. However, by the mid-1970s, significant numbers of citizens felt that support for curriculum in science was misdirected, if not in error. In the elementary school, the press for higher scores on tests and an emphasis upon isolated skills of reading and mathematics meant that science was seldom taught at all. Enrollment in high school science courses steadily decreased, with more than 50% of high school students taking no science after the tenth grade. By the late 1970s, science courses had given way to rote learning, with 90 percent of teachers using only a traditional textbook approach. By 1984, it was clear that there was a crisis in science education. The U.S. Government Printing Office announced the following about the status of the science curriculum:

1. A mismatch exists between the science curriculum and that which ninety percent of the students want and need.
2. Nearly all science teachers have goals that are directed only toward preparing students for the next academic level. Science is viewed as specific content to be mastered.
3. Nearly all science teachers use a textbook 95 percent of the time. Science is virtually never being learned by direct experiences, and most students never experience a real experiment throughout their school program.
4. No attention is given to the development of a science curriculum; the textbook is the course outline, the framework, the testing, and the view of science.
5. The science program is ineffective in influencing interest in science or scientific literacy. Teaching by textbook summarizes the status of science education; to compound the problem, the textbooks in the early 1980s were inadequate.[9-11]

Terminology was the central feature in most science textbooks. The new vocabulary in typical science classrooms exceeded the vocabulary necessary for mastering a foreign language. Indeed, more than 10,000 specialized terms were introduced in the typical chemistry course in high school, which is high considering that foreign language specialists suggest that the learning of vocabulary words in a foreign language should be limited to no more than 2,000 new words a year. Too many terms were introduced apart from their meaning.

---

[9]Norris C. Harms and R. E. Yager, *What Research Says to the Science Teacher*, 3 (Washington, DC: National Science Teachers Association, 1981).

[10]R. E. Stake and J. Easley, *Case Studies in Science Education* (Urbana: University of Illinois, 1978).

[11]I. R. Weiss, *Report to the 1977 National Survey of Science, Mathematics, and Social Studies Education* (Research Triangle Park, NC: Center for Educational Research and Evaluation, 1978).

New Approaches in Science Education

As indicated in Chapter 4, experts in science education in an undertaking called Project Synthesis predicted that the life science curriculum of the future will be organized around the theme of human adaptation in both the scientific and social senses, and that the use of ethics and values as well as biological knowledge in making decisions will be an important goal of programs dealing with social problems. Scientific topics will be presented from the human point of view. Principles of science will be learned, not as ends in themselves, but as means of coping with personal and social concerns.

The multidisciplinary approach is frequently offered as a possible solution to the problem. In addition to drawing from several scientific disciplines, this approach involves inquiry and outreach to the community, thus serving two purposes. First, it brings new depth to all disciplines. Second, it reminds us of science's relation to the political, economic, and social affairs of humankind. A major goal of science teachers in the 1990s will be to provide students with the basic problem-solving skills they will need to cope with an often dehumanizing technological society. One effort in this direction is the Inquiry Training Project of Port Colborne, Ontario, Canada. This project hopes to improve students' abilities to solve problems which a person might encounter now and in the future. To this end, instead of teaching students a single direct path between questions and answers, teachers in the inquiry project teach students to deal with questions that give rise to a number of plausible alternatives whose desirability must be thought out and ranked. The program attempts to teach children to analyze cause and effect relationships, a technique that has been profitable in the sciences. With respect to method, children are given simple scientific equipment and materials from the world around them and are encouraged to experiment. A typical activity is the raising of green plants under different conditions and observing and recording the results. Another favorite practice involves fermentation. In this project, pupils are given yeast, sugar, tubing, and a few other materials. They are asked to keep track of how the rate of fermentation is affected by changes in the amount of water used and the temperature, in order to learn about control of variables and effects of such controls. Ecological projects are also popular in science courses. As they progress, children using the discovery method are exposed to the basic concepts of many sciences, from botany and biology to physics, chemistry, and astronomy.

The broad recommendation is toward more inquiry in the science class. Two obstacles are economic and instrumental considerations. Initial investment in equipment for courses emphasizing experimentation can run as high as $500 per classroom. Also, teachers must know enough about the principles and teaching materials involved to be able to use them. One of the biggest problems in teaching science in the early grades is the teacher's insecurity about the subject matter.

Secondary schools are likely to continue to offer a few science courses of high quality for the most talented students. These courses will probably be organized around the traditional topics of biology, chemistry, and physics. Such programs are now designed for a minority of students. Indeed, data from the National Longitudinal Study of the High School Class show that entry into prestigious fields of biological sciences, business, engineering, physical sciences, and mathematics can be predicted by the science and mathematics course taken in high school.

Only 20 percent of all high school graduates take physics, primarily because it is usually the last course in the science sequence of biology and chemistry and, in fact, is an elective course for the sophisticated student.[12] The issue of whether science should be for the few or the many is alive. A recent study concludes that science at the K–12 level should enlarge the pool of science learners rather than offer opportunities for the most able students to embark on a scientific career.[13] On the other hand, many school districts have concentrated the best science students in magnet or controlled environments, which emphasize science and attenuate the distractions that interfere with learning science.

The assumption that the best course for those with science aptitude is advanced placement is now questioned. J. Myron Atkin, for example, thinks that the high school years should be used for broad intellectual exploration rather than preparation for college level specialization. An opportunity to study topics of special interest in depth might be a better use of high school time than a course focused on examinations.[14]

Recommendations for the Future Science Curriculum

There are several recommendations for improving the traditional courses. It is suggested that new materials be developed for use by the

---

[12]Michael Neuschatz and Maude Covalt, *Physics in the High School* (New York: American Institute of Physics, 1989).

[13]Robert Rothmer, "NSF Urged to Boost K-12 Effort," *The Scientist* 10, no. 5 (1987): 7.

[14]J. Myron Atkin, "The Improvement of Science Teaching," *Daedalus* 112, no. 2 (Spring 1983): 167–187.

70 percent of students now being inadequately served. These materials would deal with new areas of modern science and also would contain less encyclopedic content and detail that have little relevance to students' present problems of living. Instructional activities would be tied to the ongoing scientific enterprises in the community. Science would be treated less as an end in itself than as a field related to other aspects of life. There would be more emphasis on the power, responsibilities, and limitations of science.

The idea of having the local community serve as a learning laboratory is another recommendation. The Education Development Center in Newton, Massachusetts has developed science projects related to issues with social implications. In one such project, *The Family and Community Health,* students have health care experiences in schools, families, and agencies in the community. Units treat such topics as adolescent pregnancy, drinking, stress, and environmental and consumer health. These projects combine ideas and skills from the natural sciences, humanities, and social sciences.

F. James Rutherford is a spokesperson for the American Association of the Advancement of Science, which is now rethinking the outcomes of school science.[15] *Science for All Americans* is the first phase of *Project 2061: Education for a Changing Future.* Instead of viewing high school science as a diluted version of college science for college-bound students, Rutherford and his group argue that the science curriculum should represent a common core of knowledge for all students. Their blueprint of what scientifically literate persons need to know does not dwell on rote learning of classification lists, but recommends that more time be given to understanding concepts such as the interdependency of living things, the flow of matter and energy, how heredity works, and what cells do. Other recommendations of this first phase of *Project 2061,* which draws its name from the year Halley's comet returns, include: (a) integrating science and math with history and other disciplines (however, mathematizing science should be avoided when it makes learning science more difficult), (b) preparing students to be inquisitors and critical thinkers rather than emphasizing right answers, (c) focusing upon the connections of science to social issues of the day—population growth, environmental pollution, waste disposal, energy production, and birth control.

Instead of attempting to cover too many topics or to provide detailed

---

[15]F. James Rutherford and Andrew Ahlgren, "Rethinking the Science Curriculum," in *Content of the Curriculum,* ed. Ronald S. Brandt (Washington, DC: ASCD, 1988).

knowledge of the scientific disciplines, the curriculum should help students develop a set of cogent views of the world. Such views include the structure and evaluation of the universe, the general features of the planet, basic concepts of matter, energy, force, and motion, the living environment, biological evolution, the human organism, the human life cycle, physical and mental health, medical techniques, cultural dynamics, social change and conflict, and the mathematics of symbols.

PHYSICAL AND HEALTH EDUCATION

Its Place in the Curriculum

In the early 1960s, President John Kennedy proposed a national standard of physical fitness. Shortly thereafter, most elementary and secondary students were required to participate in annual assessments of physical fitness. This period also saw the flourishing of international sports events. Participation of highly trained foreign athletes in these events aroused American interest in the development of physical education programs.

Unfortunately, physical competition as part of the 1960s sports ethic produced disappointment and humiliation for many children. Being good was often not good enough; excellence was the goal. Physical education offerings were limited to traditional team sports, and often aggression and competitiveness were the prerequisites of sportsmanship.

Throughout the 1960s, physical education offerings gradually expanded. Communities requested that more emphasis be placed on life-long sports. As a result, courses in scuba diving, bike riding, and golf were added to the curriculum. The direction was not away from strenuous exercise, but simply away from the harshness of competition. Competition as an American virtue was slowly being replaced by individualism. Physical education established a new flexibility in course offerings. Less rigid views on sexual roles also provided new opportunities for girls. Students, for the first time, chose from a variety of programs best suited to their interests.

The role of physical education in the classroom has become a controversial issue nationwide in the face of budgetary cutbacks and the demand for renewed emphasis on basic educational forms. Nevertheless, concerns about students' lack of fitness has drawn attention to the problem.[16]

---

[16]"National Children and Youth Fitness Study," *Journal of Physical Education, Recreating and Dance* 16, no. 1 (1985): 303.

Guidelines for Future Physical Education Programs

The American Alliance for Health, Physical Education and Recreation (a 50,000-member professional organization) has suggested five guidelines for future physical education programs:

1. Break down current mass education techniques.
2. Increase flexibility of offerings and teaching methods.
3. View sports as more than athletic competition.
4. Increase coeducational classes, sailing, camp counselor training, self-defense.
5. Promote physical activities that support the desire to maintain physical fitness throughout life.

The association recommends that teaching emphasize activities that can serve as vehicles for education of the whole person. Activities should be designed to introduce students to the subtle and often overlooked potentials of the human body. Here are some suggested activities:

Movement Education. The objective is to develop an understanding of creative and expressive movement. Five-year-olds can be asked to proceed down a marked line in any fashion they desire. Some balance carefully, some run, some crawl, but all experience their own style.

Centering Oneself. Here, the student develops a state of alert calm by becoming aware of physical energy in and outside the body.

Structural Patterning. Students become aware of variations in the way people move.

Relaxation Techniques. By means of rhythmic breathing, the student learns how to gain control over habitual tensions.

The new direction in physical education curriculum is a response to four needs: (a) strength to perform expected tasks of living, (b) aerobic capacity to maintain cardiorespiratory efficiency, (c) flexibility and abdominal strength to avoid debilitating effects of lower back injuries, and (d) maintenance of appropriate levels of body fat. To these ends, some sports are deleted from the curriculum and body development activities have been added. Sports skills are alternated with fitness development units. For example, optimal aerobic capacity is met through the rhythmic action of running, jogging, bicycling, swimming, cross-country skiing, and downhill skiing at least three times per week. Information about exercise and nutrition is offered so that students understand how to balance caloric intake and exercise in maintaining appropriate body fat.

In addition to fitness activities, physical education content includes motor skills, such as supporting, suspending, moving and receiving force, and how to learn these skills. Sports and dance are common in the programs because they feature the critical elements of movement. To perform well, students learn the skills, strategies, and traditions of the specific activity.

Illustrative of newer curriculum in health is the *Health Activities Project* (HAP) developed by the Lawrence Hall of Science, University of California, Berkeley. This program offers an activity-centered health curriculum for pupils in grades five through eight. The goal of the project is to create a positive attitude toward health by giving pupils a sense of control over their own bodies and by imparting understanding about the body's potential for improvement. HAP activities, organized into modules treating such topics as fitness, interaction, growth, decision making, and skin care, supplement existing programs in health, physical education, and science.

New textbooks encourage students to evaluate their own food and fitness habits and develop better ones. Texts are beginning to reveal the role of the food industry in shaping the American diet and to feature the future of women in sports and the effects of advertising on self-image.

Those planning the health curriculum confront concerns about AIDS, drug abuse, stress, and human sexuality. Social ambivalence toward drugs as well as difficult home lives are factors in such programs. So, too, are the images students have of themselves. The role of health curriculum has been chiefly that of helping students learn how to deal with potential problems posed by dangerous practices such as alcohol abuse. Peer counseling projects, in which students work with other students in helpful relations, have replaced the use of stern lectures and frightening stories to discourage youths from abuse.

Discouraging results from earlier efforts at drug and alcohol education have provoked a new social-psychological approach which shows some promise. Social-psychological prevention programs strengthen resistance to peer pressure to use drugs and alcohol and to smoke. They also help students to cope with interpersonal relations and to reduce stress. Elements in these programs include (1) working with families, community groups, and the media to influence policies and cultural norms associated with smoking and other negative health behaviors; (2) recognizing that substance abuse is intertwined with other problem behaviors, such as dropping out, teen pregnancy, and delinquency; (3) focusing on specific knowledge, attitudes, and useful skills about alcohol and drugs by the fourth grade; (4) giving information about physiology (genetic predispositions), high-risk populations (medications), psychosocial correlates (family influences), and role of the community and media as related to alcohol and drugs so that young people can estimate their personal risk for developing substance abuse problems; (5) focusing on short-term social consequences important to the students, and (6) attitudinal inoculation, including role playing and Socratic discussions for dealing with overt and covert pressures.[17]

Sex education sometimes suffers attacks from conservative political groups, although even a majority of conservative groups supports sex education. Investigators are surprised at how badly youths in the United States fare in their understanding of the various aspects of sexuality. Although sex education is only one factor, some draw a connection between it and the incidence of teenage marriage, divorce, unwanted pregnancy, abortion, and venereal disease. Sweden with compulsory sex education has the lowest incidence of such problems, and the United States without a systematic program has the highest.

ENGLISH

English as a Subject

English as a school subject is relatively young, hardly over 100 years old. In 1865, there was a variety of studies of English—rhetoric, oratory, spelling, literary history, and reading. In the following decades, these traditional offerings were united under the teaching of a single subject—English—with literature, language, and composition forming the major components of the subject.

Early in the twentieth century, there were efforts to emancipate the teaching of English in the high schools from the college program. These efforts took the form of rejecting a traditional body of literature as the sole purveyor of culture, giving up an analytical approach to literary studies in favor of studying types of literature. In the early 1920s, there was a functional emphasis on English; committees attempted to identify the skills learned in English classes that were most useful to people in a range of social positions. An experience curriculum in English was introduced. It featured an abandonment of formal grammar in favor of functional instruction through activities in creative expression, speaking, and writing.

---

[17]Bonnie Bernard et al. "Knowing What to Do and *Not* to Do—Reinvigorates Drug Education," *Curriculum Update* (February 1987): 1–2.

The 1940s saw teachers of English trying to adapt their content to adolescent needs, the problems of family life, international relations, and other aspects of daily living. English became guidance. In the late 1950s, there was an academic resurgence, with attacks on such a conception of English. English as a discipline in the high schools followed the model of academic work in the college. There was a stress on intensive reading, the Great Books, and literary rather than personal pursuits. Language, literature, and composition remained the tripod of English. Teachers were expected to teach pupils how to give close analytical attention to what was read, asking questions about form, rhetoric, and meaning. Literary values once again prevailed over other considerations.

The middle 1960s saw the beginning of a countermovement with concern about making the English curriculum more relevant and meaningful to the disadvantaged. The emphasis again shifted to contemporary writing, including selections by black authors. In literature, there was a move away from the traditional historical and biographical approach that had focused on the social context, and toward topical units in the junior high school and thematic units in the senior high school. A theme like justice as treated by poets, playwrights, and novelists over the years often served as the basis for deeper study by the student. Reading literature was considered more important than reading what was said about it.

English teachers and curriculum workers still wonder whether courses should feature great works of literature or emphasize contemporary problems and modern psychological interpretations. The popular response is to try to include both the traditional and contemporary. One chooses important themes dealing with the human condition, such as guilt, and then selects material from traditional and modern American and British literature, folklore, and mythology that helps illuminate the theme. A danger in this approach is that it may induce a premature sophistication with respect to literary works. No single course can cover all centuries. Selectivity should govern both the scope and the details selected.

A conference on the teaching of English at Dartmouth College in 1966 brought American specialists in English in contact with British influences. The British offered the Americans a model for English that focused on the personal and linguistic growth of the child. Hence, many teachers of English began to copy the British practice of offering improvised drama, imaginative writing, personal response to literature, and informal classroom discussion. Like the British, they gave less attention to textual analysis, to the study of genres, to literary periods, and to chronology. Parallel with the reemphasis of English as a humanistic subject came technological influences. Behavioral objectives in English aroused much controversy. The skills thought necessary for speaking, listening, reading, and writing could be specified and taught. How these skills could be related to the goals of expression or response to literature is uncertain.

Trends in the Teaching of English

The 1980s saw a return to basic skills. Many freshmen were required to take a basic grammar course before enrolling in an English course in college. The basic skills movement gained support among students, teachers, parents, and administrators. Some minority members also supported the movement. Courses for studying the contributions of minority groups to literature engendered racial pride but often did not prepare minority students for the demands of a society in which standard English is the criterion for social advancement.

The basic skills movement in English was a demand for more history of classical literature, more traditional grammar, and a greater emphasis on formal than personal writing. There was a return to the workbook and hard cover anthology. Elective programs were being dismantled (they have been accused of fragmenting and diminishing the goals of an integrated approach to English), the new linguistics disappeared, "personal growth" and "creativity" were disparaged. Opponents of this movement urged English teachers not to succumb to pressures that would have them teach trivia because trivia can be easily measured, but to teach that reading and writing will help students find personal meaning in life. Some also urge including a critical study of the media, particularly television, because the media are so closely related to our quality of life.

At the beginning of the decade of the 1990s, compromise is evident. Basic English skills are taught in conjunction with themes in literature that affect all humanity. The great theme approach focuses attention on the most profound and humane questions of all time, for example, people's response to nature, to beauty, to the relationship between fate and free will. In contrast to those who teach isolated skills and neglect to show how these skills relate to current social realities, teachers consider how skills may be applied in situations relevant to students' lives. It is recognized that acquiring basic skills alone does not ensure communication of ideas. Communication of ideas requires both skill and interest. When subject matter is relevant to student interest, motivation to acquire skills is high.

The late professor, Mina Shaughnessy of the City University of New York, believed that even if a person is motivated to write and equipped with the skills needed to write, there is still no way to learn how to write unless you write. She required students to write no less than 1,000 words a week. Writing activities included a journal, essays on topics of interest, timed class writings, and term papers. To keep up with the paperwork, Dr. Shaughnessy suggested the use of peer group teaching, in which students could exchange essays and help each other to recognize areas of weakness. There is a strong belief on the part of many language arts instructors that the focus in the teaching of writing should be on designing experiences that systematically develop the students' abilities, including their sense of audience and purpose. It has been shown, for example, that even young children can be taught to formulate their writing intentions—to amuse, to inform, to praise someone or something—and to differentiate their writing according to genres such as narrative, dialogue, and exposition—and to adopt voice to suit different audiences. Attaining knowledge of stylistic conventions—paragraphing, punctuation, and so forth—leads to writing in order to affect the reader. After students start writing for others, they read their own writing, thereby improving it.

Recently there has also been a shift from "relevant" literature. There is a rising tide of criticism and displeasure about the reading material taught in schools. Book banning has risen remarkably in America during the last eight years. Because the teaching of literature is a political act, the goals for this curriculum are likely to reflect one's prior assumptions about the nature and purpose of education.

An indication of the political nature of curriculum planning in the field of English is found in the policy statement of the National Council of Teachers of English.[18] This statement, entitled *Essentials of English*, concedes something to every special interest. The authors define English as *literature* (habits, classics, human experience); *communication skills* (using media); *reading* (search for meaning, judging literature, functions in life, skills); *writing* (personal development, techniques and processes of writing, mechanics); *speaking* (self-expression, group discussion, logical argument); *listening* (purposes, details, evaluation); *thinking* (creative, logical, critical). The definitions of the essentials are not consistent with each

---

[18]National Council of Teachers of English, *Essentials of English* (Urbana IL: National Council of Teachers of English, 1983).

other and they are atheoretical (English as teaching isolated skills is incompatible with English as personally meaningful communication). The report is important for what it says about the status of English in the curriculum: English teachers are divided between utilitarian and humanistic purposes, and unsure about whether to teach performance skills or appreciation.

However, the dominant trend is to integrate the language arts using literature as the prime motivator. Through literature study, students are expected to use all the language skills. The literature program typically is composed of (a) the *core*—literary selections of recognized merit (common throughout an entire state or region); (b) extended *readings*—selections that are chosen by the teacher as appropriate for local or individual student requirements; and (c) *recreational readings*, in which a student reads independently in conjunction with library and bookstore resources.

Current trends in the teaching of English reflect three conflicting conceptions. (1) Teachers who value an academic orientation base their instruction on what scholars are doing in the field. (2) Those who think of education as personal growth concentrate on oral expression, projects, popular media, contemporary literature, and social commentary. (3) Those who think of English as a set of mechanical skills focus directly on reading, spelling, and writing.

The precedence to literature, "to reading and responding to texts written by others," has been broadened to include writing. The National Council of Teachers of English has stressed the importance of writing in its call for a consistent English from the early grades through undergraduate years.[19] Accordingly, students at all levels should read widely in both traditional literature and literature that reflects the diversity of American culture and practice writing in different styles for different purposes. Perhaps the most outstanding example of a successful writing project is the Foxfire Project involving oral history and cultural journalism.[20] This writing project is grounded in the principles of democratic experiential curriculum in which writing flows from student desire and choice, is connected to issues in the student's own environment, and evidences affirmation that student writing is important, needed, and worth doing.

---

[19]Richard Lloyd-Jones, ed., *The English Coalition Conference: Democracy Through Language* (Urbana, IL: National Council of Teachers of English, 1989).

[20]Eliot Wissington, "Foxfire Grows Up," *Harvard Educational Review* 59, no. 1 (February 1989); 24–49.

READING

The Curriculum for Reading

The curriculum for the teaching of reading in America from 1600 to the present has reflected different goals. The initial goal was religious. Children were expected to learn to read the word of God directly. With the forming of a new nation, reading was taught to help build national strength and unity—to instill patriotism. From 1840 to 1890, the teaching of reading as a means for obtaining information was the primary goal. This emphasis on enlightenment was an extension of nationalism—from patriotic sentiment to the ideal of an intelligent citizenry. To awaken a perennial interest in literary material was the overriding goal in the late 1890s and until about 1918. Thereafter, utility rather than aesthetics had priority. Reading selections were oriented more to the events of daily living than to literary appreciation.

Currently, there are three emphases in the teaching of reading. One emphasis focuses on word recognition and reading comprehension. These skills are taught without considering the purpose for which they will ultimately be used. A second emphasis focuses on the specific kinds of situations in which the student is to apply reading skills—reading want ads, Yellow Pages, job applications, and newspapers. The latter emphasis reflects a concern for those who are functionally illiterate—those who lack the reading competencies necessary to function successfully in contemporary society. Accordingly, there is increasing interest in the teaching of reading at the middle and senior high school levels. A third emphasis is to teach reading as conceptual development in which a person's background of experience is made use of in the process so that the reader creates meaning from text.

Trends and Directions

Trends in the teaching of reading during the past decade followed those in the other language arts. Instruction in reading was influenced by scholarship, technology, and humanistic concerns. The influence of scholars in linguistics, for example, can be noted in more natural language in primers, controlled spelling patterns rather than a controlled vocabulary in texts designed for teaching word recognition skills, the use of language patterns to signal the meaning of what is written (for example, word order patterns), and greater acceptance of the learner's own articulation and substitution of words. On the other hand, the influence of the technologists is seen in today's instructional materials which feature task analyses, specific objectives with matching criterion-referenced tests, relevant practice, provision for feedback to the learner, and mastery of prerequisite tasks before proceeding.

Three directions in the teaching of reading are the whole language movement, the interactive view of reading, and literature-based reading. Proponents of whole language view reading as part of general language development and not as a discrete skill isolated from listening, speaking, and writing. Beginning in kindergarten, children compose stories and learn to read from their writing. They also engage in shared reading of literature. Whole language with older students allows for learners' choice of the areas in which to become literate and encourages voices that are authentic to local reality. The interactive view of reading is that the reader creates meaning by combining text with previously acquired experiences.

Learners can be helped in the process by being taught metacognitive skills (how to monitor their understanding of the text), how to use their prior knowledge in reading, and how to integrate text with their background knowledge. The driving force behind whole language reading is teacher and student empowerment. With this approach, they are not dependent on text written by others. On the other hand, the emphasis upon teaching as comprehension or thinking is supported by the belief that higher level reasoning abilities are required in today's technological and communication society. Finally, the trend to place literature at the core of the reading program reflects a conservative social view—that of the advocates of cultural literacy, such as E.D. Hirsch, who want all readers to amass a shared content that reflects the traditions of the dominant class.

HISTORY AND SOCIAL STUDIES

History as a Subject

The "new" history of the 1960s, both in subject matter and methodology, evolved from the same forces that had affected other subject matter fields, that is, the discipline proposal and the push toward specialization. The subject matter of history was chosen in order to provide students with a conceptual foundation on which specialization could be based. Emphasis was placed on historians' methods of research, analysis, and interpretation. Students were no longer required to memorize sheer facts or chronology, but to express an understanding for general sociological theories. This conceptual approach encouraged students to doubt and openly criticize textbook interpretations of history. Students drew their own conclusions and often found previous perspectives biased and unreliable.

Campus demonstrations in the late 1960s reflected a general lack of confidence in politicians and governmental agencies. Students had been taught to examine, analyze, and interpret, and they freely applied these skills to national policy making. The Vietnam War was history in the making, and students were determined to make known their interpretations of the facts.

Public concern about campus protests resulted in a demand that history be taught in a manner that would make it applicable to constructive resolution of community problems. To accommodate this demand, curriculum specialists suggested integrating the study of history with other subjects and to life in the present. Therefore, emphasis was placed upon building a basic understanding of the historical influences on community life. Suggested learning activities included studying the influence of science and technology on various periods of history, identifying the relationship between historical movements and developments in the arts, and investigating the effects of business and industry on local history.

An Evaluation of History Curriculum

Appraisals of the curriculum in history during the 1980s were negative. Teachers were accused of having an unintegrated interpretation of history, a limited range of teaching strategies, and a narrow conception of the students' responsibilities.[21] Curriculum consisted of a prescribed, fragmented body of material to be absorbed and repeated to the teacher. Whether the focus was the Federal Reserve Act, current events, or World War II, the material was not related to the lives of students or to the larger historical process.

The appraisal of elementary and secondary history textbooks was also negative.[22] The texts were unrealistic, although they showed the

---

[21]Paula M. Evans, ''Teaching History in Libertyville,'' *Daedalus* 112, no. 3 (Spring 1983): 199–229.

[22]Frances Fitzgerald, ''Prizewinning Author Charges History Textbooks' President Distorted Picture,'' *ASCD News Exchange* 21, no. 4 (Summer 1979): 1, 7.

present as a "tangle of problems" and, paradoxically, were sanguine about the future. Economic history was conspicuously absent, an analysis of ideological conflict was missing from discussions of American wars, and the authors did not attend to continuity. "Politics is one theory to them, economics another, culture a third. . . . There is no link between the end of Reconstruction in the South and the Civil Rights movement of the sixties. . . . History is just one damn thing after another. It is, in fact, not history at all."[23] Frances Fitzgerald attributes the lack of interest in academic competence in history to the societal demand that the curriculum promote good social behavior and learning for strictly practical purposes.

History and Geography in the 1990s

At the start of the 1990s, there is renewed emphasis on history and geography, a new look at the primary curriculum, the integration of literature with history, and a more in-depth study of both the history of the world and the history of the United States. These directions are illustrated by the California curriculum for history, which was developed to meet the standards of the Bradley Commission, a group of historians.[24]

Most students study American history in grade 5 (pre-Columbian societies to 1850), grade 8 (growth and conflict 1783–1914), and grade 11 (continuity and change 1900 to present); world history in grade 6 (ancient civilizations), grade 7 (medieval and early modern times), and grade 10 (culture and geography of the modern world). Those in the elementary grades learn about local, family, and state history by studying the achievements of great men and women of different cultures. Controversial issues usually are reserved for grades 10 and 11, and high school seniors study economics and government.

In addition to emphasizing historical chronology and continuity, this curriculum features literature (fairy tales, myths, legends, and biography) in the early grades and literature, including sources from the social sciences in the secondary school units. This curriculum stresses the rights and responsibilities of citizens, contrasts government in different societies, and fosters individual initiative for historical change.

Most reviewers approve of the new framework's efforts to involve students in historical events by telling stimulating stories of colorful per-

---

[24]*Building a History Curriculum: Guidelines for Teaching History in Schools* (Washington, DC: Educational Excellence Network, 1988).

sons and dramatic episodes and having students react to what they would have done in the situations. Nevertheless, there is concern that this program will selectively reinforce a cultural memory that is univocal and uncontested. In trying to give students a solid introduction to their national past and to build national pride in American achievements, the history curriculum may ignore the conflicting voices and heterogeneity of the American experience. Furthermore, in focusing upon history, less attention is given to the study of current problems and the development of sociological, anthropological, and economic interpretations.

Social Studies

Social studies is a broad term covering several subject matters including history and the social sciences. Originally, the purpose of the social studies curriculum was the "creation of rich and many-sided personalities, equipped with practical knowledge and inspired by ideals so that they can make their way and fulfill their mission in a changing society which is part of a world complex."[25] Today, there is disenchantment with the stated purpose. It is too vague, and there is doubt that those in the social sciences are able to furnish knowledge with which to resolve complex social issues like racial strife, war, and economic depressions. Indeed, social scientists have inflated hopes and made promises beyond the means of their knowledge and capacities.

In the 1950s, the curriculum of the social studies was varied. The authors of some programs aimed at social literacy. They wanted learners to understand social change as responses to the problems and needs of human beings throughout the world. Others said their mission was to help learners develop socially desirable behavior; social scientists felt they were demonstrating social processes, promoting understanding and skill in dealing with social problems. A common curriculum premise of that time was that the social studies program should combine both content and process. Students should have the opportunity to make decisions regarding personal and social problems using the generalizations from the social sciences.

In the 1960s, more than forty major social studies curriculum projects were financed by the federal government, foundations, and institutions of higher learning. Authors of these projects all emphasized an academic structure but did not share a common view as to what the structure was.

---

[25]Charles Beard, *The Nature of the Social Sciences* (New York: Scribner & Sons, 1938), p. 179.

They tended to define structure loosely as generalizations, concepts, or modes of inquiry. There was little agreement on which concepts or ways of working in the social sciences are most fruitful and representative of structure. Like most other curriculum programs of the 1960s, social studies projects stressed inductive teaching. Students were expected to make generalizations from data. Typical goals for the social studies during this period were to interpret problems of world citizenship using concepts from the behavioral sciences; to interperet social behavior using concepts from a variety of disciplines; to analyze public controversies using the method of discussion and argument; and to recognise objective evidence using concepts from philosophy, psychology, law, and other social sciences.

In the 1960s, the social studies curriculum was in disarray. On the one hand, there were those who advocated drawing substantially from a wide range of social science disciplines in developing new social studies programs. On the other hand, there were those who recommended studying non-Western societies and organizing curriculum content around the study of world cultures and international affairs.

Today, the social studies curriculum in schools is still more social studies than social science, with history, government, and geography as the dominant subjects. In elementary schools, the social studies receive little attention, serving primarily as another opportunity to teach reading and writing skills. At all levels the social studies curriculum is a textbook curriculum; the textbook is used to organize courses and students concentrate solely on the content of the text. Few teachers have ever heard of approaches oriented toward the social sciences, and fewer still use them. They also do not connect the course with anything in the student's life, with events familiar to them. The basic skills movement has weakened efforts to promote inquiry and problem analysis. There is little agreement among teachers, advocates, and analysts within the field as to what purposes the social studies should serve or the most appropriate subject matter to teach.[26]

The Future of Social Studies

Problems concerning the social studies curriculum of the future center on the following observations. Rational discourse, critical inquiry, op-

---

[26]Howard D. Mehlinger, "The Reform of Social Studies and the Role of the National Commission for the Social Studies," *The History Teacher* 21, no. 1 (February 1988): 195–207.

portunity to exercise the skill of autonomous judgment, and other featured values in social studies programs seem to be no guarantee of behavioral change or even increased happiness of the individual or society. Inasmuch as human beings may act irrationally on impulse, emotion, pride, and passion, social studies programs that feature only facts and interpretations should not be expected to contribute much toward making students more reasonable about human and social behavior. Consequently, the future will see a movement in the direction of the affective realm. Values and attitudes will become more important, and efforts will be made to involve students in ecological and political matters of personal interest. There will be a return to the project method, stressing ways to participate in acts of citizenship and to improve and perfect our governmental system, an emphasis that may overcome students' loss of confidence in the American political system.

By way of example, eighth graders in Walnut, California, participate in an applied social studies program "We Care"[27] and undertake such projects as simplifying voting procedures, revamping fire drill regulations, promoting water conservation, and more. Each class selects a project to improve life in their community and state. In dealing with water conservation, the students make use of abstract principles of conservation in writing legislation requiring the state to use water-saving plants for landscaping. They launched a campaign for getting state-wide support for the legislation by lobbying, disseminating information through newspapers, and other forms of political behavior.

The need to construct a better world will force those in the social studies to focus on social problems rather than on transmitting knowledge. These kinds of problems require the student to draw the best current thinking from both the natural and the social sciences. Hence, we will see attempts at an integrative curriculum. The task is difficult. Teachers, for example, are not always comfortable with the inquiry methods and concepts of a single social science. Now they are asked to gain competency in several disciplines. Also, we know that scholars in a single social science have difficulty in agreeing on the objectives and content for course materials. Greater difficulty will be experienced in getting agreement from scholars in different fields about what should be taught.

In the short run, pressures will continue to make the social studies curriculum respond to the needs of special groups. Business interests

---

[27]Alan Haskvitz, "A Middle School Program That Can Change Society," *Phi Delta Kappan* 70, no. 2 (October 1988): 175–178.

will influence legislators to mandate instruction on the free enterprise system; Jewish groups will seek legislation to require detailed study of the Holocaust. Nuclear curricula, economic education, global education, and law-related studies are examples of topics that have been included in the social studies curriculum in response to special interests. The social studies curriculum across the land might be a hodgepodge of programs, but the topics should be regarded as vehicles for helping students acquire the common elements of citizenship—skills for participating in public affairs and understanding the premises of American liberty. Social studies could also be an opportunity for students to apply the concepts and generalizations acquired from concurrent study of history, geography, government, or other disciplines.

FOREIGN LANGUAGE

The Rise and Fall of Foreign Language

Six years before Sputnik, the Modern Language Association of America expressed the conviction that we were not teaching foreign languages to enough people. National concern for the advancement of scientific and technological research in the late fifties accentuated the need for international exchange of knowledge. Hence, the study of one or two foreign languages became a requirement of most secondary schools and universities. Over 8,000 elementary schools began to offer instruction in foreign languages.

An instructional method sometimes called the American method or the audiolingual approach for teaching foreign languages became popular at this time. This method was derived from the science of structural or descriptive linguistics that had proved useful in courses offered to the military during World War II. The basic principle of the method is that students' language must be learned as a system of communication by sound from mouth to ear. Students and teacher who used this method spoke the foreign language; they did not only talk about it. The first 300 to 400 hours of language learning were devoted to acquiring a skill rather than a body of facts. During this initial period, students began to comprehend the spoken word and to speak after listening; reading and writing were not emphasized. Students then practiced actively and aloud until they gained some control over the language patterns. The opportunity for such practice was generally provided by language laboratories in which the students heard recordings of a native speaker and tried to model their speech after the speaker's.

Interest in foreign languages began to decline in the mid-1960s as the national concern for space exploration subsided, and with it the push for communication with foreign scientists. Studies in language were criticized for being too specialized to be applicable. Foreign language requirements were eliminated in many colleges and secondary schools. By 1980, only 15 percent of high school students were enrolled in foreign language courses. Indeed, a presidential commission reported that only 4 percent of pupils graduating from high school had studied a foreign language for as long as two years. One-fifth of United States public high schools offered no courses in foreign language at all. Among those that did, Spanish, French, and German were most often offered, in that order. A national sampling by the University of Michigan found that more than 52 percent of Americans who were questioned would like to study a foreign language in the future, but nearly 49 percent opposed making it a requirement in high schools.

Efforts to Revive Language Instruction

To counteract the loss of student enrollment, advocates of foreign language attempted to concentrate on the human aspects of their discipline in hopes of regaining student interest. Language departments expanded their course offerings in order to meet the needs and interests of students. In discussing ways to do this, teachers typically suggested integration of language study with other subject matter areas, early introduction of language arts, and student participation in curriculum development. Subject matter integration is accomplished by introducing students to the contributions of language to all subject areas. English classes study the contribution of foreign languages to the development of American English, music classes study lyrics of foreign folk songs, and art classes share their work with those in foreign countries.

In her study of the teaching of foreign language, Marlies Mueller found that students have few classroom opportunities to speak the new language in situations that involve genuine communication.[28] Instead, the language is spoken only in dry grammar exercises as an abstract activity. Seventy-five percent of the teachers visited by Mueller used the grammar-translation method whose origin dates back to the time when Latin and Greek were taught as a means for forming the intellect. Accord-

---

[28]Marlies Mueller, ''The Tower of Babel in Libertyville,'' *Daedalus* 112, no. 3 (Summer 1983): 229–249.

ingly, grammar is deductively presented—first the rule and then the example—along with vocabulary lists to be memorized and later texts to be translated. Obviously, this method is inconsistent with the communication-oriented purpose of language study. The latter goal is better served by (a) trying to approximate the manner in which children learn their first language (the natural language learning approach); (b) insisting on the conscious understanding and use of newly acquired phrases or structures in a meaningful context (the cognitive-code approach); and (c) thinking in the foreign language so that the student uses the language in direct association with classroom objects and pictorial representations or actions by teacher and students, and (d) teaching grammar rules inductively so that students derive linguistic generalizations after being confronted with many examples (the direct method).

The early introduction of foreign languages has gained general support from everyone concerned with the development of language skills. Young children between the ages of four and ten learn foreign languages easily. Children are usually flexible, uninhibited, and eager to explore different languages. Early introduction of languages also enhances cultural awareness among children. Languages may be used to explore the typical experiences in different cultures (cooking styles and names of foods, folk songs, games played in foreign countries). Among the innovations suggested for stimulating language learning are bilingual nursery schools, home visits by bilingual teachers, tutoring of younger children by trained school-age peers during play, and mobile classrooms to teach foreign languages.

Students are now being encouraged to participate in the planning of new language courses. This trend emerged from the need to make the language arts relevant to the needs of students. In addition, it is now realized that optimum learning takes place when the learner is meaningfully involved in determining what is to be learned and how it is to be learned. However, efforts to entice students toward second language learning through exposure to language and culture in games may backfire. If students are shielded from the serious mental effort required for learning a language, the subject may be trivialized and fail to gain student respect.

Language subject matter for the 1990s probably will include emphasis on basic speaking skills as well as those needed for reading and writing. Study activities will be designed to ensure relevancy and applicability. Speaking skills will be related to foreign cultural topics ranging from dating customs to urban problems. Use of current periodicals will also enhance relevancy of reading skills.

Resource persons can bring life to the languages. Non-English-speaking persons in the community may be invited to participate in classroom learning activities. Community businesses that employ bilingual persons may be encouraged to offer internship experiences. Field trips and opportunities for travel can be used to introduce students to the language in use, making language studies alive and vital.

Among the new methodologies is the *confluent approach* drawn from the humanistic orientation. Accordingly, students participate in group activities designed to elicit open interpersonal communication. Students in such classes explore and discuss various aspects of themselves, as well as less personal information, in the language. The most original of the new methods is *suggestopedia* which uses hypnotic and subliminal learning techniques, such as sleep learning.

Optimism for increased instruction in foreign language is found in such recent developments as the reinstatement of foreign language as a graduation requirement and as a college entrance requirement, language instruction beginning in the fifth and sixth grades, and the public's general awareness of the commercial and social value of learning another language.

THE ARTS

Fine Arts in the Curriculum

The broad direction of curriculum revision needed in the arts was set in 1958. At that time, the American Council of Learned Societies' panel on curriculum made two recommendations: (1) that the basic approach be creative, allowing the student in studios and workshops to be personally involved and (2) that historical matter be incorporated to develop the student's sense of heritage in the arts. Instead of survey courses, an attempt should be made to involve the student in the study of art as it represents various epochs and cultures and as it might affect his or her own creativity. Critical judgment is to be developed by practice and by seeing good examples, reading, and hearing about original works.[29]

Subsequently, some educators based their curriculum on aesthetic theory; others, mindful of learning theory's emphasis on conceptual structure, turned their efforts toward defining the structure of art in

---

[29]American Council of Learned Societies, "Secondary School Curriculum Problems," *Newsletter 9,* no. 9 (1959).

terms of concepts. The pronouncement that any subject could be effectively taught to any child at any stage of development had eventually influenced curriculum developments in art as it had in other subjects.

Art curriculum of the mid-1960s was designed to provide students with an appreciation for the basic aesthetic themes expressed in all art forms. Subject matter covered basic concepts such as rhythm, movement, harmony, and texture. These concepts were to be experienced through listening (music appreciation), performing (acting, playing traditional instruments), and composing (emphasizing classical techniques). The main weakness of this instructional approach was that it served the needs of only a small portion of the student population. Subject matter was too specialized for the average student's basic artistic needs. The narrow range of course offerings could not encompass growing interest in art forms of ethnic minorities, use of a wide variety of musical instruments, art forms of different countries, and use of new art media.

To help show the usefulness of art, curriculum specialists suggested integrating art with other subject matter fields. Examples of integration are when music instruction includes an examination of the cultural and historical influences and the development of lyrics is studied in English courses. Public schools in Columbus, Ohio, are known for their integration of the arts with other areas of the curriculum. In many of the schools, for example, music is used in the teaching of poetry (rhythm), history (songs of people in history), mathematics (patterns and frequencies), and science (the physics of sound). Students studying future utopias might examine the authenticity of the proposed systems in science classes. Later, they could write a play in conjunction with a creative writing course. Finally, their play could be produced in a drama class.

Instruction in the arts should be related to actual experiences. Students will have increased interest and will be able to see how the arts can become an intrinsic part of life. Resident artists can help students plan a career in the arts. Local artists are participating in school art curriculum programs. Poets, musicians, sculptors, actors, craftspersons, designers, environmental planners, and filmmakers are a sample of the artists bringing the outside world to the classroom.

Use of peer group and cross-age teaching gained support in the 1980s. Dr. Robert Pace, chairman of the piano department at Columbia University's Teachers College, developed a system of musical training which made the most of peer teaching. Groups of eight to ten students of various ages learned the techniques of music by participating in sight-reading games, ear-training musical drills, and exercises in musical improvisation. The program was cost-effective, and students enjoyed sharing their musical development with peers.

New methods are being developed for the teaching of music, based on the interests and capacities of the average child. Some schools offer programs that begin in kindergarten, based on children's natural affinity for jazz. Other schools teach rock music and electronic music. Guitars have become major teaching tools. An art curriculum specialist faces only one fear for art in the 1990s: "Will art, music, dance, and drama be regarded as frills by an increasingly cost-conscious public?"

The basic skills movement is a threat to courses in the arts, although the Council for Basic Education thinks art is among the basics.

The best private or independent schools are as proud of their instruction in the arts as in science and mathematics. Such schools are concerned with the whole person, with creativity as well as performance on test scores. Instruction in the arts is viewed as an essential part of preparation for life.

The idea that the arts merit attention in all schools underlies the Rockefeller Brothers Fund, which awards prizes to exemplary art programs in public schools. The variety of exemplary programs being offered is illustrated in arts essays produced by the American Academy of Arts and Sciences.

In the Great Smoky Mountains, the Swain County High School arts program introduces students to the foundations of aesthetic awareness—line, form, color, and design—through the works of major artists and through individual projects. The forms of arts and crafts include macramé, pottery, fibers, weaving, drawing, photography, silk screening, papermaking, batik, stitchery, quilting, lettering, and airbrushing. The program is strongly vocational, equipping students with the knowledge skills for becoming commercial artists, artisans, and craftspersons. Nevertheless, it is the development of individual self-expression and personal aesthetic values that make the program successful.

The Fillmore Arts Center in Washington, DC, is devoted to teaching the arts and offers a good education in the visual arts, music, dance, and drama. From kindergarten through eighth grade, pupils rotate through all four basic arts during the year. Beginning at grade four, children take courses such as "discovery art," "music for voice, recorder, and xylophone," "puppet pizzary" and "video techniques." In grades five and six, among the choices are painting and drawing, modern and jazz dance, calligraphy, poetry and fabric design. Students in grades seven and eight can take percussion, story dramatization, woodworking, filmmaking, cartooning, or sculpture. The arts in this school are taught as a means for strengthening personal growth in many ways—intellectual (solving problems), emotional (finding ways for self expression), and perceptual (experiencing the environment through the senses). Cognitive development corresponds to the development of oral and motor skills, reading and writing skills. It is a true curriculum in the sense of extending important elements. For example, in music, the physical expression of rhythmic patterns to body movement lays the foundation for reading notes; reading and writing music leads to sharper perception when listening to a symphony; listening for patterns in a symphony gives children ideas for expressing their own music.

Thus, the reasons for art in the curriculum are many—for self-expression, appreciation, a future career. Also, art is valued for its intellectual content, historical importance, and key role in culture. In an essay that is highly critical of the vague, lofty, and unexamined list of aims for teaching art, Jacques Barzun says we do not have to have eighteen reasons to justify it in the schools. One reason is enough: "Art is an important part of our culture. It corresponds to a deep instinct in man; hence it is enjoyable. We therefore teach its rudiments."[30] Harry S. Broudy, on the other hand, believes that the schools should cultivate the aesthetic mode of experience, not because it is a delight, but because it is necessary for the development of the intellect. He argues for teaching sensitivity to the appearance of things, the expressive properties of color, sound, texture, and movement organized into aesthetic objects, and the perception and construction of images that portray intimations of reality in forms of feeling.[31] Those who are giving the arts a firm place in the school program seem to say that both viewpoints are necessary.

The issue of whether the arts are academic or affective is clearly seen in two distinctly different programs that are trying to breathe new life into the American art curriculum. The Los Angeles Getty Center advocates a discipline-based curriculum in which the arts are treated as a cognitive discipline through the teaching of art history, criticism, and aesthetics along with production, i.e., to learn about art, not merely to "do" art.[32]

---

[30]Jacques Barzun, "Art and Educational Inflation," *The Education Digest* 45, no. 1 (September 1979): 12–16.

[31]Harry S. Broudy, "A Common Curriculum in Aesthetics and Fine Arts," in *Individual Differences and the Common Curriculum*, NSSE Yearbook, Gary Festermaker and John I. Goodlad, eds. (Chicago: The University of Chicago Press, 1983).

[32]*The Place for Art in America's Schools* (Los Angeles: The Getty Center for Education in the Arts, 1985).

Virginia Beach approaches the standards. In that city, programs offered are a standardized art program for its students in K–6, an elective junior high art course, and five high school courses. In all of these courses, students study and critically evaluate works of art. Even in the second grade, students learn the difference between realistic, abstract, and other forms of painting so that they can see the principles behind their own original artwork.

In contrast, the Lincoln Center Institute for the Arts in Education aims at producing both cognitive and affective outcomes through a non-academic approach.[33] Those at the center believe that the primary purpose of the art curriculum is *art*, with no need to justify the teaching of art on the grounds that art is teaching something else. Experiential learning methods take precedence. Although teaching objectives and a prescriptive sequence are not discussed, there is an effort to bring excitement to the arts by analyzing experiences of the student and manipulating, recreating, and reassembling major elements. In drama, for example, students deal separately with plot, character, and setting, and the role of the director, using the concept of choice as an organizing theme. Similarly, in dance, the concept of contrast might provide unity, while students work with space, energy, and time. Always students are taught to see the interconnections among the basic components.

In brief, the arts and music curricula are moving toward the creation of art forms (production and performance), the promotion of creative expression, along with discourse about the arts and students critiquing of their experience with art.

CONCLUDING COMMENTS

Most subjects are influenced by the same social, economic, political, and technological forces. Hence, it is no great surprise to see most of them moving in the same direction. We have just undergone a period of great renewal in the academic curriculum. Policy makers have demanded that more students complete more work in the academic subjects, particularly mathematics, science, writing, and the humanities. This renewal was accompanied by three problems: a crisis in purpose, a concern about student interest, and a desire for open access to knowledge.

There is a revival in all the academic subjects to find clear-cut goals

[33]Carol Sienkiewicz, *Report* (New York: Lincoln Center, January/February 1985).

and a body of essential content. In part, this activity is a response to the many incoherent programs developed at a period when individualization was prized. Thus far, there is no final agreement on central purposes in any field. Curriculum policy statements in the respective fields reflect pluralistic interests: functional competency, intellectual development, traditional values, social relevancy, and self-actualization. There is a lack of agreement regarding essential content and strong disagreement between those who prefer the traditional curriculum as the standard of excellence and those who want the academic content to reflect new conceptions of the fields. Even the new college board specialists for college preparation reveal inconsistent expectations, which are more in keeping with political compromise (something for everybody) than an educational philosophy.

A new rationale for redefining goals in academic subjects is needed. It would be better to have separate curriculum programs reflecting specific philosophies, such as in some distinguished magnet, specialized, and private schools, than to create programs with conflicting purposes.

Student interest and access reflect the fact that most academic subjects are taught in a sterile manner—primarily textbook information with corresponding emphasis on terminology and definitions. Also, only some students are given the opportunity to pursue subjects in an inspired way, asking new questions, thinking critically and imaginatively.

Studies of fields such as science reveal much student alienation from knowledge. Less than 50 percent of high school graduates express interest in further study of science, and there is little evidence that school science prepares them either for college or for life. Less than 10 percent of secondary students are interested in the field of science. If additional mandates for more work in the "hard" subjects, such as science, result in more of the same inferior curriculum, the alienation from knowledge is likely to be even greater.

A serious challenge is a curriculum design that will enable large numbers of students (particularly those from less academically privileged classes) to have success with content formerly available only to a small elite group. Obviously, to define subjects in terms of the ways in which experts view their subjects is not enough. Nor is it adequate to offer a subject as a means of advancing up the academic ladder. Students expect to apply what they are learning to current issues and to their personal needs. Where in the new academic curriculum will there be opportunities for the students' active learning in exploring, drawing inferences, problem solving, collaborative learning, and creativity?

Curriculum makers in all fields are trying to relate subject matter to the developmental stages of various learners. This effort is putting curriculum makers ahead of academic specialists in the redefinition and integration of subject matter. The relationship of vocational education to academic achievement in mathematics and science is one example.

It is clear that closer attention must be paid to the relationships among the ideal academic curricula as stated by national and state policy makers, the perceptions of teachers about what they are teaching, and the perceptions of students about what they are learning. Course content, regardless of course title, is dependent upon the skills, interests, and preferences of individual teachers.

QUESTIONS

1. Sometimes academic trends reflect a desired future; others warn of practices that should be stopped. Identify some trends that you feel attempt to bring about a desirable future and some that you see as warnings.
2. Try your hand at anticipating a likely future trend in a subject field by (a) identifying or analyzing political, economic, or other social factors that have the potential for shaping curriculum and (b) indicating how this force might affect the curriculum in this field.
3. Subject matter was never really viewed as an end in itself. The learning of a subject is always justified as useful for some social purpose. What social purpose or interests have been served by your academic field?
4. It is sometimes suggested that teachers offer various courses like technology science, surgical science, science and pollution, health care science and the science of music so that students' interests and local needs are better served. What scientific themes might run through these courses?
5. What, if anything, should be done about the practice of offering a different academic content, pedagogy, and class climate to upper track students from those offered to lower track students studying the same subject?

SELECTED REFERENCES

Art and Music
Eisner, Elliot W. *The Role of Discipline Based Art Education in American Schools.* Los Angeles: The Getty Center for Education in the Arts, 1987.

Frank Hodsoll, ed., *Toward Civilization: A Report on Arts Education*, Washington, DC: National Endowment for the Arts, 1988.

K-12 Arts Education in the United States: Present Context, Future Needs. Reston, VA: Arts Education Community, 1986.

English, the Language Arts, and Reading

Becoming a Nation of Readers. Washington, DC: National Academy of Education, 1984.

Jane C. Davidson, ed., *Counterpoint and Beyond: A Response to a ''Nation of Readers,''* Urbana, IL: National Council of Teachers of English, 1988.

Richard Lloyd-Jones, ed., *The English Coalition Conference: Democracy Through Language*, Urbana, IL: National Council of Teachers of English, 1989.

Dorothy J. Watson, ed., *Ideas and Insights: Language Arts in the Elementary School*, Urbana, IL: National Council of Teachers of English, 1987.

Wigginton, Eliot. *Sometimes a Shining Moment: The Foxfire Experience*. New York: Doubleday, 1985.

Foreign Language

Academic Preparation in Foreign Language: Teaching for Transition from High School to College. New York: College Entrance Exam Board, 1986.

Hawkins, Eric W. *Modern Language in the Curriculum*. New York: Cambridge University Press, 1987.

Yalden, Janice. *Principles of Course Design for Language Teachers*. New York: Cambridge University Press, 1987.

Physical Education and Health

Compendium of Exemplary School Health Education Programs. Atlanta, GA: Center for Disease Control, 1989.

Physical Activity in Early and Modern Populations. Champaign, IL: American Academy of Physical Education, 1988.

Science

Science for All Americans. Washington, DC: American Association for the Advancement of Science, 1989.

Zeitler, William R. *Elementary School Science: A Perspective for Teachers*. New York: Longman, 1988.

History and Social Studies

Engle, Shirley H., and Ochoa, Anna S. *Education for Democratic Citizens*. New York: Columbia University, Teachers College Press, 1988.

History in the Schools: What Shall We Teach?, Bernard R. Gifford, ed. New York: Macmillan, 1988.

Social Studies for Early Childhood and Elementary School Children: Preparing for the 21st Century. Newark, NJ: National Council for the Social Studies, 1989.

Mathematics

Curriculum and Evaluation Standards for School Mathematics. Reston, VA: National Council for Teachers of Mathematics, 1989.

Research Theory
and Curriculum

A popular publication carried the title *The Curriculum—Retrospect and Prospect.* This would be a good title to apply to this part. The emergence of curriculum as a professional study is treated in a historical chapter. The views of a number of influential curriculum theorists and developers are examined to cast light on the nature of curriculum and the central concerns of curriculum specialists. A second chapter is devoted to appraising curriculum as a field of inquiry today, giving attention to future directions. The work of curriculum scholars is described, making it possible to see successes, gaps, and trends in curriculum research and development. The reader will find specific suggestions by which research in curriculum can be most fruitfully pursued.

14

A Historical Perspective of Curriculum Making

There are at least two reasons for attending to the history of curriculum thought and practice. First, a review of the past can help us identify problems with which dedicated persons have struggled and are struggling.

Admittedly, we still have to decide whether these problems are unsolvable, and, therefore, should be abandoned as unfruitful areas of inquiry, or whether their very persistence makes them worthy of our attention. For example, the issue of curriculum correlation (the relating of ideas from different subject matter) which is so pressing today was central in 1895. Then, some viewed correlation with suspicion and as a threat to the inviolability of the basic divisions of subject matter. Others saw it as an answer to the problem of an overcrowded program of studies and of value in helping the child's untrained mind relate an enormous number of topics.

Now, in the 1990s, as in 1895, some ask not so much whether there should be correlation of subject matter but how it should be accomplished. Should we group subjects around problems, using the facts from one discipline to illuminate another? Or, should we put within a comprehensive course the important generalizations from many fields?

A second reason for studying the history of curriculum thought and practice is to gain a clearer understanding of the processes of curriculum making by examining the work of prominent exponents in the field. By examining what curriculum meant to those who developed the field during this century, we can see more clearly what curriculum now means. For example, few issues are more important to current theorists than the formulation of an adequate concept of curriculum. Theorists believe that its clarification may contribute to the improvement of curriculum and that it will increase our understanding of curricular phenomena. Some concepts of curriculum are

1. A set of guidelines for developing products, books, and materials for the curriculum
2. A program of activities; a listing of course offerings, units, topics, and content
3. All learning guided by the school
4. The process by which one decides what to teach
5. The study of the processes used in curriculum making
6. What learners actually learn at school
7. What one plans for students to learn
8. A design for learning.

In 1890, extensive professional preparation for curriculum making was nonexistent, and there were no curriculum experts in the United States. Yet less than fifty years later, curriculum was a recognized field of specialization. One way to illustrate this development and at the same time illuminate the nature of the specialization is to look at the work of the persons who have been most associated with curriculum making.

CONTEXT FOR FORMULATION OF THE CURRICULUM FIELD

By the late 1890s, the conventional classifications of knowledge were seen by many as unsatisfactory in preparing students for new social demands. The curriculum was to respond to vast social changes inherent in industrialization, a large and different school population, and new psychologies emphasizing either fitting the curriculum to the nature of the child (developmentalists) or the training of specific capacities rather than trying to develop the elements of the mind through different subject matter (behavioristic connectionism).

Herbert Kliebard interprets this period as a struggle among different interest groups about what should be taught.[1] He identifies four competitors: (a) *classical humanists,* like Charles A. Eliot, who favored the liberal arts and the transmission of traditional values and culture; (b) *child-centered* leaders, like G. Stanley Hall, who argued that the content of the curriculum could be determined from data of child development (Hall's pedocentric curriculum upset the dominant ideal of fitting the child to the school with the new ideal of fitting the school to the child.); (c) *social efficiency* advocates represented by John Franklin Bobbitt, who saw the curriculum as a mechanism for preparing students for adult roles in the new industrial society (As described later, his work had great influence on the practice of curriculum development by stressing specifications and responses to current social needs rather than on transmitting classical subjects.); and (d) *social reconstructionists,* such as Harold Rugg, who wanted the curriculum to provide social change by giving students a new vision of justice and equality with which to remake the society.

According to Kliebard, each of these interest groups was the dominant force at a given time. The classics dominated the nineteenth century; social efficiency and scientific curriculum making were predominant in the first two decades of the twentieth century; child development, with the popularity of the project and activity curriculum, had center stage in the twenties; and social reconstructionism through critical social studies texts was strongest in the thirties. Kliebard holds that John Dewey did not fit comfortably in any of the four camps, nor did his vision take hold as powerfully as those of the competing factions.

David Larabee has provided additional insights regarding the interest groups identified by Kliebard.[2] Larabee sees these groups caught by two opposing elements in American ideology: *capitalism,* with its emphasis upon individualism and competition, and *democracy,* with the pursuit of equality. The classical traditionalists concerned themselves with the college preparatory track, sharpening the differentiation between the college-oriented middle class top stratum and the vocational working class stratum. Members of the child-centered group were democratically oriented in their insistence upon adapting the curriculum to the heterogeneous needs and capacities of students. Those of the social efficiency group tended to stress the market orientation and preparation of stu-

---

[1] Herbert M. Kliebard, *The Struggle for the American Curriculum, 1893-1951* (Boston: Routledge & Kegan Paul, 1986).

[2] David F. Larabee, "Politics, Markets and the Compromised Curriculum," *Harvard Educational Review* 57, no. 4 (1987): 483-495.

dents for the world's work; while the social reconstructionists went against the capitalistic position that school should be responsive to the demands of the marketplace and instead argued for reconstructing the curriculum around the standards of political democracy.

In his analysis of the history of the twentieth century American curriculum, Barry Franklin concentrates on the social efficiency interest group and indicates how these curriculum reformers were more interested in promoting socialization than in imparting intellectual content. Franklin advances the thesis that the middle class intellectuals of the time established the field of curriculum as a way of shaping the curriculum so that it would reconcile traditional liberal democratic values with a transformed American society. He sees social efficiency educators, like Franklin Bobbitt and Warrett W. Charters as dominating the curriculum field during its formative period and as being preoccupied with the question of how the curriculum (course of study) could socially control the twin forces of urbanization and industrialization.

The immediate focus of the emergent curriculum field in the early twenties was on how to make the curriculum. For a two-year period beginning in 1924, major figures from the different interest groups tried to achieve a consensus on the questions that the field should address.[3] Among the questions were the following: How can curriculum best preface effective participation in adult life? Should curriculum makers formulate a point of view concerning the merits or deficiencies of American civilization? Should the school fit students into the social order or educate them to change it? What is the place and function of subject matter in the education process—an end, something to be learned or a tool for problem solving? What portion of the curriculum should be general, specialized, vocational, and optional? Should the curriculum be made in advance? To what extent is the organization of subject matter to be structured by the learner or constructed by curriculum planners? To what degree should the curriculum provide for individual differences and "minimum essentials"? What use should be made of the spontaneous interests of learners?

In assessing these questions, the participants, though recognizing the importance of organized subject matter of the academic disciplines, favored helping learners to solve problems relevant to their own lives.

---

[3]Harold Rugg, ed., *The Foundations of Curriculum Making*, 26th Yearbook of the NSSE, Part 1 (Bloomington, IL: Public School Publishing Co., 1927).

Hence, they held that content should be drawn in interdisciplinary fashion rather than divided and taught as separate subjects.

In their own work in the curriculum field, early specialists answered the basic questions differently. The accounts that follow illustrate the contrasts between those who would fit students to an existing order and those who would prepare students to change it.

The persons chosen for review span a period from 1890 to the present and represent a much larger group of specialists. One basis for their selection is that they both studied the theory of curriculum and engaged in making it. In all instances, these curriculum workers contributed to the development of curriculum as an academic study and established its central questions.

HERBARTISM AND THE McMURRYS

Charles A. McMurry (1857–1929) and his brother, Frank W. McMurry (1862–1936), taught for several years in elementary schools before going abroad to study at the University of Jena in Germany, a mecca for educators in the late 1890s. There, they became profoundly influenced by the pedagogical theory of Johann Herbart whose *Outlines of Educational Doctrine* was the basis for many of the ideas and practices at Jena.[4]

Basic Tenets of Herbartism

Essentially, Herbartism was a rationalized set of philosophical and psychological ideas applied to instructional method. It rested on the assumption that only large, connected units of subject matter are able to arouse and keep alive a child's deep interest. Hence, it stressed "the doctrine of concentration," which occurs when the mind is wholly immersed in one interest to the exclusion of everything else. This doctrine was supplemented with "the doctrine of correlation," which makes one subject the focus of attention but sees to it that connections are made with related subjects.

---

[4]Johann F. Herbart, *Outlines of Educational Doctrine*, trans. Alex F. Lange (New York: Macmillan, 1904).

Instructional Procedure. Specifically, Herbartians recognized five steps as essential in the procedure of instruction:

1. *Preparation*—to revive in the student's consciousness the related ideas from past experience that will arouse interest in the new material and prepare the pupil for its rapid understanding
2. *Presentation*—to present the new material in concrete form, unless there is already ample sensory experience, and to relate it to the students' past experiences, such as reading, conversing, experimenting, lecturing, and so forth
3. *Association*—to analyze and to compare the new and the old, thus evolving a new idea
4. *Generalization*—to form general rules, laws, or principles from the analyzed experience, developing general concepts as well as sensations and perceptions
5. *Application*—to put the generalized idea to work in other situations, sometimes to test it, sometimes to use it as a practical tool

The Goal of Education. Herbart's followers believed that moral action was the highest educational goal and that education should prepare a person for life with the highest ideals of the culture. Furthermore, they believed that some subjects, such as history and literature, were superior for the development of moral ideas. They thought that if learners were guided by correct ideas and motivated by good interests, they would be prepared to discharge life's duties properly. Among the interests or motives to be advanced were sympathetic interest (a kindly disposition toward people), social interest (participation in public affairs), and religious interest (contemplation of human destiny).

The McMurrys' Thinking

The McMurrys recognized in Herbartian pedagogy a systematic method of selecting, arranging, and organizing the curriculum, something that had been missing in American schooling. On their return from Germany, they joined with others to apply the Herbartian methods and ideals in American schools. During his career, Charles McMurry wrote thirty books and prepared a course of study for the eight elementary grades describing how to select and arrange ideas for instruction. Principally, he addressed himself to teachers. His own teaching in the schools of Illinois and at George Peabody College for Teachers centered on the making of lesson plans according to the Herbartian five formal steps. He also concerned himself with the special instructional methods required for the teaching of specific subject fields.

Frank McMurry taught and wrote at Teachers College, Columbia University. His students were chiefly teachers who would train and supervise other teachers. His course in general methods reflected the Herbartian concern about the ends of education, the means for their attainment, the relative worth of studies, and the doctrines of concentration and correlation. Both brothers participated in national organizations devoted to the study and improvement of school programs. The effect of their efforts was great. Charles's course of study provided an overall framework for teachers, giving details for conducting lessons, the types of studies, and the special methods thought best for organizing the content in each subject. Their influence on lesson planning was especially noteworthy. In the period between 1900 and 1910, "every good teacher was supposed to have a lesson plan for each class period, and the five formal steps were much in evidence."[5] Even today military instructors are expected to design their lessons according to the formal steps outlined by the McMurrys. Analysis of the McMurrys' work shows the questions and answers that define the nature of curriculum thought in this early period.

Basic Questions. Implicit in the McMurrys' thinking were five basic questions:

1. *What Is the Aim of Education?* The McMurrys broadened Herbartian concerns for the moral development of the child to include the desire to lead children into the ways of good citizenship and into a wise physical, social, and moral adjustment to the world.
2. *What Subject Matter Has the Greatest Pedagogical Value?* Initially the McMurrys regarded literature as most useful in bringing the aesthetic and the intellectual into helpful association: they saw geography as the most universal, concrete correlating study. When the development of good character was the primary aim, they saw literature and history as the most important subjects. Later, the McMurrys differentiated between subjects that primarily helped the learner to express thought and those which primarily helped the learner receive or furnish thought. They noted that about one-half of schoolwork (that is,

---

[5]William H. Kilpatrick, "Dewey's Influence on Education," in *The Philosophy of John Dewey,* ed. Paul A. Schilpp (Evanston, IL: Northwestern University, 1939), p. 465.

beginning reading, writing, spelling, grammar, music, numbers, modeling, drawing, and painting), depends on the other half for its motive and force. In their later years, the McMurrys came to see that new subjects would claim favor. These new studies were nature study, science, industrial arts, health, agriculture, civics, and modern languages. Indeed, the introduction of new branches of knowledge and activity was seen by them as one of the greatest achievements of the age.

3. *How Is Subject Matter Related to Instructional Method?* The McMurrys believed there were formal elements of method and concepts for each subject, whether geology, arithmetic, or literature. They insisted that the child learn to think with these elements just as the specialists did in these fields and that the learner develop a consciousness of the right method of thinking in each subject. They saw that teachers at that time were not equipped with the fundamental concepts of each subject and, therefore, found it difficult to order instruction to clarify concepts in the respective fields. They were disturbed when curriculum workers ignored the fact that each subject matter makes particular demands on the organization of the curriculum.

4. *What Is the Best Sequence of Studies?* The McMurrys thought that suitable subject matter varies according to age and stage of development. Initially, they believed in the *theory of the culture epochs.* This theory holds that the child passes through the same general stages of development through which the race or culture has passed. Hence, what interested humanity at a certain historical stage would appeal most to a child at the corresponding stage of development. It was thought, for example, that teachers should present the stories of Ulysses to younger children. *The Odyssey* was seen as a means by which the heroic impulses of childhood could be related to an ideal person who achieved what the child would like to achieve. This work was deemed of pedagogical value, because it portrayed the primitive human struggle and at the same time revealed a higher plane of reason. Similarly, *Robinson Crusoe* was viewed as a good source for showing humankind's struggle with nature and at the same time helping the learner see that myths were attempts to interpret nature. Myths, legends, and heroic tales were followed by biography and formal history.

By 1923, Charles McMurry, at least, saw the theory of culture epochs as vague in its implications and admitted he knew of no sound basis for the placement of studies. For him, any particular scheme for placement of subject matter had come to be no better than the broad plan for organization that ordered it. The importance of organizing studies in relation to the child's mode of thought was seen as the more pressing problem.

5. *How Can the Curriculum Best Be Organized?* Faced with new school studies and activities, the imposition of scholarly works on children, and the isolation of each study, Charles McMurry gave highest priority to organization of the curriculum. His first answer was to organize the school studies on a life basis. Knowledge from different subject fields was coordinated into a single project or unit of study. Pupils were to become absorbed in pragmatic life problems or centers of interest. There was, for instance, applied science, like "the problem of securing a pure milk supply"; there were geographic projects like "the Salt River Irrigation Project in Arizona"; and there were historic projects like "Hamilton's project for funding the national debt." Most of these projects drew on history, geography, science, mathematics, and language. Also, each project or series of projects was to reveal the scope and meaning of a larger idea, which "like a view from the mountain top, at one glance brings into simple perspective and arrangement a whole vast grouping of minor facts."[6] The idea of evolution, for example, derived from a series of animal studies, becomes a principle of interpretation for use in other studies of animals and plants. A well-devised continuity of thoughts was kept steadily developing from grade to grade. The growth of institutions in history was one element chosen to ensure continuity over the span of several years of study.

Central Problem of Curriculum. Charles McMurry saw that the central problem of curriculum was to select the right centers of organization. These centers were to be points where older forms of knowledge and new studies could be combined. The relationship of centers of organization to the aim of education was most important. Furthermore, McMurry was concerned about who would develop the big topics or themes and organize them into effective instructional plans and materials. Experienced teachers seemed too absorbed with their teaching duties; scholarly specialists were too involved in the academic instruction of university students; and the pedagogical specialists were identified as members of an educational cult dealing solely in generalities and verbal distinctions.

---

[6]Charles A. McMurry, *How To Organize the Curriculum* (New York: Macmillan, 1923), p. 76.

JOHN DEWEY OPPOSES HERBARTISM

Dewey's School

In his own laboratory school at the University of Chicago, John Dewey introduced manual training, shopwork, sewing, and cooking on the ground that the traditional curriculum no longer met the needs of the new society created by the forces of industrialism. He wanted the school to take on the character of an embryonic community life, active with occupations that reflect the life of the larger society.

Younger children in the school played at actual occupations, simplifying but not distorting adult roles. Older children followed the Herbartian idea of recapitulating primitive life, but in a childhood social setting as they reconstructed the social life of other times and places. These children were expected to relate their own activities to the consequences of those activities. Primitive human life was supposed to reveal to the child the social effects of introducing tools into a culture. Still older children reflected on the meaning of social forces and processes found in occupations. They were to sense questions, doubts, and problems and to find a means of resolving them.

Dewey used his experiences in the laboratory school in formulating philosophical views that were different from those of the Herbartians. He insisted that the Herbartian interpretations of morality were too narrow and too formal. He protested the teaching of particular virtues without regard for the motives of children. Instead, he proposed that moral motives would develop when children learned to observe and note relationships between the means and the ends in social situations. It was not enough for the teacher to be the model of moral behavior for the children to emulate. Children should be asked to judge and respond morally to their present situations, which are real to them. Indeed, Dewey wanted life in the school to offer opportunities for children to act morally and to learn how to judge their own behavior in terms of the social ideas of cooperation, participation, and positive service. Thus, Dewey challenged the view that morality was an individual matter between oneself and God.

Dewey attacked the view that one's social duty should be done within a traditional framework of values, proposing instead that the method of social intelligence be a critical and creative force. The method of social intelligence means deciding what is right through experimental procedures and the judgment of participants. It requires recognition of different points of view and accommodations of one's own perspective.

Whereas the Herbartians relied on ideas as the basic guide to conduct and conceived of knowledge as something to be acquired, Dewey thought more in terms of the child's discovery and evaluation of knowledge than of mere acquisition. He recommended that the learner become the link between knowledge and conduct. His was a relative view of knowledge, not a fixed one. In contrast to the Herbartians' assumption that there was a body of known knowledge, which was indispensable and which could be made interesting to pupils, Dewey argued that subject matter was interesting only when it served the purposes of the learners. Hence, he emphasized learners' participation in formulating the purposes that were the basis for the selection of subject matter.

Dewey's Curriculum

By setting purposes, Dewey meant, however, not only expressing desires but studying means by which those desires can best be realized. Desire was not the end, but only the occasion for the formulation of a plan and method of activity. Thus, Dewey would not have the curriculum start with facts and truth that are outside the range of experience of those taught. Rather, he would start with materials for learning that are consistent with the experience learners already have and then introduce new objects and events that would stimulate new ways to observe and to judge. Subject matter was not to be selected on the basis of what adults thought would be useful for the learner at some future time. Instead, the present experience of the learners was to become the primary focus. The achievements of the past (organized knowledge) were to serve as a resource for helping learners both to understand their present condition and to deal with present problems.

In short, Dewey did not believe that the goal of the curriculum should be merely the acquisition of subject matter. He believed in a new goal for curriculum, namely, that organized subject matter become a tool for understanding and intelligently ordering experience. He generated many of the fundamental questions that guide current inquiries: What is the best way to relate the natural view of the child and the scientific view of those with specialized knowledge? How can knowledge become a method for enriching social life? How can we help learners act morally rather than merely have ideas about morality? How can the curriculum best bring order, power, initiative, and intelligence into the child's experience? How can the teacher be helped to follow the individual internal authority of truth about a learner's growth when curriculum decisions are made by external authority above the teacher?

SCIENTIFIC CURRICULUM MAKING

Scientific curriculum making is the attempt to use empirical methods (surveys and analysis of human conduct) in deciding *what* to teach. The history of the scientific movement in curriculum making shows very well that curriculum cannot be separated from the general history of American education or divorced from the broader stream of cultural and intellectual history. Both Franklin Bobbitt and Warrett Charters were greatly influenced by these developments in their lifetimes.

Societal Influences

Industrialism. Large numbers of persons began engaging in manufacturing instead of agriculture. The technological revolution wrought many changes, including a concern for efficiency and economy. For the first time, there was a societal interest in the systematic study of jobs, practices, and working conditions as related to objectives. Also a concern was about how to set standards for both products and processes.

Changing Concepts of School. From an institution with fixed subject matter and with the primary concern of improving intellectual ability by disciplining the mind, the school was increasingly conceived as an agency with no less a goal than satisfying individual and social needs.

Scientific Methods and Techniques. The nineteenth century was characterized by great developments in the pure sciences such as biology, physics, and chemistry and in the application of science to agriculture, manufacture, and almost every other phase of practical life. Yet it wasn't until early in the twentieth century that the spirit of scientific experimentation began to push its way into the thinking of educators. Bobbitt and Charters brought a scientific way of thinking into the emerging field of curriculum making.

Much of what was called scientific at the time is now labeled scientism, mere technology, or nose counting. Modern critics like to say pejoratively that educational scientists of those days equated efficiency with science. It is true that these early educational scientists were attempting to solve educational problems by means of experimental and statistical techniques. They particularly emphasized the measurement of ability and achievement with their development of intelligence and achievement tests. The zeal for measurement brought forth an abundance of facts about school buildings, school finance, pupil achievement and pupil traits, and learners' physical, emotional, intellectual, and social growth. The field of curriculum also caught this zeal for measurement. Data were collected about the content of textbooks, courses of study, school subjects, and appraisal of results. Studies were undertaken to find out how pupils learn and to design new methods for overcoming pupil difficulties.

Key Ideas

Two ideals were frequently associated with the scientific movement in education. One was the idea of an open attitude, the expectation that the school staff would be willing to consider new proposals and be alert to new methods and devices. Teachers, for example, were expected to join their pupils in asking questions. Second, there was an assumption that natural laws govern not only things and their forces, but also humans and their ways. Hence, it was the duty of education to shape the will into a desire to move in harmony with these laws. Science was seen as a guarantor of social progress.

Bobbitt's Contribution

Franklin Bobbitt articulated for the first time the importance of studying the processes for making a curriculum. He realized that it was not enough to develop new curricula; there was also a need to learn more about how new curricula can best be developed. This insight came through long experience in curriculum matters.

In his book, *The Curriculum,* Bobbitt tells of a personal experience that caused him to look at curriculum from the point of view of social needs rather than mere academic study.[7] He had gone to the Philippines early in the American occupation as a member of a committee sent to draw up an elementary school curriculum for the islands. Free to recommend almost anything to meet the needs of the population, the committee had the opportunity to create an original, constructive curriculum.

And what happened? The members assembled American textbooks for reading, arithmetic, geography, United States history, and other subjects with which they had been familiar in American schools. Without being conscious of it, they had organized a course of study for the tradi-

---

[7]Franklin Bobbitt, *The Curriculum* (Boston: Houghton Mifflin, 1918), p. 35.

tional eight elementary school grades, on the basis of their American prejudices and preconceptions about what an elementary course ought to be.

Bobbitt was lucky. A director of education in the Philippines helped him and the committee to look at the social realities, and they then unceremoniously threw out time-hallowed content. Instead, they brought into the course a number of things to help the people gain health, make a living, and enjoy self-realization. The activities they introduced came from the culture of the Philippines and were quite different from those found in the American textbooks.

From this experience, Bobbitt saw his difficulty: his complete adherence to traditional curriculum beliefs had kept him from realizing the possibility of more useful solutions. He had needed something to shatter his complacency. As Bobbitt himself said,

> We needed principles of curriculum making. We did not know that we should first determine objectives from a study of social needs. We supposed education consisted only of teaching the familiar subjects. We had not come to see that it is essentially a process of unfolding the potential abilities of a population and in particularized relation to the social conditions. We had not learned that studies are means, not ends. We did not realize that any instrument or experience which is effective in such unfoldment is the right instrument and right experience; and that anything which is not effective is wrong, however time-honored and widely used it may be.[8]

Bobbitt was little different from most people who are entering the field of curriculum for the first time today. They are unaware that what they have personally experienced in school may not be the final answer. They have difficulty creating something different and more appropriate.

After his experience in the Philippines, Bobbitt stimulated other workers in the field. His book, *How To Make a Curriculum*, was the forerunner of others in the subject and had great influence on school practice.[9] Students of curriculum now see Bobbitt as the first to recognize the need for a new specialization, the study of curriculum making. It was Bobbitt who saw that professional agreement on a *method* of discovery is more important than agreement on the details of curriculum content. He offered the profession his method with the intention that others would

---

[8]Ibid., p. 283.
[9]Franklin Bobbitt, *How to Make a Curriculum* (Boston: Houghton Mifflin, 1924).

try it, improve it, or suggest a better one. Bobbitt's method helps to define what is meant by curriculum making.

His method was guided by a fundamental assumption that would not be accepted by all curriculum makers today—namely, that education is to prepare us for the activities that ought to make up a well-rounded adult life. It is primarily for adult life, not childhood.

Steps in Making Curriculum. Bobbitt envisions five steps in curriculum making:

1. *Analysis of Human Experience.* The first step in curriculum making, according to Bobbitt, is to separate the broad range of human experience into major fields. One such classification includes language, health, citizenship, social life, recreation, religious life, home, vocation. The whole field of human experience should be reviewed in order that the portions belonging to the schools may be seen in relation to the whole.
2. *Job Analysis.* The second step is to break down the fields into their more specific activities. In this step, Bobbitt had to compromise with his ideal. He recognized the desirability of using a scientific method of analysis, yet knew that thus far there was not adequate technique for the work. Hence, he tended to fall back on practical and personal experiences to prove that a given activity was crucial to one or more of the categories of human experience.

   Bobbitt knew that only a few activity analyses had ever been made and that most of them were in the fields of spelling, language, arithmetic, history, geography, and vocation. He did, however, believe that activity analysis was a promising technique and turned to his colleague, W. W. Charters, for examples of how best to determine specific activities from larger units. Charters, in turn, drew from the idea of job analysis already common in industry. Business and industry at that time made an analysis for each job and prepared training programs for the tasks identified. For the position of application clerk the analysis would include these tasks: meets people who want to open accounts, asks them to fill out blanks, looks up rating in Dunn and Bradstreet. A course of study was prepared to teach future clerks each of the identified duties.

   It should be clear, however, that job analysis could result in either a list of duties or a list of methods for performing duties. The procedures for the analysis included introspection, interview, and investigation. In introspection, an expert related his or her duties and methods. Then, in an interview, a number of experts reviewed a list of duties to verify the tasks. Finally, the investigator actually carried out the operations on the job. A problem in making a complete analysis occurred in trying to describe the mental operations necessary for the task when one cannot see the steps carried out with the material. The analyses indicated only what the activities were if one were to learn the duties of a position.

3. *Deriving Objectives.* The third step is to derive the objectives of education from statements of the abilities required to perform the activities. In *How To Make a Curriculum,* Bobbitt presented more than 800 major objectives in ten fields of human experience. Here is a partial list of the general objectives within a language field: (1) to pronounce words properly; (2) to use voice in agreeable ways; (3) to use grammatically correct language; (4) to effectively organize and express thoughts; (5) to express thought to others in conversation, in recounting experiences, in serious or formal discussion, in an oral report, in giving directions, and before an audience; (6) to command an adequate reading, speaking, and writing vocabulary; (7) to write legibly with ease and speed; (8) to spell correctly the words of one's writing vocabulary; (9) to use good form and order in all written work (margins, spacing, alignment, paragraphing, capitalization, punctuation, syllabification, abbreviation). These objectives illustrate the level of generality needed to help curriculum makers decide what specific educational results were to be produced. Bobbitt also realized that each of the objectives could be broken down further into its component parts; indeed, he illustrated such detailed analysis.

4. *Selecting Objectives.* The fourth step is to select from the list of objectives those which are to serve as the basis for planning pupil activities. Guidelines for making this final selection of objectives include:

> Eliminate objectives that can be accomplished through the normal process of living. Only the abilities that are not sufficiently developed by chance should be included among the objectives of systematic education. Possibly the more important portions of education are not accomplished in schools but through nonscholastic agencies.
>
> Emphasize objectives that will overcome deficiencies in the adult world. Avoid objectives opposed by the community. Specific objectives in religion, economics, and health are especially likely to be opposed.
>
> Eliminate objectives when there are practical constraints hindering

their achievement. Involve the community in the selection of objectives. Consult community members who are proficient in practical affairs and experts in their fields.

Differentiate between objectives that are for all learners and those that are practical for only part of the population. Sequence the objectives, indicating how far pupils should go each year in attaining the general goals.

5. *Planning in Detail.* The fifth step is to lay out the kinds of activities, experiences, and opportunities involved in attaining the objectives. Details for the day-to-day activities of children at each age or grade level must be laid out. These detailed activities make up the curriculum. As project activity and part-time work at home and in the community are introduced, there must be cooperative planning. Teachers, nurses, play activity directors, and parents together should plan the detailed procedures of the courses. Their plans should then be approved by the principal, superintendent, and school board.

Charters' Contribution

Although Charters enunciated a method of curriculum formulation that was very similar to Bobbitt's, he differed in the emphasis on ideals and systematized knowledge in determining the content of the curriculum. Charters saw ideals as objectives with observable consequences. He believed that honesty, loyalty, and generosity contributed to satisfaction. Ideals did not necessarily lead to immediate satisfaction but to satisfaction in the long run or to satisfaction as defined by social consensus. However, he knew of no scientific measurement that would determine which ideals should operate in a school. There was no scientific way to determine whether open-mindedness or artistic taste should be the ideal of the school or student. Hence, Charters thought it defensible for a faculty to vote on the ideals it believed to be most valuable. Faculty selection of ideals was not to be arbitrary, however. The opinion of thoughtful men and women in public and private life needed to be carefully weighed and the needs of the student investigated.

After ideals were selected they had to serve as standards for actions and were not to be abstracted from activities. The teacher who wished to inculcate ideals in the lives of pupils needed to analyze activities to which an ideal applied and to see that the selected ideal was applied in the pupils' activities. For Charters, the curriculum consisted of both ideals and activities. Unlike Bobbitt, Charters gave explicit attention to knowledge in his method for making the curriculum.[10] He wanted subject matter useful for living and of motivational import to the learner. But he also wanted to reassure those who feared that organized information in such fields as chemistry, history, physics, and mathematics would have no place in a curriculum built around objectives derived from studies of life in the social setting. His answer showed how job analyses revealed the importance of both primary subjects (mathematics and English in application) and derived subjects (subjects necessary for understanding the activity or the reason for the activity). Psychology, for example, was needed in order to explain methods of supervision.

On the one hand, Charters would determine subject material from analysis of life projects in order that one would know which elements of the subjects are most important and require the most attention. On the other hand, he would select school projects that would give instruction in the subject items and allow the pupil to use the knowledge in a broader range of activities.

As representatives of the scientific movement in curriculum making, Bobbitt and Charters brought forth the following conceptions and dimensions of curriculum: It is a process which, if followed, will result in an evolving curriculum. The process of curriculum making is itself a field of study. The relation of goals (ideals), objectives, and activities is a curriculum concern. The selection of goals is a normative process. The selection of objectives and activities is empirical and scientific. Objectives and activities are subject to scientific analysis and verification. The relationship of organized systematic fields of knowledge to the practical requirements of daily living is a central question for students of the curriculum.

IMPROVEMENT OF INSTRUCTION

Local Development of Curriculum

Until the end of World War I, major influences on curriculum came from outside the local school system. Academic scholars set the direction for purposes and content through national committees and textbook writing. Usually, local schools participated only to the extent of deciding which subjects to add and which textbooks to use. The high school curriculum was standardized on the basis of what college presidents thought students needed for college. After 1920, the scientific movement

---

[10]W. W. Charters, *Curriculum Construction* (New York: Macmillan, 1923), pp. 103–106.

directly influenced the curriculum through new types of school textbooks stressing skills related to the everyday needs of adults and children. College scholars found their power to determine the curriculum challenged by the scientific method of curriculum formulation. The first local systematic curriculum making also began around 1920 when several school systems tried to develop courses of study in single subjects and the study of particular problems, such as learning difficulties in spelling and how to overcome them through instruction.

A course of study was a guide to the teaching of a particular subject or subjects. The course of study included a philosophy, suggested content (topics and their ordering for study), a structure (discipline-centered or interdisciplinary), and the relation of the content to the life of the learner and the larger society. Major themes and other abstractions were outlined for relating activities, and suggested activities and resources were given.

The Course of Study Movement

By 1926, practically all schools were revising their curricula. They attacked the problem of curriculum development in a comprehensive way by defining the general objectives on which the entire curriculum was based and by which all subjects were correlated. It is true, however, that members of state education departments often chose the objectives and left the selection of activities to the teachers. Sometimes, the principals or representatives of teachers selected the objectives according to local needs. In these schools teachers worked in committees in order to list activities to be tested. A director was provided to supervise the preparation of the course of study for an individual school district or an entire state, and a curriculum specialist served as general consultant. Not all professional educators viewed the movement with favor:

> Too much of the present-day curriculum is amateurish, trifling, and a sheer waste of time—worse than that, an injection of pernicious confusion into what should be orderly progress. The let-everybody-pitch-in-and-help method is ludicrous when applied to curriculum building. It is too much like inviting a group of practical electricians to redesign a modern power plant.[11]

---

[11]Guy M. Whipple, "What Price Curriculum Making," *School and Society* 31 (March 15, 1930): 368.

Caswell's Influence

The late Hollis Leland Caswell extended our view of the curriculum field through his concern about the relationships between the course of study, teaching, and the learner's role. Caswell was one of the first to see the making of a course of study as too limiting in purpose. He shifted the emphasis from production of a course of study to the actual improvement of instruction. He saw curriculum development as a means of helping teachers apply in their daily tasks of instruction the best information on subject matter, the interests of children, and contemporary social needs. He involved 16,000 Virginia teachers and administrators in making a course of study for that state.[12] His involvement of all teachers instead of just a few selected representatives was a new thrust. Caswell considered the course of study as only one of several aids to the teacher and believed that when teachers made the course of study together they would learn the limits of its usefulness. He looked on the course of study as a means of providing source materials for teachers to use in planning their work rather than a prescription to be followed in detail.

Help for the Teacher in Curriculum Making. Caswell attempted to help teachers improve curricula by providing them with a syllabus of carefully chosen readings under seven topics. These topics or questions are important for what they tell us about the nature of curriculum and the tasks involved in making a curriculum.[13]

1. What is curriculum?
2. What developments resulted in a need for curriculum revision?
3. What is the function of subject matter?
4. How do we determine educational objectives?
5. What is the best way to organize instruction?
6. How should we select subject matter?
7. How should we measure the outcomes of instruction?

The readings Caswell suggested to help teachers answer these questions included a range of sources, some of which gave conflicting opin-

---

[12]Mary Louise Seguel, *The Curriculum Field: Its Formative Years* (New York: Columbia University, Teachers College Press, 1966), p. 148.

[13]Sidney B. Hall, D. W. Peters, and Hollis L. Caswell, "Study Course for Virginia State Curriculum," *State Board of Education Bulletin* 14, no. 2 (January 1932): 363.

ions. Caswell himself believed that the curriculum is more than the experiences made available to the child. It consists of the experiences the child actually undergoes. Hence, the teacher's interaction with the pupil is a vital aspect of curriculum. Preparing a course of study is only the starting point for curriculum improvement.

Curriculum Revision. Caswell also believed in curriculum revision. He said that curriculum revision is necessary in order for the school to meet more social and personal needs. Curriculum should help sensitize people to social problems and give pupils experience in social action. Caswell wanted the school to be an avenue of opportunity for all the people, contributing to interracial understanding and relations, strengthening home life, stressing democratic ideals, and contributing to the conservation of resources.

Evaluating Demands. Caswell thought that the demands for curriculum change must be evaluated. He recommended that any proposed change be screened, and that changes be accepted only if they are (1) consistent with democratic values, (2) consistent with the development needs of the learner, (3) something that other agencies cannot accomplish, (4) something that has or will gain the support of leaders in the community, (5) something that does not replace other existing curriculum areas of relatively higher value.

Curriculum Design. Caswell agreed that a curriculum design should synthesize the three basic elements of the curriculum—children's interests, social functions, and organized knowledge. In the tentative course of study for Virginia elementary schools, for example, he helped developers provide scope and sequence. Social functions served as the scope. Some of these functions were protection and conservation of life, property, and natural resources; recreation; expression of aesthetic impulses; and distribution of rewards of production. These functions were worked on in some form in every grade. Sequenced experiences were arranged according to centers of interest. For example, home and school life were studied in the first grade; the effects of the machine on learning in the sixth. Specific activities were suggested to match both the social functions and the centers of interest using the most relevant subject matter.

Caswell saw the central task of curriculum development as a synthesis of materials from subject matter fields, philosophy, psychology, and sociology. ''Materials must be so selected and arranged as to become vital in the experience of the learner.''[14] Thus, he saw curriculum as a field of study that represents no structurally limited body of content; rather, it represents a process or procedure.

RATIONAL CURRICULUM MAKING

In 1949, Ralph Tyler sent to the University of Chicago Press a manuscript, *Basic Principles of Curriculum and Instruction,* a rationale for examining problems of curriculum and instruction.[15] The rationale was based on his experiences as a teacher of curriculum and as a curriculum maker and evaluator. He had been especially active in designing ways to measure changes in learners brought about by schools' new efforts to help learners develop interests and perform more appropriately in society. Since then, nearly 90,000 copies of Tyler's rationale have been sold, and it is regarded as the culmination of one epoch of curriculum making.

Tyler's Curriculum Inquiry

Tyler assumed that anyone engaging in curriculum inquiry must try to answer these questions:

1. What educational purposes should the school seek to attain?
2. What educational experiences can be provided that are likely to attain these purposes?
3. How can these educational experiences be effectively organized?
4. How can we determine whether these purposes are being attained?

By purposes, Tyler meant educational objectives, and he proposed that school goals would have greater validity if they are selected in light of information about learners' psychological needs and interests, contemporary life, and aspects of subject matter that would be useful to everyone, not just specialists in disciplines. In order to select from the many objectives that would be inferred from such information, Tyler recommended that a school staff ''screen'' them according to the school's philosophy of education and beliefs about the psychology of learning.

Tyler realized that having purposes was only the first step. He used the phrase *learning experiences* to include a plan for providing learning

---

[14]Hollis L. Caswell and Doak S. Campbell, *Curriculum Development* (New York: American Book Company, 1935), p. 81.

[15]Ralph W. Tyler, *Basic Principles of Curriculum and Instruction* (Chicago: The University of Chicago Press, 1949).

situations that take into account both the previous experience and perceptions that the learner brings to the situation, and whether or not the learner is likely to respond to it mentally and emotionally and in action.

Tyler then turned his attention to ordering the learning situations so that they would be focused on the same outcomes. He was preoccupied with how the curriculum could produce a maximum cumulative effect. He wanted a cumulative plan for organization that would help students learn more and learn more effectively.

His answer drew heavily from the early Herbartians' ideas of organization. Like Charles McMurry, he thought organizing elements or controlling ideas, concepts, values, and skills should be the threads, the warp and woof of the fabric of curriculum organization. Tyler approved of using the concept of a place value numeration system, for example, which can be enlarged on from kindergarten through the twelfth grade. Such concepts were seen as useful elements for relating different learning experiences in science, social studies, and other fields. He described optional ways of structuring learning experiences both within schools and in the classroom. They could, for instance, be structured within special subject courses, like English and mathematics, or as broad fields, like the language arts. Experience could also be structured within the format of lessons. He showed his own organization and curriculum preference by listing the advantages of relating content to real life through projects that allow for broader grouping of learning opportunities. He also saw merit in organizing courses that span several years rather than a single term.

Finally, Tyler regarded evaluation as an important operation in curriculum development. He saw it as a process for finding out whether the learning experiences actually produced the desired results and for discovering the strengths and weaknesses of the plans. He made a real contribution by enlarging our concept of evaluation. Rather than focusing on only a few aspects of growth, tests should, he believed, indicate attainment of all the objectives of an educational program. Furthermore, he did not believe that tests should mean only paper and pencil examinations. He thought that observations of pupils, products made by learners, records of student participation, and other methods should also be included.

Criticisms of Tyler's Rationale

Criticisms of Tyler's rationale generally stem from Tyler's statement that the selection of objectives is a prerequisite for curriculum development. The late James MacDonald, for instance, felt that statements of expected behavioral outcomes violate the integrity of learners by fragmenting their behavior and manipulating them for an end that has no present worth for them.[16]

In prescribing three sources from which objectives can be derived, the student, the society, and the subject, Tyler attempted to reconcile the conflict between those who favored one or another as the most important factor and to formulate a consensus that would allow individuals with divergent goals to work together in developing curricula. To effect a consistency among the resultant goals, he relied on the staff to apply their own philosophical and psychological criteria. On this point, critics contend, Tyler does not realize that information collected from the learner and society is biased and that, after that information has been gathered, there is no scientific way to infer what *should* follow from the facts reported. Furthermore, Tyler's proposal for filtering educational objectives through a philosophical screen is regarded as vacuous and trivial.[17] It leaves to staff in individual schools the question of which objectives to keep and which to throw out. Tyler gives no criterion to use in making a choice among objectives.

Tyler's rationale for examining problems of curriculum and instruction summed up the best thought regarding curriculum during its first half-century as a field of study. His debt to the McMurrys, Dewey, Bobbitt, and Charters is clear. The four questions he poses and the suggestions he gives for answering the questions define the field of curriculum as it was understood until very recently.

CONCLUDING COMMENTS

As indicated in Table 14–1, influential curriculum leaders have addressed themselves to significant questions about what should be taught and why. Their questions ranged from inquiries into purposes, such as whether morality can and should be taught, to questions about the selection of content, the relationship between content and method, and the

---

[16]James B. MacDonald, "The Person in the Curriculum," in *Precedents and Promise in the Curriculum Field*, ed. Helen F. Robinson (New York: Columbia University Press, Teachers College, 1966), p. 41.

[17]Herbert Kliebard, "The Tyler Rationale," in *Curriculum and Evaluation*, eds. Arno Bellack and Herbert Kliebard (Berkeley: McCutchan, 1977), pp. 56–67.

way in which organization can have a cumulative effect on learning experiences.

Any new effort in curriculum thought and action must still treat the persistent questions of purpose, activity, organization, and evaluation. The emphases on these matters and the way they are addressed, however, are changing. The 1970s saw special interest groups and governmental agencies taking over the leadership in program development; fragmentation was the result. The 1980s saw a change in leadership to state government in response to industrial and business interests in academic excellence and a growing concern for general education. In the 1990s, curriculum development at the local level is regaining importance because curriculum must be adapted to local interests and to the specific persons to be served. How best to balance the demand for programs in response to national needs with the requirements of local communities is a current dilemma. The popularity of local curriculum development also rests on the desire for effective schools, which have a strong sense of community, shared goals, and high expectations for students and staff. Through collective decision making in the design of the curriculum, the preparation of instructional materials, and the evaluation of the program, school efficiency is achieved. A good curriculum-making process requires deliberation—the coalescence of aims, data, and judgments.

A knowledge of curriculum history, including its theoretical and practical knowledge, is helpful in improving present reform efforts. For example, what better guidelines for the conduct of local curriculum development can be found than those based on Caswell's experiences? Similarly, the McMurrys' approach to correlation and the value of particular subjects in interrelating knowledge has value for current planners who want to strengthen general education. Also, Dewey's view of moral education is timely as planners consider the best response to public opinion that gives a high priority to education as a moral enterprise.

Contemporary scholars in curriculum need a manageable range of problems that can be investigated in depth. An examination of the problems undertaken by historically influential persons in the field suggests areas for research.

QUESTIONS

1. What central concerns of prominent historical figures in the field of curriculum are of importance today?

TABLE 14-1 A Summary of Early Curriculum Theorist's Ideas

Theorists	Purpose, Aims, and Objectives	Content	Method of Instruction	Organization
Charles and Frank McMurry	Moral development Good citizenship	Literature for related aesthetics and the intellectual History and literature for citizenship Geography for correlating studies Later, acceptance of new branches of knowledge	Five formal steps in lesson plans Special methods in each subject field	Studies sequenced according to age and stage of learner development Information organized around problems and projects Activities related by topics and themes
John Dewey	Intellectual control over the forces of man and nature Social intelligence Trained capacities in the service of social interest Development as an aim	The intellectual method by which social life is enriched and improved Knowledge from organized fields as it functions in the life of the child	Survey of capacities and needs of learners Arrangement of conditions that provide the content to satisfy needs The plan for meeting needs involves the participation of all group members. Intelligent activity, not aimless activity	Life experiences that learners use to carry on to more refined and better organized facts and ideas Curriculum organized around two concepts: that knowing is experimental and that knowledge is instrumental to individual and social purposes
Franklin Bobbitt	Meeting social needs Preparation of learner for adult life	Subject matter as a means, not an end	Deriving objectives from analysis of what is required in order to perform in broad categories of life Detailed activities to be planned by teachers, parents, and others	Specification of objectives to be attained each year Layout of activities involved in attaining objectives

Warren W. Charters	Satisfaction through fulfillment of ideals (e.g., honesty) that sway socially efficient persons	Organized knowledge that can be applied in activities needed for a socially efficient life	Projects and activities consistent with ideals	Experimentation to find the best way to order ideals, activities, and ideas
Hollis Caswell	Fulfillment of democratic ideals (improved intergroup relations, home life, and the conservation of resources)	No limiting body of content Key concepts most helpful in the solution of social problems	Teacher interaction with pupil Teacher applying the best of what is known about subject matter, children's interests, and social needs Key ideas to be woven into the child's performance of social functions	Selected social functions (e.g., the conservation of life) to be worked on in some form in every grade Sequence of activities to be arranged according to centers of interest
Ralph Tyler	No stated purposes Each curriculum person to evolve own purposes through a rational process, involving consideration of learner, social conditions, knowledge, and philosophical position Objectives to be behaviorally stated, but specificity to depend on one's theory of learning	Subject matter from subject specialists that could contribute to the broad functions of daily living	Opportunity to practice what the objectives of instruction call for Each opportunity to contribute to several objectives Activities that are within the learner's capacity and are satisfying	Provisions for the reiteration of concepts, skills, or values Provision for the progressive development of the concept, skill, or attitude Correlation of concepts from one field to content in other fields

2. What current curriculum doctrines and practices are carry-overs from another historical period?

3. In what way is the present curriculum situation different from the past? How does this difference make some past ideas of curriculum irrelevant?

4. It is said that a history of curriculum thought and practice cannot be separated from the broader stream of cultural and intellectual history. What conditions, movements, or ideas had the greatest influence on curriculum making in the past century? What social and intellectual forces are likely to shape the curriculum field today?

5. What the McMurrys, Dewey, Charters, Bobbitt, Caswell, and Tyler thought about curriculum is less important than what they make *you* think about curriculum. What do they have to say to you?

SELECTED REFERENCES

Bobbitt, Franklin. *The Curriculum.* New York: Houghton Mifflin, 1918.

Bobbitt, Franklin. *How To Make a Curriculum.* New York: Houghton Mifflin, 1924.

Caswell, Hollis L., and Campbell, Doak S. *Readings in Curriculum Development.* New York: American Book, 1937.

Charters, W. W. *Curriculum Construction.* New York: Macmillan, 1923.

Davis, O. L., Jr., ed. *Perspectives on Curriculum Development 1776–1976.* Washington, DC: ASCD, 1976.

Franklin, Barry M. *Building the American Community: The School Curriculum and the Search for Social Control.* London and Philadelphia: The Falmer Press, 1986.

Kliebard, Herbert M. *The Struggle for the American Curriculum 1893–1951.* Boston: Routledge & Kegan Paul, 1986.

McMurry, Charles A. *How to Organize the Curriculum.* New York: Macmillan, 1923.

National Society for the Study of Education. *The First Yearbook of the Herbart Society for the Scientific Study of Teaching.* Chicago: The University of Chicago Press, 1907.

National Society for the Study of Education. *The Curriculum—Retrospect and Prospect.* NSSE Yearbook, Part 1. Chicago: The University of Chicago Press, 1971.

Popkewitz, Thomas S. *The Formation of School Subjects: The Struggle for Creating an American Institution.* London and Philadelphia: The Falmer Press, 1987.

Seguel, Mary Louise. *The Curriculum Field: Its Formative Years.* New York: Columbia University, Teachers College Press, 1966.

Tyler, Ralph. *Basic Principles of Curriculum and Instruction.* Chicago: The University of Chicago Press, 1949.

15

The Promise of Theory and Research in Curriculum

Curriculum researchers can be divided into various camps. Some are under the banner of quantitative or empirical inquiry. They engage in surveys, experiments, and descriptive observations and use questionnaires, statistical methods, and protocols. Others are qualitative or interpretative researchers. They are interested in the meanings of interactions among students, teachers, textbooks, and other aspects of the curriculum. Often they are participant observers, drawing upon the concepts and methods of sociology and anthropology. Some within this camp use journals and autobiographies as well as psychoanalysis and meditation with the idea of understanding both themselves and what the curriculum means to students. Critical theorists are a third category of researchers. They examine curriculum practices with the purpose of showing their true nature. Critical theorists attempt to increase awareness of historical and ideological influences on our lives.

Curriculum research has multiple purposes: to advance conceptualization and understanding of the field, to conceive new visions of what and how to teach, to influence curriculum policy, to question other normative premises about curriculum, and to improve programs for learning.

In this chapter, I begin by looking at progress in six areas of curriculum research. The contributions of the various research orientations to these areas will be apparent. Later, the nature of curriculum research is illustrated by work of selected productive scholars and practitioners. Finally, several types of curriculum research are featured which are flourishing today, and the question is raised as to whether the research camps with their different aims and approaches expand our vision or whether their commitment to a paradigm leads to intolerance and restricted horizons.

STATE OF THE FIELD

In 1960 and again in 1969, John Goodlad appraised the status of curriculum research in terms of the curriculum needs for (1) theoretical constructs, (2) concepts that identify major questions, (3) determination of what can best be taught simultaneously, (4) arrangement of material for effective learning, (5) taxonomical analysis of objectives, and (6) studies indicating the relationship between specific instructional variables and the outcomes from instruction. As benchmarks to progress, let us look at each of Goodlad's 1960 concerns and the status of research in each area in 1969 and the present.

The Need for Curriculum Theory

Status of Curriculum Theory in 1969. Between 1960 and 1969, little was added to our knowledge of how to derive educational objectives. Elizabeth and George Macia and others attempted to adopt theories from outside the field of education to conceptualize phenomena related to curriculum.[1] One consequence was the differentiation of four different kinds of curriculum theory. *Formal curriculum theory* involves theorizing about the structure of the disciplines that will constitute the curriculum. Elizabeth Macia would leave this theorizing to the philosophers and members of the disciplines. *Valuational curriculum theory* involves speculation about the appropriate means to attain the most valuable objectives and to present the best content in a curriculum. *Event theory* is very much like scientific theory in that it tries to predict what will occur under certain conditions. *Praxiological theory* is speculation about the appropriate

---

[1] Several papers by Elizabeth Macia, George Macia, Robert Jewett, and others treating educational theorizing through models (Columbus: Bureau of Educational Research and Service, Ohio State University, 1963–65).

means to attain what is judged to be valuable. Praxiological theory forms the theoretical base for determining curriculum policy, the decision to adopt certain objectives and practices. Using the perspective of science in theorizing (event theory), George Beauchamp described efforts to make theory in the field of curriculum during this period. Indeed, he concluded that little theoretical research had been done. Beauchamp found theory making in curriculum a "shambles." In a seminal paper, the late Joseph Schwab said that theoretical pursuits were not appropriate in the field of curriculum. He urged instead direct study of the curriculum: what it is, how it gets that way, and how it affects the students and the teachers.[2-4]

Present Status of Curriculum Theory. There have been several attempts to act on Schwab's recommendation. Decker Walker was one of the first to offer a model for guiding the study of deliberations, processes, and assumptions of curriculum developers. Walker faulted those in the curriculum field for being so busy prescribing curriculum making that they did not pay sufficient attention to discovering how it is done.[5] Although he has not changed his opinion that curriculum theory should be applied in documenting what happens in actual important cases, Walker now writes of the value of curriculum theories in helping us to see curriculum in a different light and to interpret it in a way in which we would not have done otherwise.[6] Walker conceives of families of theories with different purposes and forms bearing on the same problem, all trying to rationalize practice, to conceptualize it, to explain it. He observes that some curriculum theories accept society as it is and others work for a new and better society to come. Walker cites Paulo Freire as an example of a person who uses theory for *program rationalization;* Franklin Bobbitt and Ralph Tyler as those who used theory in the *rationalization of procedures* for curriculum construction; John Dewey as one who used theory as a basis for thinking about *curriculum phenomena;* and Walter Ong as

---

[2]George A. Beauchamp, *Curriculum Theory* (Wilmette, IL: Kagg, 1968).

[3]George A. Beauchamp, "Curriculum Theory: Meaning, Development, and Use," *Theory into Practice,* 21, no. 1 (Winter 1982): 23–28.

[4]Joseph J. Schwab, *The Practical: A Language for Curriculum* (Washington, DC: National Education Association, 1970).

[5]Decker F. Walker, "A Naturalistic Model for Curriculum Development," *School Review* 80, no. 1 (November 1971): 51–67.

[6]Decker F. Walker, "Curriculum Theory Is Many Things to Many People," *Theory Into Practice* 21, no. 1 (Winter 1982): 62–65.

one who uses curriculum theory to explain fads, reforms, and curriculum changes.

There is opposition to Schwab's call for attention to the practical rather than to the theoretical. Some theorists are trying to develop a more comprehensive and realistic philosophy of society and the individual instead of merely engaging in the practical problems of curriculum maintenance and incremental reform. They view curriculum theorizing as a way to demythologize curriculum and to advance two concerns of modern revolutionaries: heightened consciousness about the consequences of technology, capitalism, and other institutional structures, and exploration of the inner life to broaden our ways of knowing.

William Pinar and Madeline Grumet believe that curriculum theorists must constantly question curriculum practices by interrupting the predictable in schooling with analyses that suggest alternatives.[7]

Another important theoretical development is the evaluators' usurpation of curriculum theory. As indicated in Chapter 10, theories of evaluation have been broadened to include frameworks for determining objectives, monitoring procedures for curriculum design and implementation, and guiding other curriculum decisions.

There is great disenchantment with the notion that the curriculum field will amass empirical generalizations, put them into general laws, and form these laws into a coherent theory. The idea that theory will tell us the necessary and sufficient conditions for a particular result in curriculum has given way to the assessment of local events and to the development of concepts that will help people make their own decisions.

Nevertheless, efforts in the construction of event theory continue. Garnet McDiarmid has proposed a theory with which to explain the obdurate nature of curriculum as flat, mindless recitation.[8] McDiarmid posits that curriculum activities are correlated with the attitudes of those who put pressure on the school board. Knowing their attitudes toward child rearing and other social issues, McDiarmid predicts the curriculum. For instance, right-wing beliefs about child rearing, he believes are associated with didactic methods and the teaching of history and geography rather than social studies. Furthermore, his theory attributes working class support of the status quo to such sociopsychological factors as au-

---

[7]William Pinar and Madeline R. Grumet, "Theory and Practice and the Reconceptualization of Curriculum Studies," in *Rethinking Curriculum Studies*, eds. L. Barton and M. Lawer (New York: Halsted Press, John Wiley & Sons, 1981).

[8]Garnet McDiarmid, "The Development of a Conceptual Empirical Theory of Curriculum," *Interchange* 18, no. 3 (1987): 38–62.

thoritarianism, dogmatism, xenophobia, and punitive behavior toward the powerless. Criticism of this probabilistic theory centers on its fulfilling prophecy. The invariance of the theory contributes to the status quo.[9]

The Need for Curriculum Conceptions

Status of Curriculum Conception in 1969. General theory and conceptualizations in curriculum had advanced very little in the decade before 1969. John Goodlad tried to bridge theory and practice with a conceptual scheme for rational curriculum planning. His categories and suggested processes, which build on the Tyler rationale of 1949, were intended to stimulate research and organize thinking in the curriculum field. However, he later saw no evidence that the intent was fulfilled. Also, Dwayne Huebner elaborated on a concept of curriculum as a field of study. He criticized the means–ends concept of curriculum and argued that curriculum should be conceived as a political process for effecting a just environment. One of the major questions he would have the curriculum workers ask was, "Does the present educational activity reflect the best that humans are capable of?"[10]

Present Status of Curriculum Conceptions. In 1979, John Goodlad assessed his 1966 conceptual system for curriculum, a rational decision-making model for determining purposes and selecting and organizing learning opportunities. He found that the model or system provides a reasonably accurate identification of the elements of curriculum practice in complex settings such as the United States.[11] It does not, however, adequately reflect practices at different levels of decision making. Consequently, Goodlad and his associates suggest three modifications:

1. More attention should be given to the personal and experiential as a decision-making level in the conceptual system. (This is partly in response to the work of the curriculum reconceptualists who see learners as potential generators and not mere passive recipients of curriculum.)

---

[9]William Pinar, "Comment on McDiarmid's Theory," *Interchange* 18, no. 3 (1987): 73–76.

[10]Dwayne Huebner, "Curriculum as a Field of Study," in *Precedents and Promise in the Curriculum Field,* ed. Helen Robinson (New York: Columbia University, Teachers College Press, 1966), p. 107.

[11]John I. Goodlad and associates, *Curriculum Inquiry: The Study of Curriculum Practice* (New York: McGraw-Hill, 1979).

2. Values should be recognized as playing a part in all curriculum decisions, not merely stated as a guiding educational philosophy at the beginning of curriculum planning, as it was in the original conceptual scheme.
3. The sociopolitical interests of special groups (the political milieu) should be recognized as influencing each level of decision making.

Instead of curriculum language that reveals a concern for effectiveness, objectives, and principles of learning, the language of curriculum increasingly refers to possibility, emancipation, and cooperation. The language of critical theorists reveals the economics and technical policies that affect education, as well as directs attention to the learner's choice of subject matter. For example, "How much of the richness of the world is made available to the learner?" "How can we best allow the learner to draw on all cultures of the world to create possibilities for the future?" Note that this use of culture serves the interests of the individual rather than controlling social interests.

Herbert Kliebard has proposed three possible ways of attacking the problem of conceptualization in the curriculum field. The first means of attack is the identification of critical and persistent questions that have characterized the field. Chapter 12 follows this suggestion. Second, Kliebard suggests regarding the field as a synoptic one in which the curriculum person brings perspectives from other fields to the school programs. This method means examining the more useful concepts of economists, anthropologists, sociologists, and other specialists to see whether they can guide program development. Third, Kliebard suggests creating metaphors that might promise new directions and theoretical constructs. Instead of using only the metaphors that have dominated thinking in curriculum (for example, "production" with its technological implications and "growth" with its connotations of unfolding, readiness, and nurturing), we should experiment with alternative *root metaphors*.

Kliebard points out how some social reconstructionists, such as Michael Apple and Jean Anyon, use the metaphors of culture as a form of capital.[12] Paulo Freire's use of the "banking" concept of education is an act of deposition in which the students are the depositories and the teacher is the depositor. The teacher issues communiqués and makes deposits, which the students passively receive, memorize, and repeat. These metaphors bring into focus what might otherwise be ignored—the

---

[12]Herbert Kliebard, "Curriculum Theory as Metaphor," *Theory into Practice* 21, no. 1 (Winter 1982): 11–17.

unequal distribution of knowledge through the curriculum, the question of whose interests are served by an unequal distribution of cultural capital, and the static as opposed to the creative origin of knowledge.

Philip Taylor compared the kinds of metaphors in the educational tests of 1905, 1931, 1944, and 1968.[13] He found that in 1905 the *tabula rasa* or "blank slate" view of the child dominated; in 1931, the root metaphor emphasized curriculum as activity rather than facts to be stored; in 1944, the root metaphor, "First the blade, and then the ear, then the full corn shall appear," stressed self-motivation and the idea of stages in development; in 1968, children were characterized as "natural explorers," "agents of their own language." Furthermore, the metaphors of 1905 tended to center on the teacher and to have an explanatory, logical intent, whereas the metaphors of 1968 were centered on the child and had a rhetorical and persuasive intent.

Arthur Powell's metaphor for the secondary school of the early 1980s, the shopping mall in which consumer learners negotiated their curriculum was used by conservative reformers as an argument for curriculum change in the late 1980s. Paraphrasing Henry Ford's options with the Model T, "any color you want provided it's black," became "any subject you want, providing it's math and science."

Currently, the field of curriculum is fragmented into several conceptual camps. William Pinar discriminates among the following three groups, each holding a different view of what the field should be about.[14]

1. *Traditionalists.* Traditionalists, according to Pinar, value service to practitioners in the schools above all else. He names as traditionalists such persons as Ralph Tyler, John McNeil, Daniel and Laurel Tanner, and Robert Zais. According to Pinar, service—defined as a response to the practical concern for curriculum matters—is more important to traditionalists than research or the development of theory. The close relationship between traditionalists and school teachers is said to prevent them from creating new ways of talking about curriculum which may in the future be far more fruitful than the present ways.
2. *Conceptual Empiricists.* These persons tend to be trained in social science and see service to practitioners as being subsequent to research. Their basic premise is that a scientific knowledge of human behavior,

---

[13]Philip H. Taylor, "The Metaphor as a Source of Curriculum Knowledge," *Conceptions of Curriculum Knowledge,* ed. Edmund Short (University Park: Pennsylvania State University, 1982).

[14]William Pinar, "Notes on the Curriculum Field 1978," *Educational Researcher* 7, no. 8 (September 1978): 5–12.

including curriculum, is possible. They argue that their research serves school practitioners and that by the creation of a science of curriculum the traditional aspirations of the field can be realized. They differ from traditionalists by their allegiance to social science, rather than to practitioners and to "kids."

Decker Walker is considered a conceptual empiricist and the following also seem to fit the category: George J. Posner, who explores the application of cognitive science to curriculum research and development, and S. Alan Cohen, who aims at high achievement through curriculum alignment with tests, and teaching. Pinar criticizes conceptual empiricists for producing only technical recommendations and principles based on static regularities that imply a subtle control of human behavior.

3. *Reconceptualists.* The fundamental view of the reconceptualists is that an intellectual and cultural distance from curriculum practice is required for the present in order to develop more useful comprehensive critiques and theoretical programs. Currently, reconceptualists are preoccupied with a critique of the field, a field they believe is too immersed in practical, technical modes of understanding and action. The term *reconceptualist* is credited to the late James MacDonald, who sensed a need for reconceiving the fundamental concerns, questions, and priorities that give direction to curriculum as a field of inquiry. This task contrasts with both the prevailing intents of traditionalists, who view their task as giving guidance and prescriptive assistance to the practitioners, and the scientists, who pursue research on curriculum variables.

Reconceptualists include Michael Apple and Henry Giroux, who engage in ideological and social critique; Herbert Kliebard, who illuminates the shortcomings of curriculum as science through historical critique; Max van Manen, who exposes the technological conception of curriculum through aesthetic critique; and phenomenologist Pinar who criticizes teaching by using a psychoanalytic method and devises means by which curriculum researchers can become conscious of their own participation in rigid social and psychological structures and their complicity in the arrested intellectual development characteristic of American schooling. Pinar recommends a method of self-analysis, for example, by means of which learners can study their own responses to educational situations by (a) recalling and describing the past and then analyzing its psychic relation to the present, (b) describing one's imagined future and analyzing its relation to the present, and (c) placing this analytic understanding of one's education in its cultural and political context.

Daniel and Laurel Tanner have responded negatively to Pinar's map of the field.[15] They see the reconceptualists as radical critics rather than curriculum theorists. They also fault Pinar's notion of the need for an intellectual and cultural distance from school practitioners in order to develop a more comprehensive and theoretical program. Citing Dewey, the Tanners argue for "some kind of vital current between the field worker and the research worker." Without this flow, the latter is not able to judge the real scope of the problem being addressed. The Tanners also indicate how they think traditionalists and those representing empirical–analytical sciences have contributed to curriculum's body of concepts.

Replies to the Tanners, in turn, charge that they misunderstood what Pinar is saying. Reconceptualists, for example, are not repudiating research but regard literary criticism, art history and criticism, philosophical inquiry, and historical analysis as research and as the forms from which the reconceptualists' work is derived. Intellectual and cultural distancing only means "bracketing" (the suspension of judgments about things and events), a methodological tool to aid in judging the essence of the problem to be addressed.[16]

Nelson Haggerson sees the study of actions and events within school situations as the foci for inquiry into curriculum. Haggerson's conceptual framework of research paradigms for curriculum inquiry closely follows Pinar's conceptual camps although he does not regard the paradigms as competing but as complementary ways of inquiry into curriculum.[17]

The Need for Studies of Correlation and Integration

Status of Correlation Studies in 1969. Goodlad omitted any mention of studies during the review period that treated the effects of concurrent

---

[15]Daniel Tanner and Laurel Tanner, "Emancipation from Research: The Reconceptualist Position," *Educational Research* 8, no. 6 (June 1977): 8–12.

[16]William F. Pinar, James H. Finkelstein, C. Ray Williams, and Maxine Greene, "Letters to the Editor," *Educational Researcher* 8, no. 9 (October 1979): 6, 24–25.

[17]Nelson L. Haggerson, "Reconceptualizing Inquiry in Curriculum: Using Multiple Research Paradigms to Enhance the Study of Curriculum," *The Journal of Curriculum Theorizing* 8, no. 1 (1988): 81–103.

offerings. Thus, we can assume that curriculum knowledge increased very little in the areas of integration and correlation of subject matters. Instead, the period was marked by the separation of subjects and linear organizational plans within fields.

Present Status of Correlation and Integration Studies.   Concern for general education, for a more integrated view of knowledge, for a focus on larger social questions has created increased efforts to correlation studies. Academic alliances are being formed as sociologists, psychologists, biologists, and chemists seek answers to closely related questions. Development of curriculum that will relate literature, language, composition, and popular culture is underway without a unifying theory. Perhaps the whole language framework is a move to such a theory. An emphasis on the interrelationships of things through curriculum invites inquiry about the effects of correlation. However, it is a false hope that curriculum developers can themselves effect an integration of knowledge.[18] Although curriculum scholars may encourage interdisciplinary approaches to a problem or area of interest, they are unlikely to integrate knowledge or synthesize concepts from various disciplines to create a set of new concepts.

Nathalie Gehrke found that teachers' conceptions of integrative curriculum are vague because they have not experienced an integrative curriculum. Gehrke is one of the first investigators to observe the behaviors of those engaged in integrative curriculum development. She learned that the process was not much different from other curriculum development, but is tied to assumptions about what constitutes integration. Her categorization of integration as simple relational, applicational, analogical and logical relational has been elaborated upon in Chapter 7.[19]

Practical accounts of integrated curriculum are increasing. Andrew Kaplan's "Galileo," an experiment in interdisciplinary curriculum planning by an entire faculty is an excellent example.[20] Kaplan emphasizes the need for training teachers in the deliberative process required for developing such curriculum.

With respect to administrative organizational planning, there is

---

[18]Richard L. Derr, "A Note on Curriculum Integration," *Curriculum Inquiry* 11, no. 4 (1981): 387–392.

[19]Nathalie Gehrke, "Developing Integrative Curriculum: Some Discoveries on Process," AERA paper, New Orleans, 1988.

[20]Andrew Kaplan, "Galileo: An Experiment in Interdisciplinary Education," *Curriculum Inquiry* 18, no. 3 (1988): 255–287.

much discussion about the value of intensive or total immersion courses, which are taken one at a time, in place of traditional concurrent courses, which are taken three, four, or five at a time throughout the term. Some schools are experimenting with intensive courses during the one month of 4-1-4 plans. Yet, appallingly little research has been undertaken on the educational effects of either intensive or concurrent courses.

The Need for Studies of Sequence

Status of Studies Treating Sequence in 1969. The quest for the best arrangement of material in a field was very much alive in 1969. There were many experiments with different sequences in programmed and computer-based instruction. Robert Gagné's work stimulated several investigations to assess the effects of scrambled versus hierarchical orderings of learning tasks. The findings were mixed, indicating that increasing complexity is not always the best criterion for ordering material.

Present Status of Studies Treating Sequence in 1990. Since 1976, when George Posner and Kenneth Strike completed the extensive categorization scheme for sequence described in Chapter 7, there has been little research on the topic. James Kallison, Jr., provides evidence that the most important way to judge sequence is whether or not it reveals the relationships among parts.[21] Also, developmentalists continue to take into account the cognitive capacities of learners, emphasizing that sequence should be planned from the learner's point of view rather than a priori. As seen in the next section, many ideas about the cognitive capacities of learners at different ages are being challenged.

The Need for Analyzing Educational Objectives

Status of Taxonomical Analysis of Objectives in 1969. The pioneer taxonomy or classification of objectives in the classification of objectives in the cognitive domain was completed in 1956, and taxonomies in both psychomotor and affective realms were developed after 1969. Furthermore, there was much research treating how best to refine educational objectives into precise behavioral objectives. Studies of the effects of behavioral objectives on learning were also common.

---

[21]James Kallison, Jr., "Effects of Lesson Organization on Achievement," *American Educational Research Journal* 23, no. 2 (1986): 337–347.

Present Status of Taxonomical Analysis of Objectives. The structural analysis of feelings, attitudes, and values has not kept up with similar research in the areas of mental abilities and personality. There is still interest in whether the levels of behavior given in taxonomies are cumulative or hierarchical. J. R. Calder and others found that in the *Taxonomy of Educational Objectives—Cognitive Domains*, the synthesis and evaluation of the categories did not depend on integration with lower level behaviors.[22] In his critical review of taxonomies of educational objectives, Robert M. W. Travers faults the Bloom taxonomy for being chiefly an inventory of test items and not a taxonomy of cognitive processes.[23] He views Piaget's system, by which knowledge is classified in terms of formal properties, as a better potential basis for developing a taxonomy of cognitive processes. Piaget's framework has been used in a number of curriculum projects for analyzing learning activities in terms of the logical operations they involve (Project SOAR at Xavier University of Louisiana, the STAR Program of Metropolitan State College of Denver, Project ADAPT at the University of Nebraska, and an elementary science program developed at the University of California, Berkeley).

Current research casts doubt on rigid conceptions of skill hierarchies and spiraled curriculum. Although there are some valid skill hierarchies such as teaching addition before multiplication, little evidence supports hierarchies such as those in Bloom's taxonomy.

Three principles for sequencing thinking skills show promise: increasing the complexity of the content and task, increasing the diversity of applications, and providing adequate support for learning, gradually transferring responsibility from teacher to student (scaffolding).[24]

Indeed, analysis of cognitive processes has been greatly strengthened during the last decade by studies of (a) metacognitive processes (knowledge of when and why to use various strategies for problem solving),[25] (b) the cognitive processes underlying the act of writing (planning), sentence generations and revising,[26] and (c) the processes in-

---

[22]J. R. Calder, "In the Cells of the 'Bloom Taxonomy'," *Journal of Curriculum Studies* 15, no. 3 (July-September 1983): 291–302.

[23]Robert M. W. Travers, "Taxonomies of Educational Objectives and Theories of Classification," *Educational Evaluation and Policy Analysis* 2, no. 2 (March-April 1980): 5–23.

[24]A. Collins, J. S. Brown, S. E. Newman, "Cognitive Apprenticeships: Teaching the Craft of Reading, Writing, Mathematics," in *Cognition and Instruction*, ed. Lauren Resnick (Hillsdale, NJ: Erlbaum, 1986).

[25]*Cognition and Instruction Issues and Agendas*, ed. Lauren Resnick (Hillsdale, NJ: Erlbaum, 1987).

[26]John R. Hayes and Linda S. Flower, "Writing Research and the Writer," *American Psychologist* 41, no. 10 (October 1986): 1106–1114.

volved in mathematics activities.[27] A new view of taxonomies of learning tasks marks a departure from task analysis (identifying the knowledge involved in specific tasks and a sequence of mechanical steps) to the articulation of the learning process itself—procedural knowledge constructed on the basis of schemata (concepts or structure for interpreting phenomenon).

Evidence of the great change in curriculum development as a result of cognitive psychology supplanting behaviorism can be found in military curriculum development.[28] The old methodology for analyzing the task requirements of a job and developing curriculum geared to those requirements is limited by the problems of high cost and a failure to analyze the mental structures that underlie competence. The new methodology is more interested in analyzing what must be learned in specific situations, emphasizing content rather than behavior. The new military training programs use simulations to teach principles of operations and reasoning. Students are not presented with physically faithful renditions of what they will be working with but with graphical simulations which exhibit the conceptual components of the phenomenon. Also, simplified versions of the actual equipment are easier to understand and provide better models for reasoning about the task than physically faithful simulators or the real-life equipment. Training now focuses on making relevant knowledge explicit, using problem-solving contexts for instruction in basic principles, and carefully managing information processing during learning.

The Need for Process–Product Research

Status of Process–Product Research in 1969. Process–product research attempts to relate instructional variables to learner achievement and the curriculum planning process to improved instruction and learning. Much process–product research between 1960 and 1969 dealt with instructional objectives. Most curriculum materials investigations dwelt on specific treatment variables associated with the materials (for example, organizers, relevant practice, knowledge of results and prompts). Goodlad realized, however, that there were two problems with this research.

---

[27]*The Development of Mathematical Thinking*, ed. H. P. Ginsberg (New York: Academic Press, 1983).

[28]Henry M. Halff, "Cognitive Science and Military Training," *American Psychologist* 41, no. 10 (1986): 1131-1139.

The first was methodological. It was not always clear what constituted the process or treatment, nor was it always established that the treatment had been carried out as stipulated. The second problem was theoretical. It was often difficult to know the significance of a small manageable process–product equation within some large frame of explanation.

Present Status of Process–Product Research. The methodological and theoretical problems of 1969 have not been resolved. However, they are more widely recognized now. Research into instructional effectiveness by means of the input-output approach has not yielded consistent results. Background factors tend to dominate the findings. No single resource or variable is consistently shown to exert a powerful influence on learning. Perhaps one reason for this state of affairs is the emphasis on generalizations. Instead of making the search for generalizations the major priority, investigators should look for unique personal characteristics and uncontrolled events in situations. We should try to use generalizations only as working hypotheses and then look for clues to specific factors that might cause departures from the predicted effects. These factors might be *learner variables,* such as a learner's perceptions of the curriculum event, or a learner's cognitive style; *teacher variables,* such as a teacher's attitude toward the curriculum and the learners, or teacher pressure toward student conformity rather than toward independence; and *school* or *classroom ambient variables,* such as peer group interactions, morale, expectations, and consistency with home and community values.

As indicated in Chapter 8, work has expanded from concentration on isolated variables associated with effectiveness to include analyses of life in classrooms and from unambiguous tasks with certain answers to the study of tasks with several possible answers. This work has led to a recognition of the importance of (a) improving instructional materials that carry the major academic content and (b) attending to learning tasks that have the greatest consequences for the quality of academic work.

Among current trends in process–product research are the following:

1. Making clearer distinction between curriculum issues and instructional methods used. Curriculum content must be held constant in order to study instructional methods.
2. Refining measurement instruments in order to measure how well and not just how often something is done and to assess motor instructional sequences instead of discrete behaviors. Considering the limited range of measures that have been used to assess curriculum, it is

inadvisable to equate curriculum effects in achievement with effectiveness.

3. Considering untapped questions such as what makes an effective unit of instruction and how best to accommodate individual differences.

A serious problem in process–product research is that researchers assume that certain instructional variables are directly related to student achievement. In fact, the relationship between classroom processes and achievement are usually nonlinear. Too much or too little of a good process is ineffective. Furthermore, a good practice may mask a better one. For instance, time on task is considered beneficial. However, Ann Dyson found that time off task, when children collaboratively engage in spontaneous talk, is often a more intellectually demanding opportunity than time on teacher-directed lessons.[29]

FUTURE DIRECTIONS IN CURRICULUM THEORY

The best predictor of the future is present activity. We can predict at least two directions for curriculum theory because there are two kinds of theorists at work: *soft* curricularists and *hard* curricularists. The soft curricularists may be few in number among curriculum workers in bureaucratic institutions, but increasingly they are the chief presenters at research conferences and major writers in prestigious journals of the field. Their stated purpose is not to guide practitioners but to understand the internal and existential nature of the educational experience. They are called soft curricularists because they model themselves after those in the humanities, in history, religion, philosophy, and literary criticism, not in the hard sciences. They include intuition and existence as sources of knowledge, not only the senses and reason. The hard curricularists follow a rational approach, relying on empirical data to justify means and a consistent philosophical position for validating ends proposed.

The Soft Curricularists

The reconceptualists, or soft curricularists, do not study change in behavior or decision making in the classroom, but the meaning of tem-

---

[29]Anne Haas Dyson, ''The Value of Time off Task: Spontaneous Talk and Deliberate Text,'' *Harvard Educational Review* 57, no. 4 (November 1987): 396–420.

porality, transcendence, consciousness, and politics. Dwayne Huebner writes of temporality, i.e., existence in time, and the need for an awareness of history. He would mesh a person's biography with the history of the person's society so that this person could realize his or her own potentiality for being.[30] Huebner challenges curriculum workers, for example, to present historical wisdom in a way that will be useful to specific persons at different age levels.

As another example, we can look at Philip Phenix and his regard for transcendence as surpassing any certain state. As described in Chapter 1, transcendence suggests a curriculum that has regard for the uniqueness of the human personality and is characterized by an atmosphere of freedom. Politics is very much in the minds of the soft curricularists. They are concerned about the political implications that might follow reconceptualization of curriculum theory and, in turn, curriculum development. The soft curricularists realize that the political climate does not now favor radical activities as it did in the 1960s, and they are divided about the best means for effecting social reconstruction. One group thinks it best to present what is known about the content of curriculum, stressing its racism, sexism, and classism. Another group shifts from harsh criticism to ways of working. Advocacy groups such as the Children's Defense Fund are influencing legislation for children, improving organizations for the government of institutions, and becoming better acquainted with the knowledge from which new alternatives for schooling can come.

The Hard Curricularists

The study of curricular phenomena by hard curricularists is undertaken for the immediate purpose of accurate description and for future prediction and control. Decker Walker, for example, a member of this group, prepared a naturalistic model for curriculum development in order to illuminate facets of the curriculum development process.[31] Although this model, as described in Chapter 5, was meant to be descriptive rather than prescriptive, it has been widely used as a guide to deliberative curriculum inquiry and development. The model assumes that the curriculum is developed in accordance with an idea or vision of

---

[30]Dwayne Huebner, "Curriculum as Concern for Man's Temporality," in *Curriculum Theorizing*, ed. William Pinar (Berkeley, CA: McCutchan, 1975), pp. 237–250.

[31]Decker Walker, "A Naturalistic Model, for Curriculum Development," *School Review* 80, no. 1 (November 1971): 51–67.

what ought to be (a platform) and that a curriculum design consists of a number of decisions made in producing curriculum materials. The process by which beliefs and information are used to make the design decisions is called *deliberation*. The heart of the deliberation process is the justification of choices. Walker, as a hard curricularist, defines deliberation by logical, not social or psychological criteria. Empirical confirmations (data) are seen as a most persuasive basis for justification. Good decisions are those consistent with given platforms and available information, although a platform may be changed by the curriculum designer as the work progresses. A defensible set of objectives is the result of deliberations based on a platform. The purposes of the hard curricularist can be inferred from the five intended uses of the naturalistic model:

1. *To test propositions.* For example: Do curriculum-making groups with similar platforms conduct similar deliberations and produce similar designs and objectives?
2. *To make descriptive studies.* For example: How do the platforms of those in one subject field differ from those in other fields?
3. *To establish connections between design elements (curriculum variables) and learning outcomes.* For example: What is the effect of a specific design element on a given outcome?
4. *To formulate new curriculum questions.* For example: What kinds of grounds should be given greater weight in justifying decisions during deliberation?
5. *To identify questions in curriculum making that will be of interest to colleagues in other fields.* For example: Just as the curriculum practitioners' treatment of discovery learning led to renewed interest in this topic by psychologists, might not other matters of importance to noncurricularists come to light through study of platforms and deliberations?

Another hard curricularist, Mauritz Johnson, sees the definition of curriculum and instruction as a directive force for the theorist.[32] He distinguishes among curriculum, the source of curriculum, and the relationship of curriculum to instruction. According to Johnson, a curriculum is the result of a curriculum development system, i.e., a structured series of intended outcomes. A curriculum is the result of curriculum development that occurs as cultural content is selected and ordered. Johnson is interested in the method of selecting cultural content within specific

---

[32]Mauritz Johnson, Jr., "Definitions and Models of Curriculum Theory," in *Curriculum and Instruction*, ed. Henry A. Giroux (Berkeley: McCutchan, 1981), pp. 69–86.

realms or domains (such as vocational and general education), but has not been very successful in clarifying the criteria or in devising procedures for using them.

Johnson's position on the issue of whether objectives should follow or precede instruction is clear. He believes that curriculum should guide instruction. The restrictions of curriculum should be minimal, however, in order to allow flexibility in instructional sequencing. Johnson believes that a definition of instruction must encompass all training and instructional situations and all domains of outcomes for all kinds of learners. He views learning experiences as the instructional route to intended outcomes and holds that such experiences must have both active (what the learner is to do) and substantive (what content is to be involved) components.

For Johnson, the curriculum restricts but does not prescribe the content and form of instructional activity. It influences instruction primarily through the mediation of an instructional plan. A curriculum does not guide all aspects of instruction or control for the spontaneity and effectiveness of discourse in the instructional act. Although curriculum does not specify the means of evaluation, it furnishes the criteria for evaluating instructional outcomes.

Presumably the purpose of Johnson's conceptualization is the clarification of the different components in a system. Improvement can then be enhanced by focusing on the components that are deficient, whether they are instructional techniques, materials, instructional plans, curriculum ordering, or curriculum selection. A soft curricularist might look at the language Johnson uses: "system," "detailed control tactics," "well-established rules," "review by experts," "results." The critic would assume that this technological and military-like talk with its means–ends, cause–effect structure is unlikely to answer a person's need for liberating activities.

DIRECTIONS IN CURRICULUM RESEARCH

General frameworks and specific questions for guiding inquiry in the field of curriculum have been given in prior paragraphs describing the state of the field and the trends in theoretical curriculum research. There are, however, five specific kinds of inquiry likely to be pursued by productive scholars and practitioners.

Comprehensive Curriculum Inquiry

Decker Walker believes that there are only five questions to be addressed by curricularists:

1. What are the significant features of a given curriculum?
2. What are the personal and social consequences of a given curriculum feature?
3. What accounts for stability and change in curriculum features?
4. What accounts for persons' judgments of the merit or worth of various curriculum features?
5. What sorts of curriculum features ought to be included in a curriculum intended for a certain purpose in a situation?

The last question requires a normative rather than an empirical answer.

Walker's questions reflect his assumption that the curriculum is a practical field of study. It is expected to make a difference in someone's learning. Also, the meaning of "curriculum feature" is vague in recognition of the field's lack of consensus on conceptions of curriculum. Hence, curriculum workers of different persuasions may define curriculum features according to their own purposes.[33]

Barry Franklin, for example, studied the social efficiency movement as a significant feature in curriculum.[34] He examined the social efficiency movement in the Minneapolis school systems from 1917 to 1950. The evidence Franklin obtained supported the claim that ideas of efficiency dominated policy making in the system. However, he failed to find that efficiency-minded educators used the curriculum to achieve inegalitarian aims. In fact, in terms of actual impact on the practice in the schools, the curriculum ideas of those in the social efficiency movement was slight. The curriculum differentiations were minor and the changes in course content minimal.

Synoptic Activity as Curriculum Inquiry

As mentioned previously, Herbert Kliebard has speculated that one direction for the curriculum field is to bring together widely separated fields into a larger common area. The curriculum person's competence

---

[33]Decker Walker, "What Are the Problems Curricularists Ought to Study?" *Curriculum Theory Network* 4, nos. 2-3 (1974): 217–218.

[34]Barry M. Franklin, *Building The American Community* (Philadelphia: Falmer Press, 1986).

may lie not in unearthing new knowledge, but in putting together many of the findings from other disciplines. The curriculum expert can take a number of narrow perspectives and unite them by applying them in the development of school programs that help students learn things that will be helpful to them and to society. The kinds of research borrowing that are useful in curriculum synoptic activity are the following:

1. *Concepts.* There are more concepts, such as concepts of motivation (locus of control), and concepts of learning (learned helplessness), than anything else that can be used. Developers of new courses should use such concepts in their developmental efforts.
2. *Generalizations.* There is growing concern that few generalizations have broad applicability. Generalizations depend on conditions that may not be present in particular school settings.
3. *Facts.* General facts are often less useful than generalizations. Particular facts have to be collected for each situation.
4. *Methods.* Problem-solving procedures can be borrowed from disciplines and applied to curriculum problems. For example, the anthropologist's use of naturalistic observation is currently applied in studies of classrooms.
5. *Values and Attitudes.* A commitment to truth, to the facts and an active skepticism are needed to solve our real dilemmas.

Examples of synoptic activity in curriculum, illustrating the contributions of different subject matter fields to curriculum development, are seen in *borrowings from social psychology* with its concepts about peer group learning in the selection of learning opportunities; *borrowings from personality psychology* with its notion of human needs and the self, particularly in designing curriculum for moral development; *borrowings from sociology* with its concepts of social class and social mobility; and *borrowings from the psychology of learning* with its concepts and findings about the learning process and their implications for curriculum and instruction. Synoptic activity is predicated on our willingness to question what our curriculum is doing and what we know about the changes we propose. It means using research from many sources, including historical research, in guiding our efforts.

Conceptualization as Curriculum Inquiry

As indicated previously, there is much interest in conceptualization in the curriculum field. Louise Tyler adds another level to the societal, institutional, and classroom levels of curriculum decision by specifying a *personal* level and detailing the nature of personal decision making. For example, she has contrasted an aspect of curriculum decision making at the four levels in terms of psychoanalytic constructs, such as *transference* (projecting upon another person the attitudes and responses attached to an emotionally significant person), indicating and explaining the dimensions of thought and feeling that a student might experience in responding to learning situations and to the problem of revealing what has been learned.[35]

The opportunities for inquiry at the level of the personal domain are great. For instance, there is a need to know about the meaning of various subjects for students at different developmental levels, the meaning of school itself for students, the nature of students' fears in the school setting, the function of their jokes and humor, and the meaning of their play.

Other curriculum researchers are trying to conceptualize curriculum to take into account the *inward* experience of students reacting to their educational environment. George Willis is grappling with speculative, analytical, and empirical studies in an effort to discover how students develop meaning from their educational environment and how these environments can enhance the quality of experience for the individual.[36]

Signs indicate that research in curriculum will center on new approaches to curriculum development for the teaching of nonprocedural tasks.[37] The need for a curriculum that attempts to teach intellectual tasks involving understanding and higher level cognitive processes has been mentioned previously. Newer theories of cognition and learning challenge traditional curriculum development approaches—especially competency-based models which assume that tasks are basically procedural and that the tasks can be broken down into elements which, when practiced, will yield mastery.

Alternative approaches have been suggested. James Martin and Margaret Uguroglu, for example, address the problem of teaching bodies

[35]Louise Tyler and John Goodlad, "The Personal Domain: Curricular Meaning," in *Curricular Inquiry* (New York: McGraw-Hill, 1979), pp. 191–209.

[36]George Willis, "Creating Curriculum Knowledge from Students' Phenomenologies," in *Conceptions of Curriculum Knowledge*, ed. Edmund Short (University Park: Pennsylvania State University, 1982), pp 43–49.

[37]Gary A. Klein, "Curriculum Development Versus Education," *Teachers College Record* 84, no. 4 (Summer 1983): 821–836.

of knowledge that do not have certain answers or specified educational results.[38] They offer a design approach by which groups of learners generate solutions to a problem. Students define the problem by determining the purposes to be achieved and proposing a unique solution—often one that may not be within the framework of the school as a social organization. There must be criteria for the solution, however. The solution must be cost-effective and maintain human values.

Peter Lemish also has addressed curriculum development in response to uncertainty.[39] His "praxis process" for curriculum development involves posing problems that challenge the apparent order in the school and classroom. Teachers reflect upon the assumptions, values, and meanings of the activities found in their educational setting. The process involves teachers in critical inquiry; they question, seek contradictions, and assess the consequences of their situation, leading to better understanding of themselves, students, subject matter, and potentials for change.

Qualitative Inquiry in School Settings

In the past few years, curriculum inquirers have placed themselves in direct and continuous contact with the objects of curriculum investigation: instructional materials, classroom interactions, and their meanings for learners. Often these investigators use ethnographic methods. Basic to this kind of inquiry is the nature of the interpretations given to classroom observations. Gail McCutcheon has illustrated how researchers construct meaning by relating their knowledge to the observations made.[40] McCutcheon recognizes that many qualitative researchers use a phenomenological approach. They interpret events in light of the meanings participants make of those events. Others use a critical stance, such as a Marxist orientation, and interpret events in light of wider considerations. McCutcheon offers the example of the influence of a researcher's orientation on inquiry by examining three approaches to the study of the 45-minute period. A technologist concerned with achievement and

---

[38]James L. Martin and Margaret E. Uguroglu, "Building Curricula When You Don't Have the Answer" Paper presented at the annual meeting of the American Educational Research Association, New York City, 1982.

[39]Peter Lemish, "The Technical Approach and the Praxis Orientation to Curriculum Development" Paper presented at the annual meeting of the American Educational Research Association, New York City, 1982.

[40]Gail McCutcheon, "On the Interpretation of Classroom Observations," *Educational Researcher* 10, no. 5 (May 1981): 5–10.

teaching effectiveness might approach the situation by considering the time spent on tasks within the 45-minutes; a phenomenologist might wonder what meaning 45-minute periods have for participants; a critical scientist might ask about the origin of 45-minute periods and how such time affects what students learn or how the time allocation denies some students access to knowledge, thereby producing social injustice.

McCutcheon refers to three ways in which interpretations are made. The researcher may look for patterns in the observations. There may be an unconscious order in classroom practices (raising hands, asking questions, assigning projects, grading responses). Observations may also be interpreted for their social meanings. For instance, what does movement of the students' heads mean? Boredom? Agreement? Trying to please the teacher? Fatigue? Social meanings may be interpreted by asking the teacher or students to justify an action or to describe what a particular statement *really* meant. In a third type of interpretation, the facts of a classroom are related to a theory. For example, they might be related to psychological theories of learning, to a historical movement or theme, to a particular educational philosophy, or to a theory of social classes.

The validity of interpretations depends on the reasoning used in arriving at the interpretation, the amount of evidence that supports the interpretation, and the extent to which the interpretation seems to fit with other knowledge of the real world. How far can one generalize from a single case study? The answer is similar to the answer for how far can one accept truths in great literature. It rests on the assumption that others can apply the findings to their own situation.

Action Research as Curriculum Inquiry

A popular view is that action research practitioners put the findings of research into effect in order to resolve their own areas of need. Originally, practitioners used action research in attempting to study their problems systematically, and the value of such research was not determined by the discovery of scientific laws or generalizations but by whether or not the application led to improvement in practice.

In the mid-1950s, teachers began using action research to improve their curricula. Gordon MacKenzie, Stephen Corey, and Hilda Taba were among those curriculum specialists who involved teachers in the research process. Teachers under their direction accumulated evidence to define their problems, drew on experience and knowledge to form action hypotheses to improve the situation of their daily work, tested promising procedures, and accumulated evidence of their effectiveness. The rationale and technical procedures for conducting such research is still available from several sources.[41,42] Three forces aborted the growth of action research. First, the academic curriculum reform of the 1960s put little emphasis on local development of curriculum. Standardization was prized over uniqueness. Second, educational researchers in universities, who in the 1950s might have been willing to work with teachers in curriculum inquiry, found themselves in the 1960s attending instead to the interests of government agencies that were funding certain kinds of research. Third, many persons in the 1960s believed that problems of curriculum and instruction would best be resolved by the discovery and application of generalizations and laws of learning, not by individual teachers in unique situations.

Currently, it is again being recognized that teachers (as well as students and persons not directly involved in the school) are theorists and researchers in their own right. There are signs of a shift of responsibility for curriculum development from colleges and laboratories to classrooms and communities. Networks, such as those described in Chapter 9, represent scholarly efforts aimed at helping teachers rather than at producing research for fellow scholars.

Enthusiasm for action research is cresting. Action research projects, textbooks, and journal articles on actions abound.[43,44] However, Wilfred Carr has illuminated problems with this activity.[45] Carr points out that action research now means different things to different people. While all action researchers have a contempt for academic theorizing and are disenchanted with "mainstream" research, they are divided on what the practical purposes of action research are. Some regard action research primarily as a way to deepen teachers' understanding, whereas others stress the role in stimulating improvement and change. Still others see action research as an effective way to communicate research findings to teachers. Carr warns against action researchers using the language and evaluative standards of positivist conventional research. The old practices of action researchers engaging in systematic and methodological processes for acquiring knowledge is faulted because it falls into the posi-

---

[41]ASCD, *Research for Curriculum Development* (Washington, DC: ASCD, 1957).

[42]Stephen M. Corey, *Action Research to Improve School Practice* (New York: Columbia University, Teachers College, 1953).

[43]Stephen Kemmis, ed., *The Action Research Planner* (Victoria, Australia: Deakin University Press, 1988).

[44]D. Hustler et al., eds., *Action Research in Classrooms and Schools* (London: Allen & Unwin, 1986).

[45]Wilfred Carr, "Action Research: Ten Years On." *Journal of Curriculum Studies* 21, no. 1 (1989): 85–90.

tivist tradition with its separation from philosophical questioning and its indifferences to major social, political, and moral concerns. A contrary view is that action research is a dialogical or reflective process of democratic discussion and philosophical critique. By way of example, Richard Winter describes how action research need not be confined to revealing teachers' interpretive theories, but revealing to them aspects of their practices in a way which makes practice amenable to critical transformation.[46] Instead of being primarily concerned with explicating or testing teachers' implicit theories, action research can be concerned with establishing the conditions that enable teachers to reflect critically on the contradictions between their educational ideas and beliefs and the institutionalized practices through which the ideas and beliefs are expressed. A practical illustration of this perspective is found in the work of Carr and Kemmis.[47]

According to these researchers, action research is a critical inquiry controlled by practitioners who are committed to social as well as curriculum change. Teachers reflect on the justice of their social and educational practices, their understanding of these practices, and the situation in which these practices are carried out. The latter relates to understanding the influence of broader sociocultural and political structures on the educational environment.

In *Sources of a Science of Education*, Dewey made these points[48]:

1. An inquirer can repeat the research of another to confirm or discredit it. Moreover, by using this technique, the inquirer discovers new problems and new investigations that refine old procedures and lead to new and better ones.
2. No conclusion of scientific research can be converted into an immediate rule for educators. Educational practice contains many conditions and factors not included in the scientific finding.
3. Although scientific findings should not be used as a rule of action, they can help teachers to be alert to discover certain factors that would otherwise go unnoticed and to interpret something that would otherwise be misunderstood.
4. The practitioner who knows a science (a system) can see more possi-

[46]Richard Winter, *Action Research and the Nature of Social Inquiry: Professional Innovation and Education Work* (Aldershot, England: Avebury, Gower, 1987).

[47]Wilfred Carr and Stephen Kemmis, *Becoming Critical: Knowing Through Action Research* (Victoria, Australia: Deakin University Press, 1983).

[48]John Dewey, *The Sources of a Science of Education* (New York: Horace Liveright, 1929).

bilities and opportunities and has a wide range of alternatives to select from in dealing with individual situations.

5. In education, practice should form the problems of inquiry. The worth of a scientific finding is shown only when it serves an educational purpose, and whether it really serves or not can be found only in practice.

6. Research persons connected with school systems may be too close to the practical problems and the university professor too far away from them to secure the best results.

7. Problems that require treatment arise in relations with students. Consequently, it is impossible to see how there can be an adequate investigation unless teachers actively participate.

Perhaps the most eloquent argument for action research as a form of curriculum inquiry is found in John Dewey's answer to the question of how educational objectives are to be determined. He thought it false to say that social conditions, science, or the subject matter of any field could determine objectives. He conceived education as a process of discovering what values are worthwhile and to be pursued as objectives.

> To see what is going on and to observe the results of what goes on so as to see their future consequences in the process of growth, and so on indefinitely, is the only way in which the value of what takes place can be judged. To look at some outside source to provide aims is to fail to know what education is as an ongoing process. . . .
>
> Knowledge of the objectives which society actually strives for and the consequences actually attained may be had in some measure through a study of the social sciences. This knowledge may render educators more circumspect, more critical, as to what they are doing. It may inspire better insight into what is going on here and now in the home or school; it may enable teachers and parents to look farther ahead and judge on the basis of consequences in a longer course of development. But it must operate through their own ideas, plannings, observations, judgments. Otherwise it is not *educational* science at all, but merely so much sociological information.[49]

CONCLUDING COMMENTS

In this chapter, the state of the curriculum field was appraised by reviewing the status of curriculum research in six areas. Curriculum the-

---

[49]Ibid., pp. 74–76.

ory is divided among traditionalists, scientists, and reconceptualists. A lack of common ground of professional action and responsibility is a source of concern. The status of conceptual systems for identifying major curriculum questions is giving more attention to the role of the learner as a decision maker in curriculum, the impact of social political forces in curriculum making, and curriculum criticism as a mode of inquiry in its own right. Although there has been little research in correlated studies, much activity is attempting to show how best to arrange material for effective learning. Work regarding educational objectives, which has dominated much of curriculum thought and practice, is now being extended thus revealing reasons for the learner's inability to use knowledge and the relationship between the content objectives and the cognitive processes and structure that underlie competent performance.

With respect to the methodological and theoretical problems associated with process–product research, two apparently conflicting trends are (1) acceptance of opportunity to learn and time in instruction as the key variables in designing means to *minimal* ends and (2) recognition that no single variable can consistently exert a powerful or predictable influence on student outcomes.

Future directions in curriculum theory promise to be fruitful. The soft curricularists are drawing our attention to both the political and moral aspects of curriculum making. The hard curricularists have posed specific propositions to be tested that will contribute to our understanding of curriculum making as a process. Anyone wishing to do research in the curriculum field should be greatly helped by the guidance of those advocating comprehensive curriculum inquiry, synoptic activity, conceptualization, qualitative research and action research. I leave it to you to decide whether multiple research paradigms are broadening or whether they are so self-contained that they neglect important questions outside their paradigms, clouding our visions.

QUESTIONS

1. How are the categories of traditionalist, conceptual empiricist, and reconceptualist related to humanistic, academic, technological, and social reconstructionist conceptions of curricula? Are reconceptualists contributing to both humanistic and social reconstructionist curricula? In what way are conceptual empiricists influencing technological and academic curricula?

2. Which of the six curriculum concerns used to appraise the status of curriculum research shows the least progress? What might account for the difference in progress?
3. The classroom teacher in the 1990s is likely to feel pressure to help design curriculum and instruction. Which of the research directions in this chapter do you think will be of the greatest help to the teacher in responding to this pressure?
4. Give examples of the language (metaphors) used in your discussions of curriculum. Characterize this language by its style, imagery, and what it reveals about views of learners and knowledge. What consequences does the use of this language have in creating curriculum problems?
5. Donald Chipley at Pennsylvania State University has identified three basic reasons for undertaking curriculum research. One of these purposes is to make an inventory of the content that is offered and the resources that are invested in particular educational developments. Another purpose is personal curiosity. An investigator has an interest in exploring new ideas and extending generalizable knowledge about curriculum relationships. The third purpose is decision making. A person assesses various curriculum alternatives in order to make more rational decisions in specific situations. Which of these motives is closest to your own?

SELECTED REFERENCES

Beyer, Landon E., and Apple, Michael W. *The Curriculum: Problems, Politics, and Possibilities.* Albany: State University of New York, 1988.

Cherryholmes, Cleo H. *Power and Criticism.* New York: Columbia University, Teachers College Press, 1989.

Reid, William A. *Thinking About the Curriculum.* Boston: Routledge & Kegan Paul, 1978.

Sherman, Robert R., Rodman B., and Webb B., eds. *Contemporary Curriculum Discourses.* Scottsdale, AZ: Gorsuch Scaribuck, 1988.

Winter, Richard. *Action Research and the Nature of Social Inquiry.* Avebury, England: Gower, Aldershot, 1987.

INDEX

Academic core, and liberal arts, 78–82
Academic subject curriculum, 1–2, 69–70
   approaches to, 70–84
   characteristics of, 84–92
   and cultural literacy, 82–84
   evaluation of, 88–89
   and forms of knowledge approach, 71–73
   and goals for thinking, 293
   guidelines for instructional materials in, 151–153
   liberal arts and the academic core, 78–82
   making subject matter more appealing to growing minds, 89–92
   methods in, 85
   organization of, 85–88
   purpose of, 84–85
   and reaction against a structure of knowledge, 75–77
   and revival of disciplines approach, 77–78
   and structure in disciplines approach, 73–75
Accreditation, and curriculum policy, 275
Achievement motivation, 18
Action research, as curriculum inquiry, 417–420
Add-on curriculum, 13
Adler, Mortimer, 81
Administration
   of curriculum, 193–215
   for instructional effectiveness, 209–215
Administrators. See also Principals, Superintendents
   and curriculum change, 218, 220
   and curriculum coordination, 209–211, 214–215
Adult volunteers, 203
Affect, measuring, 252–253
Affective development, and self-directed learning, 19
Affective experiences, sequencing of, 10–11
Affective techniques, in humanistic curriculum, 14–15
AFL-CIO, 281
Agassi, Joseph, 141
Airasian, Peter, 250

Alteration, 219
Alternative schools, 206–207
American Academy of Arts and Sciences, 358
American Alliance for Health, Physical Education and Recreation, 339
American Association of Advancement of Science, 337
American Civil Liberties Union, 250
American Council of Learned Societies, 356
American Education Association, 281
American method, for teaching foreign languages, 353
Anyon, Jean, 42–43, 310, 400
Apple, Michael, 40, 310, 400, 402
Arts
   computers in, 62
   in curriculum, 356–360
   and curriculum reform, 75
   personalization of, 21
   strengthening of requirements in, 88
Association for Supervision and Curriculum Development, 116, 194
Atkin, J. Myron, 336
Attributive theory, 18
Audiolingual approach for teaching foreign languages, 353
Autonomic position, on moral education, 313

Banking concept of education, 400
Bard, Beatrice, 229–230
Barzun, Jacques, 359
Basic operations, curriculum for teaching, 293–294
Basic skills movement, 343
Beauchamp, George, 397
Bell, Lee, 23
Bennett, William, 279
Berends, Mark, 201
Bernard, Claude, 81
Bilingual education, 321–322
Biofeedback, 17, 18

Biological Science Curriculum Study, curriculum designed by, 90–92
Bloom, Allan, 79
Bloom, Benjamin, 59, 154–155, 182
Bobbitt, Franklin, 113–114, 369, 370, 378, 379, 392, 397
Bode, Boyd H., 113
Bonser, Steward, 126–127
Book banning, 344
Bottom-up strategies, for curriculum change, 222, 225–226
Bowers, C. A., 47
Boyd, William, 262–263, 264–265, 270
Boyer, Ernest L., 262
Bracketing, 403
Bradley Commission, 349
Brameld, Theodore, 30, 33
Branching, 147
Brickell, Henry, 269
Broad fields structure, 164
Broudy, Harry S., 359
Brown, George I., 14–15, 24
Bruner, Jerome, 73, 76, 160
Burboles, N. C., 311
Butler, Kathleen, 137

Calder, J. R., 406
California
    "Cash for Caps" program in, 271
    cultural literacy programs in, 82–83
    and curriculum control, 274
    restructuring curriculum in, 195
    systems technology in, 53–54
    vocational education in, 305
Carmon, Arye, 21
Carnegie Colloquium on General Education, 184
Carnegie Forum, 193
Carnegie Foundation, 280
Carnegie Schools, 194
Carnegie unit, 198, 200
Carr, Wilfred, 418–419
Caswell, Hollis L., 386–388, 393
Centering oneself, 339
Centers, and course development, 170–171
Chamber of Commerce, 281
Chapter I, 279
Character education, 317
Charters, Warren W., 370, 378, 381, 383–384, 393
Cheney, Lynne V., 79
Chicago, decentralization experiment in, 273
Child-centered curriculum, 369
    arguments for shift away from, 3
Children's Defense Fund, 410
Children's interests, 78–79
China, education in, 296
Chronology, 175
CIPP (Contest, Input, Process, Product) model, 241
Cistone, Peter, 263
Clark, C. M., 169–170
Clark, Charles, 247
Classical humanists, 369
Classroom, introducing new materials into, 230–232
Classroom level, organizing structure at, 165–170
Classroom practices, effective, 212
Cognitive-code approach, to language instruction, 355
Cognitive development, and self-directed learning, 19
Cognitive psychology, 177
Cognitive Research Trust (CORT), 294
Cohen, S. Alan, 54, 402

Cohesion, 18
Collective bargaining, and curriculum decisions, 268
College Board's Admission Testing programs, 87
College Entrance Examination Board, 200
Comenius, John Amos, 135, 174
Committee of Ten, 290
Community participation, in curriculum planning, 329–330
Comparison groups, 255
Computer-assisted instruction (CAI), 146
Computers, 61–63
    in learning activities, 147–149
Conant, James B., 302
Concept learning, 176
Concepts, 414
    as organizing element, 172
    teaching of, 181
Conceptual empiricists, 401–402
Conceptualization, as curriculum inquiry, 414–416
Concern, curriculum of, 15
Concerns conferences, 111–112
Conflict avoidance, 264–265
Confluence, 137
Confluent curriculum, 356
    activities within, 14–15
    rationale for, 13–14
Conlan, John B., 77
Connoisseurship model, of curriculum evaluation, 243–244
Conrad, Melissa, 158
Conscientization, 37–38
Consensus models, for curriculum evaluation, 236, 237–242
Consummation function, 108
Context, Input, Process, Product (CIPP) model, 241
Contexturalization, 248
Controversy, politics of, and curriculum policy, 265
Core curriculum structure, 164
Corey, Stephen, 417
Cornbleth, Catherine, 311–312
Cornell, F. G., 269
Correlation studies
    need for, 403–405
    present status of, 404–405
    status of, in 1969, 403–404
Council for Basic Education, 82, 281, 300–301, 301, 358
Council for Educational Research and Development, 232
Countercultural movement, 3
Counts, George, 29
Course, 104
Course development, centers and, 170–171
Course of study movement, 385
Courts, participation in curriculum policy, 276–277
Creative indicators, to collect data for curriculum evaluation, 251–256
Creativity
    American commitment to, 4
    learning opportunities in, 142–143
Criterion-referenced tests, 249
Critical inquiry, evaluation as, 244
Cronbach, Lee, 152–153, 238
Cross-age teaching, to fine arts, 357–358
Cross-age tutoring, 203
Cross-cultural investigations, 111
Csikszentmihalyi, Mihaly, 7
Cuban, Larry, 62–63, 214, 263
Cultural diversity, and teaching multicultural education, 320
Cultural epochs, theory of, 175, 374–375
Cultural literacy, 82–84
Cultural minority, applying needs assessment to, 111

Cultural pluralism, 318–319
    approaches to multicultural education, 319–321
    bilingual education, 321–322
Curriculum
    and context of restructuring, 193–194
    coordinating, 209–211
    at different levels, 103–104
    evidence of dissatisfaction with present, 4–5
    experiential, 104
    formal, 103
    functions of, 106–108
    government influence on, 273–280
    ideal, 103
    integration in, 183–185
    international comparisons of, 299–301
    issues in organization of, 186–188
    local development of, 384–385
    operational, 104
    perceived, 103
    pressure group participation in, 281–282, 352–353
    for teaching problem solving, 294–295
    for thinking, 290–295
Curriculum administration, 193
    administrative arrangements in, 198, 200–207
    for instructional effectiveness, 209–215
    reform options in, 208–209
    and restructuring, 193–198
Curriculum alignment, 210
Curriculum change, 217–218
    bottom-up strategies for, 225–226
    conceptualizations of change process, 218–219
    conditions conducive to, 221–222
    middle-up strategy for, 227
    multiple element strategies for, 223–225
    networking for school renewal, 229–230
    research and development (R and D) model, 223
    role of administrators in, 218, 220
    role of teachers in, 217–218, 220
    sociological findings about, 219–222
    through staff development, 227–229
    top-down strategies for, 222–223
Curriculum competition
    invidious comparisons, 295–299
    validity of invidious comparisons, 299–301
Curriculum conceptions
    need for, 399–403
    present status of, 399–400
    status of, in 1969, 399
Curriculum control, conflicts in, 282–284
Curriculum coordination
    school cultural approach to, 210–211
    systems approach to, 209–210
Curriculum decision making
    and curriculum policy, 261, 262–265
    levels of, in curriculum development, 100–102
    rational and technical models in, 110–128
Curriculum development
    Caswell's influence, 386–388
    contents for, 104–108
    course of study movement, 385
    decision making in, 99–131
    Dewey on, 376–377
    Herbartism, 371–376
    historical perspective of, 367–393
    local, 384–385
    rational, 388–390
    scientific, 378–384

Curriculum evaluation, 235–237
    consensus models for, 237–242
    controversial technical issues in, 245–251
    pluralistic models for, 242–244
    techniques for collecting data, 251–256
Curriculum field, context for formulation of, 368–371
Curriculum innovations, search for, 232
Curriculum inquiry. See also Curriculum research
    action research as, 417–420
    comprehensive, 413
    conceptualization as, 414–416
    synoptic activity as, 413
Curriculum integration, 186
Curriculum management, department heads in, 197–198
Curriculum materials, technology in development of, 59–60
Curriculum policy, 104, 259–260
    community participants in determining, 271–273
    constraints on, 264–265
    courts' participation in, 276–277
    decisions in, 261
    federal government's participation in, 277–280
    forces of stability, 263–264
    foundations' participation in, 280–281
    politics in, 260–261
    pressure groups' participation in, 281–282, 352–353
    professionalization of reform, 262–263
    publishers' participation in, 275–276
    school-based participants in determining, 266–271
    state agencies' participation in, 273–274
    testing agencies' participation in, 275
Curriculum project, evaluating, 241–242
Curriculum reform movement, 74, 198
Curriculum research. See also Curriculum inquiry
    correlation studies, 403–405
    curriculum conceptions, 399–403
    directions in, 412–420
    hard curricularists, 410–412
    process-product research, 407–409
    sequence studies, 405
    soft curricularists, 409–410
    taxonomical analysis of objectives, 405–407
Curriculum restructuring, 194, 219
    administrative arrangements, 198, 200–207
    context of, 193–194
    principal as director of learning, 195
    principal in shared leadership, 195–197
Curriculum theory, 395–396
    correlation studies in, 403–405
    future directions in, 409–412
    hard curricularists on, 410–412
    need for, 396–399
    present status of, 397–399
    soft curricularists on, 409–410
    state of field, 396–409
    status of, in 1969, 396–397
Custodial function, 108

Damon, William, 317
Davies, Lee K., 272
de Bono, Edward, 143, 294
Decentralization, experiment on, in Chicago, 273
Deliberation, 411
Delphi method, 116
Dently, Robert, 227
Department heads, in curriculum management, 197–198
Depersonalization, responses to, 18–23
Design components, 59–60

Developmental consideration, 59
Developmentalism, 224
Dewey, John, 86, 182, 290, 369, 376–377, 392, 397, 403, 419–420
Disciplines approach
  revival of, 77–78
  structure in the, 73–75
Discrimination, in vocational education, 303–304
Disjointed incrementalism
  in curriculum decision making, 125
  problems with, 125–126
Domain-specific knowledge, 295
Down, A. Graham, 301–302
Doyle, Walter, 140
Drachler, Norman, 262
Dreeben, Robert, 309
Driver training programs, 274, 310
Drug education, 274
Dyads, 14

Education, as function of curriculum, 106–107
Educational objectives, need for analyzing, 405–407
Educational Products Information Exchange Institute (EPIE), 60
Educational Testing Service, 275, 297
Education and Consolidation and Improvement Act, 279
Education Development Center, 337
Effectiveness studies, implications of, 213–214
Efficiency, technology and ideal of, 52–53
Effros, Edward, 331
Ego development, and self-directed learning, 19
Einstein, A., 143
Eisner, Elliot, 108, 243
Elaborating, 293
Eliot, Charles A., 369
Elmore, Richard, 283
Emergent approaches, in curriculum decision making, 126–128
Encounter group, 9, 24
End-means approach, 117
English
  and curriculum reform, 75
  strengthening of requirements in, 88, 274
  as subject, 341–343
  trends in teaching, 343–345
Ennis, Robert, 292
Erickson, Erik, 22, 176, 178, 182
ESALEN type, 25
Essentials of English, 344
Ethnic studies, 318
  in teaching multicultural education, 320
Evaluation
  of academic subject curriculum, 88–89
  critical inquiry as, 244
  of humanistic curriculum, 11–12
  of social reconstructionist curriculum, 34
  of technological curriculum, 58–59
"Even Start," 279
Event theory, 396
Excellence Movement of 1980s, 263–264
Experiential curriculum, 104
Experimental psychologists, 74
Exploration, as function of curriculum, 107
Exploring, 293
Exposition, in academic curriculum, 85
External supports, 231
External variables, 211

Facilities, 204
Facts, 414

Fallacy of content, 89–90
Fallacy of universalism, 90
Family and Community Health, 337
Fantasy body trip, 14
Fantini, Mario, 262
Federal government, participation in curriculum policy, 277–280
Feedback, 147
Fetterman, David, 248
Fillmore Arts Center, 358
Finn, Charles, Jr., 82
Fitzgerald, Frances, 349
Flexibility, 293
Flow experiences, 7
Fluency, 293
Fluid block, 202
Ford Foundation, 280
Foreign language
  American method to, 353
  audiolingual approach to, 353
  confluent approach to, 356
  efforts to revive language instruction, 354–356
  grammar-translation method for, 354–355
  rise and fall of, 353–354
  strengthening requirements for, 88, 274
Formal curriculum, 103, 396
Formative evaluation, 238
Forms of knowledge approach, 71–73
Foundations, participation in curriculum policy, 280–281
Foxfire Project, 345
Frankenstein, Marilyn, 41–42
Franklin, Barry, 370, 413
Freedom schools, 206
Free-form structure, 164
Freire, Paulo, 36–45, 46–47, 397, 400
Freudian psychologies, 6
Freyberg, Peter, 187
Futuristic model
  common ingredients, 115–116
  in curriculum decision making, 115–117
  problems with, 116–117
Futurologists, and social reconstructionism, 43–45

Gagné, Robert, 176–177, 182, 405
Gain scores, use of, 254
"Galileo," 404
Gamoran, Adam, 201
Gardner, Howard, 196
Gehrke, Nathalie, 185, 404
Generalizations, 414
  as organizing element, 172
General systems philosophy, 52
Genetics, teaching of, 90–92
Gestalt psychology, 10
  as basis for confluent education, 13–14
  "I have available" technique, 15
Giroux, Henry, 33, 40–41, 311, 402
Goal areas
  assigning priority to, 112
  determining acceptability of learner performance in each of preferred, 112–113
Goal-free evaluation, measurement of intended outcomes versus, 247–248
Goals, translating high priority, into plans, 113
Goals statements, formulating set of tentative, in curriculum decision making, 111–112
Good, Thomas, 139
Goodlad, John, 103–104, 140, 229, 396, 399–400, 403, 407–408

Gordon, C. Wayne, 308–309
Gordon, William, 293
Grade-equivalent scores, 254
Graduated responsibility, principle of, 183
Graman, Tomas, 128
Grammar-translation method, for language instruction, 354–355
Grant, Carl, 319
Griswold, Wendy, 39
Grumet, Madeline, 398
Grundy, Shirley, 126–127

Haaken, Janice, 24n
Habermas, Jurgen, 124
Haggerson, Nelson, 403
Hall, G. Stanley, 369
Hamilton, David, 235–236
Havighurst, Robert, 176, 177–178
Hawkins-Stafford Improvement Amendment (1988), 279
Health Activities Project (HAP), 340
Health education. See Physical and health education
Heckman, Paul, 230
Herbart, Johann, 371
Herbartism, 371
  basic tenets of, 371–372
  Dewey's opposition to, 376–377
  McMurrys' thoughts on, 372–375
Heritage Foundation, 280
Herrick, Virgil, 266
Heteronomic position, on moral education, 313
Hidden curriculum, 308
  informal system within school, 308–309
  and moral growth, 311–312
  sociology of knowledge, 309–311
Higher education, liberal arts in, 79–81
Higher order thinking, learning opportunities for, 140–143
Hirsch, E. D., Jr., 83–84
Hirst, Paul, 71–72, 72–73
History. See also Social studies
  and curriculum reform, 75
  evaluation of curriculum, 348–349
  in 1990s, 349–350
  personalizing instruction in, 21
  as subject, 347–348
Holism, 248
Holocaust, teaching of, 21
Horst, Donald, 254–256
Horton, Myles, 36
Huebner, Dwayne, 399, 410
Hufstedter, Shirley, 321
Hull, Daniel, 305
Humanistic curriculum, 1, 3–27
  basis for selecting learning opportunities, 8–10
  characteristics of, 9–10
  criticisms of, 24–26
  developing learning activities, 149–151
  directions in, 12
    confluent curriculum, 13–14
    consciousness, 16–23
  evaluation of, 11–12, 236
  features of, 4
  goals for thinking, 293
  negative connotations evoked by, 3
  organization of, 10–11
  purpose, 5–6
  revival of, in 1990s, 5
  role of teacher in, 8
  support of, for individualism, 4

Humanistic psychologists, 69
Human relations approach, to multicultural education, 319
Hunter, Madeline, 57
Hurd, Paul, 296
Hurn, Christopher, 300
Husen, Torsten, 299
Hutchins, Robert Maynard, 90
Hyper-rationalization, 265

Iannaccone, Lawrence, 263
Ideal curriculum, 103
Illiteracy, eradicating, 38–39
Imaginary journeys, 17
IMPACT II, 226
Inappropriate test levels, 254–255
Incongruity, 136–137
Individualism, in technological curriculum, 57
Individual learning, connecting, and social learning, 23
Industrialism, 378
Innovation, American commitment to, 4
Inquiry, in academic curriculum, 85
Inquiry-related sequences, 182
Inquiry Training Project, 335
Institutional level
  curriculum development at, 100
  organizing structure at, 164–165
Institutional purposes, for curriculum development, 105–106
Instructional alignment, 54
Instructional effectiveness, administration for, 209–215
Instructional materials, criteria for selection of, 60
Instructional objectives, 246–247
Instructional Systems Design, 65–66
Instructional units, 104
Instrumental Enrichment, 293
Integration, in curriculum, 10, 85–86, 164, 183–185, 186
Integrative development strategy, 225–226
Interactive video, 63
Interactive view of reading, 347
Interdisciplinary teaming, 202
Internal supports, 231
International Association for Evaluation of Education Achievement (IEA), 296–297, 299
International Mathematics Olympics, 299
Internships, 307
Interrupted time series design, 239

Jackson, Jesse, 262
James, William, 290
Japan, education in, 4, 296
Job analysis, 105, 381–382
John Birch Society, 281
Johnson, Mauritz, 411–412
John-Steiner, Vera, 143
Joyce, Bruce, 160
Judgment of projected trends, in curriculum decision making, 116

Kallison, James, Jr., 405
Kaplan, Andrew, 404
Karplus, Robert, 62
Keislar, Evan, 19
Kemmis, Stephen, 419
Kennedy, John F., 338
Kettering Foundation, 280
"Kids Network," 62
Kirkland, Marjorie C., 250
Kirst, Michael W., 260–261, 266, 281

Klein, M. Frances, 159
Kliebard, Herbert, 368–369, 400, 402, 413
Knapp,Michael, 283
Knowledge
  definition of, 70
  form of, approach, 71–73
  reaction against structure of, 75–77
Kohlberg, Lawrence, 139, 176, 178–179, 314–315
Komoski, Kenneth, 158

Lampert, Magdalene, 331
Language arts. *See also* English; Literature; Reading
  use of computer in, 62
Larabee, David, 369–370
Lawton, Denis, 109
Learning activities
  criteria for selecting, 153–158
  procedures for developing, 144–153
Learning opportunities, 133–135
  criticisms of criteria for selecting, 158–159
  devices for joining, 163
  for higher order thinking, 140–143
  organizing elements in, 171–174
  organizing structures for, 164–171
  principles for developing, 135–140
  principles for integrating content, 183–185
  principles for sequencing content and activities, 174–183
  selection of, for humanistic curriculum, 8–10
  selection of, for social reconstructionist curriculum, 32–33
Learning style
  dimensions of, 137
  matching teaching style to students', 138
Lehman, David, 291, 292
Lemish, Peter, 416
Lesson plans, 104
Liberal arts
  and the academic core, 78–82
  in the elementary and secondary curriculum, 81–82
  in higher education, 79–81
Lieberman, Ann, 224
Lincoln Center Institute for the Arts in Education, 360
Lippitt, Ronald, 230–231
Liston, Daniel, 46
Literature. *See also* English; Language Arts; Reading
  personalizing instruction in, 20–21
  teaching of, 344–345
Literature-based reading, 347
Locus of control, 19
LOGO, 61, 147
Loose coupling, and curriculum policy, 265
Los Angeles Getty Center, 359
Loucks, Susan, 224
Louis, Karen, 227

MacDonald, James, 390, 402
Macia, Elizabeth, 396
Macia, George, 396
MacKenzie, Gordon, 417
MACOS (Man: A Course of Study), 76–77, 262
Magnet schools, 207
Maharishi International University (MIU), 16–17
Manipulative variables, 211
Martin, James, 415
Maslow, Abraham, 6, 7, 25
Mastery learning, 55–56
Materials, new. *See* New materials

Mathematics
  anxiety over, 42, 137, 139
  and curriculum reform, 74
  international achievement in, 297
  and international competition, 207
  new, 328
  personalizing instruction in, 21
  and pragmatic rule systems, 291
  and revival of the disciplines approach, 77
  and strengthening of requirements in, 87, 88, 274
  technological curriculum for, 57–58
  trends in, 329–332
Matrix sampling, 253–254
McCarty, F. Hanoch, 25
McCutcheon, Gail, 416–417
McDiarmid, Garnet, 398
McLaughlin, Milbray, 283
McMurry, Charles, 371, 372–375, 389, 392
McMurry, Frank, 371, 373–375, 392
McNeil, John, 401
McNeil, Linda, 139, 212
Medical education, reforms in, 5
Meditation, 7
Mendel, Gregor Johann, 81
Mental imagery, 18
Mental rehearsal, 18
Metacognition training, 294
Metfessel, Newton S., 251
Methods, 414
Metrics, 330
Michael, William B., 251
Middle school, 204–205
Middle-up strategy, for curriculum change, 227
Milner, N. A., 262
Minority group pressure, for equity in education, 322
Mismatched comparison group, assembling, 255
Modern Language Association of America, 353
Modular scheduling, 205
Module, 170
Moral development
  and hidden curriculum, 311–312
  Kohlberg's theory of, 314–315
  and self-directed learning, 19
Moral education, 312
  autonomic position on, 313
  heteronomic position on, 313
  nihilistic position on, 312–313
  telenomic position on, 313–314
  value clarification, 315–318
Mort, Paul, 269
Movement education, 339
Mueller, Marlies, 354–355
Muller, Connie, 158
Multicultural education, approaches to, 319–321
Multidisciplinary seminar, in curriculum decision making, 115
Multiple discrimination, 176
Multiple element strategies, for curriculum change, 223–225
Multiple intelligence, theory of, 196
Mysticism, 16–17

National Academy of Sciences (NAS), 332
National Assessment of Educational Progress (NAEP), 240
National Assessment of Education Project (NAEP), 297
National Association for Education of Young Children, 281
National Association of Manufacturers, 281
National Association of School Principals, 275
National Association of State Boards of Education, 198, 200

National Bank of Validated Programs, 232
National Council for Social Studies (NCSS), 101
National Council of Teachers of English (NCTE), 344, 345
National Council of Teachers of Mathematics (NCTM), 330, 332
National Education Association, learning laboratory of, 200
National Government Association, 194
National Institute of Education, 299
National Longitudinal Study of High School Class, 336
National Research Council (NRC), 18
National Science Foundation, 76–77
   funding of curriculum projects by, 69
Nation at Risk: The Imperatives for Educational Reform, 264
Needs assessment
   in curriculum decision making, 110–114
   problems in, 113–114
   steps in, 110–113
Nelkin, D., 262
Neo-Marxists, 46
   and social reconstructionism, 39–43
Network for Educational Renewal, 229
Networking, for school renewal, 229–230
Nevo, David, 241
New curriculum, distribution of, 232
New England, and curriculum control, 274
Newman, Cardinal, 302
New material
   adoption of, 231
   development of, 232
   introducing, into classroom, 230–232
   student use of, 231
   teacher use of, 231
New York, and curriculum control, 274
Nickerson, Raymond, 292
Nihilistic position on moral education, 312–313
Noncomparable pretests and posttests, 255
Noncomparable treatment, 255
Non-decision making, 264
Nongrading, 203–204
Nonjudgmentalism, 248
Norm-group comparisons, 254
Norm-referenced tests, 248–249
North Central Association of Colleges and Secondary Schools, 275

Oakes, Jeannie, 200, 303
Objectives, in curriculum evaluation, 245–247
Oldenquist, Andrew, 316
Ong, Walter, 397–398
Open structure, 165–167
Operational curriculum, 104
Options system, 207
Orff, Carl, 175
Organization
   of academic subject curriculum, 85–88
   of humanistic curriculum, 10–11
   of social reconstructionist curriculum, 32–33
   of technological curriculum, 57–58
Organizing centers, 151, 163
Organizing elements, 163
   in learning opportunities, 171–174
Osborne, Roger, 187–188
Outcomes, measurement of intended vs. goal-free evaluation, 247–248

Pace, Robert, 357
Pacing, 147
Paideia Proposal, 81–82, 90

Papert, Seymour, 51, 61
Participation, 224
Patton, Michael, 251–252
Peak experiences, 6, 7
Pedrotti, Leno, 305
Peer group teaching
   in English, 344
   in fine arts, 357–358
Peltier, Gary, 197
Perceived curriculum, 103
Perkins, Carl D., Vocational Education Act, 307
Personal growth movement, 25
Personalized systematic instruction in higher education, 54–55
Perturbations, 219
Phenix, Philip, 20, 71, 73, 312, 313, 410
Phenomology, 248
Philosophical criteria, for selecting learning activities, 153–154
Physical and health education
   and curriculum reform, 75
   guidelines for future programs, 339–341
   place in curriculum, 338
Physical manipulation, 136
Physical Science Study Committee, 271
Piaget, Jean, 176, 179–180, 182
Pinar, William, 398, 401, 403
Pluralistic models for curriculum evaluation, 236, 242–244
Political criteria, in selecting learning activities, 156–157
Political decision-making, interpreting, 262–265
Politics, in curriculum policy, 260–261
Popham, James, 238, 253
Posner, George, 181, 402, 405
Postman, Neil, 45
Posttest scores
   lack of, for each treatment participant, 255
   use of inappropriate formulas to estimate, 255–256
Powell, A., 401
Practicality as criterion, in selecting learning activities, 157–158
Practice, principle of appropriate, 136
Pragmatic rule systems, 291
Praxiological theory, 396–397
Presentism, 127
Pressure groups, participation in curriculum policy, 281–282, 352–353
Pretest/posttest control group design, 238–239
Pretest scores
   lack of, for each treatment participant, 255
   using, to select program participants, 255
Prigo, Robert, 137
Principal. *See also* Administrator; Superintendent
   as director of learning, 195
   effectiveness of, in instructional effectiveness, 211–212
   role of, in curriculum change, 228
   role of, in determining curriculum policy, 269–270
   in shared leadership, 195–197
Principal learning, 176
Principle of appropriate practice, 136
Principle of satisfaction, 136–137
Privacy, tests and invasion of, 250–251
Problem solving, 176
   curriculum for teaching, 294–295
   learning opportunities in, 140–142
Process-product research, 407–409
   present status of, 408–409
   status of, in 1969, 407–408
Productive Thinking Program, 294
Programs of study, 104
Project 2061: Education for a Changing Future, 337

Project ADAPT, 406
Project Ixtliyollotl (San Andres, Mexico), 34–35
Project SOAR, 406
Project Synthesis, 335
Project Talent, 239, 240
Psychological criteria, for selecting learning opportunities, 154
Psychology, third force, 6
Public, role of, in curriculum development, 272–273
Publishers, participation in curriculum policy, 275–276
Pull-out programs, 322
Purpose, as organizing element, 173–174
Purves, Alan C., 129

Qualitative inquiry, in school settings, 416–417
"Quick start" programs, 306

Raths, Louis, 315
Rational curriculum making, 388
    criticisms of Tyler's rationale, 389–390
    Tyler's curriculum inquiry, 388–389
Rational model
    in curriculum decision making, 117–121
    deriving objectives, 117–119
    determining occupational targets, 121–123
    problems with, 119–121
    selecting from among education goals and objectives, 119
    delete on pages 121–123
Ravitch, Diane, 82
Reaction against a structure of knowledge, 75–77
Reading. *See also* English; Language Arts; Literature
    conventional approach to, 38
    curriculum for, 346
    Freire approach to, 38
    interactive view of, 347
    literature-based, 347
    strengthening of requirements in, 87
    trends and directions in teaching of, 346–347
Reagan, Ronald, 278
Reasoning, skills needed in, 87
Reconceptualists, 402–403
Reflective deliberation, 126
Reform
    options in schools, 208–209
    professionalization of, 262–263
Regression toward the mean, 255
Relaxation, 17
Relaxation techniques, 339
"Reproductive" critical theory and knowledge, 40–43
Resch, Kenneth, 20
Research and curriculum policy, effective, 212–215
Research and development (R and D) model for curriculum
        change, 223
Resource unit, 169
Response format, 147
Responsive evaluation, of curriculum, 242–243
Revival of disciplines approach, 77–78
Riles, Wilson, 264
Risk taking, 293
Rituals, 14–15
Rockefeller Brothers Fund, 358
Rockefeller Foundation, 280
Rogers, Carl, 11–12, 160
Rotberg, Iris, 299
Rugg, Harold, 29, 369
Rutherford, F. James, 337

St. Vincent Millay, Edna, 171
Sampling, 253–254
Santayana, George, 247
Sarason, Seymour, 222
Satisfaction, principle of, 136–137
Scenario writing, in curriculum decision making, 115–116
Schaffarzick, Jon, 273, 276
Schniedewind, Nancy, 23
Scholastic Aptitude Test, 275
School board, role of, in determining curriculum policy, 271–272
School cultural approach, to curriculum coordination, 210–211
School district level, curriculum development at, 102
School renewal, networking for, 229–230
School settings, qualitative inquiry in, 416–417
Schwab, Joseph, 397, 398
Schwille, John, 266
Science
    computers in, 62
    and curriculum reform, 74
    evolution of teaching, 332–333
    international assessment of, 297
    international competition in, 207
    new approaches to, 335–336
    personalizing instruction in, 21
    and revival of the disciplines approach, 77–78
    strengthening of requirements for, 88, 274
    and the teaching of genetics, 90–92
Science—A Process Approach, 293
Science for All Americans, 337
Scientific curriculum making, 378
    Bobbitt's contribution to, 379–383
    Charters' contribution to, 383–384
    key ideas in, 379
    societal influences on, 378–379
Scientific methods and techniques, 378–379
Scriven, Michael, 247–248
Secondary school, organization of, 33
Self-actualization
    American commitment to, 4
    ideal of, 6
Self-awareness, in humanistic curriculum, 9
Self-directed learning, 18
Self-identity, 15
Sensitivity training, 24
Sequence, 164
    in academic subject matter, 86–88
    in humanistic curriculum, 10
    newer principles of, 176–180
    traditional principles of, 174–175
Sequence studies
    present status of, 405
    status of, in 1969, 405
Sequencing principles, categorizing, 181–183
Sex education, 341
Shane, Harold G., 43–44
Shapiro, Stewart B., 13
Shared curriculum leadership, 196
Shaughnessy, Mina, 344
Shavelson, 168
Shiplett, John M., 11
Shopping Mall High School, The, 311
Significant others, 137
Simon, Sidney, 314, 315
Sirotnick, Kenneth, 244
Skills, as organizing element, 172
Skinner, B. F., 53
Slavin, Robert, 59, 201

Sleep learning, 18
Sleeter, Christine, 319
Social adaptation, and social reconstructionism, 45
Social development, and self-directed learning, 19
Social efficiency advocates, 369–370
Socializing function, 108
Social learning, connecting individual learning and, 23
Social-psychological prevention programs, 340
Social reconstructionist curriculum, 1, 29–30, 369, 370, 400
  basis for selecting learning opportunities, 32–33
  characteristics of, 31–32
  criticisms of, 46–47
  developing learning activities, 144–145
  evaluation of, 34, 236
  goals of thinking, 292–293
  organization of, 33–34
  in practice, and changing the community, 34–36
  purpose of, 31
  role of teacher in, 31–32
  teaching multicultural education, 320–321
Social studies, 350–351. *See also* History
  and curriculum reform, 75
  future of, 351–353
  personalizing instruction in, 21
  strengthening of requirements in, 88
Societal level, curriculum development at, 101–102
Sociological findings, on change, 219–222
Soltis, Jonas, 72
Sorenson, Gail Paulus, 277
Soviet Union, education in, 296, 299
Specialization, as function of curriculum, 107–108
Specific subjects structure, 164
Sponsor speakups, 112
Staff development, curriculum change through, 227–229
Staffing patterns and scheduling, 201–203
Stake, Robert E., 242–243
Standardized achievement tests, 213
Staples, Esra, 269
STAR Program, 406
Statistics, 41–42
Steiner, Vera John, 293
Stern, Paula, 168
Stevenson, H. W., 296
Stipek, Deborah, 139
Strategic interaction, 193
Strategic teaching, 142
Strike, Kenneth, 181, 405
Strong sense thinkers, 292
Structural patterning, 339
Structured openness, 167–168
Structure in disciplines approach, 73–75
Student-generated curriculum, 127–128
Students
  role of, in determining curriculum policy, 271
  stratifying, 200–201
Studying, skills needed in, 87
Stufflebeam, Dan, 241
Subject-oriented curriculum, 3
Submersion, 321–322
Substitution, 218
Suggestopedia, 356
Summative evaluation, 238
Superintendents, role of, in determining curriculum policy, 270
Supplementary personnel, 203
Supplementation, as function of curriculum, 107
Support, 224
Synectics, 293

Synoptic activity, as curriculum coordination, 209–210
Systems technology, 53–54

Taba, Hilda, 266–267, 417
Tanner, Daniel, 401, 403
Tanner, Laurel, 401, 403
Taxonomical analysis of objectives
  present status of, 406–407
  status of, in 1969, 405
Taylor, Philip, 401
Teacher
  as agent of change, 226
  in curriculum change, 217–218, 220, 228
  in curriculum decision making, 197
  in curriculum making, 386–387
  in determining curriculum policy, 266–268
  in humanistic curriculum, 8
  and school society, 309
  in social reconstructionist curriculum, 31–32
  staffing patterns and scheduling of, 201–203
  in student-generated curriculum, 127–128
  and team teaching, 202
Teacher organizations, and curriculum issues, 267
Teaching style, matching, to students' learning style, 138
Teaching the culturally different approach to multicultural education, 319
Teaching unit, 169
Team teaching, 202
Technical hazards, in conducting curriculum evaluation, 254–256
Technological criteria, for selecting learning opportunities, 154–156
Technological curriculum, 1, 99
  characteristics of, 56–59
  developing learning activities in, 145–149
  evaluation of, 58–59
  instructional alignment, 54
  issues in, 63–66
  mastery learning, 55–56
  methods of, 57
  objectives of, 56–57
  organization of, 57–58
  personalized systematic instruction in higher education, 54–55
  special problems in teaching, 64–66
  systems technology, 53–54
  technical innovations, 61
    computers, 61–63
    interactive video, 63
Technology
  in development of curriculum materials, 59–60
  and ideal of efficiency, 52–53
  influence of, on curriculum, 51–52
Telenomic position, on moral education, 313–314
Testing agencies, participation in curriculum policy, 275
Tests
  careless administration of, 255
  criterion-referenced, 249
  and invasion of privacy, 250–251
  norm-referenced, 248–249
Texas, and curriculum control, 274–275
Theory curriculum, 395–396
Thinking curriculum, 290–295
  focus of, 292–295
Third force psychology, 6
Thorndike, Edward, 290–291
Tight-coupling, 210, 214–215
TM (transcendental meditation), 16–17
Tobias, Sheila, 137, 139

Top-down strategies for curriculum change, 218, 222–223
Torrance, E. Paul, 142–143
Tracking, 200–201
Traditionalists, 401
Transcendental meditation (TM), 16–17
Transition programs, 322
Travers, Robert M. W., 406
Tutoring, 203
Tyler, Louise, 414–416
Tyler, Ralph, 117–121, 136, 247, 388–389, 393, 397, 399, 401

Uguroglu, Margaret, 415–416
Unit, 169
United States, education in, 263–264, 299–301
U.S. Department of Education, 329
Unobtrusive measures, 251
Usefulness, 175
Utilitarianism, 300
Utilization-related sequence, 182

Valuation curriculum theory, 396
Value clarification, 315–318
Value orientation changes, 219
Values, 211
  as organizing element, 172
Values and attitudes, 414
Van Geel, T., 268
van Manen, Max, 402
Videodisks, 63
Virginia Beach, 360
Vocational education, 301
  access to, 303–304
  content of, 305–306
  contrasting purposes for, 301–303
  discrimination in, 304
  equity in, 302
  federal aid to, 302
  human development in, 303
  restructuring, 306–307
  trends in, 307–308
Vocational specialization, 107
Vocational or training model
  in curriculum decision making, 121–124
  determining objectives for training programs or courses, 123–124
  determining occupational targets, 121–123
  problems with, 124
Von Baer, Karl Ernst, 81

Walberg, Herbert, 295–296, 299
Walker, Decker, 260–261, 276, 281, 397, 402, 410–411, 413
Walker, Jim, 47
Weak sense thinkers, 292
Weil, Marsha, 160
Whole language movement, 347
Willis, George, 415
Winter, Richard, 419
Wirszup, Isaak, 296, 299
Wise, Arthur, 265
Wolfe, Richard, 297, 299
World Future Society, 43
Wright, E. L., 141
Writing. *See also* Language arts
  strengthening of requirements in, 87

Yoga, 7
Young, M. F. D., 310

Zais, Robert, 401
Zigler, Edward F., 262